# *Delphi*™ *COM Programming*

Eric Harmon

M
T P
MACMILLAN
TECHNICAL
PUBLISHING
U·S·A

# Delphi™ COM Programming

By Eric Harmon

Published by:
MTP
201 West 103rd Street
Indianapolis, Indiana 46290 USA

Copyright © 2000 by MTP

FIRST EDITION

International Standard Book Number: 1-57870-221-6

Library of Congress Catalog Card Number: 99-63277

03 02 01 00      7 6 5 4 3 2 1

Interpretation of the printing code: The rightmost double-digit number is the year of the book's printing; the rightmost single-digit number is the number of the book's printing. For example, the printing code 00-1 shows that the first printing of the book occurred in 2000.

Composed in Quark and MCPdigital by MTP

Printed in the United States of America

**Publisher**
*David Dwyer*

**Executive Editor**
*Linda Ratts Engelman*

**Product Marketing Manager**
*Stephanie Layton*

**Managing Editor**
*Gina Brown*

**Acquisitions Editor**
*Karen Wachs*

**Development Editor**
*Ami Frank Sullivan*

**Project Editor**
*Alissa Cayton*

**Copy Editor**
*Elise Walter*

**Proofreader**
*Debbie Williams*

**Indexer**
*Kevin Fulcher*

**Team Coordinator**
*Jennifer Garrett*

**Manufacturing Coordinator**
*Chris Moos*

**Compositor**
*Amy Parker*

**Book Designer**
*Louisa Klucznik*

**Cover Designer**
*Aren Howell*

## Trademark Acknowledgments

## Warning and Disclaimer

## About the Author

**Eric Harmon** has been a computer programmer for over 16 years. He started working extensively with Turbo Pascal, and later Delphi, in 1985. Eric is a charter member of TPX, a volunteer group of individuals who assist TurboPower Software Company in monitoring their newsgroups. He has also written a variety of magazine articles for *Visual Developer Magazine*.

Eric lives in Florida with his wife Tina, their cat Princess, and their dog Oscar. When he isn't programming, he enjoys reading, motorcycling, playing cards, and listening to music. Eric can be reached at Eric.Harmon@tpx.turbopower.com.

## About the Technical Reviewers

These reviewers contributed their considerable practical, hands-on expertise to the entire development process for *Delphi COM Programming*. As the book was being written, these folks reviewed all the material for technical content, organization, and flow. Their feedback was critical to ensuring that *Delphi COM Programming* fits our reader's need for the highest quality technical information.

**Wayne Niddery** is an independent software developer. Working in a variety of fields and with many computer languages for over 16 years, Delphi has been his preferred development tool since its inception. A member of TeamB since September 1998, Wayne can be found contributing regularly in Borland's Delphi newsgroups. Wayne co-authored the popular *Borland Delphi How-To* (1995, The Waite Group) and was a technical editor for the *Delphi 3 Super Bible* (1997, The Waite Group). Wayne makes his home in Toronto, Canada with his wife Sonoe, young son Curtis, and dog Patch.

**Danny Thorpe** is a senior engineer on the Delphi and C++ Builder R&D Team at Inprise Corporation. His current responsibilities include the ongoing evolution of the core VCL architecture, graphics classes, streaming system, RTL, grids classes, design-time property editors, and form designer architecture. He has contributed to every Pascal-based product produced by Borland/Inprise since Turbo Pascal 6.0 in 1990. Danny has also served as technical editor on more than forty Delphi programming books, and is the author of *Delphi Component Design* (1997, Addison Wesley).

## Dedication

Dedicated to the memory of my high school English teacher, Miss Mac, who pushed us just a little harder.

## Acknowledgments

I would like to thank the people who have directly influenced my decision to write this book, or who have in some way participated in making this book a reality.

First, I want to thank Jeff Duntemann, who is largely responsible for getting my writing career off the ground. Ray Konopka, Xavier Pacheco, and Kent Reisdorph evaluated my original proposal and all agreed that this idea just might fly.

The whole crew at Macmillan has been simply great: Karen Wachs sent me the innocent email message that planted the seed that grew into this finished product. Karen has been involved with the book-writing process from the very beginning to the very end. Jennifer Garrett also helped keep the wheels in motion throughout the project. Leah Williams critiqued the first chapter that I wrote, and provided a number of ideas for making subsequent chapters even better. Ami Frank Sullivan did a terrific job of patiently editing my chapters, consolidating technical review comments, and answering my questions. Alissa Cayton picked up where Ami left off, and incorporated the screen shots into the text. Elise Walter painstakingly took care of dotting the i's and crossing the t's on the finished book. I don't fully understand the jobs of any of the great ladies at Macmillan who worked with me on this, but they all assure me that their job is the most important one in the book-writing process.

Thanks to Ben Riga and Kendyl Uppstrom of Inprise/Borland, who saw to it that I had the materials I needed to do this book. Bruneau Babet, also of Borland, answered several technical questions that I had along the way.

Last, but certainly not least, I want to say a special thank you to my technical editors: Danny Thorpe and Wayne Niddery. Danny is a senior Borland engineer on the Delphi project, and one of the best technical editors imaginable for this type of book. Not only did he set me straight when I wrote something that was just plain wrong, but he also offered insight into the inner workings of Delphi, and offered ideas on better coding techniques for the example applications. Wayne is a member of Borland's TeamB, and in many ways personifies the target audience for this book.

Whereas Wayne is an excellent Delphi programmer, he is learning COM, and he provided invaluable feedback in many cases where I just didn't explain things well enough. Any errors that remain, of course, are nobody's fault but my own.

My apologies to anyone whom I may have inadvertently omitted. If I left you out, it's probably because I never interacted with you directly. So a blanket thank you to anyone else who contributed to this project. If this book is a success, it's partly because of you.

## Feedback Information

At MTP, our goal is to create in-depth technical books of the highest quality and value. Each book is crafted with care and precision, undergoing rigorous development that involves the unique expertise of members from the professional technical community.

Readers' feedback is a natural continuation of this process. If you have any comments regarding how we could improve the quality of this book, or otherwise alter it to better suit your needs, you can contact us at `networktech@newriders.com`. Please make sure to include the book title and ISBN in your message.

We greatly appreciate your assistance.

# Contents at a Glance

# Table of Contents

# *Foreword*

Every time I get together with other Delphi developers at Borland conferences worldwide or in user groups, I am always reminded of the infamous ActiveX Control creation session that I gave in Anaheim, California in 1995. There, I scared 1,400 developers by showing them in 1 hour and 15 minutes how to write an ActiveX Control in Delphi 2; 5,700 lines of code later, a Delphi button clicked on a Visual Basic 4 form.

At that time, Anders Hejlsberg, former Chief Architect of Delphi, requested that I join the Delphi development team to be a member of the Mission Impossible team, later known as the DAX team. At the time, the team was Anders, Conrad Herrmann, and myself, and then Joe "TLB" Bentley joined us from the Paradox team. Finally, not too long after that, we got the last member, my dear friend Steve "Cookie Monster" Teixeira.

The work was incredible. We knew we were working on the cutting edge of technology, but at the same time, lack of documentation, articles, and inexperience forced us to work day and night for several months to create a framework that is, arguably, the best and easiest to use to this day.

Becoming a COM developer takes a little bit of time; becoming a good COM developer takes a tremendous amount of time. But for us, it was different. Not only were we supposed to produce a framework to easily allow the creation of COM servers and clients, but we had to work with everything under the sun: Visual C++ 3, 4, and 5; Visual Basic 4 and 5; Internet Explorer 3, 4, and 5; Borland C++; Office products; and so on. Considering that each container had a "gotcha" and each "gotcha" had another "gotcha," I believe we did exceptionally well.

Don Box says, "COM is love." I say, "COM is hard." That is why I am pleased that Eric decided to write this valuable book to introduce Delphi developers to the world of COM and get them up and running fast with this great, lasting technology.

Read, enjoy, and code.

*Alain "Lino" Tadros*
*Director of Technology*
*DeVries Data Systems*
www.dvdata.com

# *Introduction*

This is a book about COM programming in Delphi. There are several excellent books available today for Delphi programmers of varying skill levels. Likewise, there are several excellent books available that discuss the details of COM. What's been missing is a book that teaches COM programming to Delphi programmers. Until now.

## Who This Book Is For

As you can tell from the title, this book targets Delphi programmers. More specifically, this book is written for programmers who are somewhat fluent in Delphi, but who lack familiarity with COM, or who are having trouble getting up to speed with COM by reading the other books that are currently available.

If you've previously read books or articles about COM, and still don't know how to even begin programming COM-related applications in Delphi, don't despair! Delphi provides a number of language features and wizards that significantly reduce or eliminate many of the headaches associated with traditional COM programming.

This book assumes that you're already a seasoned Delphi programmer, so I will not be providing any background information on Delphi programming in general. If you need to brush up on your Delphi programming, please refer to Appendix A, "Suggested Readings and Resources," for a list of excellent books on Delphi, from beginner to advanced levels.

# How This Book Is Organized

This book is composed of nine chapters. Chapters 1 through 5 discuss, in detail, the basics of COM and how it is implemented in Delphi. Although later chapters build on the material presented in earlier chapters, a particularly nice feature of COM is that you can use pieces of it without completely understanding the whole. Obviously, the more you understand, the better you'll be as a Delphi COM programmer, but you'll be able to start using what you've learned in each chapter before moving on to the next chapter.

Chapters 6 through 9 use the concepts presented in Chapters 1 through 5 to delve into specific areas of COM programming. For example, Chapter 9 shows you how you can extend the Windows shell (by writing such things as applications that make use of the tray) through COM.

As a result, this book can be used in two different, yet compatible, ways. First, you can use it as a COM tutorial, reading each chapter in order. Second, you can use it as a reference, re-reading a specific chapter in order to solidify your knowledge of the concepts presented in that chapter. For that reason, this section provides a roadmap to the rest of the chapters in this book, to help you quickly and easily find your way around.

- Chapter 1, "Using Interfaces in Delphi," introduces the concept of *interfaces*. Interfaces are the most basic building block in COM. In Chapter 1, you'll learn that interfaces are a useful language element in their own right in Delphi. I'll show you how to create Delphi applications that are built on interfaces, without ever discussing COM per se.

- Chapter 2, "Interfaces and COM," picks up where Chapter 1 leaves off. In Chapter 2, I'll show you how you can create COM servers in Delphi. You'll learn how to upgrade existing COM servers without breaking existing code that depends on an older version of that server.

- In Chapter 3, "Type Libraries," I'll introduce the concept of a *type library*. As you'll see, type libraries provide the means by which COM servers can be used by practically any compiler or language on the market today.

- Chapter 4, "Automation," accumulates the concepts discussed in the preceding chapters to create automation clients and servers. Automation provides a mechanism by which one application can be controlled by another application.

- In Chapter 5, "ActiveX Controls and ActiveForms," I'll discuss ActiveX controls and ActiveForms. I'll show you how easy is it to use existing ActiveX controls in Delphi, and I'll show you how you can create your own ActiveX controls that you can market to programmers using not only Delphi, but also Visual Basic, C++, and other languages.

- Chapter 6, "DCOM," shows you how you can take the concepts you've already learned and apply them across a network. You'll learn how to write distributed applications that can communicate with each other on a LAN or WAN.

- In Chapter 7, "Structured Storage," I introduce *structured storage*, which is a way of storing multiple types of data in a single file. You'll see how to use COM interfaces to easily use structured storage files in your Delphi applications.

- Chapter 8, "Structured Storage and OLE," builds on Chapter 7, and discusses *OLE property sets* and *OLE containers*. OLE property sets provide a universal way to store tagged data in a structured storage file. For example, one application can store the author's name in a document, and any other application (that knows about OLE property sets) can read the author's name from the file without knowing anything about the structure of the file.

- Chapter 9, "Programming the Windows Shell," explains how to write several of the common types of Windows shell extensions, including context menu handlers, copy hook handlers, applications that make use of the tray, and more.

## Components Developed in This Book

Although this isn't a book about component development, there are several places in the text where it makes sense to develop a Delphi component to encapsulate the ideas presented here. For that reason, the source code that accompanies this book includes the Delphi package DCP (for Delphi COM Programming). The DCP package is provided in three flavors: DCP3 for Delphi 3 programmers, DCP4 for Delphi 4 programmers, and DCP5 for Delphi 5 programmers. The package includes the following components:

- **EventSink**—Provides a means of easily responding to automation events in automation clients (used in Chapter 4)

- **PropertySet**—Reads and writes OLE property sets (used in Chapter 8)

- **TrayIcon**—Manages an icon in the tray (used in Chapter 9)

## Sample Applications

Each chapter in this book includes a number of sample programs to help you get up to speed with Delphi COM programming as quickly and painlessly as possible. Most of these examples were written in Delphi 4, and then recompiled with Delphi 5 after it shipped.

With few exceptions, all the examples presented in this book compile under Delphi 3, Delphi 4, and Delphi 5. In several cases, you will see compiler directives where special provisions had to be made to accommodate Delphi 3, and in a couple of isolated instances, a sample program will not work with Delphi 3 because the sample takes advantage of language and/or library enhancements introduced after Delphi 3. These instances are clearly marked in the text.

The source code for the sample programs presented in this book can be downloaded from http://www.newriders.com/delphi.

The following list provides a roadmap, by chapter, of the sample applications developed in this book:

**Chapter 1**
- **GUIDDemo**—Shows how to generate Globally Unique IDentifiers (GUIDs) programmatically.
- **IntfDemo**—Reinforces the concept of interface reference counting and lifetime management for COM objects.
- **SortDemo**—Shows a concrete example of how to implement a generic algorithm (comparison/sorting routines) using interfaces.
- **GrphDemo**—Implements a number of advanced interface features, such as multiple interfaces in a single class, method name resolution, and more. Shows how interfaces can be used to cleanly create a hierarchy of classes.

**Chapter 2**
- **Bin1Srv**—Demonstrates how to create a simple COM server that implements one-dimensional optimization (an NP-complete problem)
- **Bin1Cli**—Shows a client that accesses the Bin1Srv server
- **Bin1Srv2**—Shows how to update an existing COM server without breaking existing client code
- **Bin1Cli2**—An updated version of Bin1Cli that takes advantage of the new features of Bin1Srv2

**Chapter 3**
- **TIViewer**—Demonstrates how to read and interpret the contents of a type library

## Chapter 4

- **UnitSrv**—Demonstrates an in-process COM server that can convert between different units, such as feet, inches, meters, and so on
- **UnitCli**—A client application for UnitSrv
- **MemoDemo**—A simple application used as a base point for showing how to add automation to existing applications
- **MemoSrv**—The automated MemoDemo application
- **MemoCli**—A client application for MemoSrv
- **EventSrv**—A simple application used to demonstrate how to fire events from an automation server
- **EventCli**—A client application for EventSrv
- **EventMultSrv**—The EventSrv application enhanced to allow events to be sent to multiple clients at once
- **EventMultCli**—A client application for EventMultSrv
- **EventCli5**—A Delphi 5-specific client application for EventMultSrv
- **IntfSrv**—Shows how to implement callback interfaces in COM servers
- **IntfCli**—A client application for IntfSrv
- **ADO**—Demonstrates how to access Microsoft Active Data Objects (ADO) from Delphi

## Chapter 5

- **AgentTest**—Shows how to use an existing ActiveX control in Delphi
- **AgentDemo**—An extended example that shows some of the features of the Microsoft Agent ActiveX control
- **ActiveX**—Shows how to convert a Delphi visual component into an ActiveX control
- **ActiveForm**—Shows how to create an ActiveForm

## Chapter 6

- **DCOMServer**—A simple DCOM server used to test the DCOM setup on your computer.
- **DCOMClient**—A client application for DCOMServer.
- **PartServer**—A DCOM server application which might be used in a parts warehouse. This server demonstrates a method of accessing a remote database without costly solutions such as MIDAS.

- **PartAdmin**—One of two client applications for PartServer. This client application allows the user to perform administrative duties on the part database, such as updating prices or adding new parts to the database.

- **PartStock**—The second of two client applications for PartServer. This application allows the user to view existing inventory and remove inventory from stock.

## Chapter 7

- **CarDemo**—Shows how to take advantage of structured storage files in Delphi applications.

- **SSView**—Demonstrates how to iterate through the objects in a structured storage file. Also shows how to compact a structured storage file to remove the bloat that is commonly associated with structured storage files.

## Chapter 8

- **PropDemo**—Shows how to read and write OLE property sets in your Delphi application

- **FindProp**—A utility program that searches for files on your hard drive, based on data stored in OLE property sets

- **OLECont**—Demonstrates how to write an OLE container application in Delphi

## Chapter 9

- **CtxDemo**—Shows how to write a context menu handler
- **CHDemo**—Demonstrates a copy hook handler
- **LinkDemo**—Shows how to create and update shell links (shortcuts)
- **TrayDemo**—Shows how to write an application that places an icon in the tray
- **PropDemo**—Demonstrates how to write a property sheet handler in Delphi

In the following section, I'll give a quick overview of COM.

# About COM

This section talks about what COM is, and why you might want to use it in your Delphi applications. It also gives a short history of COM, and talks a bit about the future direction of COM.

## Defining COM

COM is an acronym for Component Object Model. COM was created to solve two problems that Windows programmers commonly face:

1. It defines a specification by which you can create objects that can be used by multiple languages or programming environments.

2. It defines a way by which client applications on one machine can interact with servers on another machine.

## A Brief History of COM

The COM technology began as OLE (Object Linking and Embedding). OLE was basically a fancy form of Dynamic Data Exchange (DDE). It allowed a client application to store data from a server application, along with enough information about the server to fire up the server when the user requested it (usually by double-clicking on an image that represented the server data).

As Microsoft enhanced OLE, they added additional features, such as Automation (discussed in Chapter 4) and OLE Controls (OCX) (discussed in Chapter 5). Eventually, the term Object Linking and Embedding became obsolete, and Microsoft declared that OLE didn't actually stand for anything, but was simply a term in its own right.

COM is technically defined as the implementation of OLE, although the two terms have gotten so confused that most people use them interchangeably. OLE actually refers to the higher-level features built on top of COM, including advise sinks, in-place activation, structured storage, and so on.

## The Future of COM

Although COM is a mature technology, it isn't finished by any means. Microsoft is currently working on the successor to COM, COM+. COM+ will add two major improvements to COM:

- Reference counting will be automatically handled.
- COM objects will be able to be inspected at runtime.

It's worthwhile to note that Delphi already provides both of these capabilities, to an extent. As you'll learn in Chapter 3, Delphi currently provides automatic reference counting for COM objects in most situations. As you're probably well aware, Delphi also allows VCL classes to be inspected at runtime, through the use of Runtime Type Information (RTTI).

You can rest assured that no matter what direction COM takes in the future, the engineers at Borland will be hard at work updating Delphi to take advantage of the latest COM technologies.

## Conventions Used in this Book

Several typographical conventions are used throughout *Delphi COM Programming*. These have been kept to a minimum in attempt to make the text as concise and clean as possible, but the ones that have been used should help clarify certain types of text. These conventions are as follows:

- **Bold** is used for keywords when they are introduced and for operators.
- *Italic* is used for parameter names.
- `Monospace font` is used for Web addresses and code listings.
- Filenames are written with lowercase letters.

## Contacting the Author

If you would like to contact me regarding any questions, comments, praise, or criticism you might have concerning this book, please feel free to email me at `Eric.Harmon@tpx.turbopower.com`. I will do my best to respond to you as quickly as possible.

# Using Interfaces in Delphi

Starting with Delphi 3, Borland introduced the **interface** keyword to Delphi. Interfaces form the cornerstone of COM programming, but interestingly, they can also be used in the development of non–COM-oriented programs. For that reason, this chapter focuses on interfaces as language elements. Most everything that you learn in this chapter applies 100% to COM, but you will not see the word COM mentioned much in this chapter.

Other than the fact that they share the same name, the interface that I'm talking about here has nothing whatsoever to do with a unit's interface section. The dual use of the word interface should not be a source of confusion, since the usage occurs in two completely unrelated contexts.

## Defining Interfaces

Perhaps the simplest way to understand an interface is that it is more or less the equivalent of an abstract class. In case you're unfamiliar with abstract classes, they are classes that define a behavior, but don't actually implement the behavior themselves. Instead, they rely on descendent classes to provide the implementation. Consider the following class declaration:

```
type
  TFormattedNumber = class
  public
    function FormattedString: string; virtual; abstract;
  end;
```

This is an abstract class, and you should recognize it as laying the foundation for a series of derived classes that all have something in common. Namely, they all have the capability to format some kind of number through a method named FormattedString.

You will never create an instance of an abstract class (or at least, you *should* never create an instance of an abstract class!). The class is created only to "lay down the law", so to speak, for its descendent classes. Consider the following code fragment:

```
var
  MyNumber: TFormattedNumber;
begin
  MyNumber := TFormattedNumber.Create;
  MyNumber.Free;
end;
```

This is legal code, and all you will get from the compiler when compiling this code is the following warning:

```
Constructing instance of 'TFormattedNumber' containing abstract methods
```

The code compiles and runs just fine. However, just try to *use* MyNumber and Delphi will throw an EAbstractError exception, indicating that you are trying to call an abstract method.

In order for TFormattedNumber to be useful, you need to derive classes from it, like this:

```
type
  TFormattedNumber = class
  public
    function FormattedString: string; virtual; abstract;
  end;

  TFormattedInteger = class(TFormattedNumber)
  private
    FValue: Integer;
  public
    function FormattedString: string; override;
  end;

  TFormattedDouble = class(TFormattedNumber)
  private
    FValue: Double;
  public
    function FormattedString: string; override;
  end;
```

After the classes are defined, you can use them like this:

```
procedure ShowFormattedNumber(F: TFormattedNumber);
begin
  ShowMessage(F.FormattedString);
end;
```

The ShowFormattedNumber procedure doesn't care whether you pass it a TFormattedInteger or a TFormattedDouble. It simply calls the FormattedString method of the appropriate class.

This should not be new to you as a seasoned Delphi programmer. Now let's look at the same construct using an interface. We'll see how an interface lets us achieve the same results, with some interesting (and useful) side effects.

```
type
  IFormattedNumber = interface
    function FormattedString: string;
  end;
```

The similarities between the declarations of TFormattedNumber and IFormattedNumber should be obvious. However, there are some subtle and important differences you need to understand. The following sections explore these differences in detail.

## Interface as a Contract

Conceptually, an interface is nothing more than a contract between the implementor of the interface and the user of the interface. By defining an interface, you are in effect saying, "I see the need for this functionality. I recognize that this functionality could be implemented in many different ways. I don't really care how the functionality is physically implemented, but it had better adhere to these specifications." The interface's user can code to the interface specification without worrying that the specification will change.

In the previous example, I have decided that I want to create a class (or actually, a set of classes) that supports formatting different types of numbers. Derived classes may include classes to format integers, floating-point numbers, and hexadecimal numbers, for example.

An interface is not a class; it's an interface. Therefore, it must be declared as such. In the next section, I'll explore more deeply that statement's importance.

## The Differences Between an Interface and a Class

Though interfaces have much in common with abstract classes, they also have several important differences. Let's examine the differences in detail. For ease of reference, here are the two declarations again:

```
TFormattedNumber = class
protected
  function FormattedString: string virtual; abstract;
end;

IFormattedNumber = interface
  function FormattedString: string;
end;
```

Interfaces have the following characteristics:

- An interface is declared as type interface, and not as type class. By convention, interface names begin with the letter I, just as class type names begin with the letter T.

- All interfaces inherit, directly or indirectly, from IUnknown. Just as TObject is the root of all classes in Delphi, IUnknown is the root of all interfaces in COM. I will explore the IUnknown interface in detail later in this chapter.

- You cannot create an instance of an interface. The following code is illegal:

```
var
  MyNumber: IFormattedNumber;
begin
  MyNumber := IFormattedNumber.Create;   // This is illegal
end;
```

The compiler generates the following error message when attempting to compile the code:

```
  Object or class type required
```

This feature is a welcome safety net. Whereas with an abstract class you can explicitly create an instance of that class, this feature allows the compiler to enforce the concept that an instance of an interface cannot be created.

- You cannot specify scoping directives in an interface. All methods defined by an interface are public, and you cannot include scoping directives (including public) in the interface declaration.

- An interface cannot declare variables. An interface only determines what functionality is to be provided. It places no restriction on how that functionality is to be achieved. If you were allowed to place a member variable in an interface declaration, you would be dictating, to some degree, what means must be used to achieve the desired functionality.

- All functions and procedures declared in an interface are, by definition, virtual abstract functions and procedures. You don't need to declare them as such; and in fact, it is not legal to do so.

## An Interface is Immutable

After you define and publish an interface, it is cast in stone. You cannot modify that interface. Obviously, while you're in the process of developing the interface, you will go through many renditions and revisions of the interface and associated code, but after you have released the interface for others to use, you cannot change it. If you need to enhance an interface, you can come out with a new "version" of the interface. For instance, let's say you decide that you want to add a method named SetCaption to the IFormattedNumber interface. You would create a new interface, named IFormattedNumber2, like this:

```
type
  IFormattedNumber2 = interface
    function FormattedString: string;
    procedure SetCaption(ACaption: string);
  end;
```

Any existing code still using the IFormattedNumber interface will continue to work unmodified. New code can take advantage of the new IFormattedNumber2 interface.

> **Note**
>
> *Just because you declare a new IFormattedNumber2 interface doesn't mean you have to completely reimplement the interface. If all IFormattedNumber2 does is add a new SetCaption method, you can derive IFormattedNumber2 from IFormattedNumber.*
>
> ```
> type
>   IFormattedNumber2 = interface(IFormattedNumber)
>     procedure SetCaption(ACaption: string);
>   end; ◆
> ```

Now you know what an interface is, and how it relates to (and differs from) an abstract class. In the next section, I'll show you how to declare an interface.

# Declaring an Interface

You've already seen an example of a simple interface declaration. Here it is again:

```
IFormattedNumber = interface
  ['{2DE825C1-EADF-11D2-B39F-0040F67455FE}']
  function FormattedString: string;
end;
```

You should notice immediately the presence of a new string just below the interface name. This string is referred to as a *Globally Unique Identifier*, or GUID for short. All COM interfaces, as well as certain interfaces that are used only internally in your own application, require a unique GUID to function properly.

## Defining GUIDs

A GUID is a 16-byte unique number. The algorithm for creating a GUID is quite complex, and is defined by the Open Software Foundation. The algorithm takes into account the current date and time, the current process number of the program used to generate the GUID, and the unique ID stored in your network card, if you have one, among other things. Fortunately, you don't need to understand the algorithm to create GUIDs for your own interfaces.

If you have a network card, all GUIDs generated on your computer are guaranteed to be unique. All network cards contain a unique serial number, referred to as a MAC address, which is included as part of the GUID. If you don't have a network card, the GUID is still statistically guaranteed to be unique, due to the large number of digits in the GUID and the algorithm used to generate the GUID.

It is vitally important that when you create a new interface, you generate a new, unique GUID for that interface. You should never copy a GUID from one interface to another.

Delphi makes it very easy to generate a GUID whenever you need one. Simply position the cursor where you want to insert the GUID and press Ctrl + Shift + G. Internally, Delphi makes a call to the Windows API function CoCreateGuid to generate GUIDs.

Listing 1.1 shows a sample program that calls CoCreateGuid directly to generate a list of GUIDs.

---

**Listing 1.1**   *The Main Form of the GUIDDemo Application*

```
unit MainForm;

interface

uses
  Windows, Messages, SysUtils, Classes, Graphics, Controls, Forms,
  Dialogs, StdCtrls, ComObj, ActiveX;

type
  TForm1 = class(TForm)
    btnGenerate: TButton;
    Memo1: TMemo;
    procedure btnGenerateClick(Sender: TObject);
  private
    { Private declarations }
  public
    { Public declarations }
  end;

var
  Form1: TForm1;

implementation
```

```
{$R *.DFM}

procedure TForm1.btnGenerateClick(Sender: TObject);
var
  Guid: TGUID;
begin
  CoCreateGuid(Guid);
  Memo1.Lines.Add(GuidToString(Guid));
end;

end.
```

Figure 1.1 shows GUIDDemo in action.

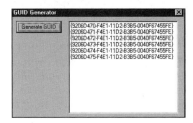

**Figure 1.1**    *GUIDDemo demonstrates how to call CoCreateGuid.*

Notice that the GUIDs appear to be sequentially numbered. However, if you close the program and run it again, a completely different set of GUIDs will be generated.

Delphi defines the TGUID structure as follows:

```
TGUID = record
  D1: LongWord;
  D2: Word;
  D3: Word;
  D4: array[0..7] of Byte;
end;
```

The four fields in TGUID correspond to the four parts of the GUID structure. GUIDS can be represented in two ways in Delphi. For instance, using IFormattedNumber's GUID as an example, the following two declarations are identical:

```
MyGuid := ['{2DE825C1-EADF-11D2-B39F-0040F67455FE}'];

MyGUID: TGUID = (D1: $2DE825C1; D2: $EADF; D3: $11D2; D4: ($B3, $9F, $00, $40, $F6,
➡$74, $55, $FE));
```

Obviously, the first line is much easier to read.

Declaring the interface is the first half of creating a useful interface. After the interface is declared, you still need to provide the implementation of the interface. In the next section, I'll show you how to implement an interface.

# Implementing an Interface

As I mentioned in the last section, you cannot create an instance of an interface. How, then, do you use the IFormattedNumber interface?

The answer is that you create a class that implements the interface, like this:

```
type
  TFormattedInteger = class(TObject, IFormattedNumber)
  private:
    FValue: Integer;
  public:
    constructor Create(AValue: Integer);
    function FormattedString: string; procedure SetValue(AValue: Integer);
  end;
```

We can now flesh out the class, in the usual way, as follows:

```
constructor TFormattedInteger.Create(AValue: Integer);
begin
  inherited Create;

  FValue := AValue;
end;

function TFormattedInteger.FormattedString: string;
begin
  Result := 'The value is ' + IntToStr(FValue);
end;

procedure TFormattedInteger.SetValue(AValue: Integer);
begin
  FValue := Value;
end;
```

If you try to compile this code at this point, you'll get the following errors:

```
Undeclared identifier: 'QueryInterface'
Undeclared identifier: '_AddRef'
Undeclared identifier: '_Release'
```

Where are these identifiers coming from? We certainly didn't define them in our code. These are the functions that are declared in the IUnknown interface. Recall that earlier I told you that all interfaces are ultimately derived from IUnknown. However, I didn't explain exactly what IUnknown is.

## Implementing IUnknown

If you look in the VCL source code for system.pas, you'll see the following declaration:

```
IUnknown = interface
  ['{00000000-0000-0000-C000-000000000046}']
  function QueryInterface(const IID: TGUID; out Obj): HResult; stdcall;
```

```
  function _AddRef: Integer; stdcall;
  function _Release: Integer; stdcall;
end;
```

IUnknown is the root of all interfaces, and is defined by Microsoft. QueryInterface, _AddRef, and _Release are functions that must be implemented by all descendents of IUnknown, which means they must be implemented by all classes that implement an interface.

Let's take a few moments to explore the IUnknown interface in detail.

### QueryInterface

QueryInterface is a function that requests a pointer to an interface. If the interface is implemented by the object in question, QueryInterface returns that interface in the Obj parameter, and returns the value 0. If the interface is not implemented by the object, QueryInterface returns the Microsoft-defined constant E_NOINTERFACE.

### _AddRef

Interfaces are reference counted, so when you obtain a pointer to an interface on an object, the number of references to the object is incremented. When you are finished with the interface, the number of references to the object is decremented. When the number of references reaches zero, the object is automatically destroyed. _AddRef is the function responsible for incrementing the reference count. How you physically store the reference count is up to you, but you will typically set up an Integer variable to hold the count.

### _Release

_Release is the function responsible for decrementing the reference count. When the reference count reaches zero, the object is automatically destroyed.

Reference counting is discussed in more detail later in the section titled "Interfaces Are Reference Counted." For now, just be aware that interfaces are reference counted, and that _AddRef increases the reference count and _Release decreases the reference count.

### Implementing IUnknown Manually

We can't compile TFormattedNumber yet because it doesn't implement the IUnknown interface. It's easy to add the necessary functions. Take a look at the new TFormattedInteger declaration, shown in Listing 1.2.

**Listing 1.2**    *Implementing IUnknown*

```
type
  TFormattedInteger = class(TObject, IFormattedNumber)
  private:
    FRefCount: Integer;
    FValue: Integer;
  public:
    Constructor Create(AValue: Integer);

    // IUnknown interface
    function QueryInterface(const IID: TGUID; out Obj): HResult; stdcall;
    function _AddRef: Integer; stdcall;
    function _Release: Integer; stdcall;

    // IFormattedNumber interface
    Function FormattedString: string; virtual;
    Procedure SetValue(AValue: Integer);
end;

constructor TFormattedInteger.Create(AValue: Integer);
begin
  Inherited Create;

  FValue := AValue;
end;

// IUnknown interface

function TFormattedInteger.QueryInterface(const IID: TGUID; out Obj): HResult; stdcall;
const
  E_NOINTERFACE = $80004002;
begin
  if GetInterface(IID, Obj) then
    Result := 0
  else
    Result := E_NOINTERFACE;
end;

function TFormattedInteger._AddRef: Integer; stdcall;
begin
  Inc(FRefCount);
  Result := FrefCount;
end;

function TFormattedInteger._Release: Integer; stdcall;
begin
  Dec(FrefCount);
  Result := FrefCount;
  If FRefCount = 0 then
    Destroy;
end;

// IFormattedNumber interface

function TFormattedInteger.FormattedString: string;
```

```
begin
  Result := 'The value is ' + IntToStr(FValue);
end;

procedure TFormattedInteger.SetValue(AValue: Integer);
begin
  FValue := Value;
end;
```

I'm going to ignore the implementation of QueryInterface for the time being. For now, just accept that it's a fairly standard implementation for that function. Later in this chapter, I'll explore QueryInterface in more detail.

As you can see, _AddRef and _Release simply increment and decrement the FRefCount variable. When the value of the variable is decremented to zero, the object is destroyed.

### Using TInterfacedObject to Implement IUnknown Automatically

Fortunately, you don't have to write that code every time you create a class that implements an interface. Delphi provides a class named TInterfacedObject that already implements the IUnknown interface for you. Listing 1.3 shows the source code for the parts of TInterfacedObject that are of interest to this discussion. TInterfacedObject is defined in system.pas.

**Listing 1.3**   *The Source Code for TInterfacedObject*

```
TInterfacedObject = class(TObject, IUnknown)
protected
  FRefCount: Integer;
  function QueryInterface(const IID: TGUID; out Obj): HResult; stdcall;
  function _AddRef: Integer; stdcall;
  function _Release: Integer; stdcall;
public
  procedure BeforeDestruction; override;
  property RefCount: Integer read FRefCount;
end;

procedure TInterfacedObject.BeforeDestruction;
begin
  if RefCount <> 0 then Error(reInvalidPtr);
end;

function TInterfacedObject.QueryInterface(const IID: TGUID; out Obj): HResult;
const
  E_NOINTERFACE = $80004002;
Begin
  if GetInterface(IID, Obj) then Result := 0 else Result := E_NOINTERFACE;
end;

function TInterfacedObject._AddRef: Integer;
```

*continues* ▶

**Listing 1.3** *continued*

```
begin
  Result := InterlockedIncrement(FRefCount);
end;

function TInterfacedObject._Release: Integer;
begin
  Result := InterlockedDecrement(FRefCount);
  if Result = 0 then
    Destroy;
end;
```

Other than for the use of InterlockedIncrement and InterlockedDecrement for thread-safety, and the RefCount property, this class' implementation of IUnknown is almost identical to the one we just developed. However, the existence of this class means that instead of deriving from TObject and repeatedly implementing IUnknown, you can simply derive from TInterfacedObject instead.

There are times, however, when you might want to provide your own implementation of the IUnknown interface. Later in this chapter, in the section titled "Circumventing Automatic Reference Counting," we will explore the reasons for doing that.

## Creating, Using, and Destroying Interfaces

After you've written the code for the class, you can use it just as you would use any other class. For example:

```
var
  MyNumber: TFormattedInteger;
begin
  MyNumber := TFormattedInteger.Create(12);
  ShowMessage(MyNumber.FormattedString);
  MyNumber.Free;
end;
```

You're probably wondering what good the interface declaration is, because it doesn't appear to provide any benefits at all. The preceding code fragment can also be written in another, similar fashion. Look at the following code, which is functionally equivalent to the last example:

```
var
  MyNumber: IFormattedNumber;
begin
  MyNumber := TFormattedInteger.Create(12);
  ShowMessage(MyNumber.FormattedString);
end;
```

There are several points of interest in this code fragment. First, MyNumber is defined as an IFormattedNumber instead of a TFormattedInteger. In this example, MyNumber is a pointer to an interface—not a pointer to an object instance. There is a very important distinction to be made here. MyNumber does not have access to any information other than what is defined in the IFormattedNumber interface. For instance, the following code will not compile:

```
MyNumber.SetValue(10);
```

The compiler will complain with

```
Undeclared identified: 'SetValue'
```

Any variable of type IFormattedNumber only "sees" the declaration of IFormattedNumber, even if it was created as a TFormattedInteger, as in the preceding code.

The next important item I would like to draw your attention to is that this code does not explicitly free MyNumber. This looks like a surefire memory leak, but *MyNumber is automatically freed at the end of the procedure.* This requires some explanation.

### Interfaces Are Reference Counted

As mentioned earlier, interfaces are reference counted. What I didn't explain, though, was exactly how the reference counting mechanism works. Delphi works hard behind the scenes to make reference counting as invisible to you as possible. I should point out that with most languages, this is not the case. If you code with C++, for example (but not with C++ Builder), you need to manually call AddRef and Release to increment and decrement the reference count, respectively.

Was that a typo in the previous paragraph? When we examined TFormattedInteger earlier, we implemented functions named _AddRef and _Release. Now I'm talking about AddRef and Release. The original names assigned to these functions by Microsoft were AddRef and Release. Borland changed the function names by prepending the underscores, in order to reinforce the concept that you will typically not call these functions yourself.

To gain an appreciation for all Delphi does for us, let's take a moment to consider how you would write code that uses an interface in a typical language. I'll use Delphi syntax for this example, because you might not be familiar with other languages, such as C or C++.

```
procedure DoSomethingWithInterfaces;
var
  MyIntf: IFormattedNumber;
begin
  MyIntf := TFormattedInteger.Create(12);
  MyIntf.AddRef;
  ShowMessage(MyIntf.FormattedString);
  MyIntf.Release;

  MyIntf := TFormattedHexInteger.Create(1024);
  MyIntf.AddRef;
```

```
ShowMessage(MyIntf.FormattedString);
  MyIntf.Release;
end;
```

As soon as we obtain a reference to an interface (which we do in the first line of code), it is our responsibility to explicitly call AddRef to add a reference to that interface. As long as someone holds a reference to an object's interface, the object will not be destroyed. Therefore, we need to increment the object's reference count as soon as possible.

After we've called AddRef, we can use the interface to call any method of that interface. After we're done with the interface, we call Release to decrement the reference count. Inside the Release function, if the reference count reaches zero, the object is automatically destroyed.

Now let's see what we need to do in Delphi to accomplish the same thing:

```
procedure DoSomethingWithInterfaces;
var
  MyIntf: IFormattedNumber;
begin
  MyIntf := TFormattedInteger.Create(12);
  ShowMessage(MyIntf.FormattedString);

  MyIntf := TFormattedHexInteger.Create(1024);
  ShowMessage(MyIntf.FormattedString);
end;
```

That's it! We can code as if _AddRef and _Release don't even exist. If you don't call _AddRef and _Release, then exactly how (and when) do they get called? Delphi will automatically make the calls for you, at the appropriate times. Let's take a look behind the scenes to see exactly what Delphi is doing for us. The code Delphi automatically injects into our application is marked as such with comments. Note that Delphi does not physically add this code to your source files—this is simply a hypothetical representation of what is added to your executable when you compile.

```
procedure DoSomethingWithInterfaces;
var
  MyIntf: IFormattedNumber;
begin
  MyIntf := TFormattedInteger.Create(12);
  MyIntf._AddRef;  // Added by Delphi
  ShowMessage(MyIntf.FormattedString);

  MyIntf._Release;  // Added by Delphi
  MyIntf := TFormattedHexInteger.Create(1024);
  MyIntf._AddRef;  // Added by Delphi
  ShowMessage(MyIntf.FormattedString);
```

```
    MyIntf._Release;  // Added by Delphi
  end;
```

By the way, if you ever want to force an interface to be released, you can simply set the interface variable to nil, like this:

```
MyIntf := nil;
```

## Obtaining a Pointer to an Interface

Delphi provides a number of ways to get a pointer to an interface. You can obtain a pointer to an interface given an object that implements the interface, or given a pointer to another interface. I will discuss multiple interfaces later in this chapter, in the section "Advanced Interface Issues."

### Direct Assignment

The easiest way to obtain an interface from an object is through direct assignment. Classes are type-compatible with the interfaces they implement, so you can write code like this:

```
var
  MyInteger: TFormattedInteger;
  MyNumber: IFormattedNumber;
begin
  MyInteger := TFormattedInteger.Create(12);
  MyNumber := MyInteger;
end;
```

This code is checked at compile time, so if the object in question does not support the interface, then you will get a compile-time error. Sometimes, though, you don't know if an object supports an interface, and you would like to find out at runtime. The GetInterface function allows you to do just that.

### GetInterface

GetInterface is defined like this:

```
function TObject.GetInterface(const IID: TGUID; out Obj): Boolean;
```

The IID parameter takes the GUID of the interface to which you want to get a pointer.

```
var
  MyObject: TObject;
  MyNumber: IFormattedNumber;
begin
  MyObject := TFormattedInteger.Create(12);
  ...
  if MyObject.GetInterface(IFormattedNumber, MyNumber) then
    ShowMessage(MyNumber.FormattedString);
end;
```

Recall that the implementation of QueryInterface we saw earlier called GetInterface to obtain the interface in question.

### The *as* Operator

Delphi makes it even easier to get an interface, though, if you know that an object supports it. Delphi overloads the **as** operator so that you can write code like this:

```
var
  MyObject: TObject;
  MyNumber: IFormattedNumber;
begin
  MyObject := TFormattedInteger.Create(12);
  ...
  MyNumber := MyObject as IFormattedNumber;
  ShowMessage(MyNumber.FormattedString);
end;
```

The difference between this code and the code which uses GetInterface is that in this example, if MyNumber does not support the IFormattedNumber interface, an exception will be raised.

In general, you can use the **as** operator if you know that the object in question supports a given interface, or if it would be an error for the object not to support the interface. Use the GetInterface function if you want to see whether an object supports an interface, but you don't want an exception to be thrown if the interface is not supported.

The **as** operator differs from GetInterface in one other important way. GetInterface is a member of TObject, and can only be used on objects. The **as** operator can be used both on objects that implement IUnknown (as determined by Delphi) and on interfaces themselves. For example:

```
procedure DoSomethingWithObject(O: TObject);
var
  MyNumber: IFormattedNumber;
begin
  if O.GetInterface(IFormattedNumber, MyNumber) then
    ShowMessage(MyNumber.FormattedString);
end;

procedure DoSomethingWithInterface(I: IUnknown);
var
  MyNumber: IFormattedNumber;
begin
  ShowMessage((I as IFormattedNumber).FormattedString);
end;
```

*GetInterface and the **as** operator will only work if the interface is declared with a GUID. That's why I mentioned earlier that you should always create a GUID for an interface, even though is not strictly required for a non-COM interface. If you don't associate a GUID with an interface, you'll get the following cryptic compiler error when compiling an **as** statement:*

```
Operator not applicable to this operand type
```

*GetInterface will generate the following, more informative, compile error:*

```
Interface 'IFormattedNumber' has no interface identification ♦
```

## Object Model and Interface Model Do Not Mix

In the examples presented so far, I've been showing you both object references and interface references as if they work together and are interchangeable. That is not the case. The interface model is an alternative to the reference model. When implementing one or more interfaces in a class, you should manipulate objects of the class using only interfaces. This section shows you how you can get into trouble by mixing the object model and the reference model, and a hack you can use if you are in a situation which absolutely requires mixing the two models.

*When you feel you're in a situation that requires mixing the object model and interface model, it more than likely means you have a design flaw in your application. ♦*

The **as** operator has one side effect you need to be aware of. Using the **as** operator causes Delphi to make a call to _AddRef. When you are done with the interface, of course, Delphi will call _Release, and your object will be destroyed (assuming the reference count goes to zero). Here is an example that mixes the object model with the interface model and suffers for it:

```
procedure DoSomethingWithInterface(Intf: IFormattedNumber);
begin
  ShowMessage(Intf.FormattedString);
end;

procedure CreateAndUseObject;
var
  MyInteger: TFormattedInteger;
begin
  MyInteger := TFormattedInteger.Create(12);
  DoSomethingWithInterface(MyInteger as IFormattedNumber);

  MyInteger.SetValue(10);
end.
```

In this example, MyInteger is an object of class TFormattedInteger. It is created using the object model (in other words, the result of TFormattedInteger.Create is assigned to an object variable). An interface is obtained on IFormattedNumber for the duration of the function call to DoSomethingWithInterface (this is where the code switched to the interface model). Delphi automatically calls _AddRef just before the function call is made. At this point, the reference count is incremented to 1. When the function call returns, Delphi calls _Release, and the reference count is decremented to 0, destroying the object in the process.

The net result is that after the call to DoSomethingWithInterface, MyInteger is no longer valid. Any reference to MyInteger is sure to cause an access violation.

Note that if DoSomethingWithInterface is declared as either

```
procedure DoSomethingWithInterface(var Intf: IFormattedNumber)
```

or

```
procedure DoSomethingWithInterface(const Intf: IFormattedNumber)
```

then the interface won't be released, and the object won't be automatically destroyed. The reasoning behind this is simple enough: A const or var parameter causes Delphi to pass the interface by reference instead of by value. Passing the interface by value forces _AddRef and _Release to be called.

The correct way to write the previous code (following the interface model) is this:

```
procedure DoSomethingWithInterface(Intf: IFormattedNumber);
begin
  ShowMessage(Intf.FormattedString);
end;

procedure CreateAndUseInterface;
var
  MyInteger: IFormattedInteger;
begin
  MyInteger := TFormattedInteger.Create(12);
  DoSomethingWithInterface(MyInteger);

  MyInteger.SetValue(10);
end.
```

This code uses only the interface model (there are no variables of type TFormattedInteger in this code). As a result, the reference count of MyInteger is 1 when it is created. During the call to DoSomethingWithInterface, the reference count gets incremented momentarily to 2 and then decremented back to 1, leaving the MyInteger variable intact.

**Circumventing Automatic Reference Counting**

I showed you what can happen when you mix reference models in your application. Now I'll show you two ways that you can circumvent automatic reference counting if you feel you must mix reference models.

Take a look at the following code:

```
procedure DoSomethingWithInterface(Intf: IFormattedNumber);
begin
  ShowMessage(Intf.FormattedString);
end;

procedure CreateAndUseObject;
var
  MyInteger: TFormattedInteger;
begin
  MyInteger := TFormattedInteger.Create(12);
  MyInteger._AddRef;

  DoSomethingWithInterface(MyInteger as IFormattedNumber);

  MyInteger.SetValue(10);
  MyInteger._Release;
end.
```

This solution works, but you have to remember to call _AddRef and _Release on each object after you've finished with it. Another solution is to attack the problem at the root by implementing a class that doesn't destroy itself when the reference count goes to zero.

Delphi does not provide such a class for us, but it's easy to create one. The following is a simple implementation of a class that is not automatically destroyed by reference counting:

```
  TNonRefCountedObject = class(TInterfacedObject, IUnknown)
  protected
function _AddRef: Integer; stdcall;
    function _Release: Integer; stdcall;
  end;

    function TNonRefCountedObject._AddRef: Integer;
begin
  Result := -1;
end;

function TNonRefCountedObject._Release: Integer;
begin
  Result := -1;
end;
```

Notice what's going on here. I simply derived TNonRefCountedObject from TInterfacedObject, and re-implemented the methods required to circumvent reference counting.

*Even though _AddRef and _Release aren't declared as virtual in
TInterfacedObject, you can override the implementation of those methods by simply redeclaring the interface and the methods in the descendent class. If they were declared as virtual, you could still override them by adding the override directive onto the end of the definition in the TNonRefCountedClass, but the compiler would actually generate more code for each method. ♦*

As you can see, the _AddRef and _Release methods now return –1, instead of implementing any actual reference counting. This code will never attempt to destroy the object, so assuming that TFormattedInteger is derived from TNonRefCountedObject, we can use it like this:

```
procedure DoSomethingWithInterface(Intf: IFormattedNumber);
begin
   ShowMessage(Intf.FormattedString);
end;

procedure CreateAndUseObject;
var
   MyInteger: TFormattedInteger;
begin
   MyInteger := TFormattedInteger.Create(12);

   DoSomethingWithInterface(MyInteger as IFormattedNumber);

   MyInteger.SetValue(10);
   MyInteger.Free;
end.
```

Please remember that neither of these "solutions" is anything more than a dirty hack. The *real* solution is to avoid mixing the object model and interface model altogether.

Perhaps not obviously, what this means is that you shouldn't arbitrarily add interface support to a class after the class has already been written. If you're going to use interfaces, the class should be designed for interfaces right from the start, and interfaces should be the only access method used for the class.

## Example: Interface Demo

This example program illustrates most of the concepts discussed so far. Figure 1.2 shows a screen shot of IntfDemo's main form.

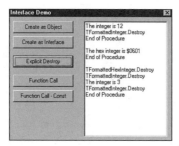

**Figure 1.2**    *The IntfDemo sample application.*

This example takes the IFormattedNumber interface you're so familiar with by now and creates two classes that implement the interface: TFormattedInteger and TFormattedHexInteger. Because TFormattedHexInteger derives from TFormattedInteger, it doesn't have to explicitly list the IFormattedNumber interface; TFormattedNumber has already taken care of that requirement.

The destructors for both TFormattedInteger and TFormattedHexInteger have been overridden so you can see exactly when they get called.

The main form has five buttons and a memo. The top button creates an object, calls a method of that object, and then destroys the object—nothing out of the ordinary.

The second button also creates an object, but it assigns the object to an interface variable. The interface goes out of scope at the end of the procedure, and the object is automatically destroyed—you don't need to explicitly free the object.

The third button does the same thing as button two, except it demonstrates how to set an interface variable to nil in order to force it to be released immediately. Consequently, the object is destroyed immediately.

The fourth button creates an object, and then makes a function call that implicitly obtains an interface from the object. When the function call returns, the object is automatically destroyed. It is important to understand exactly what's going on here, since this can be a source of memory problems if you're not careful.

The final button does the same thing as button four, except the parameter to the function call is defined as const. This circumvents the automatic calls to _AddRef and _Release, and the object is not automatically destroyed.

The file intfunit.pas defines the IFormattedNumber interface, and the two classes that implement it (see Listing 1.4).

**Listing 1.4**    *IntfDemo Source: intfunit.pas*

```
unit IntfUnit;

interface

uses
  Classes, SysUtils, Dialogs;

type
  IFormattedNumber = interface
    ['{2DE825C1-EADF-11D2-B39F-0040F67455FE}']
    function FormattedString: string;
    function GetName: string;
  end;

  TFormattedInteger = class(TInterfacedObject, IFormattedNumber)
  private
    FValue: Integer;
  public
    constructor Create(AValue: Integer);
    destructor Destroy; override;
    function FormattedString: string; function GetName: string; end;

  TFormattedHexInteger = class(TFormattedInteger, IFormattedNumber)
  public
    destructor Destroy; override;
    function FormattedString: string; function GetName: string; end;

implementation

uses
  MainForm;

{ TFormattedInteger }

constructor TFormattedInteger.Create(AValue: Integer);
begin
  inherited Create;

  FValue := AValue;
end;

destructor TFormattedInteger.Destroy;
begin
  Form1.Memo1.Lines.Add('TFormattedInteger.Destroy');

  inherited Destroy;
end;

function TFormattedInteger.FormattedString: string;
begin
  Result := 'The integer is ' + IntToStr(FValue);
end;

function TFormattedInteger.GetName: string;
```

```
begin
  Result := 'TFormattedInteger.GetName';
end;

{ TFormattedHexInteger }

destructor TFormattedHexInteger.Destroy;
begin
  Form1.Memo1.Lines.Add('TFormattedHexInteger.Destroy');

  inherited Destroy;
end;

function TFormattedHexInteger.FormattedString: string;
begin
  Result := 'The hex integer is $' + IntToHex(FValue, 4);
end;

function TFormattedHexInteger.GetName: string;
begin
  Result := 'TFormattedHexInteger.GetName';
end;

end.
```

Listing 1.5 shows the source code for the IntfDemo's main form.

**Listing 1.5**   *IntfDemo Source: mainform.pas*

```
unit MainForm;

interface

uses
  Windows, Messages, SysUtils, Classes, Graphics, Controls, Forms,
  Dialogs, StdCtrls, IntfUnit;

type
  TForm1 = class(TForm)
    btnAsObject: TButton;
    Memo1: TMemo;
    btnAsInterface: TButton;
    btnExplicitDestroy: TButton;
    btnFunction: TButton;
    btnConstFunction: TButton;
    procedure btnAsObjectClick(Sender: TObject);
    procedure btnAsInterfaceClick(Sender: TObject);
    procedure btnExplicitDestroyClick(Sender: TObject);
    procedure btnFunctionClick(Sender: TObject);
    procedure btnConstFunctionClick(Sender: TObject);
  private
    { Private declarations }
    procedure ShowName(Intf: IFormattedNumber);
    procedure ShowNameConst(const Intf: IFormattedNumber);
```

*continues* ▶

**Listing 1.4**  *continued*

```
public
  { Public declarations }
end;

var
  Form1: TForm1;

implementation

{$R *.DFM}

procedure TForm1.btnAsObjectClick(Sender: TObject);
var
  MyInt: TFormattedInteger;
begin
  MyInt := TFormattedInteger.Create(12);
  Memo1.Lines.Add(MyInt.FormattedString);
  MyInt.Free;  // You must free MyInt

  Memo1.Lines.Add('End of Procedure');
  Memo1.Lines.Add('');
end;

procedure TForm1.btnAsInterfaceClick(Sender: TObject);
var
  MyIntf: IFormattedNumber;
begin
  MyIntf := TFormattedHexInteger.Create(1537);
  Memo1.Lines.Add(MyIntf.FormattedString);

  Memo1.Lines.Add('End of Procedure');
  Memo1.Lines.Add('');

  // MyIntf is automatically destroyed here
end;

procedure TForm1.btnExplicitDestroyClick(Sender: TObject);
var
  MyIntf: IFormattedNumber;
begin
  MyIntf := TFormattedInteger.Create(3);
  Memo1.Lines.Add(MyIntf.FormattedString);
  MyIntf := nil;    // Explicitly destroy object

  Memo1.Lines.Add('End of Procedure');
  Memo1.Lines.Add('');
end;

procedure TForm1.ShowName(Intf: IFormattedNumber);
begin
  Memo1.Lines.Add(Intf.GetName);
end;
```

```
procedure TForm1.btnFunctionClick(Sender: TObject);
var
  MyInt: TFormattedInteger;
  MyHexIntf: IFormattedNumber;
begin
  MyInt := TFormattedInteger.Create(27);
  ShowName(MyInt);
  // MyInt is automatically destroyed here

  // MyInt.Free;  This will cause an access violation!

  MyHexIntf := TFormattedHexInteger.Create(2047);
  ShowName(MyHexIntf);

  Memo1.Lines.Add('End of Procedure');
  Memo1.Lines.Add('');
end;

procedure TForm1.ShowNameConst(const Intf: IFormattedNumber);
begin
  Memo1.Lines.Add(Intf.GetName);
end;

procedure TForm1.btnConstFunctionClick(Sender: TObject);
var
  MyInt: TFormattedInteger;
begin
  MyInt := TFormattedInteger.Create(27);
  ShowNameConst(MyInt);
  MyInt.Free;

  Memo1.Lines.Add('End of Procedure');
  Memo1.Lines.Add('');
end;

end.
```

Listing 1.6 shows the source code for the IntfDemo's project file.

**Listing 1.6**   *IntfDemo Source: intfdemo.dpr*
```
program IntfDemo;

uses
  Forms,
  MainForm in 'MainForm.pas' {Form1},
  IntfUnit in 'IntfUnit.pas';

{$R *.RES}

begin
  Application.Initialize;
  Application.CreateForm(TForm1, Form1);
  Application.Run;
end.
```

This example shows several illustrations of accessing the TFormattedInteger and TFormattedHexInteger classes through both objects and interfaces. Because the objects and interfaces are created, used, and destroyed all within the same event handler, I'm not really mixing reference models in this code. Rather, I'm trying to show you how lifetime management differs between objects and interfaces.

In this section, you've learned how to define and implement interfaces. I stressed that if you're going to use interfaces, you should use them as the only means of access to your objects. I also showed you a nasty hack or two that you can use to force the object model and interface model to coexist if you feel you must.

In the next section, I'll show you some concrete sample programs that are built on interfaces.

# Programming with Interfaces

So far in this chapter, we really haven't looked at any real-life examples of using interfaces in your Delphi code. Let's stop now and look at an example that puts interfaces to good use in a familiar programming concept: sorting.

## SortDemo Example: Algorithms with Interfaces

Many programs make use of sorting to some extent. Simpler programs might use a well-placed bubble sort algorithm here or there, whereas more complex programs may require a workhorse quicksort or mergesort algorithm. Usually when you implement a sort routine in your application, it is tightly bound to the data you want to sort. How many times have you written code such as the following?

```
procedure SortEmployees;
// - sort an array of employees by name
var
  I, J: Integer;
begin
  for I := 1 to MAX_EMPLOYEES -1 do
    for J := I + 1 to MAX_EMPLOYEES do
      if EmployeeArray[J].Name < EmployeeArray[I].Name then begin
        Temp := EmployeeArray[I];
        EmployeeArray[I] := EmployeeArray[J];
        EmployeeArray[J] := Temp;
      end;
end;
```

The only thing this procedure is ever going to sort is an array of employee records. You probably justify implementing the procedure this way because it's just a quick bubble-sort procedure, and you can bang out the code so fast that you don't even have to think about it.

Wouldn't it be nicer to have a stock routine in your bag of tricks that could be used not only for sorting, but also for ordering elements in a sorted list, and anywhere else a comparison function is needed? Using interfaces, you can accomplish this easily.

Let's define an interface called ICompare. ICompare's job will be to compare an object (ObjectA) to another similar object (ObjectB), and return –1 if ObjectA comes *before* ObjectB, 0 if the two objects are equal, or 1 if ObjectA comes *after* ObjectB. To make this example more useful, I'm going to add to this interface the capability to support multiple ordering methods for an object. Here is the interface declaration:

```
type
  ICompare = interface
  ['{DDFE0840-E8FB-11D2-9085-0040F6741DE2}']
    function CompareWith(ACompareTo: ICompare; AOrderBy: Integer): Integer;
  end;
```

This interface's sole purpose in life is to provide an object with the means of ordering itself in some way. This illustrates another important point about interfaces: When creating an interface, make it as specific as possible. You don't want to create the Swiss army knife of interfaces. An interface that is multipurpose will not be useful in very many situations. More than likely, it will be specific only to a single application you're writing. Instead of one general-purpose interface, create several smaller, more focused interfaces that you can reuse in many different situations.

The usage for this interface will be like this:

```
if MyObject1.CompareWith(MyObject2, SortIndex) < 0 then
  // MyObject1 comes before MyObject2
```

The parameter AOrderBy is intended to let this interface's implementor define many ordering methods. For example, a TStudent class in a college enrollment program might need to order students by name or social security number. The TStudent class can define the number 1 to mean order by name, and the number 2 to mean order by social security number.

Listing 1.7 shows the source code for unit IntfUnit, which declares the ICompare interface and implements a simple, yet reusable, bubble sort.

**Listing 1.7**    *SortDemo Source: intfunit.pas*

```
unit IntfUnit;

interface

type
  ICompare = interface
  ['{DDFE0840-E8FB-11D2-9085-0040F6741DE2}']
    function CompareWith(ACompare: ICompare; ASortBy: Integer): Integer;
  end;
```

*continues* ▶

**Listing 1.7**  *continued*

```
procedure SortArray(var A: Array of IUnknown; ASortBy: Integer);

implementation

procedure SortArray(var A: Array of IUnknown;
  ASortBy: Integer);
var
  I, J: Integer;
  Temp: IUnknown;
begin
  for I := Low(A) to High(A) - 1 do begin
    for J := I + 1 to High(A) do begin
      if (A[J] as ICompare).CompareWith(A[I] as ICompare, ASortBy) < 0 then begin
        Temp := A[I];
        A[I] := A[J];
        A[J] := Temp;
      end;
    end;
  end;
end;

end.
```

Note that SortArray takes an array of IUnknown. If I passed in an array of TInterfacedObjects, for example, then the following line of code would cause the objects to be destroyed prematurely:

```
if (A[J] as ICompare).CompareWith(A[I], AOrderBy) < 0 then begin
```

The **as** operator would cause Delphi to call _AddRef and _Release on the ICompare interface, which would destroy all the objects I'm sorting right in the middle of the sort. This is a classic example of when mixing reference models can get you into trouble.

The SortDemo example defines two different classes that implement the ICompare interface: TEmployee and TInventoryItem. These classes are defined in the units EmpUnit and InvUnit, respectively. Listing 1.8 shows the source code for the EmpUnit unit.

**Listing 1.8**  *SortDemo Source: empunit.pas*

```
unit EmpUnit;

interface

uses
  SysUtils, IntfUnit;

type
  TEmployeeOrder = (eoName, eoSalary);
```

```
  IEmployee = interface
    ['{FFCD24F0-4FE8-11D3-B84D-0040F67455FE}']
    function GetName: string;
    function GetSalary: Double;
  end;

  TEmployee = class(TInterfacedObject, IEmployee, ICompare)
  private
    FName: string;
    FSalary: double;
  public
    constructor Create(AName: string; ASalary: Double);
    function CompareWith(ACompare: ICompare;
      ASortBy: Integer): Integer;
    function GetName: string;
    function GetSalary: Double;
  end;

implementation

{ TEmployee }

function TEmployee.CompareWith(ACompare: ICompare;
  ASortBy: Integer): Integer;
var
  Emp: IEmployee;
begin
  Result := 0;

  Emp := ACompare as IEmployee;

  case ASortBy of
    Ord(eoName):
      Result := CompareStr(FName, Emp.GetName);

    Ord(eoSalary):
      if FSalary < Emp.GetSalary then
        Result := -1
      else if FSalary> Emp.GetSalary then
        Result := 1
      else
        Result := 0;
  end;
end;

constructor TEmployee.Create(AName: string; ASalary: Double);
begin
  inherited Create;

  FName := AName;
  FSalary := ASalary;
end;
```

*continues* ▶

**Listing 1.8** *continued*

```
function TEmployee.GetName: string;
begin
  Result := FName;
end;

function TEmployee.GetSalary: Double;
begin
  Result := FSalary;
end;

end.
```

TEmployee is a simple class used to track employee names and salaries. Employees can be sorted by either name or salary. I have implemented the enumerated type TEmployeeOrder to specify valid ordering methods for the TEmployee class.

Listing 1.9 shows the source code for the InvUnit unit.

**Listing 1.9** *SortDemo Source: invunit.pas*

```
unit InvUnit;

interface

uses
  SysUtils, IntfUnit;

type
  TInventoryItemOrder = (iioPartNumber, iioDescription,
    iioUnitPrice, iioInStock);

  IInventoryItem = interface
    ['{FFCD24F1-4FE8-11D3-B84D-0040F67455FE}']
    function GetPartNumber: string;
    function GetDescription: string;
    function GetInStock: Integer;
    function GetUnitPrice: Double;
  end;

  TInventoryItem = class(TInterfacedObject, IInventoryItem, ICompare)
  private
    FPartNumber: string;
    FDescription: string;
    FInStock: Integer;
    FUnitPrice: Double;
  public
    constructor Create(APartNumber: string; ADescription: string;
      AInStock: Integer; AUnitPrice: Double);
    function CompareWith(ACompare: ICompare; ASortBy: Integer): Integer;
    function GetPartNumber: string;
    function GetDescription: string;
```

```
    function GetInStock: Integer;
    function GetUnitPrice: Double;
  end;

implementation

{ TInventoryItem }

function TInventoryItem.CompareWith(ACompare: ICompare;
  ASortBy: Integer): Integer;
var
  Inv: IInventoryItem;
begin
  Result := 0;

  Inv := ACompare as IInventoryItem;

  case ASortBy of
    Ord(iioPartNumber):
      Result := CompareStr(FPartNumber, Inv.GetPartNumber);

    Ord(iioDescription):
      Result := CompareStr(FDescription, Inv.GetDescription);

    Ord(iioInStock):
      Result := FInStock - Inv.GetInStock;

    Ord(iioUnitPrice):
      if FUnitPrice < Inv.GetUnitPrice then
        Result := -1
      else if FUnitPrice> Inv.GetUnitPrice then
        Result := 1
      else
        Result := 0;
  end;
end;

constructor TInventoryItem.Create(APartNumber, ADescription: string;
  AInStock: Integer; AUnitPrice: Double);
begin
  inherited Create;

  FPartNumber := APartNumber;
  FDescription := ADescription;
  FInStock := AInStock;
  FUnitPrice := AUnitPrice;
end;

function TInventoryItem.GetDescription: string;
begin
  Result := FDescription;
end;
```

*continues* ▶

**Listing 1.9** *continued*

```
function TInventoryItem.GetInStock: Integer;
begin
  Result := FInStock;
end;

function TInventoryItem.GetPartNumber: string;
begin
  Result := FPartNumber;
end;

function TInventoryItem.GetUnitPrice: Double;
begin
  Result := FUnitPrice;
end;

end.
```

TInventoryItem is similar in nature to TEmployee, but it is used to track inventory items, and can be sorted by part number, description, unit price, or quantity in stock (iioPartNumber, iioDescription, iioUnitPrice, or iioInStock).

The reason for creating these two disparate classes is to show you that you can easily use the same ICompare interface to sort completely independent sets of data.

Listing 1.10 shows the code for SortDemo's main form.

**Listing 1.10**    *SortDemo Source: mainform.pas*

```
unit MainForm;

interface

uses
  Windows, Messages, SysUtils, Classes, Graphics, Controls, Forms,
  Dialogs, StdCtrls, ComCtrls, IntfUnit, EmpUnit, InvUnit;

const
  MAX_EMPLOYEES = 5;
  MAX_INVENTORYITEMS = 3;

type
  TfrmMain = class(TForm)
    PageControl1: TPageControl;
    tabBubbleSort: TTabSheet;
    tabListView: TTabSheet;
    lbEmployees: TListBox;
    Label1: TLabel;
    btnByName: TButton;
    btnBySalary: TButton;
    lvInventory: TListView;
    Label2: TLabel;
```

```
    procedure FormCreate(Sender: TObject);
    procedure btnByNameClick(Sender: TObject);
    procedure btnBySalaryClick(Sender: TObject);
    procedure lvInventoryColumnClick(Sender: TObject;
      Column: TListColumn);
    procedure lvInventoryCompare(Sender: TObject;
      Item1, Item2: TListItem; Data: Integer; var Compare: Integer);
  private
    { Private declarations }
    FEmpArray: Array[1 .. MAX_EMPLOYEES] of IUnknown;
    FInvArray: Array[1 .. MAX_INVENTORYITEMS] of IUnknown;
    procedure LoadListBox;
    procedure CreateInventoryItem(AIndex: Integer; APartNo,
      ADescription: string; AInStock: Integer; AUnitPrice: Double);
  public
    { Public declarations }
  end;

var
  frmMain: TfrmMain;

implementation

{$R *.DFM}

procedure TfrmMain.CreateInventoryItem(AIndex: Integer;
  APartNo: string; ADescription: string; AInStock: Integer;
  AUnitPrice: Double);
var
  ListItem: TListItem;
begin
  FInvArray[AIndex] := TInventoryItem.Create(APartNo, ADescription,
    AInStock, AUnitPrice);
  ListItem := lvInventory.Items.Add;
  ListItem.Caption := APartNo;
  ListItem.SubItems.Add(ADescription);
  ListItem.SubItems.Add(FloatToStrF(AUnitPrice, ffCurrency, 5, 2));
  ListItem.SubItems.Add(IntToStr(AInStock));
  ListItem.Data := Pointer(FInvArray[AIndex]);
end;

procedure TfrmMain.FormCreate(Sender: TObject);
begin
  // Create some employees
  FEmpArray[1] := TEmployee.Create('Smith, Tom', 19200.00);
  FEmpArray[2] := TEmployee.Create('Doe, John', 38000.00);
  FEmpArray[3] := TEmployee.Create('Williams, Fred', 26500.00);
  FEmpArray[4] := TEmployee.Create('Jones, Bob', 90000.00);
  FEmpArray[5] := TEmployee.Create('Adams, Tim', 42500.00);

  // Load employees into the list box
  LoadListBox;
// Create some inventory items
  CreateInventoryItem(1, 'P5409', 'Widget', 35, 1.19);
```

*continues* ▶

**Listing 1.10**    *continued*

```
  CreateInventoryItem(2, 'X1234', 'Gadget',  4, 14.95);
  CreateInventoryItem(3, 'J7749', 'Doodad', 17,  8.79);
end;

procedure TfrmMain.LoadListBox;
var
  Index: Integer;
  Emp: IEmployee;
begin
  lbEmployees.Items.BeginUpdate;
  try
    lbEmployees.Items.Clear;
    for Index := 1 to MAX_EMPLOYEES do begin
      Emp := FEmpArray[Index] as IEmployee;
      lbEmployees.Items.Add(Emp.GetName + #9 +
        FloatToStrF(Emp.GetSalary, ffCurrency, 8, 2));
    end;
  finally
    lbEmployees.Items.EndUpdate;
  end;
end;

procedure TfrmMain.btnByNameClick(Sender: TObject);
begin
  SortArray(FEmpArray, Ord(eoName));

  LoadListBox;
end;

procedure TfrmMain.btnBySalaryClick(Sender: TObject);
begin
  SortArray(FEmpArray, Ord(eoSalary));

  LoadListBox;
end;

procedure TfrmMain.lvInventoryColumnClick(Sender: TObject;
  Column: TListColumn);
begin
  lvInventory.CustomSort(nil, Column.Index)
end;

procedure TfrmMain.lvInventoryCompare(Sender: TObject; Item1,
  Item2: TListItem; Data: Integer; var Compare: Integer);
var
  I1, I2: IUnknown;
begin
  I1 := IUnknown(Item1.Data);
  I2 := IUnknown(Item2.Data);

  Compare := (I1 as ICompare).CompareWith(
    (I2 as ICompare), Data);
end;
end.
```

TfrmMain's FormCreate method creates an array of employees and an array of inventory items. Obviously, a real application would get its data from a database or data file of some type, but these hardcoded arrays will suffice for demonstration purposes.

When you run this program, you'll see a TPageControl with two pages on it. The first page contains a TListBox that is used to display the list of employees.

Figure 1.3 shows the first page of the SortDemo application.

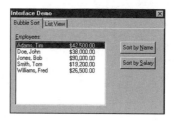

**Figure 1.3**    *SortDemo application: Employee list.*

By default, the employee names are displayed in the order that we created them. Clicking on the **Sort by Name** or **Sort by Salary** buttons sorts the employee array by name or salary, respectively. The sort routine used is a simple bubble sort that orders the objects based on the ICompare interface's CompareWith method. Click the List View tab to display the list of inventory items, again, in the order that we created them. Click any of the four headers: Part #, Description, Unit Price, or In Stock to sort the list by that column. This code uses the ICompare interface in a completely different manner.

Figure 1.4 shows the second page of the SortDemo application.

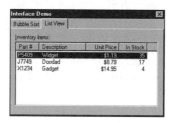

**Figure 1.4**    *SortDemo application: Inventory item list.*

If you're not familiar with the TListView's sorting capabilities, take a look at the following code snippet from Listing 1.10:

```
procedure TfrmMain.lvInventoryColumnClick(Sender: TObject;
  Column: TListColumn);
begin
  lvInventory.CustomSort(nil, Column.Index)
end;

procedure TfrmMain.lvInventoryCompare(Sender: TObject; Item1,
  Item2: TListItem; Data: Integer; var Compare: Integer);
var
  I1, I2: IUnknown;
begin
  I1 := IUnknown(Item1.Data);
  I2 := IUnknown(Item2.Data);

  Compare := (I1 as ICompare).CompareWith(
    (I2 as ICompare), Data);
end;
```

TListView's CustomSort method uses the method assigned to its OnCompare event to compare two items in the list view. Because I used the Data property of the list view items to hold a pointer to the TInventoryItem's IUnknown interface, I can simply typecast the Data property back to an IUnknown and call the TInventoryItem.CompareWith method to compare the items.

Obviously, TListView has its own internal sort engine that calls TListView's OnCompare method at the appropriate times. What's important to understand here is that by declaring the ICompare interface generically, it can be used in numerous instances. If instead of declaring an ICompare interface, we had declared an ISort interface, then that code would not have been usable in this particular situation.

At this point, we've pretty well covered the basics of interfaces. The next section discusses some additional features of interfaces that are slightly more advanced.

# Advanced Interface Issues

In this section, we'll explore some advanced uses of interfaces in Delphi, including

- Implementing multiple interfaces in a class
- Delegation of interfaces
- Interface properties

The last part of this section will create a graphics demo that shows how to use some of these advanced features.

## Implementing Multiple Interfaces in a Class

Object Pascal does not support multiple inheritance as do some other languages, such as C++. The main reason for avoiding multiple inheritance is that multiple ancestors in the inheritance tree with duplicate method names leads to an ambiguity as to which method should become bound to the descendent class.

In some isolated situations multiple inheritance is desirable, or even necessary. Fortunately, with interfaces you can achieve most of the benefits of multiple inheritance without the associated headaches. Implementing multiple interfaces in a class is easy; you simply list the interfaces one after another in the class declaration, like this:

```
type
  TMyMultiplyInterfacedClass = class(TInterfacedObject, IInterface1, IInterface2)
```

TMyMultiplyInterfacedClass can now implement all the methods of both IInterface1 and IInterface2.

### Multiple Interfaces Is Not Multiple Inheritance

Even though the class declaration shown earlier might look like multiple inheritance, it is not. TMyMultiplyInterfacedClass has one and only one parent class: namely, TInterfacedObject. The fact that it implements all the methods of both IInterface1 and IInterface2 does not change that fact.

### Method Resolution Clauses

What do you do when more than one interface defines a method with the same name? Consider the following (simple) interfaces:

```
type
  IInterface1 = interface
    procedure DoIt;
  end;

  IInterface2 = interface
    procedure DoIt;
  end;
```

Both of these interfaces are perfectly legal. Now, what if you want to create a class that implements both the IInterface1 and IInterface2 interfaces? Assuming that the implementation of IInterface1.DoIt is different from the implementation of IInterface2.DoIt, your class would require two methods named DoIt, which is not possible.

> **Note**
>
> *If the implementations of IInterface1.DoIt and IInterface2.DoIt are the same, you can implement a single DoIt method in your class, and Delphi will map both interfaces to the same method.* ♦

To work around this problem, Delphi provides a feature called *method resolution clauses*. A method resolution clause lets you change the interface method's name when it's implemented in a class. Consider the following class declaration:

```
type
  TMyObject = class(TInterfacedObject, IInterface1, IInterface2)
    procedure Iinterface1.DoIt = DoIt1;
    procedure Iinterface2.DoIt = DoIt2;

    procedure DoIt1;
    procedure DoIt2;
  end;
```

TMyObject maps IInterface1.DoIt to the procedure DoIt1, and IInterface2.DoIt to the procedure DoIt2. The following code snippet actually calls TMyObject.DoIt1.

```
Var
  MyInt1: IInterface1;
Begin
  MyInt1 := TMyObject.Create;
  MyInt1.DoIt;
End;
```

You don't need to rename all the conflicting method names. The following code is perfectly legal as well:

```
type
  TMyObject = class(TInterfacedObject, IInterface1, IInterface2)
    procedure Iinterface2.DoIt = DoIt2;

    procedure DoIt;
    procedure DoIt2;
  end;
```

In this example, IInterface1.DoIt maps to method DoIt, as usual, and IInterface2.DoIt maps to DoIt2.

## Interface Delegation

Let's say you have a well thought-out class named TObject1 that implements IInterface1. You want to create a class named TCombinedObject that implements both IInterface1 and IInterface2. It would appear that you need to re-implement the methods of IInterface1, possibly copying the source code from TObject1 into TCombinedObject, right?

Not necessarily. Delphi lets you delegate the implementation of an interface to another class. Delegation means that a class contains a pointer to another class. The contained class implements the functionality of one or more interfaces. Instead of re-implementing the interface(s) in question, the outer class simply passes those methods to the contained class.

The following code implements interface IInterface1 in class TObject1. TCombinedObject contains a reference to TObject1, and *delegates* the implementation of IInterface1 to FObj1.

```
type
  IInterface1 = interface
    ['{72B1C430-A021-11D3-B8AC-0040F67455FE}']
    procedure DoIt1;
  end;

  IInterface2 = interface
    ['{72B1C431-A021-11D3-B8AC-0040F67455FE}']
    procedure DoIt2;
  end;

  TObject1 = class(TInterfacedObject, IInterface1)
  protected
    procedure DoIt1;
  end;

  TCombinedObject = class(TInterfacedObject, IInterface1, IInterface2)
  protected
    FObj1: IInterface1;
  public
    constructor Create;
    destructor Destroy; override;

    procedure DoIt2;
    property MyIntf: IInterface1 read FObj1 implements IInterface1;
  end;

implementation

{ TObject1 }

procedure TObject1.DoIt1;
begin
  ShowMessage('Inside TObject.DoIt1');
end;

{ TCombinedObject }

constructor TCombinedObject.Create;
begin
  inherited Create;

  FObj1 := TObject1.Create;
end;
```

```
destructor TCombinedObject.Destroy;
begin
  FObj1 := nil;

  inherited;
end;

procedure TCombinedObject.DoIt2;
begin
  ShowMessage('Inside TCombinedObject.DoIt2');
end;
```

To use TCombinedObject in your code, you could write something like this:

```
procedure TForm1.Button1Click(Sender: TObject);
var
  I1: IInterface1;
  I2: IInterface2;
begin
  I2 := TCombinedObject.Create;
  I2.DoIt2;

  I1 := I2 as IInterface1;
  I1.DoIt1;
end;
```

Notice that the statement I2 as IInterface1 automatically extracts the IInterface1 interface from the TCombinedObject object, even though IInterface1 is actually implemented by TObject1. That's the beauty of delegation: Your code doesn't need to be aware how the interface is actually implemented.

### Aggregated Objects Require Special Care

*When you create an object intended to be used as an aggregated object, you should not inherit from TInterfacedObject. If you do, then once you obtain a reference to an interface implemented by the aggregated object, you cannot use that interface to obtain a reference to an interface implemented by the containing object.*

*For example, the following application will fail:*

```
unit Unit1;

interface

uses
  Windows, Messages, SysUtils, Classes, Graphics, Controls, Forms, Dialogs,
  StdCtrls;

type
  IInterface1 = interface
    ['{72B1C430-A021-11D3-B8AC-0040F67455FE}']
    procedure DoIt1;
  end;
```

```
  IInterface2 = interface
    ['{72B1C431-A021-11D3-B8AC-0040F67455FE}']
    procedure DoIt2;
  end;

  TAggObject = class(TInterfacedObject, IInterface1)
  protected
    procedure DoIt1;
  end;

  TCombinedObject = class(TInterfacedObject, IInterface1, IInterface2)
  protected
    FAggObj: IInterface1;
  public
    constructor Create;
    destructor Destroy; override;

    procedure DoIt2;
    property AggObj: IInterface1 read FAggObj implements IInterface1;
  end;

  TForm1 = class(TForm)
    Button1: TButton;
    procedure Button1Click(Sender: TObject);
  private
    { Private declarations }
  public
    { Public declarations }
  end;

var
  Form1: TForm1;

implementation

{$R *.DFM}

{ TAggObject }

procedure TAggObject.DoIt1;
begin
  ShowMessage('Inside TAggObject.DoIt1');
end;

{ TCombinedObject }

constructor TCombinedObject.Create;
begin
  inherited Create;

  FAggObj := TAggObject.Create;
end;
```

*continues* ▶

▶ *continued*

```
destructor TCombinedObject.Destroy;
begin
  FAggObj := nil;

  inherited;
end;

procedure TCombinedObject.DoIt2;
begin
  ShowMessage('Inside TCombinedObject.DoIt2');
end;

procedure TForm1.Button1Click(Sender: TObject);
var
  I1: IInterface1;
  I2: IInterface2;
begin
  I2 := TCombinedObject.Create;
  I2.DoIt2;

  I1 := I2 as IInterface1;  // This succeeds
  I1.DoIt1;

  // Use delegated interface IInterface2 to get a
  // reference to interface IInterface2
  I2 := I1 as IInterface2;  // This fails
  I2.DoIt2;
end;

end.
```

*Delphi will raise an "Interface not supported" exception when trying to cast I1 as IInterface2. The reason is that once the compiler has a reference to the aggregated object, it has no way to know how to get back to the containing object.*

*Delphi provides the TAggregatedObject class specifically for this situation. The above application works correctly if we add comobj.pas to the uses clause, derive TAggObject from TAggregatedObject instead of TInterfacedObject, and change TCombinedObject.Create to the following:*

```
constructor TCombinedObject.Create;
begin
  inherited Create;

  FAggObj := TAggObject.Create(self);
end;
```

*Note that TAggregatedObject's constructor requires a reference to the container object ("self" in the above code snippit). You will run into a snag if you want to use the same object both as a standalone object and also as an aggregated object, since you cannot pass nil to TAggregatedObject's constructor.*

*Hallvard Vossbotn suggests the following class as an alternative to
TAggregatedObject. If you want to use the class as a standalone class, call the
Create constructor with no arguments. If you want to use the class as an aggregated object, call the Create constructor and pass a reference to the containing
object (self).*

```
TAggregatedOrStandaloneObject = class(TInterfacedObject, IUnknown)
  private
    FController: Pointer;
    function GetController: IUnknown;
  protected
    { IUnknown }
    function QueryInterface(const IID: TGUID; out Obj): HResult; stdcall;
    function _AddRef: Integer; stdcall;
    function _Release: Integer; stdcall;
  public
    constructor Create(Controller: IUnknown); overload;
    property Controller: IUnknown read GetController;
  end;

{ TAggregatedOrStandaloneObject }

constructor TAggregatedOrStandaloneObject.Create(Controller: IUnknown);
begin
  FController := Pointer(Controller);
end;

function TAggregatedOrStandaloneObject.GetController: IUnknown;
begin
  if Assigned(FController) then
    Result := IUnknown(FController)
  else
    Result := Self;
end;

{ TAggregatedOrStandaloneObject.IUnknown }

function TAggregatedOrStandaloneObject.QueryInterface(const IID: TGUID; out
Obj): HResult;
begin
  if Assigned(FController) then
    Result := IUnknown(FController).QueryInterface(IID, Obj)
  else
    Result := inherited QueryInterface(IID, Obj);
end;

function TAggregatedOrStandaloneObject._AddRef: Integer;
begin
  if Assigned(FController) then
    Result := IUnknown(FController)._AddRef
  else
    Result := inherited _AddRef;
end;
```

*continues* ▶

▶ *continued*

```
function TAggregatedOrStandaloneObject._Release: Integer; stdcall;
begin
  if Assigned(FController) then
    Result := IUnknown(FController)._Release
  else
    Result := inherited _Release;
end;
```

## Interface Properties

It might not be immediately obvious, but you can also define properties in an interface. You can define read-only, write-only, or read/write properties, but all access must be through access functions, because interfaces cannot define storage.

For example, the following interface declaration defines a read-only, a write-only, and a read/write property:

```
IPropertyInterface = interface
  function GetAge: Integer;
  procedure SetShoeSize(Value: Double);
  function GetHeight: Double;
  procedure SetHeight(Value: Double);
  property Age: Integer read GetAge;
  property ShoeSize: Double write SetShoeSize;
  property Height: Double read GetHeight write SetHeight;
end;
```

When you implement this interface in a class, realize that the class's users will have access to both the access functions and the properties. In other words, a user could either call function GetAge or access the Age property. Because most languages don't support properties, and interfaces are designed to be portable between languages, the GetXxx and SetXxx functions need to be accessible to users of the interface.

## Example: A Graphics Demo

The final example in this chapter illustrates some of the advanced techniques discussed in this section, as well as concepts from earlier in this chapter. Specifically, this example demonstrates

- Inheriting from a class that implements an interface
- Implementing multiple interfaces in a class
- Interface properties

Many industries use object-oriented graphics in their applications. CAD-type software can draw, resize, and drag graphic shapes around the screen. Prototyping software can move various shapes around the screen and depict relationships between them. And the list goes on.

GrphDemo is a simple program that randomly places blue Xs (marks) and black rectangles on a form. The marks and rectangles are similar in that they both have a color, and they both have a position. The rectangles are different in that they also have a size. (The marks in this particular demo application can't be sized.)

GrphDemo uses Delphi's TInterfaceList class to hold the list of shapes. Delphi 3 does not include TInterfaceList, so this example will not compile under Delphi 3 as-is.

Listing 1.11 shows the code for the interfaces defined by GrphDemo. As you can see, each graphic attribute (color, size, and position) is defined as a separate interface. The graphics objects in this application implement the individual interfaces they support.

**Listing 1.11**   *GrphDemo Source: intfform.pas*

```
unit IntfUnit;

interface

uses
  Windows, graphics;

type
  IColor = interface
    ['{EAE054E1-EB94-11D2-9086-0040F6741DE2}']
    function GetColor: TColor;
    procedure SetColor(AColor: TColor);
    property Color: TColor read GetColor write SetColor;
  end;

  IPosition = interface
    ['{162EDFE1-EB8C-11D2-9086-0040F6741DE2}']
    function GetXY: TPoint;
    procedure SetXY(APoint: TPoint);
    procedure NudgeUp;
    procedure NudgeDown;
    procedure NudgeLeft;
    procedure NudgeRight;
    property Point: TPoint read GetXY write SetXY;
  end;

  ISize = interface
    ['{162EDFE0-EB8C-11D2-9086-0040F6741DE2}']
    function GetWidth: Integer;
    function GetHeight: Integer;
    procedure SetWidth(AWidth: Integer);
    procedure SetHeight(AHeight: Integer);
    property Height: Integer read GetHeight write SetHeight;
    property Width: Integer read GetWidth write SetWidth;
  end;
```

*continues* ▶

**Listing 1.11**   *continued*

```
IDraw = interface
  ['{FFCD24F3-4FE8-11D3-B84D-0040F67455FE}']
  procedure Draw(ACanvas: TCanvas);
end;

implementation

end.
```

Listing 1.12 shows the code for the two graphic objects that implement the interfaces.

**Listing 1.12**   *GrphDemo Source: shapes.pas*

```
unit Shapes;

interface

uses
  Windows, IntfUnit, graphics, dialogs;

type
  TMark = class(TInterfacedObject, IColor, IPosition, IDraw)
  private
    FColor: TColor;
    FPoint: TPoint;
  public
    constructor Create(APoint: TPoint; AColor: TColor);
    function GetColor: TColor;
    procedure SetColor(AColor: TColor);
    function GetXY: TPoint;
    procedure SetXY(APoint: TPoint);
    procedure NudgeUp;
    procedure NudgeDown;
    procedure NudgeLeft;
    procedure NudgeRight;
    procedure Draw(ACanvas: TCanvas);
  end;

  TSquare = class(TMark, IColor, IPosition, ISize, IDraw)
  private
    FHeight: Integer;
    FWidth: Integer;
  public
    constructor Create(AUpLeft: TPoint; AHeight: Integer;
      AWidth: Integer; AColor: TColor);
    function GetWidth: Integer;
    function GetHeight: Integer;
    procedure SetWidth(AWidth: Integer);
    procedure SetHeight(AHeight: Integer);
    procedure Draw(ACanvas: TCanvas);
  end;
```

```
implementation

{ TMark }

constructor TMark.Create(APoint: TPoint; AColor: TColor);
begin
  inherited Create;

  FPoint := APoint;
  FColor := AColor;
end;

procedure TMark.Draw(ACanvas: TCanvas);
begin
  ACanvas.Pen.Color := FColor;
  ACanvas.MoveTo(FPoint.X - 2, FPoint.Y - 2);
  ACanvas.LineTo(FPoint.X + 3, FPoint.Y + 3);
  ACanvas.MoveTo(FPoint.X - 2, FPoint.Y + 2);
  ACanvas.LineTo(FPoint.X + 3, FPoint.Y - 3);
end;

function TMark.GetColor: TColor;
begin
  Result := FColor;
end;

function TMark.GetXY: TPoint;
begin
  Result := FPoint;
end;

procedure TMark.NudgeDown;
begin
  Inc(FPoint.Y);
end;

procedure TMark.NudgeLeft;
begin
  Dec(FPoint.X);
end;

procedure TMark.NudgeRight;
begin
  Inc(FPoint.X);
end;

procedure TMark.NudgeUp;
begin
  Dec(FPoint.Y);
end;

procedure TMark.SetColor(AColor: TColor);
begin
  FColor := AColor;
```

*continues* ▶

**Listing 1.12**    *continued*

```pascal
end;

procedure TMark.SetXY(APoint: TPoint);
begin
  FPoint := APoint;
end;

{ TSquare }

constructor TSquare.Create(AUpLeft: TPoint; AHeight: Integer;
  AWidth: Integer; AColor: TColor);
begin
  inherited Create(AUpLeft, AColor);

  FHeight := AHeight;
  FWidth := AWidth;
end;

procedure TSquare.Draw(ACanvas: TCanvas);
begin
  ACanvas.Pen.Color := FColor;
  ACanvas.Rectangle(FPoint.X, FPoint.Y, FPoint.X + FWidth,
    FPoint.Y + FHeight);
end;

function TSquare.GetHeight: Integer;
begin
  Result := FHeight;
end;

function TSquare.GetWidth: Integer;
begin
  Result := FWidth;
end;

procedure TSquare.SetHeight(AHeight: Integer);
begin
  FHeight := AHeight;
end;

procedure TSquare.SetWidth(AWidth: Integer);
begin
  FWidth := AWidth;
end;

end.
```

Listing 1.13 shows the code for the main form, shown in Figure 1.5.

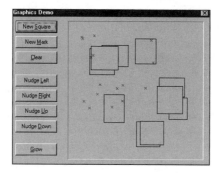

**Figure 1.5**   *The GrphDemo main form.*

**Listing 1.13**   *GrphDemo Source: mainform.pas*

```
unit MainForm;

interface

uses
  Windows, Messages, SysUtils, Classes, Graphics, Controls, Forms,
  Dialogs, ExtCtrls, StdCtrls, IntfUnit;

type
  TForm1 = class(TForm)
    btnNewSquare: TButton;
    btnNewMark: TButton;
    btnClear: TButton;
    btnNudgeLeft: TButton;
    btnNudgeRight: TButton;
    btnNudgeUp: TButton;
    btnNudgeDown: TButton;
    btnGrow: TButton;
    Bevel1: TBevel;
    PaintBox1: TPaintBox;
    procedure FormCreate(Sender: TObject);
    procedure FormDestroy(Sender: TObject);
    procedure btnNewSquareClick(Sender: TObject);
    procedure btnNewMarkClick(Sender: TObject);
    procedure btnClearClick(Sender: TObject);
    procedure btnNudgeLeftClick(Sender: TObject);
    procedure btnNudgeRightClick(Sender: TObject);
    procedure btnNudgeUpClick(Sender: TObject);
    procedure btnNudgeDownClick(Sender: TObject);
    procedure btnGrowClick(Sender: TObject);
    procedure PaintBox1Paint(Sender: TObject);
  private
    { Private declarations }
    FShapes: TInterfaceList;
    procedure Clear;
  public
```

*continues* ▶

**Listing 1.13**  *continued*

```
    { Public declarations }
  end;

var
  Form1: TForm1;

implementation

uses
  Shapes;

{$R *.DFM}

procedure TForm1.FormCreate(Sender: TObject);
begin
  FShapes := TInterfaceList.Create;
end;

procedure TForm1.FormDestroy(Sender: TObject);
begin
  Clear;

  FShapes.Free;
end;

procedure TForm1.btnNewSquareClick(Sender: TObject);
var
  Square: IUnknown;
begin
  Square := TSquare.Create(Point(10 + Random(200), 10 + Random(200)),
    40 + Random(20), 40 + Random(20), clBlack);
  FShapes.Add(Square);

  PaintBox1.Invalidate;
end;

procedure TForm1.btnNewMarkClick(Sender: TObject);
var
  Mark: IUnknown;
begin
  Mark := TMark.Create(Point(10 + Random(200), 10 + Random(200)),
    clBlue);
  FShapes.Add(Mark);

  PaintBox1.Invalidate;
end;

procedure TForm1.Clear;
begin
  // TInterfaceList.Clear automatically releases all of the
  // interfaces destroyed in the list.
  FShapes.Clear;
end;
```

```
procedure TForm1.btnClearClick(Sender: TObject);
begin
  Clear;

  PaintBox1.Invalidate;
end;

procedure TForm1.PaintBox1Paint(Sender: TObject);
var
  Index: Integer;
  Shape: IUnknown;
begin
  for Index := 0 to FShapes.Count - 1 do begin
    Shape := FShapes[Index];

    (Shape as IDraw).Draw(PaintBox1.Canvas);
  end;
end;

procedure TForm1.btnNudgeLeftClick(Sender: TObject);
var
  Index: Integer;
  Shape: IUnknown;
begin
  for Index := 0 to FShapes.Count - 1 do begin
    Shape := IUnknown(FShapes[Index]);

    (Shape as IPosition).NudgeLeft;
  end;

  PaintBox1.Invalidate;
end;

procedure TForm1.btnNudgeRightClick(Sender: TObject);
var
  Index: Integer;
  Shape: IUnknown;
begin
  for Index := 0 to FShapes.Count - 1 do begin
    Shape := IUnknown(FShapes[Index]);

    (Shape as IPosition).NudgeRight;
  end;

  PaintBox1.Invalidate;
end;

procedure TForm1.btnNudgeUpClick(Sender: TObject);
var
  Index: Integer;
  Shape: IUnknown;
begin
  for Index := 0 to FShapes.Count - 1 do begin
    Shape := IUnknown(FShapes[Index]);
```

*continues* ▶

---

**Listing 1.13**  *continued*

```
  (Shape as IPosition).NudgeUp;
  end;

  PaintBox1.Invalidate;
end;

procedure TForm1.btnNudgeDownClick(Sender: TObject);
var
  Index: Integer;
  Shape: IUnknown;
begin
  for Index := 0 to FShapes.Count - 1 do begin
    Shape := IUnknown(FShapes[Index]);

    (Shape as IPosition).NudgeDown;
  end;

  PaintBox1.Invalidate;
end;

procedure TForm1.btnGrowClick(Sender: TObject);
var
  Index: Integer;
  Shape: IUnknown;
  SizeIntf: ISize;
begin
  for Index := 0 to FShapes.Count - 1 do begin
    Shape := IUnknown(FShapes[Index]);

    if Shape.QueryInterface(ISize, SizeIntf) = S_OK then begin
      SizeIntf.Width := SizeIntf.Width + 1;
      SizeIntf.Height := SizeIntf.Height + 1;
    end;
  end;

  PaintBox1.Invalidate;
end;

end.
```

---

Listing 1.14 shows the source code for the GrphDemo's project file.

**Listing 1.14**  *GrphDemo Source: grphdemo.dpr*

```
program GrphDemo;

uses
  Forms,
  MainForm in 'MainForm.pas' {Form1},
  IntfUnit in 'IntfUnit.pas',
  Shapes in 'Shapes.pas';
```

```
{$R *.RES}

begin
  Application.Initialize;
  Application.CreateForm(TForm1, Form1);
  Application.Run;
end.
```

## Summary

In this chapter, we've examined interfaces in detail. I've shown you how you can use interfaces internally in your Delphi applications, and laid the groundwork for the rest of the chapters in this book. By now, you should know how to

- Declare an interface
- Implement an interface in a class
- Implement the required functionality of IUnknown
- Bypass reference counting to disable automatic object destruction
- Get a pointer to an interface, given another interface
- Implement multiple interfaces in your classes
- Delegate the implementation of an interface to a contained object
- Define and implement interface properties

At this point, you should have a clear understanding of how you can use interfaces in your Delphi programs. In the next chapter, I'll discuss interfaces as they relate to COM programming.

# 2

## Interfaces and COM

In the last chapter, we looked at interfaces as Delphi language elements. You learned that interfaces can be used internally to develop an application. The main purpose of an interface, however, is for developing COM applications.

In this chapter, we will look at how interfaces are used in COM objects. We will discuss the two types of COM servers, and we will build some small, but useful, COM servers.

The example COM servers presented in this chapter are atypical of most COM servers in that they lack type libraries. In an effort to introduce one concept at a time, I defer the discussion of type libraries until Chapter 3, "Type Libraries." As a result, the COM servers that we create in this chapter are really only useful if you're creating both the server and client applications in Delphi (or another language that fully supports virtual method tables). After I've introduced type libraries, I'll show you how to create COM servers that are usable by just about every programming environment available today.

## GUIDs and COM

In Chapter 1, "Using Interfaces in Delphi," I explained what a GUID is. I told you that most internal interfaces and *all* COM interfaces require a GUID. Let's take a moment to understand the role that GUIDs play in COM programming.

Inside the Windows Registry, there is a key named HKEY_CLASSES_ ROOT\CLSID. If you open this node and page down a few times, you'll see line after line of GUIDs. Figure 2.1 shows a portion of the CLSID section of the Registry on my computer.

> **Note**
>
> *A CLSID (pronounced "class ID") is nothing more than a name for a particular type of GUID.* ◆

**Figure 2.1**    *The Windows Registry contains a list of registered COM classes.*

Each CLSID, or GUID, represents an implementation of a COM interface. For example, the very first CLSID listed on my machine is {00000010-0000-0010-8000-00AA006D2AE4}. This CLSID provides the interface to the Microsoft *Data Access Objects* (DAO) engine. The InprocServer32 key below the GUID contains information that is used by Windows to locate the DAO DLL on my machine. In-process servers are discussed in detail later in this chapter, in the section titled "In-Process COM Servers."

The ProgID key specifies the human-readable name by which this interface can be referred to for automation purposes. Automation is discussed in detail in Chapter 4, "Automation."

## COM Objects and Class Factories

As mentioned previously, a COM Object is really nothing more than an object that implements one or more interfaces. COM objects are implemented in either a DLL or an executable file for client software to use. All the classes we wrote in Chapter 1 were used inside our own Delphi applications only. In this chapter, we're going to write objects that can be used by any COM-compliant language. (Well, theoretically, anyway. Visual Basic, for example, doesn't understand true object-oriented programming methods, so the objects that we create in this chapter will not be usable by VB programmers. In Chapter 4, we'll focus on writing COM servers that can be used not only by Delphi, C++, and Visual Basic, but also by applications, such as Microsoft Word and Internet Explorer. But we'll take it one step at a time...)

A COM Object resides either inside a DLL or an EXE. COM Objects that live in DLLs are referred to as *in-process servers*. COM Objects that live in EXEs are referred to as *out-of-process servers*. I'll discuss in-process and out-of-process servers later in this chapter.

COM servers may contain one or more COM objects. COM objects are discussed in the following section.

### COM Objects

In Chapter 1, we derived most of our classes from TInterfacedObject. In this chapter, we're going to derive from TComObject instead, because TInterfacedObject does not provide the necessary functionality for implementing COM objects.

Here is the declaration of TComObject, from the file comobj.pas:

```
TComObject = class(TObject, IUnknown, ISupportErrorInfo)
private
  FController: Pointer;
  FFactory: TComObjectFactory;
  FNonCountedObject: Boolean;
  FRefCount: Integer;
  FServerExceptionHandler: IServerExceptionHandler;
  function GetController: IUnknown;
protected
  { IUnknown }
  function IUnknown.QueryInterface = ObjQueryInterface;
  function IUnknown._AddRef = ObjAddRef;
  function IUnknown._Release = ObjRelease;
  { IUnknown methods for other interfaces }
  function QueryInterface(const IID: TGUID; out Obj): HResult; stdcall;
  function _AddRef: Integer; stdcall;
  function _Release: Integer; stdcall;
  { ISupportErrorInfo }
  function InterfaceSupportsErrorInfo(const iid: TIID): HResult; stdcall;
public
  constructor Create;
  constructor CreateAggregated(const Controller: IUnknown);
  constructor CreateFromFactory(Factory: TComObjectFactory;
    const Controller: IUnknown);
  destructor Destroy; override;
  procedure Initialize; virtual;
  function ObjAddRef: Integer; virtual; stdcall;
  function ObjQueryInterface(const IID: TGUID; out Obj): HResult; virtual; stdcall;
  function ObjRelease: Integer; virtual; stdcall;
  function SafeCallException(ExceptObject: TObject;
    ExceptAddr: Pointer): HResult; override;
  property Controller: IUnknown read GetController;
  property Factory: TComObjectFactory read FFactory;
  property RefCount: Integer read FRefCount;
  property ServerExceptionHandler: IServerExceptionHandler
    read FServerExceptionHandler write FServerExceptionHandler;
end;
```

Notice that TComObject is derived from TObject, not TInterfacedObject, so it needs to provide an implementation for _AddRef, _Release, and QueryInterface. TComObject uses method resolution clauses to map these methods to ObjAddRef, ObjRelease, and ObjQueryInterface, respectively.

TComObject looks complicated, but fortunately we don't need to deal with most of it because Borland has provided the implementation for us. All we need to do is derive our COM objects from TComObject, and VCL (and COM) does the rest.

### HResult and OleCheck

In COM programming, most functions (with the exception of _AddRef and _Release) return a value of type HResult. An HResult is a special return value that indicates whether the function call succeeded or failed, and it also contains an error code in case of failure. In traditional COM programming, it is not uncommon to see code like this:

```
if Failed(MyComObject.SomeFunction) then begin
  ShowMessage('Couldn''t perform SomeFunction');
  exit;
end;

if Failed(MyComObject.SomeOtherFunction) then begin
  ShowMessage('Couldn''t perform SomeOtherFunction');
  exit;
end;
```

As you can see, most of this code is dedicated to checking for errors that might occur during a function call. The Delphi philosophy is to separate return values from exception handling. Clearly, the preceding code is not in keeping with this philosophy. Fortunately, Delphi provides a procedure named OleCheck, which allows us to rewrite the preceding code like this:

```
OleCheck(MyComObject.SomeFunction);
OleCheck(MyComObject.SomeOtherFunction);
```

Obviously, this code is shorter, easier to write, and easier to understand. You should use OleCheck when you make calls to COM functions that return an HResult.

### Class Factories

COM objects are not instantiated directly by your application. Instead, COM uses a class factory to create the object. A class factory is an object whose express purpose is to create other objects. Every COM object has an associated class factory. The class factory is responsible for creating the COM object, which is implemented in the server.

#### Dual Classes in Class Factories

*You may wonder why this duality of classes exists. It may seem like overkill to require a class factory for each and every COM object. However, COM doesn't require a different class factory for each COM object. One class factory can handle the creation of multiple COM objects. In fact, in Delphi there is only one class factory instance that COM sees. This class factory owns a list of all the internal Delphi class factory objects in the COM server. When COM calls the class factory to request an instance of a new COM object, the class factory looks through its internal list of helper classes for a match.*

*Class factories insulate COM from the actual process of constructing an object. If it weren't for the class factory, COM would have to make direct calls to the object's constructor in order to create the object. COM places no restriction on how COM objects are implemented, and construction is an integral part of the implementation process, so it is important that COM not have direct knowledge of the object construction process.*

*Although DLLs can export standard functions that COM could call to get an instance of an object, EXEs cannot. For example, a DLL could export a function named ConstructMyCOMObject, and tell COM to call that function whenever it needs to create an instance of MyCOMObject.*

*EXEs must register their class factories when they create them, and COM makes calls to the class factory interface in order to create COM objects. For consistency, DLLs create and register class factories in the same manner as EXEs.* ◆

Class factories support the IClassFactory interface, which is defined as follows:

```
type
  IClassFactory = interface(IUnknown)
    ['{00000001-0000-0000-C000-000000000046}']
    function CreateInstance(const unkOuter: IUnknown; const iid: TIID;
      out obj): HResult; stdcall;
    function LockServer(fLock: BOOL): HResult; stdcall;
  end;
```

### Tip

*When you see a GUID composed of very low numbers, such as the one used in IClassFactory (['{00000001-0000-0000-C000-000000000046}']), you can assume that interface is probably one of the core COM interfaces defined by Microsoft. GUIDs generated by third-party companies, such as Inprise/Borland or yours, will be more random, and will not consist mainly of zeroes.*

*You can still find the definition for Microsoft's interfaces in Delphi's source code— more specifically, in activex.pas. If you need additional information on these Microsoft-defined interfaces, however, the best reference is the Microsoft Developer's Network (MSDN). MSDN is available online at* http://www.msdn.microsoft.com, *or through a quarterly CD subscription that you can purchase through Microsoft. The online content is more current than the quarterly CDs, but if you don't have a fast Internet connection, it could take longer to find the information you're looking for. ◆*

As you can see, IClassFactory defines only two functions: CreateInstance and LockServer.

CreateInstance is the function that is responsible for creating an instance of the COM object this class factory references. You will typically not call this function yourself. As you'll see in a bit, COM calls this function for you.

COM servers are typically unloaded from memory when there are no active clients using the server. LockServer can be called to force the server to remain in memory. Call LockServer(True) to increment an internal lock count. Call LockServer(False) to decrement the lock count. When the lock count reaches zero, the server may be unloaded from memory if there are no clients referencing the server.

Note that the calls to LockServer(True) and LockServer(False) must be balanced for everything to work correctly. Issuing a call to LockServer(True) with no corresponding call to LockServer(False) is a surefire way to keep the COM server hanging around in memory forever!

**Note**

*You'll probably never need to call LockServer. LockServer is a remnant of the old OLE document embedding days when COM servers were separate EXEs that took a long time to load (such as Microsoft Word). For performance reasons, it was beneficial to keep the server loaded in memory even when it wasn't being used. ◆*

When you use Delphi's wizards (more on this later) to create a COM object, Delphi automatically writes the code necessary to create the corresponding class factory for that object.

Now you have a fair understanding of what COM objects and class factories are. The next section describes in-process COM servers in detail.

# In-Process COM Servers

The first COM server that we're going to look at is an in-process server. In-process servers get their name because they are implemented inside a DLL. Therefore, the server occupies the same address space (process) as the application that uses it. All in-process COM servers export four standard functions: DllRegisterServer, DllUnregisterServer, DllGetClassObject, and DllCanUnloadNow. Borland has provided a default implementation of these functions in comserv.pas. Therefore, you don't need to code these functions yourself, but you should understand their purpose.

- **DllRegisterServer.** DllRegisterServer is called automatically in two ways. The IDE's Register ActiveX Server menu item calls it, and Windows' RegSvr32.exe command-line utility (or the Borland utility TRegSvr) calls it. Regardless of the means by which it is called, DllRegisterServer registers your COM objects with the Windows Registry. Earlier, I showed you a screen shot that displayed a number of COM objects in the Registry. In-process COM servers have a subkey named InprocServer32 that contains the full path name to the COM server.

- **DllUnregisterServer.** DllUnregisterServer reverses the process of DllRegisterServer. It removes all entries in the Windows Registry that were put there by DllRegisterServer.

- **DllGetClassObject.** DllGetClassObject is responsible for providing a class factory to COM, given a COM object to create. Recall that each COM server will implement a class factory for each COM object that it exports.

- **DllCanUnloadNow.**   COM is responsible for calling DllCanUnloadNow to see if it is okay to unload the COM server from memory. If any application has a reference to any COM object in this server, DllCanUnloadNow returns S_FALSE. If there are no open references to any COM objects in this server, then DllCanUnloadNow returns S_TRUE, and COM removes the COM server from memory.

## Threading Support

Threading support pertains to in-process servers only, and does not apply to out-of-process servers. In-process servers can adhere to one of several threading models. The threading model for an in-process server is stored in the Windows Registry. The threading models that an in-process server can support are

- **Single.**   Single-threaded COM objects really have no support for threads at all. All access to the COM server is serialized by Windows, so you don't need to worry about multiple threads trying to access the server at the same time. All access to the COM server occurs on the thread in which the COM server DLL was created.

- **Apartment.**   Apartment-threaded (or single-threaded apartment, as they are sometimes called) COM objects can only process requests from the thread that created them. One server can export a number of COM objects, and each COM object may be created from a different thread. For this reason, access to any global data defined in the server must be synchronized through the use of a mutex, event, critical section, or some other synchronization method.

- **Free.**   Free-threaded servers remove the restriction imposed by apartment-threaded servers. In the free-threaded model, multiple threads may be active on any given COM object at the same time. Because of this fact, not only must access to global data be synchronized, but access to local data must also be synchronized for multiple thread access.

- **Both apartment and free.**   COM servers that support this option adhere to both the apartment-threaded model and also the free-threaded model. This is the most difficult threading model to support, because COM servers that support both apartment threading and free threading must synchronize their own access to apartment-threaded object instances and marshal parameter data across threads.

In most cases, you'll want to write COM servers that adhere to the apart-ment-threaded model. Delphi 5's RTL and COM classes (implemented in comserv.pas and comobj.pas) support all threading models, including free threading. Free threading offers a noticeable performance increase in MTS and IIS hosted COM servers, where the host manages a number of worker threads to handle a large number of client requests, and where most COM methods are read access rather than write access.

In most situations, including normal applications and visual controls, there is no advantage to free threading. Therefore, the additional work that is required to make your COM classes free-threaded safe is not warranted. On the other hand, single-threaded COM servers are often too restrictive in that they really don't support threaded access at all. Unless you need the performance boost associated with a free-threaded COM server under MTS or IIS, or you have a compelling reason to stay with a single-threaded COM server, you should write apartment-threaded COM servers.

## Registering the Server

All COM servers need to be registered with Windows to function properly. The registration process involves making the necessary entries into the Windows Registry so that Windows knows the location and type of the server (in-process or out-of-process).

As a Delphi programmer, you can register your COM servers by selecting Run, Register ActiveX Server from the Delphi main menu. Obviously, your typical end user will not have Delphi installed on his or her machine. Windows comes with a registration utility called RegSvr32. To register a COM server, you can simply type RegSvr32 *<ServerName>*. An even easier approach, however, is to register the server from within your installation program. Most installation software, such as WISE and InstallShield, provides a way to register a COM server as part of the installation process.

Regardless of the method used to register the server, the details are the same. The program (RegSvr32, WISE, and so on) simply makes a call to the DllRegisterServer function inside the COM Server DLL. The DllRegisterServer function is responsible for making the Registry entries necessary for the in-process server to function properly.

As mentioned earlier, Delphi's implementation of DllRegisterServer does all this for you. If you want to investigate the details of this function, you can find it in the file comserv.pas.

If you remove an in-process server from your computer, you can unregis-ter it either from Delphi by selecting Run, Unregister ActiveX Server from the main menu, or by running RegSvr32 –u *<ServerName>*. Most installation programs also have the capability to remove an in-process server during an uninstall procedure.

## Custom Constructors

You should not attempt to override the constructor for a COM object.
The constructors defined in TComObject all call the virtual method
Initialize. If you need to provide your COM object with initialization code,
override the Initialize method instead. Initialize is defined as follows:

```
procedure Initialize; virtual;
```

The reason for putting initialization code in Initialize rather than the constructor is this: The COM object base classes in Delphi contain a number of
non-virtual constructors. Depending on the scenario, the class factory will
call different constructors in different instances. The Initialize method is
virtual and is the only method that is called regardless of which constructor
is used to construct the COM object.

## Creating an Instance of an In-Process COM Object

When you want to create an instance of an in-process COM object in your
Delphi client code, you will typically use the function CreateComObject,
declared in comobj.pas as follows:

```
Function CreateComObject(const ClassID: TGUID): IUnknown;
```

CreateComObject takes as a parameter the GUID of the COM object you
want to create, and returns a pointer to the IUnknown interface on that
object. If the requested GUID cannot be located in the Windows Registry,
CreateComObject raises an exception.

I'm going to take a few moments to look at the implementation of
CreateComObject, because it's quite short:

```
function CreateComObject(const ClassID: TGUID): IUnknown;
begin
  OleCheck(CoCreateInstance(ClassID, nil, CLSCTX_INPROC_SERVER or
    CLSCTX_LOCAL_SERVER, IUnknown, Result));
end;
```

As you can see, all CreateComObject does for us is expand a call to the
Windows function CoCreateInstance, providing some default parameters.
CoCreateInstance takes five parameters, and is defined like this:

```
function CoCreateInstance(const clsid: TCLSID; unkOuter: IUnknown;
  dwClsContext: Longint; const iid: TIID; var pv): HResult; stdcall;
```

The first parameter, clsid, is the GUID of the COM server that we want to
create. This is the one and only parameter that we specifically pass to
CreateComObject. The next parameter, unkOuter, is used only if this COM
object is part of an aggregation. I discussed aggregation briefly in Chapter 1,
and I will not discuss it further here. If you are interested in COM aggregation, please see the VCL class TAggregatedObject, defined in comobj.pas.

Next, dwClsContext determines the type of server that you want to create. CreateComObject automatically requests either an in-process server (CLSCTX_INPROC_SERVER) or a local out-of-process server (CLSCTX_LOCAL_SERVER). The other flag that is sometimes used with this function is CLSCTX_REMOTE_SERVER. This flag is used in DCOM. I'll be discussing DCOM in detail in Chapter 5, "ActiveX Controls and ActiveForms."

iid is the interface that we want to get a reference to. Delphi always requests a reference to the IUnknown interface, because most class factories will fail if you ask for anything else. This parameter is mostly intended by Microsoft to be used for future expansion.

The last parameter, pv, receives the pointer to the IUnknown interface.

### Note

*One thing you will want to be aware of is that CoCreateInstance internally creates an instance of the class factory responsible for creating the COM object, and then uses the class factory to create the object. After the COM object has been created, the class factory is destroyed.*

*Obviously, if you want to create numerous instances of the same COM object, this is very inefficient. In these cases, you will want to create an instance of the class factory yourself and use its CreateInstance method to create the COM objects before disposing of it.* ◆

As mentioned earlier, CreateComObject always returns a pointer to IUnknown. To obtain a pointer to the interface that you're interested in, you should use the **as** operator, as follows:

```
MyIntf := CreateComObject(CLSID_MyServer) as IMyInterface;
```

This technique will be illustrated in the examples in this chapter.

### Virtual Method Tables

*Delphi implements interfaces as separate method tables that appear in memory next to the class virtual method table (VMT). As an example, consider the following interfaces and class definition:*

```
type
  IInterface1 = interface
    procedure DoInt1;
    function GetName1: WideString;
  end;

  IInterface2 = interface
    procedure DoInt2;
```

*continues* ▶

▶ *continued*

```
      procedure DoSomethingElse;
    end;

    TMyClass = class(TComObject, IInterface1, IInterface2)
    protected
      // IInterface 1 implementation
      procedure DoInt1;
      function GetName1: WideString;

      // IInterface2 implementation
      procedure DoInt2;
      procedure DoSomethingElse;

      // TMyClass virtual methods
      procedure WorkHard; virtual;
      function IsDone: Boolean; virtual;
    end;
```

*GUIDs were eliminated from this sample source code for brevity.*

*In memory, the class method tables are conceptually laid out as shown in Figure 2.2.*

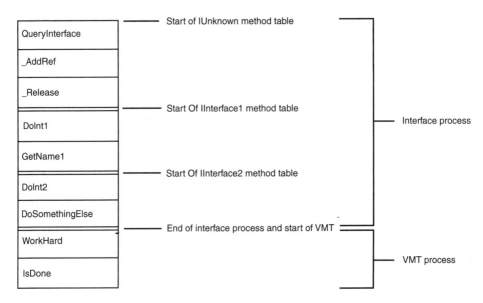

**Figure 2.2**    *The interface method tables occur one after another in memory, and the VMT occurs just after the last interface method table.*

*Because the different interface tables occupy different portions of memory, you can't simply typecast one interface to another. The following code:*

```
MyIntf1 := IInterface1(CreateComObject(CLSID_MyServer));
```

*will fail miserably, because it attempts to magically convert an IUnknown inter-*
*face to IInterface1. Always use the **as** operator to convert from one interface to*
*another, as described in Chapter 1.* ♦

Now that you know what an in-process COM server is, the next section
will lead you through the steps of creating a useful in-process COM server.

## Example: One-Dimensional Bin Packing

Let's say you have an application that you've written for the trucking industry. One of this application's duties is to load each truck as close to capacity
as possible, without exceeding some predetermined weight limit. Let's say
for sake of argument that the maximum weight limit on these trucks is
10,000 pounds.

It is your application's responsibility to ship all items, using the fewest
number of trucks possible. Obviously, if you have 40,000 pounds of material to ship, it's going to require more than one truck.

This problem is an example of an *n-complete* problem. N-complete problems have the dubious distinction of not having an optimal solution that can
be calculated in linear time. The only way to come up with the best solution
to the problem is to test every single combination of item placements on the
trucks. For anything other than very small sets of items, the time required to
test every combination is excessive.

Consider the case in which there are 100 items to ship. If five trucks are
required to ship the items, then there are $5^{100}$ possible combinations of
ways to distribute the items among the trucks. Clearly, there isn't time to
consider every combination, especially if we hope to ship the items any time
in the near future.

What we need, then, is a *heuristic*, or a way of determining a near-
optimal solution in a reasonable amount of time. A number of such
solutions exist. The purpose of this chapter is not to teach you about
bin-packing algorithms, but rather to illustrate how a COM server can
be used to implement one or more bin-packing algorithms.

The application we're writing is under a severe time crunch (what application isn't?), so we don't have time to investigate a number of algorithms
to determine which one is the best. After just a few seconds' thought, we
come up with a workable, but far from optimal solution. To understand
how this algorithm works, let's assume we have to ship the items listed in
Table 2.1.

*Table 2.1    A List of Items to Ship*

| Quantity | Item | Weight |
|----------|------|--------|
| 4 | Sofa | 300 |
| 6 | Table | 200 |
| 4 | Bed | 150 |
| 20 | Chair | 50 |

The total weight of these items is 4,000 pounds. For simplicity's sake, let's assume a truck can carry only 1,000 pounds. To implement this algorithm, we'll loop through each item in the list. If the current truck can hold the item, the item is placed on the truck. Otherwise, the truck is considered full, and a new truck is started.

Look at the first item, a sofa. We need to start a new truck to hold the sofa. The second item, another sofa, can also fit on the truck, as can the third sofa. We still have one sofa left, which would exceed the weight capacity of the truck (for purposes of this demonstration, I'm ignoring size considerations). The first truck is sent off to its destination, and a second truck is called in to load the last sofa.

Obviously, the first truck still had 100 pounds of carrying capacity left, and it could have carried two of the 20 chairs. That's a limitation of the NextFit algorithm that we're going to address later in this chapter.

Table 2.2 is how the breakdown of items will occur.

*Table 2.2    Result of Packing Items Using Next-Fit Algorithm*

| Truck # | Load |
|---------|------|
| 1 | 3 sofas |
| 2 | 1 sofa, 3 tables |
| 3 | 3 tables, 2 beds |
| 4 | 2 beds, 14 chairs |
| 5 | 6 chairs |

As you can see, the optimal number of trucks for this list of items is 4 (4,000 pounds / 1,000 pounds per truck), but this algorithm has required the use of 5 trucks. Our client has given us the go-ahead for this implementation due to time constraints, but has requested that in the future, we try to implement a better algorithm.

### Creating a Bin-Packing COM Server

To create a COM server to implement this algorithm, select File, New. In the New Items dialog box that appears, select the ActiveX tab. The ActiveX tab is displayed in Figure 2.3.

**Figure 2.3** *The ActiveX tab of the Object Repository.*

Double-click the ActiveX Library item, or select the ActiveX Library item and click OK. This will create the in-process COM server DLL.

```
library Project1;

uses
  ComServ;

exports
  DllGetClassObject,
  DllCanUnloadNow,
  DllRegisterServer,
  DllUnregisterServer;

{$R *.RES}

begin
end.
```

Notice that Delphi has automatically added DllGetClassObject, DllCanUnloadNow, DllRegisterServer, and DllUnregisterServer to the exports section of the module. We don't have to write any code at all to support these functions.

Save this file by selecting File, Save from the menu. Name it Bin1Srv.

Now we need to create the interface declaration. Let's name the interface IOneDBin (for one-dimensional bin packing). We'll define the IOneDBin interface as follows:

```
type
  IOneDBin = interface
    ['{7856B7E3-EF75-11D2-B3AB-0040F67455FE}']
    procedure SetMaxValue(AMaxValue: Integer);
    procedure AddItem(AQuantity: Integer; ADescription: Integer; AValue: Integer);
    procedure Optimize;
    function NextBin: Boolean;
    function NextItem(var ADescription: Integer; var AValue: Integer;
  end;
```

Once again, the GUID in the preceding interface declaration was generated by pressing Ctrl + Shift + G in Delphi. You should never copy a GUID from another object.

**Warning**

*You may see me say that over and over again in this book. I just can't stress enough that every interface that you create requires a unique GUID. Don't worry about running out of GUIDs on your machine. You could generate a new GUID every second and not run out of available GUIDs for something like millions of years!* ◆

Select File, New, and select the ActiveX tab in the New Items dialog box. Select the COM Object item and click OK.

**Note**

*Delphi 3 does not provide a COM Object Wizard. If you're a Delphi 3 user, you'll need to manually type in the code generated by the COM Object Wizard. The amount of code generated by this wizard is minimal, and is shown in Listing 2.1.*

*Also, Delphi 3 does not directly support threading in COM objects, and as a result, the call to TComObjectFactory.Create is slightly different under Delphi 3 than under later versions. Leave off the final parameter, tmApartment, under Delphi 3.* ◆

Delphi presents you with the COM Object Wizard. Fill out the wizard as shown in Figure 2.4, and click OK. You can ignore the Instancing option, as that only pertains to out-of-process servers. Leave the option for Include Type Library unchecked. I'll discuss type libraries in detail in Chapter 3. Delphi generates the following code:

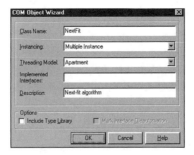

**Figure 2.4**    *Delphi's COM Object Wizard.*

Save this file as NextFit.pas. The code for NextFit.pas is shown in Listing 2.1.

**Listing 2.1**   *NextFit.pas*

```
unit NextFit;

interface

uses
  Windows, ActiveX, ComObj;

type
  TNextFit = class(TComObject, IOneDBin)
  protected
    {Declare IOneDBin methods here}
  end;

const
  Class_NextFit: TGUID = '{7856B7E2-EF75-11D2-B3AB-0040F67455FE}';

implementation

uses ComServ;

initialization
  TComObjectFactory.Create(ComServer, TNextFit, Class_NextFit,
    'NextFit', 'Next-fit algorithm', ciMultiInstance, tmApartment);
end.
```

TNextFit is the class that is generated for us. Recall that in the wizard, we specified NextFit as the class name. Delphi automatically adds the leading T.

The constant Class_NextFit is a GUID that represents the COM server. Each interface implemented in the server will also have its own GUID.

The initialization section of the unit contains a single, although complex, constructor call. This call sets up the class factory responsible for creating the TNextFit COM object. TComObjectFactory.Create is defined in comobj.pas:

```
constructor Create(ComServer: TComServerObject; ComClass: TComClass;
  const ClassID: TGUID; const ClassName, Description: string;
  Instancing: TClassInstancing; ThreadingModel: TThreadingModel = tmSingle);
```

Let's take a closer look at this function.

In 99% of all cases, you'll simply pass the global ComServer object as the parameter ComServer. I will not discuss any other use of this parameter in this book.

The second parameter, ComClass, accepts the class that will be created by this class factory. In this example, we want the class factory to create instances of TNextFit.

ClassID takes the GUID assigned to the TNextFit class. Delphi's wizard automatically created one for us: Class_NextFit.

Next, we pass the class name—NextFit—and a description of the class.

The Instancing parameter applies only to out-of-process COM servers, so I'll ignore it for the time being. Delphi's COM Object wizard fills in a default value for us, ciMultiInstance.

The final parameter accepts a value indicating the threading model supported by this object. Threading models were discussed in the section titled "Threading Support." Note that simply setting this value to tmApartment, for example, does not automatically mean the COM object is apartment-threaded. It is our responsibility to ensure that the code we write adheres to the apartment model specifications. This flag simply determines how the object is advertised in the Windows Registry.

I moved the IOneDBin interface declaration and GUID to a separate unit named BinIntf.pas to make them easy to reference from the client code (which we'll write in the next section). Listings 2.2 through 2.4 show the entire source code for the Bin1Srv server, after creating the implementation for the TNextFit class.

**Listing 2.2**    *Bin1Srv—Bin1Srv.dpr*

```
library Bin1Srv;

uses
  ComServ,
  NextFit in 'NextFit.pas',
  Bin1Srv_TLB in 'Bin1Srv_TLB.pas',
  BinIntf in 'BinIntf.pas';

exports
  DllGetClassObject,
  DllCanUnloadNow,
  DllRegisterServer,
  DllUnregisterServer;

{$R *.TLB}

{$R *.RES}

begin
end.
```

## Listing 2.3     *Bin1Srv—BinIntf.pas*

```
unit BinIntf;

interface

type
  IOneDBin = interface
    ['{7856B7E3-EF75-11D2-B3AB-0040F67455FE}']
    procedure SetMaxValue(AMaxValue: Integer);
    procedure AddItem(AQuantity: Integer; ADescription: WideString; AValue: Integer);
    procedure Optimize;
    function NextBin: Boolean;
    function NextItem(var ADescription: WideString; var AValue: Integer): Boolean;
  end;

const
  Class_NextFit: TGUID = '{7856B7E2-EF75-11D2-B3AB-0040F67455FE}';

implementation

end.
```

## Listing 2.4     *Bin1Srv—NextFit.pas*

```
unit NextFit;

interface

uses
  Windows, ActiveX, ComObj, classes, BinIntf;

type
  TBinItem = class
  protected
    FDescription: string;
    FValue: Integer;
  end;

  TBin = class
  protected
    FValue: Integer;
    FItems: TList;
  public
    constructor Create;
    destructor Destroy; override;
  end;

  TNextFit = class(TComObject, IOneDBin)
  protected
    FMaxValue: Integer;
    FItems: TList;
```

*continues* ▶

**Listing 2.4**   *continued*

```
    FBins: TList;
    FCurrentBin: TBin;
    FBinIndex: Integer;
    FItemIndex: Integer;
  public
    procedure Initialize; override;
    destructor Destroy; override;
    {Declare IOneDBin methods here}
    procedure SetMaxValue(AMaxValue: Integer);
    procedure AddItem(AQuantity: Integer; ADescription: WideString; AValue: Integer);
    procedure Optimize;
    function NextBin: Boolean;
    function NextItem(var ADescription: WideString; var AValue: Integer): Boolean;
  end;

implementation

uses ComServ;

{ TBin }

constructor TBin.Create;
begin
  FItems := TList.Create;
end;

destructor TBin.Destroy;
begin
  FItems.Free;
end;

{ TNextFit }

procedure TNextFit.AddItem(AQuantity: Integer; ADescription: WideString;
  AValue: Integer);
var
  Item: TBinItem;
  Index: Integer;
begin
  for Index := 1 to AQuantity do begin
    Item := TBinItem.Create;
    Item.FDescription := ADescription;
    Item.FValue := AValue;
    FItems.Add(Item);
  end;
end;

destructor TNextFit.Destroy;
var
  Index: Integer;
begin
```

```
  for Index := 0 to FBins.Count - 1 do
    TBin(FBins[Index]).Free;
  FBins.Free;

  for Index := 0 to FItems.Count - 1 do
    TBinItem(FItems[Index]).Free;
  FItems.Free;
end;

procedure TNextFit.Initialize;
begin
  FItems := TList.Create;
  FBins := TList.Create;
end;

function TNextFit.NextBin: Boolean;
begin
  if FBinIndex < FBins.Count - 1 then begin
    Inc(FBinIndex);
    FCurrentBin := TBin(FBins[FBinIndex]);
    FItemIndex := -1;
    Result := True;
  end else
    Result := False;
end;

function TNextFit.NextItem(var ADescription: WideString;
  var AValue: Integer): Boolean;
begin
  if FItemIndex < FCurrentBin.FItems.Count - 1 then begin
    Inc(FItemIndex);
    ADescription := TBinItem(FCurrentBin.FItems[FItemIndex]).FDescription;
    AValue := TBinItem(FCurrentBin.FItems[FItemIndex]).FValue;
    Result := True;
  end else
    Result := False;
end;

procedure TNextFit.Optimize;
var
  Index: Integer;
  Item: TBinItem;
begin
  FCurrentBin := nil;
  for Index := 0 to FItems.Count - 1 do begin
    Item := TBinItem(FItems[Index]);
    if (FCurrentBin = nil) or (FCurrentBin.FValue + Item.FValue> FMaxValue) then begin
      FCurrentBin := TBin.Create;
      FBins.Add(FCurrentBin);
    end;
```

*continues* ▶

**Listing 2.4** *continued*

```
  FCurrentBin.FItems.Add(Item);
  FCurrentBin.FValue := FCurrentBin.FValue + Item.FValue;
  end;

  FBinIndex := -1;
end;

procedure TNextFit.SetMaxValue(AMaxValue: Integer);
begin
  FMaxValue := AMaxValue;
end;

initialization
{$IFDEF VER100}
  TComObjectFactory.Create(ComServer, TNextFit, Class_NextFit,
    'NextFit', 'Next-fit algorithm', ciMultiInstance);
{$ELSE}
  TComObjectFactory.Create(ComServer, TNextFit, Class_NextFit,
    'NextFit', 'Next-fit algorithm', ciMultiInstance, tmApartment);
{$ENDIF}
end.
```

It will be worth taking a few moments to explain the code in this file.

TNextFit implements the IOneDBin algorithm as discussed previously. The client program will make repeated calls to TNextFit.AddItem to specify the items to optimize. For example, for the furniture pieces listed in Table 2.1, the client application would include the following code:

```
NextFit.AddItem(4, 'Sofa', 300);
NextFit.AddItem(6, Table, 200);
NextFit.AddItem(4, 'Bed', 150);
NextFit.AddItem(20, 'Chair', 50);
```

As the items are added, TNextFit creates a TBinItem object for each item. For example, TNextFit creates four TBinItem objects to represent the four sofas. Pretty straightforward so far. Next, the client application sets the bin size (or in our case, truck capacity):

```
NextFit.SetMaxValue(1000);
```

At this point, the items are ready to be optimized, so the client programs calls TNextFit.Optimize, which does all the actual work of optimizing the pieces.

Optimize uses an additional helper class to aid in the optimization process. The TBin class is used to represent the truck or whatever container is holding the items. TNextFit.Optimize creates a new TBin object whenever it needs a new container.

Each of the TBin objects contains a TList, FItems, which represents the items that are in that bin. The list contained by FItems coincides with the TBinItem objects created by the calls to AddItem. In other words, the TBinItem objects only exist once, but they are contained in both the TNextFit.FItems list and the TBin.FItems list to conserve memory.

After the items have been optimized, it is an easy process to traverse the bins and pull the contents for each bin. The following simple loop shows how to do that:

```
while NextFit.NextBin do begin
  // Start a new bin
  while NextFit.NextItem(Description, Value) do begin
    // Do something with Description and Value
  end;
end;
```

Before we can use this COM server, we must register it. Select Run, Register ActiveX Server from Delphi's main menu. After a moment, you'll receive a confirmation message similar to the one shown in Figure 2.5. Your drive and directory will differ from the one shown in the figure.

Figure 2.5    *Successfully registering Bin1Srv.*

At this time, Delphi also creates a type library Bin1Srv.tlb, and a type library import file Bin1Srv_TLB.pas. You might think this is strange because we didn't request a type library when creating the COM object TNextFit. However, this type library contains information about the COM server Bin1Srv, and not about the COM object TNextFit. Listing 2.5 shows the source code for Bin1Srv_TLB.pas.

Chapter 3, "Type Libraries," discusses type libraries in detail.

**Listing 2.5**    *Bin1Srv—Bin1Srv_TLB.pas*

```
unit Bin1Srv_TLB;

// ********************************************************************* //
// WARNING                                                             //
// -------                                                             //
// The types declared in this file were generated from data read from a //
// type library. If this type library is explicitly or indirectly (via  //
// another type library referring to this type library) re-imported, or the //
// 'Refresh' command of the Type Library Editor activated while editing the //
```

*continues* ▶

**Listing 2.5** *continued*

```
// type library, the contents of this file will be regenerated and all     //
// manual modifications will be lost.                                       //
// *************************************************************************  //

// PASTLWTR : $Revision:   1.11.1.75  $
// File generated on 4/19/1999 10:50:01 AM from type library described below.


// *************************************************************************  //
// Type Lib: B:\Book\samples\Chap04\Bin1Srv\Bin1Srv.tlb
// IID\LCID: {E97BFEF5-F664-11D2-9099-0040F6741DE2}\0
// Helpfile:
// HelpString: Bin1Srv Library
// Version:    1.0
// *************************************************************************  //

interface

uses Windows, ActiveX, Classes, Graphics, OleCtrls, StdVCL;


// *************************************************************************//
// GUIDS declared in the TypeLibrary. Following prefixes are used:         //
//   Type Libraries     : LIBID_xxxx                                       //
//   CoClasses          : CLASS_xxxx                                       //
//   DISPInterfaces      : DIID_xxxx                                       //
//   Non-DISP interfaces: IID_xxxx                                        //
// *************************************************************************//
const
  LIBID_Bin1Srv: TGUID = '{E97BFEF5-F664-11D2-9099-0040F6741DE2}';

implementation

uses ComObj;

end.
```

In the next section, we'll create a client application to drive this server.

### Creating a Bin-Packing Client Application

Now we can write a client program to test this server. Figure 2.6 shows the UI for the test program.

Using this program is simple. Enter the quantity, description, and value of an item and press the Add button. The program beeps to give you some rudimentary feedback that the item has been recorded. After you've added all items, press the Optimize button to place the items into bins of the size specified by the Bin Size edit control.

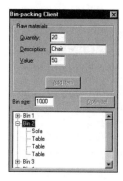

**Figure 2.6**  *Bin1Cli in action.*

The application will load up a tree indicating how many bins are required, and what items are to be placed in each bin. I have not implemented any error checking in either this application or the COM server, so the program will not check for things like trying to place a 2000-pound item in a 1000-pound bin.

Listings 2.6 and 2.7 contain the source code for the Bin1Cli application.

**Listing 2.6**  *Bin1Cli—Bin1Cli.dpr*

```
program Bin1Cli;

uses
  Forms,
  MainForm in 'MainForm.pas' {Form1},
  BinIntf in '..\Bin1Srv\BinIntf.pas';

{$R *.RES}

begin
  Application.Initialize;
  Application.CreateForm(TForm1, Form1);
  Application.Run;
end.
```

**Listing 2.7**  *Bin1Cli—MainForm.pas*

```
unit MainForm;

interface

uses
  Windows, Messages, SysUtils, Classes, Graphics, Controls, Forms, Dialogs,
  ComObj, StdCtrls, ComCtrls, BinIntf;
```

*continues* ▶

**Listing 2.7**    *continued*

```
type
  TForm1 = class(TForm)
    grpItems: TGroupBox;
    Label4: TLabel;
    ecQuantity: TEdit;
    Label5: TLabel;
    ecDescription: TEdit;
    Label6: TLabel;
    ecValue: TEdit;
    btnAdd: TButton;
    btnOptimize: TButton;
    treeBins: TTreeView;
    Label1: TLabel;
    ecBinSize: TEdit;
    procedure btnAddClick(Sender: TObject);
    procedure FormCreate(Sender: TObject);
    procedure btnOptimizeClick(Sender: TObject);
  private
    { Private declarations }
    FOneD: IOneDBin;
  public
    { Public declarations }
  end;

var
  Form1: TForm1;

implementation

{$R *.DFM}

procedure TForm1.btnAddClick(Sender: TObject);
begin
  FOneD.AddItem(StrToInt(ecQuantity.Text), ecDescription.Text,
    StrToInt(ecValue.Text));

  Beep;
  ActiveControl := ecQuantity;
end;

procedure TForm1.FormCreate(Sender: TObject);
begin
  FOneD := CreateComObject(Class_NextFit) as IOneDBin;
end;

procedure TForm1.btnOptimizeClick(Sender: TObject);
var
  Desc: string;
  Value: Integer;
  BinCount: Integer;
  Node: TTreeNode;
```

```
begin
  FOneD.SetMaxValue(StrToInt(ecBinSize.Text));

  FOneD.Optimize;
  BinCount := 0;

  treeBins.Items.BeginUpdate;
  try
    while FOneD.NextBin do begin
      Inc(BinCount);
      Node := treeBins.Items.AddChild(nil, 'Bin ' + IntToStr(BinCount));
      while FOneD.NextItem(Desc, Value) do
        treeBins.Items.AddChild(Node, Desc);
    end;
  finally
    treeBins.Items.EndUpdate;
  end;

  btnAdd.Enabled := False;
  btnOptimize.Enabled := False;
end;

end.
```

## Updating the Bin-Packing Server

Some months go by, and our application is working flawlessly. Our client is happy with the application, but the NextFit algorithm gives less-than-optimal results in many cases. They'd like us to implement a more optimal bin-packing algorithm. Perhaps after doing some research, we stumble on a better algorithm called FirstFit. FirstFit works much like NextFit, except it doesn't close a bin when it finds an item that will not fit in it. Instead, it considers all available bins when attempting to place an item. Only if no open bins have space for an item does it start a new bin.

For this example, I'm going to add the new TFirstFit object to the existing server, rather than creating a new server. As long as I don't change the interface, I'm free to modify the code inside the DLL as I see fit. Obviously, if I modify any code, I should thoroughly test the code so that I don't send out a broken update!

Most of the code for TFirstFit will be exactly the same as the code for TNextFit. Therefore, I'm going to create an abstract class named TAbstractBinPacker, that implements most of the base functionality. I will derive TNextFit and TFirstFit from TAbstractBinPacker. My point here is that I can change the implementation all I want without breaking existing code. As long as I leave the interface alone, client programs that use this server will not be broken in any way.

Of course, as often happens, I've thought of a couple of enhancements that I'd like to make to the IOneDBin interface. I want to add a routine to tell me how many bins are required, and a routine to tell me the percent of wasted space. This way, I can run both algorithms and compare the results. Whichever algorithm yields the least amount of wasted space will be the most efficient algorithm for that particular set of input data.

**Note**

*Actually, I implemented both TFirstFit and TBestFit, because the additional code required to implement TBestFit was trivial.* ◆

Because an interface is immutable once published, we can't just arbitrarily modify the IOneDBin interface. Instead, we'll create an IOneDBin2 interface (one-dimensional bin-packing, version 2). I have modified the server to do just that. Listings 2.8 through 2.13 show the source code for the updated COM server.

To update the server, I ran the Delphi COM Object Wizard twice more, creating both a TFirstFit and a TBestFit COM object. Delphi put these objects into separate source files. I then manually cut the GUIDs from those two files and moved them into BinIntf.pas so that the client application can reference them.

Next, I created the BinBase.pas file, which defines an abstract class used internally by the server. Because most of the functionality between the three bin-packing methods (NextFit, FirstFit, and BestFit) is identical, it makes sense to have the common functionality implemented by a common ancestor class.

The files NextFit.pas, FirstFit.pas, and BestFit.pas implement the two methods GetName and Optimize, which differ between the bin-packing methods.

**Listing 2.8**   *Bin1Srv2—Bin1Srv.dpr*

```
library Bin1Srv;

uses
  ComServ,
  Bin1Srv_TLB in 'Bin1Srv_TLB.pas',
  BinIntf in 'BinIntf.pas',
  BinBase in 'BinBase.pas',
  NextFit in 'NextFit.pas',
  FirstFit in 'FirstFit.pas',
  BestFit in 'BestFit.pas';
```

```
exports
  DllGetClassObject,
  DllCanUnloadNow,
  DllRegisterServer,
  DllUnregisterServer;

{$R *.TLB}

{$R *.RES}

begin
end.
```

**Listing 2.9**   *Bin1Srv2—BinIntf.pas*

```
unit BinIntf;

interface

type
  IOneDBin = interface
    ['{7856B7E3-EF75-11D2-B3AB-0040F67455FE}']
    procedure SetMaxValue(AMaxValue: Integer);
    procedure AddItem(AQuantity: Integer; ADescription: WideString; AValue: Integer);
    procedure Optimize;
    function NextBin: Boolean;
    function NextItem(var ADescription: WideString; var AValue: Integer): Boolean;
  end;

  IOneDBin2 = interface(IOneDBin)
    ['{15B382F0-F0E0-11D2-908E-0040F6741DE2}']
    function GetName: WideString;
    function NumBins: Integer;
    function PercentWaste: Double;
  end;

const
  Class_NextFit: TGUID = '{7856B7E2-EF75-11D2-B3AB-0040F67455FE}';
  Class_FirstFit: TGUID = '{E97BFEF7-F664-11D2-9099-0040F6741DE2}';
  Class_BestFit: TGUID = '{E97BFEF8-F664-11D2-9099-0040F6741DE2}';

implementation

end.
```

**Listing 2.10**    *Bin1Srv2—BinBase.pas*

```pascal
unit BinBase;

interface

uses
  Windows, ActiveX, ComObj, classes, BinIntf;

type
  TBinItem = class
  protected
    FDescription: string;
    FValue: Integer;
  public
    property Description: string read FDescription;
    property Value: Integer read FValue;
  end;

  TBin = class
  protected
    FValue: Integer;
    FItems: TList;
  public
    constructor Create;
    destructor Destroy; override;
    property Items: TList read FItems;
    property Value: Integer read FValue write FValue;
  end;

  TAbstractOneDBin = class(TComObject, IOneDBin, IOneDBin2)
  protected
    FMaxValue: Integer;
    FItems: TList;
    FBins: TList;
    FCurrentBin: TBin;
    FBinIndex: Integer;
    FItemIndex: Integer;
  public
    procedure Initialize; override;
    destructor Destroy; override;
    {Declare IOneDBin methods here}
    procedure SetMaxValue(AMaxValue: Integer);
    procedure AddItem(AQuantity: Integer; ADescription: WideString; AValue: Integer);
    procedure Optimize; virtual; abstract;
    function GetName: WideString; virtual; abstract;
    function NextBin: Boolean;
    function NextItem(var ADescription: WideString; var AValue: Integer): Boolean;
    function NumBins: Integer;
    function PercentWaste: Double;
  end;
```

```
implementation

uses ComServ;

{ TBin }

constructor TBin.Create;
begin
  FItems := TList.Create;
end;

destructor TBin.Destroy;
begin
  FItems.Free;
end;

{ TAbstractOneDBin }

procedure TAbstractOneDBin.AddItem(AQuantity: Integer; ADescription: WideString;
  AValue: Integer);
var
  Item: TBinItem;
  Index: Integer;
begin
  for Index := 1 to AQuantity do begin
    Item := TBinItem.Create;
    Item.FDescription := ADescription;
    Item.FValue := AValue;
    FItems.Add(Item);
  end;
end;

destructor TAbstractOneDBin.Destroy;
var
  Index: Integer;
begin
  for Index := 0 to FItems.Count - 1 do
    TBinItem(FItems[Index]).Free;
  FItems.Free;

  for Index := 0 to FBins.Count - 1 do
    TBin(FBins[Index]).Free;
  FBins.Free;
end;

procedure TAbstractOneDBin.Initialize;
begin
  FItems := TList.Create;
  FBins := TList.Create;
end;
```

*continues* ▶

**Listing 2.10** *continued*

```
function TAbstractOneDBin.NextBin: Boolean;
begin
  if FBinIndex < FBins.Count - 1 then begin
    Inc(FBinIndex);
    FCurrentBin := TBin(FBins[FBinIndex]);
    FItemIndex := -1;
    Result := True;
  end else
    Result := False;
end;

function TAbstractOneDBin.NextItem(var ADescription: WideString;
  var AValue: Integer): Boolean;
begin
  if FItemIndex < FCurrentBin.FItems.Count - 1 then begin
    Inc(FItemIndex);
    ADescription := TBinItem(FCurrentBin.FItems[FItemIndex]).FDescription;
    AValue := TBinItem(FCurrentBin.FItems[FItemIndex]).FValue;
    Result := True;
  end else
    Result := False;
end;

function TAbstractOneDBin.NumBins: Integer;
begin
  Result := FBins.Count;
end;

function TAbstractOneDBin.PercentWaste: Double;
var
  TotalWeight: Integer;
  UsedWeight: Integer;
  BinIndex: Integer;
  Bin: TBin;
  ItemIndex: Integer;
  Item: TBinItem;
begin
  TotalWeight := 0;
  UsedWeight := 0;

  for BinIndex := 0 to FBins.Count - 1 do begin
    Inc(TotalWeight, FMaxValue);
    Bin := TBin(FBins[BinIndex]);
    for ItemIndex := 0 to Bin.FItems.Count - 1 do begin
      Item := TBinItem(Bin.FItems[ItemIndex]);
      Inc(UsedWeight, Item.FValue);
    end;
  end;

  Result := (1.0 - UsedWeight / TotalWeight) * 100.0;
end;
```

```
procedure TAbstractOneDBin.SetMaxValue(AMaxValue: Integer);
begin
  FMaxValue := AMaxValue;
end;

end.
```

## Listing 2.11     *Bin1Srv2—NextFit.pas*

```
unit NextFit;

interface

uses
  Windows, ActiveX, ComObj, classes, BinIntf, BinBase;

type
  TNextFit = class(TAbstractOneDBin)
    procedure Optimize; override;
    function GetName: WideString; override;
  end;

implementation

uses
  ComServ;

{ TNextFit }

function TNextFit.GetName: WideString;
begin
  Result := 'Next Fit';
end;

procedure TNextFit.Optimize;
var
  Index: Integer;
  Item: TBinItem;
begin
  FCurrentBin := nil;
  for Index := 0 to FItems.Count - 1 do begin
    Item := TBinItem(FItems[Index]);
    if (FCurrentBin = nil) or (FCurrentBin.Value + Item.Value> FMaxValue) then begin
      FCurrentBin := TBin.Create;
      FBins.Add(FCurrentBin);
    end;

    FCurrentBin.Items.Add(Item);
    FCurrentBin.Value := FCurrentBin.Value + Item.Value;
  end;
```

*continues* ▶

**Listing 2.11**    *continued*

```
  FBinIndex := -1;
end;

initialization
{$IFDEF VER100}
  TComObjectFactory.Create(ComServer, TNextFit, Class_NextFit,
    'NextFit', 'Next Fit algorithm', ciMultiInstance);
{$ELSE}
  TComObjectFactory.Create(ComServer, TNextFit, Class_NextFit,
    'NextFit', 'Next Fit algorithm', ciMultiInstance, tmApartment);
{$ENDIF}
end.
```

**Listing 2.12**    *Bin1Srv2—NextFit.pas*

```
unit FirstFit;

interface

uses
  Windows, ActiveX, ComObj, classes, BinIntf, BinBase;

type
  TFirstFit = class(TAbstractOneDBin)
    procedure Optimize; override;
    function GetName: WideString; override;
  end;

implementation

uses
  ComServ;

{ TFirstFit }

function TFirstFit.GetName: WideString;
begin
  Result := 'First Fit';
end;

procedure TFirstFit.Optimize;
var
  Index: Integer;
  Item: TBinItem;
  BinFound: Boolean;
  BinIndex: Integer;
begin
  FCurrentBin := nil;
  for Index := 0 to FItems.Count - 1 do begin
    Item := TBinItem(FItems[Index]);
```

```
    // Find a bin with enough room
    BinFound := False;
    BinIndex := 0;
    while (not BinFound) and (BinIndex < FBins.Count) do begin
      FCurrentBin := TBin(FBins[BinIndex]);
      if FCurrentBin.Value + Item.Value <= FMaxValue then
        BinFound := True
      else
        Inc(BinIndex);
    end;

    // if no available bin, create a new one
    if not BinFound then begin
      FCurrentBin := TBin.Create;
      FBins.Add(FCurrentBin);
    end;

    FCurrentBin.Items.Add(Item);
    FCurrentBin.Value := FCurrentBin.Value + Item.Value;
  end;

  FBinIndex := -1;
end;

initialization
{$IFDEF VER100}
  TComObjectFactory.Create(ComServer, TFirstFit, Class_FirstFit,
    'FirstFit', 'First Fit algorithm', ciMultiInstance);
{$ELSE}
  TComObjectFactory.Create(ComServer, TFirstFit, Class_FirstFit,
    'FirstFit', 'First Fit algorithm', ciMultiInstance, tmApartment);
{$ENDIF}
end.
```

---

## Listing 2.13   *Bin1Srv2—BestFit.pas*

```
unit BestFit;

interface

uses
  Windows, ActiveX, ComObj, classes, BinIntf, BinBase;

type
  TBestFit = class(TAbstractOneDBin)
    procedure Optimize; override;
    function GetName: WideString; override;
  end;

implementation
```

*continues* ▶

**Listing 2.13**   *continued*

```
uses
  ComServ;

{ TBestFit }

function TBestFit.GetName: WideString;
begin
  Result := 'Best Fit';
end;

procedure TBestFit.Optimize;
var
  Index: Integer;
  Item: TBinItem;
  BinIndex: Integer;
  BestBinIndex: Integer;
  BestValue: Integer;
begin
  FCurrentBin := nil;
  for Index := 0 to FItems.Count - 1 do begin
    Item := TBinItem(FItems[Index]);

    // Find a bin with enough room
    BestBinIndex := -1;
    BestValue := 0;
    for BinIndex := 0 to FBins.Count - 1 do begin
      FCurrentBin := TBin(FBins[BinIndex]);
      if FCurrentBin.Value + Item.Value <= FMaxValue then begin
        if (BestBinIndex = -1) or
           (FCurrentBin.Value> BestValue) then begin
          BestBinIndex := BinIndex;
          BestValue := FCurrentBin.Value;
        end;
      end;
    end;

    // if no available bin, create a new one
    if BestBinIndex = -1 then begin
      FCurrentBin := TBin.Create;
      FBins.Add(FCurrentBin);
    end;

    FCurrentBin.Items.Add(Item);
    FCurrentBin.Value := FCurrentBin.Value + Item.Value;
  end;

  FBinIndex := -1;
end;

initialization
{$IFDEF VER100}
```

```
TComObjectFactory.Create(ComServer, TBestFit, Class_BestFit,
   'BestFit', 'Best Fit algorithm', ciMultiInstance);
{$ELSE}
TComObjectFactory.Create(ComServer, TBestFit, Class_BestFit,
   'BestFit', 'Best Fit algorithm', ciMultiInstance, tmApartment);
{$ENDIF}
end.
```

### Updating the Bin-Packing Client

I've also made some minor adjustments to the client program to run
TNextFit and TFirstFit, and to report the results of whichever algorithm
yields the best results. Listings 2.14 and 2.15 show the source code for the
updated client application.

**Listing 2.14**   *BinCli2—BinCli.dpr*

```
program Bin1Cli;

uses
  Forms,
  MainForm in 'MainForm.pas' {Form1},
  BinIntf in '..\Bin1Srv2\BinIntf.pas';

{$R *.RES}

begin
  Application.Initialize;
  Application.CreateForm(TForm1, Form1);
  Application.Run;
end.
```

**Listing 2.15**   *BinCli2—MainForm.pas*

```
unit MainForm;

interface

uses
  Windows, Messages, SysUtils, Classes, Graphics, Controls, Forms,
  Dialogs, ComObj, StdCtrls, ComCtrls, BinIntf;

const
  MAXITEMS = 10;

type
  TForm1 = class(TForm)
    grpItems: TGroupBox;
    Label4: TLabel;
```

*continues* ▶

**Listing 2.15**  *continued*

```
  ecQuantity: TEdit;
  Label5: TLabel;
  ecDescription: TEdit;
  Label6: TLabel;
  ecValue: TEdit;
  btnAdd: TButton;
  btnOptimize: TButton;
  treeBins: TTreeView;
  Label1: TLabel;
  ecBinSize: TEdit;
  lblAlgorithm: TLabel;
  lblWaste: TLabel;
  procedure btnAddClick(Sender: TObject);
  procedure btnOptimizeClick(Sender: TObject);
private
  { Private declarations }
  FQty: array[1 .. MAXITEMS] of Integer;
  FDesc: array[1 .. MAXITEMS] of string;
  FValue: array[1 .. MAXITEMS] of Integer;
  FItemCount: Integer;
  FBestIntf: IOneDBin2;
  FBestPercentWaste: Double;
  procedure TestPackingMethod(MethodID: TGUID);
public
  { Public declarations }
end;

var
  Form1: TForm1;

implementation

{$R *.DFM}

procedure TForm1.btnAddClick(Sender: TObject);
begin
  if FItemCount = MAXITEMS then begin
    ShowMessage('This demo does not accept more than ' + IntToStr(MAXITEMS) + ' items.');
    exit;
  end;

  Inc(FItemCount);
  FQty[FItemCount] := StrToInt(ecQuantity.Text);
  FDesc[FItemCount] := ecDescription.Text;
  FValue[FItemCount] := StrToInt(ecValue.Text);

  Beep;
  ActiveControl := ecQuantity;
end;
```

```
procedure TForm1.TestPackingMethod(MethodID: TGUID);
var
  TestIntf: IOneDBin2;
  Index: Integer;
begin
  TestIntf := CreateComObject(MethodID) as IOneDBin2;
  TestIntf.SetMaxValue(StrToInt(ecBinSize.Text));
  for Index := 1 to FItemCount do
    TestIntf.AddItem(FQty[Index], FDesc[Index], FValue[Index]);
  TestIntf.Optimize;
  if TestIntf.PercentWaste < FBestPercentWaste then begin
    FBestPercentWaste := TestIntf.PercentWaste;
    FBestIntf := TestIntf;
  end;
end;

procedure TForm1.btnOptimizeClick(Sender: TObject);
var
  BinCount: Integer;
  Node: TTreeNode;
  Desc: WideString;
  Value: Integer;
begin
  FBestPercentWaste := 100.0;

  TestPackingMethod(Class_NextFit);
  TestPackingMethod(Class_FirstFit);
  TestPackingMethod(Class_BestFit);

  BinCount := 0;

  lblAlgorithm.Caption := FBestIntf.GetName;
  lblWaste.Caption := FloatToStrF(FBestIntf.PercentWaste, ffFixed, 8, 2) + '% waste';

  treeBins.Items.BeginUpdate;
  try
    while FBestIntf.NextBin do begin
      Inc(BinCount);
      Node := treeBins.Items.AddChild(nil, 'Bin ' +
        IntToStr(BinCount));
      while FBestIntf.NextItem(Desc, Value) do
        treeBins.Items.AddChild(Node, Desc);
    end;
  finally
    treeBins.Items.EndUpdate;
  end;

  btnAdd.Enabled := False;
  btnOptimize.Enabled := False;
end;

end.
```

As you can see from Listing 2.15, procedure btnOptimizeClick creates an instance of each COM server and runs its Optimize method. Whichever COM server reports the least amount of waste is the one that is ultimately used to load the tree control.

Figure 2.7 shows the new version of Bin1Cli at runtime.

**Figure 2.7**   *The modified Bin1Cli application.*

The modified client program operates in much the same fashion as the original. However, the raw list of materials is stored in an array until you click the Optimize button. At that time, the program connects to each COM server (NextFit, FirstFit, and BestFit) in turn, optimizing the placement of the raw materials. Whichever method yields the least amount of waste is used to load up the tree view.

Note that there are numerous other one-dimensional bin-packing algorithms available, such as WorstFit, LastFit, and others. I'm not going to go through the tedium of implementing all the various algorithms here. I simply wanted to show you how a COM server can be enhanced after it is released.

### Recap of Example
This was certainly a long section, and I want to recap the steps that we went through and the concepts that were reinforced by this exercise.

1. First, we created the server application.

2. After we created the server, we created a client to access it.

3. Next, we enhanced the server by providing support for different algorithms (FirstFit and BestFit), and also by introducing the new methods PercentWaste and NumBins.

4. Finally, we updated the client application to run all three bin-packing algorithms and determine which is the best for a given set of input.

The following concepts were reinforced during the implementation of step 3:

- The IOneDBin interface was already released and in use, so we could not modify that interface without breaking existing client applications.

- The IOneDBin2 interface is derived from IOneDBin. It requires a new GUID, because it is a new interface, but we didn't have to redeclare the methods already declared in IOneDBin.

- Even though the structure of the source files changed (we created the new base class TAbstractOneDBin, for example), as long as the new class structure completely implements the defined interfaces, existing client applications will continue to operate correctly.

- We implemented both the IOneDBin and IOneDBin2 interfaces in the abstract class TAbstractOneDBin without having to implement the methods common to both interfaces twice. IOneDBin and IOneDBin both support the Optimize method, but they map to the same implementation of Optimize in the TAbstractOneDBin class.

With in-process COM servers behind us, the next section discusses out-of-process COM servers.

# Out-of-Process COM Servers

Out-of-process COM servers are implemented in an EXE, instead of in a DLL. Consequently, they run in a separate address space from the client application. This has several implications, which we will explore later in detail.

Out-of-process COM servers do not export the four functions required of an in-process COM server. Therefore, they use a different method to register themselves in the Windows Registry. To register an out-of-process COM server, simply run the server, placing /regserver on the command line. Delphi will register the server and COM objects, and then exit. To unregister the server, use the command-line switch /unregserver.

Delphi will also register the server if you run it normally, without any command-line options. However, the server application will then continue to run.

## Instancing

Out-of-process COM servers can support one of three *instancing* methods. Instancing refers to how many instances of the COM object are created for client requests.

- *Single Instance* means only one instance of the COM object is allowed per application. Each application requesting an instance of the COM object will launch a separate copy of the COM server.

- *Multiple Instance* means that the COM server is able to create multiple copies of a COM object. When a client requests an instance of the COM object, a new server is not started (unless the server is not yet running). Instead, the currently running server creates a new instance of the COM object.

- *Internal Only* is used for COM objects that are not meant to be made available to client applications. The only application that can create the COM object is the COM server in which they reside.

In general, you'll want to create COM servers that support multiple instancing. For example, say you've written a COM server that controls access to a serial port. Two concurrently running client applications need to be able to send data to the port (through the COM server). A COM server that supports multiple instancing can open the port and service both client applications simultaneously.

On the other hand, if the COM server were a single instance server, the first client to request access to the server would cause an instance of the server to be started. When the second client requested access to the server, a separate server would be started to service the second client. Because the first instance of the server has the serial port opened, the second instance of the server will not be able to access the port, effectively preventing the second client application from running.

Of course, there are cases in which this may be the desired effect. For those cases, create a single instance COM server. However, unless you have a reason for doing otherwise, create a multiple instance server. As you'll see in the next section, when you create a COM server using Delphi's COM Object Wizard, it assumes you want multiple instancing by default.

> **Note**
>
> *You aren't locked into an instancing method once you've selected it. After you've created the server, you can easily change instancing methods by altering a single line of code.* ◆

## Creating an Instance of an Out-of-Process COM Object

The method for creating a COM object that resides in an out-of-process server is the same as that used for creating one that lives in an in-process server. You can still call CreateComObject, passing the GUID of the COM object that you want to create.

Delphi itself needs to do some different processing for you in this case. Instead of using the Registry key InProcServer32, the LocalServer32 Registry key is used to point to the full path name of the server EXE. CreateComObject then starts up the server application. As part of the Application.Initialization process, the server registers its class factories with Windows' internal *running object table*. The running object table tracks all active COM objects. I'll discuss the running object table a little more in Chapter 4.

I will not show you how to create an out-of-process COM server in this chapter, because to use out-of-process COM servers effectively, you need to create a type library. Type libraries are discussed in Chapter 3. I'll present several concrete examples of out-of-process COM servers in Chapter 4.

## Marshaling Data

When a program uses an out-of-process COM server, the program is loaded at one address in memory, and the COM server is loaded at a different address. Variables declared in the calling application are loaded at a given memory address, which represents an address in virtual memory. For instance, say the client application declares an integer variable MyInt, whose memory address is $00442830. The out-of-process COM server does not have access to that location in memory.

Because one executable program doesn't have direct access to the address space of another executable, Windows moves data between the calling application and the out-of-process COM server through a process called *marshaling*. Windows can automatically marshal the following Delphi data types: Smallint, Integer, Single, Double, Currency, TDateTime, WideString, IDispatch, SCODE, WordBool, OleVariant, IUnknown, Shortint, Byte, Word, UINT, int64, Largeuint, SYSINT, SYSUINT, HResult, Pointer, SafeArray, PChar, and PWideChar.

Of the preceding types, Smallint, Integer, Single, Double, Currency, TDateTime, WideString, IDispatch, SCODE, WordBool, OleVariant, IUnknown, Shortint, and Byte are Automation-compatible, meaning they can safely be used in COM Automation Servers. I will discuss COM Automation Servers in detail in Chapter 4.

You may notice that records and arrays are conspicuously absent from the above list. Windows cannot automatically marshal a record or array variable.

What if you have a record or array that you need to marshal? One
thing you can do is manually provide marshaling support for that structure.
To do this, you would implement the IMarshal interface for your data.
Implementing IMarshal is an advanced issue that is beyond the scope of this
book. If you want more information on the IMarshal interface, perhaps the
best reference is the Microsoft Developer's Network (MSDN).

In Chapter 6, "DCOM," I'll develop an extended example that shows
how you can use *variant arrays* to marshal record structures across process
boundaries. Variant arrays are discussed in the following section.

# Variant Arrays

Before I move on to the subject of out-of-process COM servers, I'm going
to take some time and introduce you to another Delphi language element
called *variant arrays*. A variant is a variable that can hold various types of
data. Typically, when you define a variable, you specify the exact data type
that is stored in that variable, as in the following:

```
var
  I: Integer;
```

Variable I is declared to hold an integer value. No matter how hard you try,
you're not going to stuff a floating point number or a string into variable I.

A variant, on the other hand, can hold numerous forms of data.
Furthermore, it can also tell you what type of data is currently stored.
A variant always occupies 16 bytes of memory. You can think of a variant
as being similar to a variant record (notice the name similarity), although
variants have additional benefits, such as the capability to coerce the value
into a different type.

You can determine the type of data stored in a variant by using the
VarType function. The System unit defines the legal variant types:

```
{ Variant type codes (wtypes.h) }

  varEmpty    = $0000; { vt_empty    }
  varNull     = $0001; { vt_null     }
  varSmallint = $0002; { vt_i2       }
  varInteger  = $0003; { vt_i4       }
  varSingle   = $0004; { vt_r4       }
  varDouble   = $0005; { vt_r8       }
  varCurrency = $0006; { vt_cy       }
  varDate     = $0007; { vt_date     }
  varOleStr   = $0008; { vt_bstr     }
  varDispatch = $0009; { vt_dispatch }
  varError    = $000A; { vt_error    }
  varBoolean  = $000B; { vt_bool     }
  varVariant  = $000C; { vt_variant  }
  varUnknown  = $000D; { vt_unknown  }
```

```
                    { vt_decimal $e  }
                    { undefined  $f  }
                    { vt_i1      $10 }
varByte      = $0011; { vt_ui1          }
                    { vt_ui2     $12 }
                    { vt_ui4     $13 }
                    { vt_i8      $14 }
{ if adding new items, update varLast, BaseTypeMap and OpTypeMap }
varStrArg    = $0048; { vt_clsid    }
varString    = $0100; { Pascal string; not OLE compatible }
varAny       = $0101;
varTypeMask  = $0FFF;
varArray     = $2000;
varByRef     = $4000;
```

The value varArray is used to indicate that the variant contains an array
(it is a variant array). The value varByRef indicates that the variant holds a
pointer to the data—the actual data is not stored directly in the variant.

To determine the type of data stored in a variant, you can use code
like this:

```
VType := VarType(V) and varTypeMask
```

'And'ing the value with varTypeMask strips off the varArray and varByRef
flags, if they are present. A variant that holds an array of doubles would
have a type of $2005 (varDouble or varArray). A variant that holds a
double would have a type of $0005 (varDouble).

```
var
  V: Variant;
begin
  V := 'I love Delphi';
  V := 5;
  if VarType(V) and varTypeMask = varInteger then
    V := V + 10;
  ShowMessage(IntToStr(V));
  V := 3.5;
end;
```

Notice that you can assign different types of data to the same variant. Also
note that you can perform arithmetic on variants, as long as they contain
numeric values. If you try to add a number to a non-numeric variant (such as
a string), you'll receive the following error, shown in Figure 2.8, at runtime.

**Figure 2.8**    *Don't try to add a number to a non-numeric variant!*

I should point out that it *is* possible to add two variants together when one
is a string and one is a number. For instance, the following code will run
just fine:

```
var
  V1: Variant;
  V2: Variant;
begin
  V1 := '123';  // string value
  V2 := 5;       // integer value

  ShowMessage(IntToStr(V1 + V2));
end;
```

In this example, variant V1 will automatically be coerced to an integer value
before being added to V2. However, if the value stored in V1 can't be converted to a number, you'll receive the same type of error message shown in
Figure 2.8.

Now that you know what a variant is, it stands to reason that a variant
array is simply an array of variants. Variant arrays don't have to contain
homogenous data. Each element in the variant array can contain a different
data type. We'll take advantage of that fact in Chapter 6, but right now
we're going to demonstrate how to create a variant array.

## Creating a Variant Array

There are two basic ways to create a variant array. The first method that I'll
discuss, VarArrayCreate, is the most flexible. The second method,
VarArrayOf, must be resolved at compile time, and so is much less flexible.

### VarArrayCreate

The most basic way to create a variant array is by using the VarArrayCreate
function. VarArrayCreate is defined in system.pas as the following:

```
function VarArrayCreate(const Bounds: array of Integer;
  VarType: Integer): Variant;
```

The first parameter tells the function the lower and upper bounds of the
array. VarType determines what type of data will be stored in the array. To
create an array of integers, you could write the following code:

```
MyIntArray := VarArrayCreate([1, 10], varInteger);
```

This declares a one-dimensional array with room to store 10 integers. If you want to create a two-dimensional array, you can write something like this:

```
MyIntArray := VarArrayCreate([1, 10, 1, 5], varInteger);
```

This declares an array with 10 "columns" and 5 "rows".

One of the most common uses of variant arrays is to create an array of variant, like this:

```
MyVarArray := VarArrayCreate([1, 10], varVariant);
```

This creates an array of 10 variants. The individual elements of the array can then hold an array:

```
MyVarArray[1] := VarArrayCreate([1, 5], varVariant);
```

In this way, you can create arrays of arrays, so you can model almost any type of data structure, including lists, trees, and so on.

### VarArrayOf

Because creating a one-dimensional array is so common, Delphi provides the VarArrayOf function, which can be used to create a one-dimensional variant array on-the-fly. VarArrayOf is defined in system.pas like this:

```
function VarArrayOf(const Values: array of Variant): Variant;
```

You can use VarArrayOf like this:

```
MyVarArray := VarArrayOf([10, 100, 1000, 10000]);
```

This code constructs a 4-element array that contains the numbers 10, 100, 1000, and 10000.

One thing you need to remember is that internally, VarArrayOf creates an array of variants. You cannot use VarArrayOf to create an array of integers, for example. However, you can create an array of disparate values, like this:

```
MyVarArray := VarArrayOf(['John', 'Smith', 40, 60000.00, 'Main Street', 'West Palm
⮕Beach', 'FL']);
```

If you're thinking that looks a lot like a record definition, you're exactly correct. As a matter of fact, Delphi's database code makes good use of variant arrays in certain places.

## Accessing a Variant Array

After you have created a variant array, you will want to access the individual elements of that array. Accessing a variant array is pretty much the same as accessing a standard Delphi array. Consider the following variant array declaration:

```
MyIntArray := VarArrayCreate([1, 10, 1, 5], varInteger);
```

You can access an element in the array like this:

```
I := MyIntArray[1, 1];
```

Just as you can use Low and High to compute the bounds of a standard Delphi array, you can use VarArrayLowBound and VarArrayHighBound to compute the bounds of a variant array. VarArrayDimCount can be used to calculate the number of dimensions in the array.

```
Procedure TraverseArray(V: Variant);
Var
  Index: Integer;
Begin
  ShowMessage('Array has ' + IntToStr(VarArrayDimCount(V)) + ' dimensions';
  For Index := VarArrayLowBound(V) to VarArrayHighBound(V) do
    ShowMessage(V[Index]);
End;

Procedure TForm1.Button1Click(Sender: TObject);
Var
  MyArray: Variant;
Begin
  MyArray := VarArrayOf(['Jones', 'Smith', 'Adams']);
  TraverseArray(MyArray);
End;
```

## Improving Variant Array Performance

As I mentioned earlier, using variant arrays exacts a performance penalty. If you need to make a number of accesses to a variant array (for example, when looping through the array), you can use VarArrayLock and VarArrayUnlock to speed access to the array.

VarArrayLock returns a Delphi array with the same characteristics of the variant array. For this reason, the variant array must be declared as an array of one of the standard data types that Delphi is familiar with. In particular, you can't use VarArrayLock and VarArrayUnlock with an array of variants. This means that you can't use them on an array created with VarArrayOf.

```
Procedure TraverseArray2(V: Variant);
type
  PIntArray = ^TIntArray;
  TIntArray = array[1..100] of Integer;
Var
  Index: Integer;
  PI: PIntArray;
Begin
  ShowMessage('Array has ' + IntToStr(VarArrayDimCount(V)) + ' dimensions';

  PI := VarArrayLock(V);
  try
    For Index := VarArrayLowBound(V) to VarArrayHighBound(V) do
```

```
      ShowMessage(IntToStr(PI^[Index]));
    finally
      VarArrayUnlock(V);
    End;
  End;

  Procedure TForm1.Button1Click(Sender: TObject);
  Var
    MyArray: Variant;
  Begin
    MyArray := VarArrayCreate([1, 3], varInteger);
    MyArray[1] := 100;
    MyArray[2] := 200;
    MyArray[3] := 300;
    TraverseArray2(MyArray);
  End;
```

Note that you must remember to call VarArrayUnlock after you call VarArrayLock. For this reason, I created a try-finally block that ensures that VarArrayUnlock will get called.

## Variant Array Example

Let's build a sample program that accesses variant arrays in the three ways just described. This example will also time each array primitive, such as creating the array, reading and writing to the array, and so on.

Listings 2.16 and 2.17 show the entire source code for the VarDemo application.

**Listing 2.16** *VarDemo—VarDemo.dpr*

```
program VarDemo;

uses
  Forms,
  MainForm in 'MainForm.pas' {Form1};

{$R *.RES}

begin
  Application.Initialize;
  Application.CreateForm(TForm1, Form1);
  Application.Run;
end.
```

**Listing 2.17**    *VarDemo—MainForm.pas*

```pascal
unit MainForm;

interface

uses
  Windows, Messages, SysUtils, Classes, Graphics, Controls, Forms,
  Dialogs, StdCtrls, ExtCtrls;

type
  TForm1 = class(TForm)
    Label1: TLabel;
    Label2: TLabel;
    Label3: TLabel;
    Label4: TLabel;
    Label5: TLabel;
    Label6: TLabel;
    Label7: TLabel;
    Label8: TLabel;
    Label9: TLabel;
    lblArrayCreate: TLabel;
    lblVariantCreate: TLabel;
    lblLockedVariantCreate: TLabel;
    lblLockedVariantLock: TLabel;
    lblArrayWrite: TLabel;
    lblVariantWrite: TLabel;
    lblLockedVariantWrite: TLabel;
    lblArrayRead: TLabel;
    lblVariantRead: TLabel;
    lblLockedVariantRead: TLabel;
    lblLockedVariantUnlock: TLabel;
    lblArrayDestroy: TLabel;
    lblVariantDestroy: TLabel;
    lblLockedVariantDestroy: TLabel;
    btnRun: TButton;
    Bevel1: TBevel;
    Bevel2: TBevel;
    Bevel3: TBevel;
    procedure btnRunClick(Sender: TObject);
  private
    procedure TestArray;
    procedure TestLockedVariant;
    procedure TestVariant;
    { Private declarations }
  public
    { Public declarations }
  end;

  TTestArray = array[1 .. 1000] of Integer;
  PTestArray = ^TTestArray;

var
  Form1: TForm1;
```

```
implementation

{$R *.DFM}

procedure TForm1.TestArray;
var
  T1, T2: DWord;
  A: PTestArray;
  Index: Integer;
  I: Integer;
  Count: Integer;
begin
  T1 := GetTickCount;
  New(A);
  T2 := GetTickCount;
  lblArrayCreate.Caption := IntToStr(T2 - T1);

  T1 := GetTickCount;
  for Count := 1 to 10000 do
    for Index := 1 to 1000 do
      A^[Index] := Index;
  T2 := GetTickCount;
  lblArrayWrite.Caption := IntToStr(T2 - T1);

  T1 := GetTickCount;
  for Count := 1 to 10000 do
    for Index := 1 to 1000 do
      I := A^[Index];
  T2 := GetTickCount;
  lblArrayRead.Caption := IntToStr(T2 - T1);

  T1 := GetTickCount;
  Dispose(A);
  T2 := GetTickCount;
  lblArrayDestroy.Caption := IntToStr(T2 - T1);
end;

procedure TForm1.TestVariant;
var
  T1, T2: DWord;
  Index: Integer;
  I: Integer;
  Count: Integer;
  V: Variant;
begin
  T1 := GetTickCount;
  V := VarArrayCreate([1, 1000], varInteger);
  T2 := GetTickCount;
  lblVariantCreate.Caption := IntToStr(T2 - T1);
```

*continues* ▶

**Listing 2.17** *continued*

```
T1 := GetTickCount;
for Count := 1 to 10000 do
  for Index := 1 to 1000 do
    V[Index] := Index;
T2 := GetTickCount;
lblVariantWrite.Caption := IntToStr(T2 - T1);

T1 := GetTickCount;
for Count := 1 to 10000 do
  for Index := 1 to 1000 do
    I := V[Index];
T2 := GetTickCount;
lblVariantRead.Caption := IntToStr(T2 - T1);

T1 := GetTickCount;
VarClear(V);
T2 := GetTickCount;
lblVariantDestroy.Caption := IntToStr(T2 - T1);
end;

procedure TForm1.TestLockedVariant;
var
  T1, T2: DWord;
  A: PTestArray;
  Index: Integer;
  I: Integer;
  Count: Integer;
  V: Variant;
begin
  T1 := GetTickCount;
  V := VarArrayCreate([1, 1000], varInteger);
  T2 := GetTickCount;
  lblLockedVariantCreate.Caption := IntToStr(T2 - T1);

  T1 := GetTickCount;
  A := VarArrayLock(V);
  T2 := GetTickCount;
  lblLockedVariantLock.Caption := IntToStr(T2 - T1);

  T1 := GetTickCount;
  for Count := 1 to 10000 do
    for Index := 1 to 1000 do
      A^[Index] := Index;
  T2 := GetTickCount;
  lblLockedVariantWrite.Caption := IntToStr(T2 - T1);

  T1 := GetTickCount;
  for Count := 1 to 10000 do
    for Index := 1 to 1000 do
      I := A^[Index];
  T2 := GetTickCount;
  lblLockedVariantRead.Caption := IntToStr(T2 - T1);
```

```
  T1 := GetTickCount;
  VarArrayUnlock(V);
  T2 := GetTickCount;
  lblLockedVariantUnlock.Caption := IntToStr(T2 - T1);

  T1 := GetTickCount;
  VarClear(V);
  T2 := GetTickCount;
  lblLockedVariantDestroy.Caption := IntToStr(T2 - T1);
end;

procedure TForm1.btnRunClick(Sender: TObject);
begin
  Screen.Cursor := crHourglass;
  try
    TestArray;
    TestVariant;
    TestLockedVariant;
  finally
    Screen.Cursor := crDefault;
  end;
end;

end.
```

Figure 2.9 shows the output after running VarDemo on my 450 MHz
Pentium II.

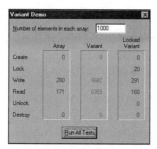

**Figure 2.9**  *VarDemo shows the relative speed of
Delphi arrays, variant arrays, and locked variant arrays.*

As you can see, the UI for this application is straightforward. Type in the
number of elements in the array, and press the **Run All Tests** button to run
each test automatically.

I will not spend any time discussing the source code for this application,
because the previous section already explained everything you need to
know about the sample. VarDemo simply pulls all the code together in one
cohesive unit.

I do want to take a few moments to discuss the times produced by this application, however. First, you should notice that the time required to create and destroy either a Delphi array or a variant array is negligible. You don't need to take initialization and cleanup time into account when determining whether to use a Delphi array or variant array.

Accessing a variant array directly is quite costly, compared to accessing a Delphi array. The performance penalty is close to 20x on my particular computer. However, note what happens when we lock the variant array before using it. The locking process provides direct access to the variant array. From that point on, the access times are the same as for any standard Delphi array.

Further note that the time required to lock and unlock the variant array is negligible. Locking a variant array does not create a copy of it – it simply sets a flag that prevents other users of the array from changing it while it is locked.

## Using COM Objects with Other Languages

At this point, you might be wondering how users of other languages might access the COM servers we've written. All the code is Delphi code, so if you need to interface with Visual C++, for example, how would you do that?

As I mentioned earlier in this chapter, COM objects can be used by any language that can support a VMT (or *vtable*, in COM parlance.) The problem with what we've written so far is that to use these objects with another language, you would need to recreate the interface definition in that language. Clearly, this isn't a reasonable solution for anything other than trivial interfaces.

Additionally, automatic marshaling of data requires a type library in order to know what parameters are passed to and from interface methods and how to marshal them. In the next chapter, I'll discuss type libraries, which are a language-neutral way to declare interfaces for your COM objects.

## Summary

In this chapter, you learned exactly what a GUID is, and why it is so critical to COM development. You also learned how you can create GUIDs for your own use.

I then discussed in-process COM servers at length, and showed you how to create and use an in-process COM server in Delphi.

You also learned what variant arrays are, why they are useful, and how to use them. I showed you how you can lock a variant array to increase performance dramatically.

From there, I introduced out-of-process COM servers, although we didn't create any in this chapter. Chapter 4 will show you how to create a number of out-of-process COM servers. I discussed marshaling, why it is important to out-of-process servers, and the types of data that Windows can automatically marshal.

Finally, I indicated that only object-oriented languages that understand vtables can access the COM servers created in this chapter.

The next chapter looks at type libraries, which are a language-independent way to expose the objects in your COM servers. After that, we'll take a long look at automation servers, which can be used by just about any language on the market today.

# 3

## Type Libraries

In Chapter 2, "Interfaces and COM," I showed you how to create COM servers. As you learned, the servers we created in that chapter can only be used by languages that understand virtual method tables, such as Delphi and C++. Not only that, but the developer of the client application must somehow obtain a copy of the interface(s) implemented by the COM server in order to utilize the server.

In cases where you are writing both the server and client in Delphi, you can simply reference the COM server's interface declaration unit in the **uses** clause of the client application. However, in many cases, you will be using a COM server written by someone else, perhaps in C or C++. Or you might be writing a COM server and distributing it to developers who are not working in Delphi. There needs to be some way to share interface declarations between programmers using different languages, and there is.

This chapter discusses type libraries, which are language-independent methods of defining interfaces and documenting COM servers.

## Type Libraries Defined

As I alluded to in the previous section, a type library provides a language-neutral way of completely documenting a COM object. Type libraries contain information, such as which interfaces are implemented by an object, which properties and methods are defined by the interface, and the number and type of the arguments for each method.

In general, type libraries may be integrated into COM servers as a resource, or they may be distributed separately as a .TLB file. Delphi automatically adds the type library to the COM server as a resource, and also generates a .TLB file for you.

Delphi (as well as most other modern-day compilers) can read the information stored in type libraries and automatically create an import file for use in writing a client application. For that reason, you typically need only to redistribute the COM server to the programmer writing the client application. If you run into someone who cannot extract the type library from your COM server, you can redistribute the .TLB file also.

## Reasons to Use Type Libraries

Type libraries are a requirement of certain types of COM servers, such as Automation servers and ActiveX controls. Automation servers are discussed in Chapter 4, "Automation," and ActiveX controls are discussed in Chapter 5, "ActiveX Controls and ActiveForms."

Even when you're writing a COM server that doesn't require a type library, you might want to create one. Type libraries provide a number of benefits, including:

- Early binding when writing Automation controllers. (Early binding and late binding are discussed in detail in Chapter 4.)

- Many compilers can automatically generate language-specific code from a type library.

- Utility programs, such as type browsers, can be used to read and display information about COM servers that contain a type library.

- Automatic marshaling of parameters between COM clients and servers. In Chapter 2, I discussed the marshaling support provided by Windows. Type libraries enable Windows to perform marshaling without any special effort on the part of either the server or client application.

## TTypedComObject

Delphi provides support for type libraries through TTypedComObject and its descendents. If you'll recall from Chapter 2, when we used Delphi's COM Object Wizard, it asked us if we'd like to create a type library. For reference, the COM Object Wizard is shown again in Figure 3.1.

If you select the **Include Type Library** checkbox, Delphi generates code similar to that shown in Listing 3.1.

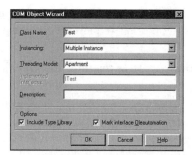

**Figure 3.1**   *Delphi's COM Object Wizard.*

*Remember that Delphi 3 does not provide the COM Object Wizard. If you're a Delphi 3 user, you'll need to enter the code shown in Listing 3.1 by hand.* ◆

**Listing 3.1**   *Code Generated by Delphi's COM Object Wizard*

```
unit Unit2;

interface

uses
  Windows, ActiveX, ComObj, Project1_TLB, StdVcl;

type
  TTest = class(TTypedComObject, ITest)
  protected
    {Declare ITest methods here}
  end;

implementation

uses ComServ;

initialization
  TTypedComObjectFactory.Create(ComServer, TTest, Class_Test,
    ciMultiInstance, tmApartment);
end.
```

The code shown in Listing 3.1 looks very similar to the template code that Delphi generates when you don't request a type library. There are three main differences:

- Delphi automatically creates the import file Project1_TLB.pas, shown in Listing 3.2.

- The COM object (in this case TTest) is derived from TTypedComObject instead of TComObject.

- In the initialization section of the unit, Delphi calls TTypedComObjectFactory.Create instead of TComObjectFactory.Create.

Here is the entire definition of class TTypedComObject, declared in ComObj.pas:

```
TTypedComObject = class(TComObject, IProvideClassInfo)
  protected
    { IProvideClassInfo }
    function GetClassInfo(out TypeInfo: ITypeInfo): HResult; stdcall;
  end;
```

As you can see, there isn't much to it. As a matter of fact, TTypedComObject implements the IProvideClassInfo interface, which only defines one method. IProvideClassInfo simply provides a means of accessing the ITypeInfo interface, which is discussed later in this chapter.

**Listing 3.2**  *Code Generated by Delphi's COM Object Wizard*

```
unit Project1_TLB;
// ******************************************************************** //
// WARNING                                                             //
// -------                                                             //
// The types declared in this file were generated from data read from a //
// Type Library. If this type library is explicitly or indirectly (via //
// another type library referring to this type library) re-imported, or the //
// 'Refresh' command of the Type Library Editor activated while editing the //
// Type Library, the contents of this file will be regenerated and all  //
// manual modifications will be lost.                                   //
// ******************************************************************** //

// PASTLWTR : $Revision:   1.11.1.75  $
// File generated on 05/11/1999 2:00:13 PM from Type Library described below.

// ******************************************************************** //
// Type Lib: B:\Book\samples\Chap03\Empty\Project1.tlb
// IID\LCID: {39D07A50-07CB-11D3-90AF-0040F6741DE2}\0
// Helpfile:
```

```
// HelpString: Project1 Library
// Version:    1.0
// ********************************************************************* //

interface

uses Windows, ActiveX, Classes, Graphics, OleCtrls, StdVCL;

// *********************************************************************//
// GUIDS declared in the TypeLibrary. Following prefixes are used:    //
//   Type Libraries     : LIBID_xxxx                                  //
//   CoClasses          : CLASS_xxxx                                  //
//   DISPInterfaces     : DIID_xxxx                                   //
//   Non-DISP interfaces: IID_xxxx                                    //
// *********************************************************************//
const
  LIBID_Project1: TGUID = '{39D07A50-07CB-11D3-90AF-0040F6741DE2}';
  IID_ITest: TGUID = '{39D07A51-07CB-11D3-90AF-0040F6741DE2}';
  CLASS_Test: TGUID = '{39D07A53-07CB-11D3-90AF-0040F6741DE2}';
type

// *********************************************************************//
// Forward declaration of interfaces defined in Type Library          //
// *********************************************************************//
  ITest = interface;

// *********************************************************************//
// Declaration of CoClasses defined in Type Library                   //
// (NOTE: Here we map each CoClass to its Default Interface)           //
// *********************************************************************//
  Test = ITest;


// *********************************************************************//
// Interface: ITest
// Flags:     (0)
// GUID:      {39D07A51-07CB-11D3-90AF-0040F6741DE2}
// *********************************************************************//
  ITest = interface(IUnknown)
    ['{39D07A51-07CB-11D3-90AF-0040F6741DE2}']
  end;

  CoTest = class
    class function Create: ITest;
    class function CreateRemote(const MachineName: string): ITest;
  end;

implementation

uses ComObj;
```

*continues* ▶

**Listing 3.2** *continued*

```
class function CoTest.Create: ITest;
begin
  Result := CreateComObject(CLASS_Test) as ITest;
end;

class function CoTest.CreateRemote(const MachineName: string): ITest;
begin
  Result := CreateRemoteComObject(MachineName, CLASS_Test) as ITest;
end;

end.
```

At this point, you know what a type library is and what it's used for. In the following section, I'll lead you through the basics of how to create a type library using Delphi.

# Creating a Type Library with Delphi

Before the advent of Delphi, most programming languages forced you to code type libraries by hand using a language known as *Interface Definition Language* (IDL). Consider the following simple interface declaration:

```
type
  ITest = interface
    procedure DoSomething;
    function GetValue: Integer;
  end;
```

The IDL for a COM server implementing the ITest interface is shown in Listing 3.3.

**Listing 3.3** *IDL for the ITest Interface*

```
[
  uuid(1F415FD5-F132-11D2-B3B0-0040F67455FE),
  version(1.0),
  helpstring("Project1 Library")
]
library Project1
{

  importlib("STDOLE2.TLB");
  importlib("STDVCL50.DLL");

  [
    uuid(1F415FD6-F132-11D2-B3B0-0040F67455FE),
    version(1.0),
    helpstring("Interface for Test Object")
```

```
]
  interface ITest: IUnknown
{
  [id(0x00000001)]
  void _stdcall DoSomething( void );
  [id(0x00000002)]
  long _stdcall GetValue( void );
};

[
  uuid(1F415FD8-F132-11D2-B3B0-0040F67455FE),
  version(1.0),
  helpstring("Test Object")
]
coclass Test
{
  [default] interface ITest;
};

};
```

Tucked away in the middle of that code, we can discern the declaration of the ITest interface itself. It is repeated here for ease of reference.

```
interface ITest: IUnknown
  {
    [id(0x00000001)]
    void _stdcall DoSomething( void );
    [id(0x00000002)]
    long _stdcall GetValue( void );
  };
```

As you can see from Listing 3.3, developing COM applications (or at least type libraries) before Delphi was a major undertaking, unless you speak fluent IDL (which I don't).

### Note

*The preceding IDL code was actually generated by Delphi's Type Library Editor.* ◆

## Using the Type Library Editor

Enter Delphi, and the Delphi Type Library Editor. A good portion of this chapter focuses on how to use the Type Library Editor, which makes creating and editing type libraries a relative piece of cake. In keeping with the underlying Delphi philosophy, Delphi's two-way tools keep your source code up-to-date as you create interface declarations using the Type Library Editor.

The Type Library Editor has undergone substantial changes from Delphi 3 to Delphi 4 to Delphi 5. The screen shots shown in this chapter are from Delphi 5, so if you're using a previous version of Delphi they may not match exactly what you see on your screen. However, you should still be able to follow along, and I'll point out major differences between versions of the Type Library Editor where appropriate.

Create a new in-process COM server in Delphi by selecting File, New from the main menu. Click the ActiveX tab in the Object Repository, and double-click the ActiveX Library icon. Again, select File, New from the main menu, but this time, double-click the COM Object icon on the ActiveX tab of the Object Repository.

Fill out the COM Object Wizard to look like Figure 3.2.

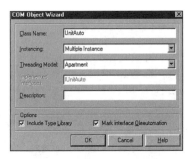

**Figure 3.2**   *Creating a COM server with a type library.*

Be sure to check the option labeled **Include Type Library** (it should be checked by default). When you click OK, Delphi generates the (by now familiar) COM object unit, and then automatically starts up the Type Library Editor. If you ever want to start the Type Library Editor manually, simply select View, Type Library from the Delphi main menu. Figure 3.3 shows what the Type Library Editor looks like when invoked by Delphi for the TUnitAuto COM Object just created.

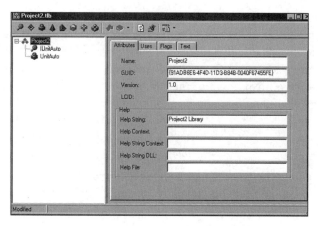

**Figure 3.3**   *The Type Library Editor.*

The Type Library Editor is divided into three sections. On the top of the window is a toolbar that you use to add interfaces, methods, and properties to your COM server. The left side of the main window is a tree control that shows the interfaces, methods, and so on that are defined for this server. This is referred to as the *object list*. The object list is conceptually very similar to the Code Explorer in Delphi itself in that it shows interface declarations, methods, and other information contained in the type library.

The remainder of the Type Library Editor is taken up by a page control that shows *type information* for the currently selected node in the tree. Oddly enough, there is no main menu in the Type Library Editor—all functionality is available through the toolbar and context menus that pop up when you right-click the object list.

**Tip**

*You can turn on captions for the toolbar by right clicking the toolbar and selecting* **Text Labels** *from the context menu.* ◆

Our newly created type library has three nodes in the object list: Project2, IUnitAuto, and UnitAuto. Project2 represents the project we're working on. The first thing we're going to do is rename the project. Either click the Project2 node to rename it, or click the Name edit box in the type information pane. Change the name to **DCPTypeServer**. Also, change the help string to **DCP TypeInfo Server**.

The next node in the object list, IUnitAuto, refers to the interface that was automatically created for us. The default values are acceptable for this interface.

The last node, UnitAuto, refers to the CoClass, or TTypedComObject-derived class, that implements the IUnitAuto interface. The default values are also acceptable for this node.

I'll discuss each button on the toolbar in the subsections below (see Figure 3.4 for a breakdown of the toolbar).

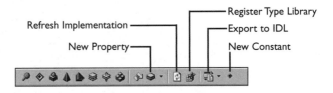

Refresh Implementation ⎯⎯⎯⎯

New Property⎯

Register Type Library⎯⎯

Export to IDL

New Constant

**Figure 3.4**    *Type Library Editor toolbar.*

The Type Library Editor toolbar looks like this. Each of the buttons discussed in the following sections is shown on this figure.

> **Note**
>
> *As I'm explaining the Type Library Editor, we're going to create a type library that is used in the first example of Chapter 4. The reason for creating a legitimate type library is that later in this chapter, I'm going to show you how to write a program that reads and interprets a type library. Though you already have a number of type libraries on your computer (whether you realize it or not), I have no way of knowing what's installed on your individual machine, so creating this sample type library keeps us both on the same page. ◆*

### New Interface
Press this button to add an interface to a type library. Our server is only going to support the IUnitAuto interface, but if you want to support additional interfaces in your own servers, you certainly can. Delphi automatically generates a GUID for any new interfaces that you create.

### New Dispinterface
A dispinterface is very similar to an interface, but it uses a different dispatching mechanism to call the methods of the server. I will discuss dispinterfaces in detail in Chapter 4, so we won't add a dispinterface to our server now.

### New CoClass

**CoClass** is the term given to the COM object that implements the interface(s). In this example, we're only writing one CoClass, UnitAuto, which Delphi created for us automatically.

### New Enumeration

An enumeration in a type library is analogous to an enumerated type in Delphi. Enumerations are designated by integer IDs, rather than set types. Let's add an enumeration to our type library.

1. Press the New Enumeration toolbar button. Delphi creates a new enumeration named Enum1.
2. Because Enum1 isn't a very descriptive name, change it to AreaUnit by typing over the name Enum1.

Delphi automatically assigns a GUID and a version number (1.0) to the new enumeration.

Simply creating an enumeration does not specify the values that belong to that enumeration. You need to add constants to the enumeration, as explained next.

### New Constant

I'll skip a few toolbar buttons and discuss the New Constant button next. This button is only enabled when you highlight an enumeration in the object list. Let's add some values to the AreaUnit enumeration now.

1. Click the AreaUnit enumeration in the object list.
2. Click the New Constant button to add a value to the AreaUnit enumeration.
3. Change the constant name to **auSquareMeters**.
4. Add another constant and give it the name **auSquareCentimeters**.
5. Add constants for auSquareYards, auSquareFeet, auSquareInches, auSquareKilometers, auSquareMiles, and auAcres.

As you're adding these constants, Delphi automatically assigns a value of 0 to auSquareMeters, 1 to auSquareCentimeters, and so forth.

Note that I like to prefix enumerations with a two- or three-letter prefix, like au (for Area Unit). This is strictly personal preference, and neither COM, the Type Library Editor, nor Delphi enforces this.

### New Alias

An alias in a type library is used to define a type that you want to include in a record or union. Most type libraries don't have this information, and I won't discuss it further in this book.

## New Record
Press this button to define a record structure in the type library. Most type libraries don't define record structures, and I won't discuss them further in this book.

## New Union
Press this button to define a union in the type library. A union is the equivalent of the Pascal variant record. Most type libraries don't define unions, and I won't discuss them further in this book.

## New Module
Click this button to create a new module. A module is a set of methods and constants. You won't find modules defined in most type libraries, and I won't discuss them further in this book.

## New Method
If you click an interface (or dispinterface) in the object list, a New Method button will light up on the toolbar. We'll add a new method to the IUnitAuto interface now.

1. Click the IUnitAuto enumeration in the object list.
2. Click the New Method button to add a new method to the IUnitAuto interface.
3. Change the name of the new method to Convert.

   The Type Library Editor automatically assigns the Convert method an ID of 1. Method IDs are discussed in Chapter 4.
4. Click the Parameters tab of the information pane. Notice that the Return Type is defined as HResult (see Figure 3.5).
5. Select Double from the Return Type combo box.

Now we're going to add a parameter to the Convert method. Convert will accept three parameters: the quantity that we want to convert, the unit we're converting from, and the unit we're converting to. Before we actually add the parameters, I want to take a few moments and talk about Parameter Modifiers.

Recall that in Chapter 2 I spoke about marshaling. Marshaling involves some detailed work on the part of Windows. Obviously, the less data that needs to be marshaled across process boundaries, the faster the method call will be.

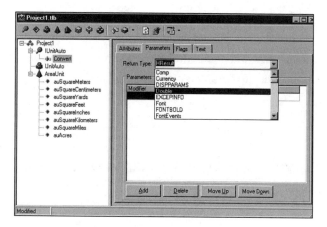

**Figure 3.5**   *Default method parameters.*

For that reason, you should consider the parameters that will be passed to the method. Some parameters only need to be sent to the server. The server won't change the value of the parameters, so they don't need to be marshaled back to the client. If the server didn't make any changes to the parameters, why send them back to the client? The client already knows the value of the parameters; after all, it sent them to the server. These parameters are referred to as *in* parameters.

On the other side of the coin are values that are computed on the server, and only need to be marshaled back to the client. These values don't need to be sent from the client to the server at all. These parameters are referred to as *out* parameters.

Rounding out the field are parameters that have a value on the client side, and are changed in the server. These parameters need to be marshaled in both directions, and are referred to as *var* parameters.

Let's consider the Convert method. The quantity passed to the function obviously needs to be sent from the client to the server. The server will use that value, but won't change it, so it doesn't have to be sent back to the client. (The quantity will be converted to a different unit, but it will be passed back to the client as the function result.) Therefore, this is a perfect example of an *in* parameter.

Now that you understand parameter modifiers, let's add the three parameters to the Convert method.

1. Click the Add button on the information pane.

    The Type Library Editor creates a new parameter named Param1.

2. Click the parameter name and change it to Quantity.

3. Click the Type and change it to double.

The Modifier defaults to in, so you can leave that as-is.

4. Click the Add button again, and add an int parameter named InUnit.

5. Add another int parameter named OutUnit.

When you're finished, the Type Library Editor should look like Figure 3.6. That's all you need to do to create the Convert method.

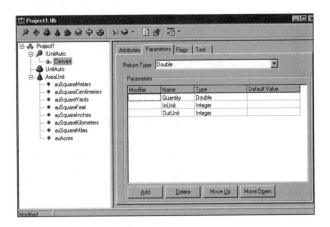

**Figure 3.6**    *Adding a method to a type library.*

**New Property**
If you click an interface (or dispinterface) in the tree, a New Property button will also light up on the toolbar. You can press this button to add a new property to the interface.

You can create read-only, write-only, and read-write properties, just as you can in Delphi classes.

The IUnitAuto interface as created in Chapter 4 doesn't require any properties. However, COM properties are common enough that I want to show you how to create one anyway.

1. Click the IUnitAuto node in the object list.

2. Click the down arrow by the New Property button.

You'll see menu options for adding a Read | Write, Read Only, Write Only, or Read | Write | Write by Ref property.

3. Select the Read | Write menu item.

The Type Library Editor will add two properties under the IUnitAuto node, both named Property1. The first instance of Property1 is the *Get* accessor for the property, and the second instance is the *Put* accessor.

4. Change the name of one of the instances of the property name to Name.

   The Type Library Editor automatically changes the name of the other instance for you.

5. Click the Name property in the object list that corresponds to the *Put* accessor.

6. On the Parameters tab of the information page, set the return type to void.

7. Also on the Parameters tab, set the Type of the automatically generated parameter to BSTR (if you're using Delphi 3 or Delphi 4, use WideString instead of BSTR).

8. Click the Name property in the object list that corresponds to the Get accessor.

9. On the Parameters tab of the information page, set the return type to BSTR. You'll have to type in the word BSTR, as it will not show up in the combo box by default. (Again, Delphi 3 and Delphi 4 users should use WideString instead of BSTR.)

Figure 3.7 shows the Type Library Editor after adding the Name property.

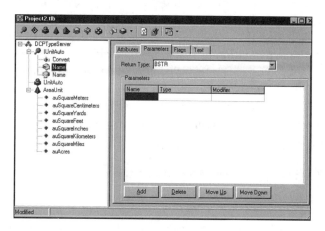

**Figure 3.7**   *Adding a property to a type library.*

**Refresh Implementation**

Typically, Delphi keeps your source code up-to-date with the information entered in the Type Library Editor. You can click this button to force Delphi to update the source files for you.

In order to make sure your source code is in sync with the Type Library Editor, click the Refresh Implementation button now.

### Register Type Library
When you click this button, Delphi compiles your COM server, and automatically registers the server with Windows. You can accomplish the same thing manually by compiling and then selecting Run, Register ActiveX Server from Delphi's main menu.

### Export to IDL
Select this button to generate source code in either MIDL or CORBA format. This can be useful if you want to inspect the IDL that Delphi generates, or if you are using another tool that requires an IDL file.

You have now created a valid type library. Close the Type Library Editor, and select File, Save All from the Delphi main menu. Save Unit1 (the COM object implementation file) as AreaIntf.pas. Save Project2 (the main project file) as TIServer.dpr. Delphi will automatically create a file named TIServer.tlb, which is the actual type library. Don't forget that the type library is also included in TIServer.dll as a resource (to build TIServer.dll, select Project, Build TIServer from the Delphi main menu).

If you look at AreaIntf.pas, you'll see that there are three stub functions (TUnitAuto.Convert, TUnitAuto.Get_Name, and TUnitAuto.Set_Name) we didn't flesh out. If we were writing a real COM server, of course, we'd provide an implementation for these methods. However, in this chapter all we're trying to do is create a type library, so we can ignore the actual implementation of those methods.

In the next section, we'll build a utility program that can read and display some of the more common content from the type library that we just created.

### Out-of-Process COM Servers and Type Libraries

*You may have noticed that an example of an out-of-process COM server is conspicuously absent from Chapter 2. The reason is simple: Out-of-process servers require marshaling support to work. As I indicated in the last chapter, it is possible to provide marshaling support yourself, but that is a topic beyond the scope of this book. Automation servers automatically marshal automation-compatible data types. These types were listed in Chapter 2, and will be discussed again in Chapter 4.*

*What do you do if you want to write a non-Automation out-of-process server? There is a little-known method for creating a non-Automation out-of-process COM server, but it's almost more trouble than it's worth. In the Type Library Editor, if you go to the Flags page (in Delphi 3, it's the Attributes page) for the interface, you'll see a checkbox titled OleAutomation. Selecting this checkbox forces Windows to use its automatic marshaling mechanism for the interface. However, if you're going to go to the trouble to add a type library to your project, you might as well create a real Automation server—it's actually easier than going through the process just described, as you'll learn in Chapter 4. (Delphi 5 simplified this process somewhat. At the bottom of the COM Object Wizard, there's a checkbox titled Mark interface OleAutomation. Selecting this checkbox—it is selected by default—automatically flags the interface for you.)*

*If you don't check the OleAutomation checkbox, you won't be able to get a reference to any interface on your COM object except IUnknown. For instance, calling CreateComObject and trying to cast the result to an ITest interface is guaranteed to produce the following error:*

*This error message is a little misleading, because the ITest interface is supported by the COM server. The real problem is that Windows doesn't know it can marshal the ITest interface, and you haven't provided a marshaling mechanism yourself.* ♦

# Creating a Type Library Viewer

In this section, we're going to build a program that can read the type information from a type library and display it in a tree view. The amount of information stored in a type library is vast, and the documentation for retrieving the information is sketchy at best. For those reasons, this example will only interpret the most common pieces of data found in a type library editor—namely, CoClasses, interfaces, dispinterfaces, and enumerations. If you want to enhance this example on your own, the Microsoft Developer's Network Library (MSDN) is the best source of information for this material.

Of course, the Type Library Editor can already read, display, and edit all the information found in a type library, so this example is strictly for educational purposes.

Figure 3.8 shows the Type Information example program (TIViewer) at runtime.

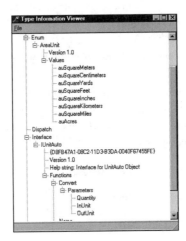

**Figure 3.8**    *TIViewer.*

Listings 3.4 and 3.5 show the entire source code for the TIViewer application.

---

**Listing 3.4**    *TIViewer Application—MainForm.pas*

```
unit MainForm;

interface

uses
  Windows, Messages, SysUtils, Classes, Graphics, Controls, Forms,
  Dialogs, Menus, ComCtrls, ExtCtrls, ActiveX;
type
  TForm1 = class(TForm)
    MainMenu1: TMainMenu;
    treeTI: TTreeView;
    StatusBar1: TStatusBar;
    FileMenu: TMenuItem;
    FileExit1: TMenuItem;
    FileOpen1: TMenuItem;
    OpenDialog1: TOpenDialog;
    procedure FileExit1Click(Sender: TObject);
    procedure FileOpen1Click(Sender: TObject);
  private
    { Private declarations }
    FLib: ITypeLib;
    FEnumRoot: TTreeNode;
    FDispatchRoot: TTreeNode;
    FInterfaceRoot: TTreeNode;
    FCoClassRoot: TTreeNode;
    FUnknownRoot: TTreeNode;
    procedure LoadTypeLibrary;
```

```
    procedure LoadEnum(TypeInfo: ITypeInfo; TypeAttr: PTypeAttr);
    procedure LoadInterface(TypeInfo: ITypeInfo; TypeAttr: PTypeAttr);
    procedure LoadCoClass(TypeInfo: ITypeInfo; TypeAttr: PTypeAttr);
  public
    { Public declarations }
  end;

var
  Form1: TForm1;

implementation

uses
  ComObj;

{$R *.DFM}

procedure TForm1.FileExit1Click(Sender: TObject);
begin
  Close;
end;

procedure TForm1.LoadEnum(TypeInfo: ITypeInfo; TypeAttr: PTypeAttr);
var
  TypeLibNode: TTreeNode;
  AName: WideString;
  ADocString: WideString;
  AHelpContext: LongInt;
  ValuesNode: TTreeNode;
  ValueNode: TTreeNode;
  ValueIndex: Integer;
  VarDesc: PVarDesc;
begin
  TypeInfo.GetDocumentation(-1, @AName, @ADocString, @AHelpContext,
    nil);
  TypeLibNode := treeTI.Items.AddChild(FEnumRoot, AName);

  treeTI.Items.AddChild(TypeLibNode, 'Version ' +
    IntToStr(TypeAttr.wMajorVerNum) + '.' +
    IntToStr(TypeAttr.wMinorVerNum));
  if ADocString <> '' then
    treeTI.Items.AddChild(TypeLibNode, 'Help string: ' + ADocString);
  if AHelpContext <> 0 then
    treeTI.Items.AddChild(TypeLibNode, 'Help context: ' +
      IntToStr(AHelpContext));

  ValuesNode := treeTI.Items.AddChild(TypeLibNode, 'Values');
  for ValueIndex := 0 to TypeAttr.cVars - 1 do begin
    TypeInfo.GetVarDesc(ValueIndex, VarDesc);
    try
      TypeInfo.GetDocumentation(VarDesc.memid, @AName, @ADocString,
        @AHelpContext, nil);
```

*continues* ▶

**Listing 3.4**    *continued*

```
      ValueNode := treeTI.Items.AddChild(ValuesNode, AName);
      if ADocString <> '' then
        treeTI.Items.AddChild(ValueNode, 'Help string: ' +
          ADocString);
      if AHelpContext <> 0 then
        treeTI.Items.AddChild(ValueNode, 'Help context: ' +
          IntToStr(AHelpContext));
    finally
      TypeInfo.ReleaseVarDesc(VarDesc);
    end;
  end;
end;

procedure TForm1.LoadInterface(TypeInfo: ITypeInfo;
  TypeAttr: PTypeAttr);
var
  TypeLibNode: TTreeNode;
  AName: WideString;
  ADocString: WideString;
  AHelpContext: LongInt;
  FunctionsNode: TTreeNode;
  FunctionNode: TTreeNode;
  FuncIndex: Integer;
  FuncDesc: PFuncDesc;
  ParametersNode: TTreeNode;
  ParamIndex: Integer;
  Names: PBStrList;
  cNames: Integer;
begin
  TypeInfo.GetDocumentation(-1, @AName, @ADocString, @AHelpContext,
    nil);
  if TypeAttr.typeKind = TKIND_DISPATCH then
    TypeLibNode := treeTI.Items.AddChild(FDispatchRoot, AName)
  else
    TypeLibNode := treeTI.Items.AddChild(FInterfaceRoot, AName);

  treeTI.Items.AddChild(TypeLibNode, GUIDToString(TypeAttr.GUID));
  treeTI.Items.AddChild(TypeLibNode, 'Version ' +
    IntToStr(TypeAttr.wMajorVerNum) + '.' +
    IntToStr(TypeAttr.wMinorVerNum));
  if ADocString <> '' then
    treeTI.Items.AddChild(TypeLibNode, 'Help string: ' + ADocString);
  if AHelpContext <> 0 then
    treeTI.Items.AddChild(TypeLibNode, 'Help context: ' +
      IntToStr(AHelpContext));

  New(Names);
  try
    // load functions
    FunctionsNode := treeTI.Items.AddChild(TypeLibNode, 'Functions');
    for FuncIndex := 0 to TypeAttr.cFuncs - 1 do begin
```

```
      TypeInfo.GetFuncDesc(FuncIndex, FuncDesc);
      try
        TypeInfo.GetDocumentation(FuncDesc.memid, @AName,
          @ADocString, @AHelpContext, nil);
        FunctionNode := treeTI.Items.AddChild(FunctionsNode, AName);
        if ADocString <> '' then
          treeTI.Items.AddChild(FunctionNode, 'Help string: ' +
            ADocString);
        if AHelpContext <> 0 then
          treeTI.Items.AddChild(FunctionNode, 'Help context: ' +
            IntToStr(AHelpContext));

        if FuncDesc.cParams> 0 then begin
          // load parameters
          ParametersNode := treeTI.Items.AddChild(FunctionNode,
            'Parameters');

          TypeInfo.GetNames(FuncDesc.memid, Names, sizeof(TBStrList),
            cNames);

          // Skip Names[0] - it's the function name
          for ParamIndex := 1 to FuncDesc.cParams do
            treeTI.Items.AddChild(ParametersNode, Names[ParamIndex]);
        end;
      finally
        TypeInfo.ReleaseFuncDesc(FuncDesc);
      end;
    end;
  finally
    Dispose(Names);
  end;
end;

procedure TForm1.LoadCoClass(TypeInfo: ITypeInfo;
  TypeAttr: PTypeAttr);
var
  TypeLibNode: TTreeNode;
  AName: WideString;
  ADocString: WideString;
  AHelpContext: LongInt;
  FunctionsNode: TTreeNode;
  FuncIndex: Integer;
  RefType: Cardinal;
  TypeInfo2: ITypeInfo;
begin
  TypeInfo.GetDocumentation(-1, @AName, @ADocString, @AHelpContext,
    nil);
  TypeLibNode := treeTI.Items.AddChild(FCoClassRoot, AName);

  treeTI.Items.AddChild(TypeLibNode, GUIDToString(TypeAttr.GUID));
  if ADocString <> '' then
```

*continues* ▶

**Listing 3.4**   *continued*

```
    treeTI.Items.AddChild(TypeLibNode, 'Help string: ' + ADocString);
  if AHelpContext <> 0 then
    treeTI.Items.AddChild(TypeLibNode, 'Help context: ' +
      IntToStr(AHelpContext));

  FunctionsNode := treeTI.Items.AddChild(TypeLibNode, 'Implements');
  for FuncIndex := 0 to TypeAttr.cImplTypes - 1 do begin
    TypeInfo.GetRefTypeOfImplType(FuncIndex, RefType);
    TypeInfo.GetRefTypeInfo(RefType, TypeInfo2);
    TypeInfo2.GetDocumentation(-1, @AName, nil, nil, nil);
    treeTI.Items.AddChild(FunctionsNode, AName);
  end;
end;

procedure TForm1.LoadTypeLibrary;
var
  LibAttr: PTLibAttr;
  TypeInfo: ITypeInfo;
  TypeLibIndex: Integer;
  AName: WideString;
  ADocString: WideString;
  AHelpContext: LongInt;
  AHelpFile: WideString;
  TypeAttr: PTypeAttr;
  RootNode: TTreeNode;
begin
  Screen.Cursor := crHourglass;
  try
    treeTI.Items.BeginUpdate;
    try
      treeTI.Items.Clear;

      FLib.GetDocumentation(-1, @AName, @ADocString, @AHelpContext,
        @AHelpFile);

      // Load help information
      RootNode := treeTI.Items.AddChild(nil, AName);

      // GUID, version, LCID
      OleCheck(FLib.GetLibAttr(LibAttr));
      try
        treeTI.Items.AddChild(RootNode, GUIDToString(LibAttr.GUID));
        treeTI.Items.AddChild(RootNode, 'Version ' +
          IntToStr(LibAttr.wMajorVerNum) + '.' +
          IntToStr(LibAttr.wMinorVerNum));
        treeTI.Items.AddChild(RootNode, 'LCID: ' +
          IntToStr(LibAttr.lcid));
      finally
        FLib.ReleaseTLibAttr(LibAttr);
      end;
```

```
      // Help information
      if ADocString <> '' then
        treeTI.Items.AddChild(RootNode, 'Help string: ' + ADocString);
      if AHelpContext <> 0 then
        treeTI.Items.AddChild(RootNode, 'Help context: ' +
          IntToStr(AHelpContext));
      if AHelpFile <> '' then
        treeTI.Items.AddChild(RootNode, 'Help file: ' + AHelpFile);

      // Set no nodes for various types
      FEnumRoot := treeTI.Items.AddChild(RootNode, 'Enum');
      FDispatchRoot := treeTI.Items.AddChild(RootNode, 'Dispatch');
      FInterfaceRoot := treeTI.Items.AddChild(RootNode, 'Interface');
      FCoClassRoot := treeTI.Items.AddChild(RootNode, 'CoClass');
      FUnknownRoot := treeTI.Items.AddChild(RootNode, 'Unknown');

      for TypeLibIndex := 0 to FLib.GetTypeInfoCount - 1 do begin
        FLib.GetTypeInfo(TypeLibIndex, TypeInfo);
        OleCheck(TypeInfo.GetTypeAttr(TypeAttr));
        try
          case TypeAttr.typeKind of
            TKIND_ENUM:
              LoadEnum(TypeInfo, TypeAttr);

            TKIND_DISPATCH,
            TKIND_INTERFACE:
              LoadInterface(TypeInfo, TypeAttr);

            TKIND_COCLASS:
              LoadCoClass(TypeInfo, TypeAttr);

            else
              treeTI.Items.AddChild(FUnknownRoot,
                'Unrecognized type: ' + IntToStr(TypeAttr.typeKind));
          end;
        finally
          TypeInfo.ReleaseTypeAttr(TypeAttr);
        end;
      end;

      RootNode.Expand(False);
    finally
      treeTI.Items.EndUpdate;
    end;
  finally
    Screen.Cursor := crDefault;
  end;
end;
```

*continues* ▶

**Listing 3.4**    *continued*

```
procedure TForm1.FileOpen1Click(Sender: TObject);
begin
  if OpenDialog1.Execute then begin
    OleCheck(LoadTypeLib(PWideChar(WideString(OpenDialog1.FileName)),
      FLib));
    LoadTypeLibrary;
  end;
end;

end.
```

**Listing 3.5**    *TIViewer Application—TIViewer.dpr*

```
program TIViewer;

uses
  Forms,
  MainForm in 'MainForm.pas' {Form1};

{$R *.RES}

begin
  Application.Initialize;
  Application.Title := 'Type Information Viewer';
  Application.CreateForm(TForm1, Form1);
  Application.Run;
end.
```

The code shown in Listing 3.4 makes considerable use of the ITypeInfo interface, which is defined in activex.pas like this:

```
ITypeInfo = interface(IUnknown)
  ['{00020401-0000-0000-C000-000000000046}']
  function GetTypeAttr(out ptypeattr: PTypeAttr): HResult; stdcall;
  function GetTypeComp(out tcomp: ITypeComp): HResult; stdcall;
  function GetFuncDesc(index: Integer; out pfuncdesc: PFuncDesc): HResult;
    stdcall;
  function GetVarDesc(index: Integer; out pvardesc: PVarDesc): HResult;
    stdcall;
  function GetNames(memid: TMemberID; rgbstrNames: PBStrList;
    cMaxNames: Integer; out cNames: Integer): HResult; stdcall;
  function GetRefTypeOfImplType(index: Integer; out reftype: HRefType): HResult;
    stdcall;
  function GetImplTypeFlags(index: Integer; out impltypeflags: Integer): HResult;
    stdcall;
  function GetIDsOfNames(rgpszNames: POleStrList; cNames: Integer;
    rgmemid: PMemberIDList): HResult; stdcall;
  function Invoke(pvInstance: Pointer; memid: TMemberID; flags: Word;
    var dispParams: TDispParams; varResult: PVariant;
    excepInfo: PExcepInfo; argErr: PInteger): HResult; stdcall;
```

```
    function GetDocumentation(memid: TMemberID; pbstrName: PWideString;
      pbstrDocString: PWideString; pdwHelpContext: PLongint;
      pbstrHelpFile: PWideString): HResult; stdcall;
    function GetDllEntry(memid: TMemberID; invkind: TInvokeKind;
      bstrDllName, bstrName: PWideString; wOrdinal: PWord): HResult;
      stdcall;
    function GetRefTypeInfo(reftype: HRefType; out tinfo: ITypeInfo): HResult;
      stdcall;
    function AddressOfMember(memid: TMemberID; invkind: TInvokeKind;
      out ppv: Pointer): HResult; stdcall;
    function CreateInstance(const unkOuter: IUnknown; const iid: TIID;
      out vObj): HResult; stdcall;
    function GetMops(memid: TMemberID; out bstrMops: WideString): HResult;
      stdcall;
    function GetContainingTypeLib(out tlib: ITypeLib; out pindex: Integer): HResult;
      stdcall;
    procedure ReleaseTypeAttr(ptypeattr: PTypeAttr); stdcall;
    procedure ReleaseFuncDesc(pfuncdesc: PFuncDesc); stdcall;
    procedure ReleaseVarDesc(pvardesc: PVarDesc); stdcall;
  end;
```

Looking at this class, you can see such methods as GetFuncDesc, GetVarDesc, and others that are used in TIViewer to retrieve details from a type library such as the interfaces defined, their methods, and the declarations of those methods.

As you will see in Chapter 4, certain automation controllers (namely, those that support late binding) will automatically make calls to the ITypeInfo functions GetIDsOfNames and Invoke. FileOpen1Click is the event handler responsible for starting everything. It calls the Windows API function LoadTypeLib to obtain a reference to the type library that the user selected in the open dialog.

LoadTypeLib takes two parameters: the name of the file containing the type library, and an ITypeLib interface in which to return the reference to the type library. The filename may be either a .TLB file or a DLL or executable file that contains a type library.

After the type library is loaded, LoadTypeLibrary deciphers the information stored in the type library and populates the tree.

LoadTypeLibrary makes a call to GetDocumentation to retrieve information about the library itself, such as the name, help file, and help context. GetDocumentation is defined like this:

```
function GetDocumentation(memid: TMemberID; pbstrName: PWideString;
    pbstrDocString: PWideString; pdwHelpContext: PLongint;
    pbstrHelpFile: PWideString): HResult; stdcall;
```

The first parameter, *memid*, accepts the index of the item whose documentation is to be returned. Specify –1 to get documentation for the library itself. We'll use this function again later to return information for the interfaces in the type library.

The parameters *pbstrName*, *pbstrDocString*, *pdwHelpContext*, and *pbstrHelpFile* return the name, documentation string, help context, and help file, respectively, of the item in question. In the Type Library Editor, this information is entered in the information pane for the library.

If any of this information is not important to you, you can pass nil for the parameter. For instance, there is only one help file for a type library, so you'll see that after I determine what the help file is here, I pass nil to GetDocumentation in all subsequent calls.

Next, LoadTypeLibrary creates some nodes in the tree view. After that comes the meat of the procedure.

```
for TypeLibIndex := 0 to FLib.GetTypeInfoCount - 1 do begin
  FLib.GetTypeInfo(TypeLibIndex, TypeInfo);
  OleCheck(TypeInfo.GetTypeAttr(TypeAttr));
  try
    case TypeAttr.typeKind of
      TKIND_ENUM:
        LoadEnum(TypeInfo, TypeAttr);

      TKIND_DISPATCH,
      TKIND_INTERFACE:
        LoadInterface(TypeInfo, TypeAttr);

      TKIND_COCLASS:
        LoadCoClass(TypeInfo, TypeAttr);

      else
        treeTI.Items.AddChild(FUnknownRoot,
          'Unrecognized type: ' + IntToStr(TypeAttr.typeKind));
    end;
  finally
    TypeInfo.ReleaseTypeAttr(TypeAttr);
  end;
end;
```

GetTypeInfoCount returns the number of type descriptions in the type library. The code then loops through each of the type descriptions, getting a reference to the type information for the item through the call to GetTypeInfo.

GetTypeInfo obtains a reference to the type information for a given item in the type library. Simply pass in the index of the item in question. GetTypeInfo retrieves a reference to a ITypeInfo interface.

The ITypeInfo interface then allows us to obtain a reference to a ITypeAttr interface, through the call to GetTypeAttr. ITypeAttr will tell us what kind of item we're dealing with (for instance, interface, dispinterface, and so on).

In order to make the code more readable, LoadTypeLibrary passes off control to one of several procedures, depending on the type of information we're retrieving. You can see from the code that LoadTypeLibrary can deal with enumerations, interfaces, dispinterfaces, and CoClasses. Any other type of information found in the library is ignored. Figure 3.9 shows the Word 97 type library (found in C:\Program Files\Microsoft Office\Office\ MSWORD8.OLB for a normal install of Word).

For ease of use, in the FormCreate event handler, TIViewer also checks to see whether the user specified a file on the command line. If so, TIViewer attempts to open that file immediately. If the operation fails for any reason, TIViewer displays an error message and quits.

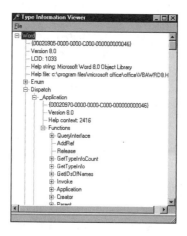

**Figure 3.9**  *The Microsoft Word 97 type library in TIViewer.*

# Interpreting Enumerations

When LoadTypeLibrary detects an enumeration, it calls the procedure LoadEnum to decipher the enumeration.

First, LoadEnum makes a call to GetDocumentation to retrieve the name, documentation, and help context for the enumeration. Notice that I pass nil for the help file, because I already obtained it at the beginning of the program.

ITypeAttr.cVars returns the number of constants defined in this particular enumeration. By looping through the cVars and calling GetDocumentation for each one, we can determine the names of each of the constants in the enumeration. ITypeInfo.GetVarDesc returns a structure that describes the value, including an ID that we can pass to GetDocumentation.

Note that the call to GetVarDesc allocates memory internally. You must match the call with a call to ReleaseVarDesc to free the memory when you're done with it. I put this code in a try-finally block so that no matter what happens, the memory will be released.

## Interpreting Interfaces and Dispinterfaces

When LoadTypeLibrary detects an interface or dispinterface, it calls the procedure LoadInterface to decipher the interface.

LoadInterface starts out much the same as LoadEnum. It calls GetDocumentation to retrieve the name, documentation string, and help context of the interface. Then, the code loops through the functions (methods) defined in the interface.

As ITypeAttr.cVars returns the number of constants in an enumeration, ITypeAttr.cFuncs returns the number of methods supported by an interface.

Analogous to GetVarDesc, we must call GetFuncDesc to retrieve information about the function in question. Again, we're interested in the memid field of the structure, so we can pass it to GetDocumentation in order to get the name of the function.

The FuncDesc also tells us how many parameters the function accepts, in the cParams field. We can call the GetNames method to load up a list of parameter names.

Note that when we're done with FuncDesc, we must call ReleaseFuncDesc to release the memory allocated by GetFuncDesc. Again, I've enclosed these calls in a try-finally block to ensure that allocated memory gets released properly.

## Interpreting CoClasses

The last item that this sample recognizes and parses is a CoClass. LoadCoClass is the procedure responsible for analyzing the CoClass information.

As per usual, at the beginning of the procedure, I've made a call to GetDocumentation to get the name of the CoClass along with the documentation string and help context.

ITypeAttr provides a field named cImplTypes, which tells you how many interfaces this particular CoClass implements. If you'll refer back to Listing 3.2, you can see that LoadCoClass makes a call to GetRefTypeOfImplType.

This returns a reference number of the implemented interface. GetRefTypeInfo then returns the type information for that interface. The type information returned here is identical to the type information retrieved for the interface in procedure LoadInterface. At this point, all TIViewer does is get the name of the interface (again, through GetDocumentation) to display in the tree.

## Extending TIViewer

As you can see, the code for this example isn't particularly difficult. The worst part about writing this code is sifting through the Microsoft documentation to try and decipher what's going on internally.

> **Note**
>
> *As explained to me by the Delphi architects, even after you've gone through all the available Microsoft documentation, you've still got your work cut out for you in terms of trying to establish just how everything is supposed to work. For example, the first interface listed in the CoClass is supposed to be the default interface, and the second interface is supposed to be the events interface. Some type libraries don't follow the rules, so you can't always assume that ordering.* ◆

If this example piques your interest, you might try to extend it to display the values of the constants in an enumerated type, or to display the types of method parameters. The best source of information for the interfaces used in this example (ITypeLib, ITypeInfo, and ITypeAttr) is, again, the Microsoft Developer's Network (MSDN).

## Summary

In this chapter, I've shown you what a type library is, and how to add one to your COM server. You've learned how to edit a type library in order to add methods, properties, and enumerated types to your servers.

I also showed you how your applications can read and interpret the information stored in a type library.

In the next chapter, we'll be using type libraries extensively in our Automation servers. As you'll see, it isn't necessary to read the type library directly in a client application, as Delphi provides tools to automatically generate Object Pascal code from a type library.

# 4

## _Automation_

In the past three chapters, I've spent a lot of time discussing interfaces and how to create COM objects. I also introduced you to type libraries in Chapter 3, "Type Libraries." This chapter is where everything comes together. If you've been feeling a little disheartened about COM up until now, this is where that will change. This chapter is long, but it has many sample programs in it. I personally feel that this is probably the most important chapter in the book. I want to make sure you have a handle on what's being discussed here. In this chapter, I'll discuss

- Interfaces and automation
- Variants and automation
- Dispinterfaces
- Dual interfaces
- Automating Microsoft ADO

In Chapter 3, I showed you what a type library is, how to create one, and how you can read the information out of a type library. As you saw, extracting the type information manually is tedious at best. The good news is that you typically won't need to work directly with type library data. In most cases, you will work with a type library indirectly through _automation._

## Defining Automation

As its name suggests, automation is a way to automatically control an application from within another application. Actually, you can build both in-process and out-of-process automation servers. As you'll see later in this chapter, each type of automation controller has its benefits.

Delphi makes it so easy to create and use automation servers that you almost do not need to know much, if anything, about COM basics. It's very easy to create a simple automation client.

```
procedure TForm1.Button1Click(Sender: TObject);
var
  V: Variant;
begin
  V := CreateOleObject('Word.Basic');
  V.AppShow;
  V.FileNew;
  V.Insert('Automation is easy!');
end;
```

Believe it or not, this little snippet of code will start Word, create a new document, and insert the text "Automation is easy!" into the document.

Later in this chapter, in the section titled "Variants," I'll explain exactly what's going on in this code, but my goal at this point is to show you just how simple automation can be in Delphi.

## Interfaces

By now I assume that you understand what interfaces are and how to use them. Interfaces are one of the two main methods used to gain access to an automation server's COM objects.

When you control an automation server through an interface, you use *early binding*. Early binding simply means that all calls made to interface methods are checked for the correct parameters at compile time. As a Delphi programmer, you should be familiar with early binding.

You've seen numerous examples of interfaces in previous chapters, so I won't show a procedure here for controlling an automation server through interfaces. This chapter provides many examples that use interfaces to control an automation server.

## Variants

I discussed variants briefly in Chapter 2, "Interfaces and COM," mainly with respect to variant arrays. Not obviously, variants can also be used to control an automation server.

When you control an automation server through variants, you are using *late binding*. Late binding means that method calls are not resolved until runtime. This has some interesting ramifications. Consider the following code, which connects to Microsoft Word and instructs it to create a new file:

```
procedure TForm1.Button1Click(Sender: TObject);
var
  V: Variant;
```

```
begin
  V := CreateOleObject('Word.Basic');
  V.AppShow;
  V.FileNew;
  V.Insert('Automation is easy!');
end;
```

I'm not going to go into detail about the CreateOleObject at this moment. Suffice it to say that it is used to create an instance of an automation server. I'll come back and discuss that function in more detail later.

What CreateOleObject actually does in this example is start a copy of Microsoft Word. It then obtains a reference to the Word.Basic interface, and stores that reference in the variant V.

By default, automation servers typically start up as hidden. The AppShow method displays the Word application.

Then, a call is made to V.FileNew, which creates a new Word document. Delphi (and Windows) performs a tremendous amount of work behind the scenes to transform V.FileNew into a function call that creates a new document.

It's interesting to note that a variant is not a pointer to an object. How can you call methods on that "object," then? The answer is late binding. Delphi will actually accept anything you type here, without performing any type checking at all at compile time—in other words, Delphi does not perform early binding on variants. For instance, I could just as easily write the following code:

```
V.DelphiRules;
```

Delphi will compile this code just fine, but you can be fairly certain that Word doesn't implement a method called DelphiRules. If you attempt to execute this statement, you will receive the runtime error shown in Figure 4.1.

**Figure 4.1** *Calling a non-existent automation method results in this screen.*

To understand how Delphi turns this code into method calls, we need to take a look at the IDispatch interface.

IDispatch is defined in the file system.pas like this:

```
IDispatch = interface(IUnknown)
  ['{00020400-0000-0000-C000-000000000046}']
  function GetTypeInfoCount(out Count: Integer): HResult; stdcall;
  function GetTypeInfo(Index, LocaleID: Integer; out TypeInfo): HResult; stdcall;
  function GetIDsOfNames(const IID: TGUID; Names: Pointer;
```

```
    NameCount, LocaleID: Integer; DispIDs: Pointer): HResult; stdcall;
  function Invoke(DispID: Integer; const IID: TGUID; LocaleID: Integer;
    Flags: Word; var Params; VarResult, ExcepInfo, ArgErr: Pointer): HResult;
stdcall;
  end;
```

The methods GetTypeInfoCount and GetTypeInfo should trigger something in your brain. IDispatch *must* consult the type library associated with the automation controller in order to resolve function calls at runtime.

That's exactly correct. As a matter of fact, what happens is the following:

1. Delphi passes the name of the method to IDispatch.GetIDsOfNames.

2. GetIDsOfNames returns an integer ID representing the method name.

3. Delphi calls the Invoke method, using the ID returned in Step 2.

This sequence of steps occurs for every method that you call on an object through a variant. The time required to execute these three steps is considerably longer than accessing the same object directly through an interface.

As a Delphi programmer, you might wonder why on earth anyone would want to use IDispatch to access an automation server. There are two very good reasons for doing so:

1. You're writing a program or macro in an application that doesn't support interfaces. Examples are Visual Basic or Microsoft Word.

2. You're writing a quick and dirty client program in Delphi, and you don't want to go through the bother of importing a type library.

## Dispinterfaces

Somewhere between interfaces and variants are dispinterfaces. A dispinterface declaration looks almost identical to an interface declaration, except it uses the keyword dispinterface instead of interface. Here is a simple interface declaration, and then the corresponding dispinterface declaration.

```
// **********************************************************************//
// Interface: IUnitAuto
// Flags:     (4416) Dual OleAutomation Dispatchable
// GUID:      {A1E420C1-F75F-11D2-B3B9-0040F67455FE}
// **********************************************************************//
  IUnitAuto = interface(IDispatch)
    ['{A1E420C1-F75F-11D2-B3B9-0040F67455FE}']
    function Convert(Quantity: Double; InUnit: Integer; OutUnit: Integer): Double;
➥safecall;
  end;
```

```
// *****************************************************************//
// DispIntf:   IUnitAutoDisp
// Flags:      (4416) Dual OleAutomation Dispatchable
// GUID:       {A1E420C1-F75F-11D2-B3B9-0040F67455FE}
// *****************************************************************//
  IUnitAutoDisp = dispinterface
    ['{A1E420C1-F75F-11D2-B3B9-0040F67455FE}']
    function Convert(Quantity: Double; InUnit: Integer; OutUnit: Integer): Double;
➥dispid 1;
  end;
```

This Delphi-generated code is taken directly from the first example program
later in this chapter, so I'm not going to explain it in detail right now.

You should notice several things about this code right away.

- The IUnitAuto interface is derived from IDispatch, so if you create
  an automation server that implements IUnitAuto, clients can use late
  binding to talk to it.

- The IUnitAuto method Convert is declared as safecall.

- The IUnitAuto interface and IUnitAutoDisp dispinterface both use the
  same GUID.

- The IUnitAutoDisp dispinterface defines the same method (Convert)
  that the IUnitAuto interface defines. However, the dispinterface
  includes dispid 1 at the end of the method name.

When you use a dispinterface, you eliminate the first two steps associated with
IDispatch. The automation controller does not have to call GetIDsOfNames,
and the server does not have to respond with the dispid of the method in question. Instead, the dispid is determined at compile time. At runtime, the client
program simply calls Invoke with the predetermined dispid.

Dispinterfaces are for client convenience only. You do not actually
implement a dispinterface on the server. The server implements interfaces.
The client application can elect to connect to the server using variants or
dispinterfaces, assuming that the server's COM object also supports the
IDispatch interface.

## Dual Interfaces

A dual interface is simply defined as an automation server that supports
clients connecting to it using interfaces (early bound) as well as clients
connecting to it using variants (late bound). Any automation servers that
you create with Delphi will automatically support a dual interface. This is
desirable because it means that any automation server that you write can
be accessed by almost any piece of software on the market today.

This section thoroughly covered automation and the way clients can access automation servers through use of interfaces, variants, dispinterfaces, and dual interfaces. The next section will take that information and apply it to the creation and use of in-process automation servers.

# In-Process Automation Servers

The first automation server we're going to develop is a simple in-process automation server. You should remember from Chapter 2 that in-process servers execute in the same address space as the client application.

## Example: Unit Conversion Server

This automation server will be able to convert between different area measurements. It can convert between square meters, square centimeters, square yards, square feet, square inches, square kilometers, square miles, and acres. You've already seen the method that will be responsible for the conversion, which appears as follows:

```
function Convert(Quantity: Double; InUnit: Integer; OutUnit: Integer): Double;
safecall;
```

In a nutshell, Convert converts a given quantity from the unit of measure designated by InUnit to the unit of measure designated by OutUnit. The actual code that performs the conversion is quite simple, and is shown in the following example:

```
const
  auSquareMeters = $00000000;
  auSquareCentimeters = $00000001;
  auSquareYards = $00000002;
  auSquareFeet = $00000003;
  auSquareInches = $00000004;
  auSquareKilometers = $00000005;
  auSquareMiles = $00000006;
  auAcres = $00000007;
function TUnitAuto.Convert(Quantity: Double; InUnit,
  OutUnit: Integer): Double;
const
  AreaFactor: Array[auSquareMeters .. auAcres] of Double =
    (10000.0, 1.0, 8361.2736, 929.0304, 6.4516, 10000000000.0,
     25899881103.4, 40468726.0987);
begin
  Result := Quantity * AreaFactor[InUnit] / AreaFactor[OutUnit];
end;
```

The AreaFactor array contains the factors necessary to convert between a given unit of measure and square centimeters. For example, one square meter is 10,000 square centimeters, and one acre is 40,468,726.0987 square centimeters. The Convert function simply converts from InUnit to square centimeters, and then from square centimeters to the OutUnit.

Now that you know how the process works, let's create an automation server to expose this functionality.

1. Select File, New from Delphi's main menu. In the ActiveX tab of the Object Repository, select the ActiveX Library icon. So far, the steps are identical to those we took when we created an in-process COM server.

2. Select File, New from the main menu again, and in the ActiveX tab of the Object Repository, select Automation Object. Delphi displays the Automation Object Wizard, shown in Figure 4.2.

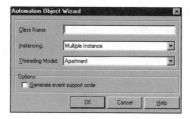

**Figure 4.2**  *The Automation Object Wizard.*

3. Enter a Class Name of AreaUnitConverter, and click OK. Delphi creates a unit for the class, and also creates a type library. The type library editor will automatically be displayed.

4. Click IAreaUnitConverter in the Object List. Notice in the Information Pane that the IAreaUnitConverter interface descends from IDispatch (Figure 4.3).

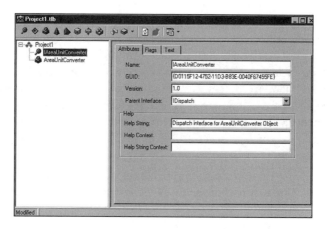

**Figure 4.3**  *The Type Library Editor.*

We already know what the Convert method needs to do, so let's add it to the interface.

5. Click the New Method icon on the toolbar, and name the method Convert. Notice that in the Information Pane, Delphi has assigned a dispid of 1 to this method.

6. Click the Parameters tab, and set the Return Type to Double. Now add a parameter named Quantity, of type Double. Add an Integer parameter named InUnit and another Integer parameter named OutUnit.

When you're finished, your screen should look like Figure 4.4.

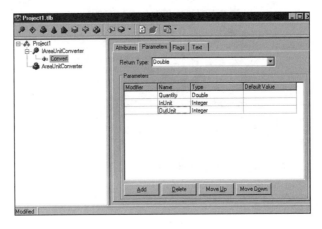

**Figure 4.4**  *The Type Library Editor after adding a method.*

Now, rather than forcing users of this automation server to remember that 0 means square meters and so on, let's add an enumeration to the type library.

7. Click the New Enumeration button on the toolbar. Name the enumeration AreaUnit. Now click the NewConst button and add a constant named auSquareMeters. Do the same for auSquareCentimeters, auSquareYards, auSquareFeet, auSquareInches, auSquareKilometers, auSquareMiles, and auAcres. Delphi will automatically assign the values zero through seven to the enumeration constants.

8. Click the Refresh Implementation button on the type library toolbar to ensure that the Delphi code reflects the additions made to the type library. You can now close the Type Library Editor.

**9.** Save the Delphi unit as AreaUnit.pas, and the project as UnitSrv.dpr. Now flesh out the Convert method so it appears as follows:

```
function TUnitAuto.Convert(Quantity: Double; InUnit,
  OutUnit: Integer): Double;
const
  AreaFactor: Array[auSquareMeters .. auAcres] of Double =
    (10000.0, 1.0, 8361.2736, 929.0304, 6.4516, 10000000000.0,
      25899881103.4, 40468726.0987);
begin
  Result := Quantity * AreaFactor[InUnit] / AreaFactor[OutUnit];
end;
```

That's all we need to do for this server. Compile it to make sure you didn't make any typos, and then select Run, Register ActiveX Server to register the server with the Windows registry.

I'm not going to bother listing the source code for the server, because you've already seen most of it, and what you have not seen, Delphi automatically created for you. Now we can concentrate on writing a client application to access the server.

> ### Note
>
> *You might be thinking that this process seemed entirely too easy. We didn't even press Ctrl+Shift+G to generate a GUID for the IAreaUnitConverter interface. The fact is that we've done all the work required to write a dual-interface automation server. Delphi's wizard automatically generated the necessary GUIDs for us.*
>
> *You might have noticed that it was even easier to create this COM automation server than it was to create the plain COM servers in Chapter 2. When I write COM code, I almost always create automation servers. They're a snap to create, and they're much more flexible than standard COM objects.* ◆

## CreateOleObject and GetActiveOleObject

Earlier, I showed you how CreateOleObject is used to start a new instance of an automation server. CreateOleObject is declared in the file comobj.pas as follows:

```
function CreateOleObject(const ClassName: string): IDispatch;
var
  ClassID: TCLSID;
begin
  ClassID := ProgIDToClassID(ClassName);
  OleCheck(CoCreateInstance(ClassID, nil, CLSCTX_INPROC_SERVER or
    CLSCTX_LOCAL_SERVER, IDispatch, Result));
end;
```

As you can see, this function first obtains the GUID of the class that we're creating. Then, it passes that GUID to CoCreateInstance. I discussed CoCreateInstance in Chapter 2. ProgIDToClassID is basically a wrapper around the Windows API called CLSIDFromProgID. So, in a nutshell, CreateOleObject works similarly to CreateComObject, except CreateOleObject takes a class name as a parameter instead of a GUID.

However, CreateOleObject always creates a new instance of a given server. What if you want to connect to an already running instance of a server? Or maybe you do not know whether the server is running or not. You'd like to start it if it is not running, and connect to it if it is.

GetActiveOleObject can be used to obtain a reference to a server that is running in memory. In Chapter 2, I discussed the Running Object Table in Windows, which tracks all active COM objects. GetActiveOleObject looks in the Running Object Table to see if the given server is running. If it is, it returns a reference to the IDispatch interface on that server. If the server is not running, GetActiveOleObject raises an exception.

With that information in mind, the following procedure will start a new copy of Word if it isn't running, and will connect to an already-running copy if it is:

```
procedure StartOrLinkToWord;
var
  V: Variant;
begin
  try
    V := GetActiveOleObject('Word.Basic');
  except
    V := CreateOleObject(Word'.Basic');
  end;

  // Do something with V here...
end;
```

## Example: Unit Conversion Client

Now we can concentrate on writing a client program to access the automation server we just created. Figure 4.5 shows the main form of the UnitCli application at runtime.

As you can see, this program's interface is composed of six buttons. The left column of buttons creates and accesses the automation server in each of the three possible ways: by interface, by variant, and by dispinterface. The right column of buttons operates the same as the left column, except it makes 100,000 calls in a row for timing purposes.

**Figure 4.5**    *UnitCli performs time tests on interfaces, dispinterfaces, and variants.*

The code required to access the server is small, in all three cases. Let's view an example of the code for accessing the server through an interface first.

```
procedure TForm1.btnInterfaceClick(Sender: TObject);
var
  I: IUnitAuto;
begin
  I := CoUnitAuto.Create;
  ShowMessage(FloatToStr(I.Convert(1.0, 0, 1)));
end;
```

You've seen similar code in Chapter 2. The call to CoUnitAuto creates an instance of the automation server, and I.Convert converts 1.0 square meters to square centimeters. Do not forget that due to reference counting, the server is automatically destroyed at the end of the procedure.

Now let's look at accessing the same server through a variant.

```
procedure TForm1.btnVariantClick(Sender: TObject);
var
  V: Variant;
begin
  V := CreateOleObject('UnitSrv.UnitAuto');
  ShowMessage(FloatToStr(V.Convert(1.0, 0, 1)));
end;
```

This code is very similar to the code required to access the server through an interface. The first line of code makes a call to CreateOleObject to create an instance of the server. You're probably wondering how I knew to use UnitSrv.UnitAuto as the class name to pass to CreateOleObject. Delphi creates this string for you by concatenating the name of the server, a dot, and the name of the CoClass. For reference, the type library for the UnitSrv server is shown in Figure 4.6.

As you can see, the name of the library is UnitSrv. The CoClass is highlighted in the Object List, and is named UnitAuto. Therefore, the classname for the object is UnitSrv.UnitAuto.

A second method you can use to determine the class name of the server is to look up the GUID in the Windows Registry. The GUID for UnitAuto is {A1E420C3-F75F-11D2-B3B9-0040F67455FE}. In the Registry, you'll see an entry like that shown in Figure 4.7.

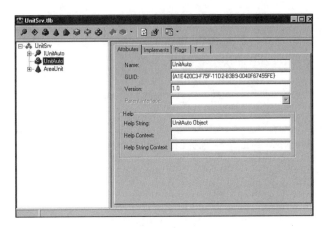

Figure 4.6    *UnitSrv type library.*

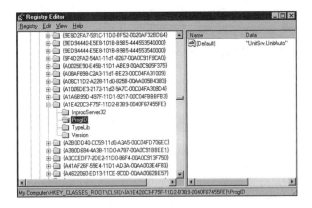

Figure 4.7    *UnitAuto entry in RegEdit.*

You cannot use these methods if you are using somebody else's automation server that might not have been created in Delphi, or if you do not know the GUID of the object in question. In those cases, the documentation for that server should give you the class name(s) available for you to use.

After CreateOleObject works its magic and stores a reference to the automation server in the variant V, we can make calls to that server just as if we were using an interface. As I explained before, the internal mechanism for making variant calls is considerably different (and slower) than that used for interfaces.

The final method for accessing the automation server is through a dispinterface.

```
procedure TForm1.btnDispInterfaceClick(Sender: TObject);
var
  DI: IUnitAutoDisp;
begin
  DI := CoUnitAuto.Create as IUnitAutoDisp;
  ShowMessage(FloatToStr(DI.Convert(1.0, 0, 1)));
end;
```

As you can see, this code is almost identical to the code used for interfaces. The only difference is that the interface obtained through CoUnitAuto.Create is converted to a dispinterface.

Listing 4.1 shows the code for the main form of the client application.

**Listing 4.1**    *UnitCli Application—MainForm.pas*

```
unit MainForm;

interface

uses
  Windows, Messages, SysUtils, Classes, Graphics, Controls, Forms, Dialogs,
  StdCtrls;

type
  TForm1 = class(TForm)
    btnVariant: TButton;
    btnInterface: TButton;
    btnDispInterface: TButton;
    btnTimeInterface: TButton;
    btnTimeVariant: TButton;
    btnTimeDispInterface: TButton;
    lblInterface: TLabel;
    lblVariant: TLabel;
    lblDispInterface: TLabel;
    procedure btnVariantClick(Sender: TObject);
    procedure btnInterfaceClick(Sender: TObject);
    procedure btnDispInterfaceClick(Sender: TObject);
    procedure btnTimeInterfaceClick(Sender: TObject);
    procedure btnTimeVariantClick(Sender: TObject);
    procedure btnTimeDispInterfaceClick(Sender: TObject);
  private
    { Private declarations }
  public
    { Public declarations }
  end;

var
  Form1: TForm1;
```

*continues* ▶

**Listing 4.1**    *continued*

```
implementation

uses
  ComObj, UnitSrv_TLB;

{$R *.DFM}

procedure TForm1.btnVariantClick(Sender: TObject);
var
  V: Variant;
begin
  V := CreateOleObject('UnitSrv.UnitAuto');
  ShowMessage(FloatToStr(V.Convert(1.0, 0, 1)));
end;

procedure TForm1.btnInterfaceClick(Sender: TObject);
var
  I: IUnitAuto;
begin
  I := CoUnitAuto.Create;
  ShowMessage(FloatToStr(I.Convert(1.0, 0, 1)));
end;

procedure TForm1.btnDispInterfaceClick(Sender: TObject);
var
  DI: IUnitAutoDisp;
begin
  DI := CoUnitAuto.Create as IUnitAutoDisp;
  ShowMessage(FloatToStr(DI.Convert(1.0, 0, 1)));
end;

procedure TForm1.btnTimeInterfaceClick(Sender: TObject);
var
  I: IUnitAuto;
  Count: Integer;
  Dbl: Double;
  T1, T2: DWord;
begin
  I := CoUnitAuto.Create;
  T1 := GetTickCount;
  for Count := 1 to 100000 do
    Dbl := I.Convert(1.0, 0, 1);
  T2 := GetTickCount;
  lblInterface.Caption := IntToStr(T2 - T1) + ' ms';
end;

procedure TForm1.btnTimeVariantClick(Sender: TObject);
var
  V: Variant;
  Count: Integer;
  Dbl: Double;
```

```
  T1, T2: DWord;              .
begin
  V := CreateOleObject('UnitSrv.UnitAuto');
  T1 := GetTickCount;
  for Count := 1 to 100000 do
    Dbl := V.Convert(1.0, 0, 1);
  T2 := GetTickCount;
  lblVariant.Caption := IntToStr(T2 - T1) + ' ms';
end;

procedure TForm1.btnTimeDispInterfaceClick(Sender: TObject);
var
  DI: IUnitAutoDisp;
  Count: Integer;
  Dbl: Double;
  T1, T2: DWord;
begin
  DI := CoUnitAuto.Create as IUnitAutoDisp;
  T1 := GetTickCount;
  for Count := 1 to 100000 do
    Dbl := DI.Convert(1.0, 0, 1);
  T2 := GetTickCount;
  lblDispInterface.Caption := IntToStr(T2 - T1) + ' ms';
end;

end.
```

This application can access our server either through an interface, a dispinterface, or IDispatch. A real application would simply choose one of the three methods. My purpose in showing all three methods is two-fold:

1. I want you to see how to use each method in your own applications.

2. This program performs some timing tests to show you the relative times for each method.

If you'll refer back to Figure 4.5, you'll see the timing results on my own computer. These values represent the time required to call the Convert method 100,000 times.

As you can see, interfaces are by far the fastest way to call a method on an automation server. Variants are more than an order of magnitude slower, and dispinterfaces lie somewhere in between.

By now, you should be familiar with in-process Automation serviers. However, in-process Automation servers are not always appropriate. If you want to create COM servers that run in a separate address space from the client application, you'll need to create an out-of-process Automation server. The next section will guide you through the creation and uses of out-of-process Automation servers.

# Out-of-Process Automation Servers

In Chapter 2, I discussed the need for marshaling in out-of-process COM
servers. Briefly, the data types that are automation compatible are Smallint,
Integer, Single, Double, Currency, TDateTime, WideString, IDispatch,
SCODE, WordBool, OleVariant, IUnknown, Shortint, and Byte. As you'll
learn in a moment, Delphi also provides marshaling support for pictures,
string lists, and fonts through the interfaces IPicture, IStrings, and IFonts.

Out-of-process Automation servers are desirable in cases where the
Automation server should act as a standalone application in its own right,
and they're required in cases where you want to access the server from a
remote machine using DCOM (DCOM is discussed in Chapter 6, "DCOM").

## HResult and Safecall

All methods in an Automation server must return an HResult, which indicates whether the method succeeded or failed. Any other return values must
be returned in *out* parameters, discussed in Chapter 3.

This doesn't sound logical, given that the Convert method used in
UnitSrv returns a Double. Once again, Delphi shields us from some of the
complexities of COM. In a typical programming environment, you would
need to write the Convert method as follows:

```
function Convert(Quantity: Double; InUnit: Integer; OutUnit: Integer; out Result:
Double): HResult; stdcall;
```

The safecall calling convention allows you to code as if the method looked
like the following:

```
function Convert(Quantity: Double; InUnit: Integer; OutUnit: Integer): Double;
stdcall;
```

The safecall directive also tells Delphi to perform another major function
behind the scenes. Safecall on the server side of the COM implementation
instructs Delphi to automatically wrap all methods in a try/except block.
For example, when you write the following code in an automation server,

```
function TMyServer.DoSomething: Integer;
begin
  Result := SomeFunctionThatReturnsAnInteger;
end;
```

Delphi compiles the equivalent of the following code into your application:

```
function TMyServer.DoSomething(out Ret: Integer): HResult;
begin
  try
    Ret := SomeFunctionThatReturnsAnInteger;
    Result := S_OK;
  except
    Result := E_UNEXPECTED;
  end;
end;
```

In other words, Delphi prevents an exception from escaping from a method of an automation server. Instead, it channels the exception back to the client application as an HResult.

On the client side, safecall causes the client to check the method for a HResult failure code and raise a Delphi exception if the method returns an error.

To understand why it's desirable for this to occur, consider the fact that an Automation server might not have a user interface. It could have a hidden main window, for example, or no window at all. If an exception suddenly popped up, it would be disconcerting for the end user, at best. Further, as you'll learn in Chapter 6, automation objects don't even have to reside on the same machine as the clients that use them. If the computer that hosts the automation object resides down the hall (or halfway around the world), the client app has no way of knowing when an exception is displayed on the server machine.

### Marshaling Strings, Fonts, and Pictures

*As I briefly mentioned earlier, Delphi provides marshaling support for pictures, string lists, and fonts. This is a welcome feature, because Delphi makes considerable use of both string lists and fonts in the VCL. I'm not going to list the declaration of those interfaces here, but if you're interested in looking into them on your own, IStrings is declared in stdvcl.pas, and IFont and IPicture are declared in activex.pas. The sample program shown in the next section shows how to use IStrings and IFonts in your applications.* ♦

## Automating an Existing Application

In this section, we're going to take an existing application and add automation capability to it. The application is a very simple program with a memo and two buttons on the main form. One button changes the font of the memo, and the other button changes the color. Not very exciting, but it serves to illustrate the points I want to make here.

There are many cases in which you might want to automate an existing application. For instance, let's say you have written a checkbook application (ala Quicken) that contains functionality for looking up stock prices online. If you automate the price lookup functionality, you (or another programmer) could later write a client application that instructs the checkbook application to download the latest stock prices at certain intervals.

In this example, you'll learn not only how to add automation capability to an existing application, but you'll also see how to pass string lists, colors, and fonts as parameters to an automation method.

> **Note**
>
> *In actuality, many out-of-process Automation servers, unlike the example shown here, are complete programs within themselves. Consider the fact that Microsoft Word is an Automation server. Word is a very complete (read: large) program in itself, yet it also makes almost all its functionality available through automation.*◆

Listing 4.2 shows the source code for the main form of the MemoDemo application.

**Listing 4.2**    *MemoDemo Application—MainForm.pas*

```
unit MainForm;

interface

uses
  Windows, Messages, SysUtils, Classes, Graphics, Controls, Forms, Dialogs,
  StdCtrls;

type
  TForm1 = class(TForm)
    Memo1: TMemo;
    btnFont: TButton;
    btnColor: TButton;
    FontDialog1: TFontDialog;
    ColorDialog1: TColorDialog;
    procedure btnFontClick(Sender: TObject);
    procedure btnColorClick(Sender: TObject);
  private
    { Private declarations }
  public
    { Public declarations }
  end;

var
  Form1: TForm1;

implementation

{$R *.DFM}

procedure TForm1.btnFontClick(Sender: TObject);
begin
  if FontDialog1.Execute then
    Memo1.Font.Assign(FontDialog1.Font);
end;
```

```
procedure TForm1.btnColorClick(Sender: TObject);
begin
  if ColorDialog1.Execute then
    Memo1.Color := ColorDialog1.Color;
end;

end.
```

As you can see, the source code for the application is almost insignificant. Figure 4.8 shows MemoDemo's main form at runtime.

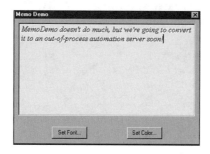

**Figure 4.8**   *MemoDemo isn't much, but it's a good starting point.*

Enter some text into the memo. Click the Font button to change the font used in the memo, or the Color button to change the background color of the memo.

### Adding an Automation Object

Now that you've seen MemoDemo—which isn't going to win any industry awards, I'm afraid—let's see what's required to add automation capabilities to it.

One of the most important things you can do when adding automation to an existing application is make use of the code that's already in the application. Ideally, the bodies of your automation methods should contain exactly one line of code, which is a call to an already existing function in your main application.

If you're writing a new application with automation in mind, it's not difficult to take this fact into account from the beginning. However, suppose automation was the farthest thing from my mind when I wrote MemoDemo. The fastest and easiest way to prepare for automation is to add the necessary support functions to the application first. For example, for MemoDemo, we want to be able to read and control the font, color, and text of the memo from another application. To state the obvious, we're going to want to add methods GetColor, SetColor, GetFont, SetFont, GetText, and SetText to the main form object. Listing 4.3 shows the result of these straightforward additions.

**Listing 4.3**   *MemoSrv Application—MainForm.pas*

```pascal
unit MainForm;

interface

uses
  Windows, Messages, SysUtils, Classes, Graphics, Controls, Forms, Dialogs,
  StdCtrls;

type
  TForm1 = class(TForm)
    Memo1: TMemo;
    btnFont: TButton;
    btnColor: TButton;
    FontDialog1: TFontDialog;
    ColorDialog1: TColorDialog;
    procedure btnFontClick(Sender: TObject);
    procedure btnColorClick(Sender: TObject);
  private
    { Private declarations }
  public
    { Public declarations }
    function GetColor: TColor;
    procedure SetColor(AColor: TColor);
    function GetFont: TFont;
    procedure SetFont(AFont: TFont);
    function GetText: TStrings;
    procedure SetText(AText: TStrings);
  end;

var
  Form1: TForm1;

implementation

{$R *.DFM}

procedure TForm1.btnFontClick(Sender: TObject);
begin
  if FontDialog1.Execute then
    Memo1.Font.Assign(FontDialog1.Font);
end;

procedure TForm1.btnColorClick(Sender: TObject);
begin
  if ColorDialog1.Execute then
    Memo1.Color := ColorDialog1.Color;
end;
```

```
procedure TForm1.SetColor(AColor: TColor);
begin
  Memo1.Color := AColor;
end;

procedure TForm1.SetFont(AFont: TFont);
begin
  Memo1.Font.Assign(AFont);
end;

procedure TForm1.SetText(AText: TStrings);
begin
  Memo1.Lines.Assign(AText);
end;

function TForm1.GetColor: TColor;
begin
  Result := Memo1.Color;
end;

function TForm1.GetFont: TFont;
begin
  Result := Memo1.Font;
end;

function TForm1.GetText: TStrings;
begin
  Result := Memo1.Lines;
end;

end.
```

Now that the main form supports the access functions we need, it's time to add the automation object to MemoSrv. Select File, New from the Delphi main menu. Click the ActiveX tab of the Object Repository, and select Automation Object. Call the object MemoIntf, and click OK. Delphi creates a new source file for MemoIntf and displays the Type Library Editor.

We're going to add three properties to the type library: Color, Font, and Text.

1. Click the New Property button. If a popup menu is displayed, select Read, Write from the menu. Name the property Color, and set the Type to OLE_COLOR.

2. Add a read/write property named Font, and set the Type to IFontDisp. You won't find IFontDisp in the drop-down list of types, but the Type Library Editor will accept the declaration if you type it in.

3. Add a read/write property named Text, and set the Type to IStrings.

4. Click the Refresh Implementation button and close the Type Library Editor.

5. Save the source file as MemoIntf.pas.

6. Add ActiveX, StdVCL, and AxCtrls to the **uses** clause of the interface section of the unit, as these units define IFont, IStrings, and the GetOLEXxx procedures respectively.

7. Add MainForm to the **uses** clause of the implementation section.

8. Flesh out each of the methods in MemoIntf so that they call the corresponding TForm1 methods (see Listing 4.4).

You can now compile the program. Run it once to register the automation server with the Windows registry, and quit the application.

---

**Note**

*Remember that out-of-process COM servers are registered with the Windows Registry every time you run them. To register an out-of-process server without actually running the application, you could run MemoSrv.exe /regserver. To unregister the server, run MemoSrv.exe /unregserver.* ♦

---

The source code for MemoIntf is shown in Listing 4.4.

**Listing 4.4**    *MemoSrv Application—MemoIntf.pas*

```
unit MemoIntf;

interface

uses
  ComObj, ActiveX, AXCtrls, StdVCL, MemoSrv_TLB;

type
  TMemoIntf = class(TAutoObject, IMemoIntf)
  protected
    function Get_Color: OLE_COLOR; safecall;
    procedure Set_Color(Value: OLE_COLOR); safecall;
    function Get_Font: IFontDisp; safecall;
    function Get_Text: IStrings; safecall;
    procedure Set_Font(const Value: IFontDisp); safecall;
    procedure Set_Text(const Value: IStrings); safecall;
    { Protected declarations }
  end;

implementation

uses ComServ, MainForm;
```

```
function TMemoIntf.Get_Color: OLE_COLOR;
begin
  Result := Form1.GetColor;
end;

procedure TMemoIntf.Set_Color(Value: OLE_COLOR);
begin
  Form1.SetColor(Value);
end;

function TMemoIntf.Get_Font: IFontDisp;
begin
  GetOleFont(Form1.GetFont, Result);
end;

function TMemoIntf.Get_Text: IStrings;
begin
  GetOleStrings(Form1.GetText, Result);
end;

procedure TMemoIntf.Set_Font(const Value: IFontDisp);
begin
  SetOleFont(Form1.GetFont, Value);
end;

procedure TMemoIntf.Set_Text(const Value: IStrings);
begin
  SetOleStrings(Form1.GetText, Value);
end;

initialization
  TAutoObjectFactory.Create(ComServer, TMemoIntf, Class_MemoIntf,
    ciMultiInstance, tmApartment);
end.
```

### Building an Automation Client

Now that we have an application to automate, we're going to concentrate on writing a client application that automates it.

In most cases, when you want to use an Automation server, you won't have any source code for the interfaces that are provided by that server. In this book, we've written both the servers and the clients, so the source code was readily available to us. What if some other programmer had written MemoSrv?

I'm going to show you how you can import a type library into Delphi and have it automatically recreate the necessary source code for you.

Create a new Delphi application, and then select Project, Import Type Library from the Delphi main menu. You'll see the screen shown in Figure 4.9.

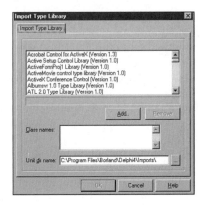

**Figure 4.9**    *Importing a type library.*

Scroll down through the list until you find MemoSrv (Version 1.0).
If it does not appear in the list, click the Add... button, and select the file
MemoSrv.exe from whatever directory it is installed in on your hard drive.

Highlight MemoSrv (Version 1.0) and click the OK button. Delphi will
generate an import library named MemoSrv_TLB.pas for the MemoSrv
Automation server. By default, the file will be placed in the Imports
directory on your hard driver. If you installed Delphi with the default configuration, this directory will be C:\Program Files\Borland\DelphiX\Imports,
where DelphiX represents the version of Delphi that you're using (Delphi4,
Delphi5, and so on). Listing 4.5 shows the imported MemoSrv type library.

---

**Listing 4.5**    *MemoCli Application—MemoSrv_TLB.pas*

```
unit MemoSrv_TLB;

// ************************************************************************** //
// WARNING                                                                  //
// -------                                                                   //
// The types declared in this file were generated from data read from a     //
// Type Library. If this type library is explicitly or indirectly (via      //
// another type library referring to this type library) re-imported, or the //
// 'Refresh' command of the Type Library Editor activated while editing the //
// Type Library, the contents of this file will be regenerated and all      //
// manual modifications will be lost.                                       //
// ************************************************************************** //

// PASTLWTR : $Revision:   1.11.1.75  $
// File generated on 7/31/99 10:50:09 AM from Type Library described below.

// ************************************************************************** //
// Type Lib: J:\Book\samples\Chap04\MemoSrv\MemoSrv.exe
// IID\LCID: {A1E420C7-F75F-11D2-B3B9-0040F67455FE}\0
// Helpfile:
```

```
// HelpString: MemoSrv Library
// Version:    1.0
// ********************************************************************** //

interface

uses Windows, ActiveX, Classes, Graphics, OleCtrls, StdVCL;

// **********************************************************************//
// GUIDS declared in the TypeLibrary. Following prefixes are used:    //
//   Type Libraries     : LIBID_xxxx                                  //
//   CoClasses          : CLASS_xxxx                                  //
//   DISPInterfaces     : DIID_xxxx                                   //
//   Non-DISP interfaces: IID_xxxx                                    //
// **********************************************************************//
const
  LIBID_MemoSrv: TGUID = '{A1E420C7-F75F-11D2-B3B9-0040F67455FE}';
  IID_IMemoIntf: TGUID = '{A1E420C8-F75F-11D2-B3B9-0040F67455FE}';
  CLASS_MemoIntf: TGUID = '{A1E420CA-F75F-11D2-B3B9-0040F67455FE}';
type

// **********************************************************************//
// Forward declaration of interfaces defined in Type Library         //
// **********************************************************************//
  IMemoIntf = interface;
  IMemoIntfDisp = dispinterface;

// **********************************************************************//
// Declaration of CoClasses defined in Type Library                  //
// (NOTE: Here we map each CoClass to its Default Interface)          //
// **********************************************************************//
  MemoIntf = IMemoIntf;


// **********************************************************************//
// Interface: IMemoIntf
// Flags:     (4416) Dual OleAutomation Dispatchable
// GUID:      {A1E420C8-F75F-11D2-B3B9-0040F67455FE}
// **********************************************************************//
  IMemoIntf = interface(IDispatch)
    ['{A1E420C8-F75F-11D2-B3B9-0040F67455FE}']
    function Get_Color: OLE_COLOR; safecall;
    procedure Set_Color(Value: OLE_COLOR); safecall;
    function Get_Font: IFontDisp; safecall;
    procedure Set_Font(const Value: IFontDisp); safecall;
    function Get_Text: IStrings; safecall;
    procedure Set_Text(const Value: IStrings); safecall;
    property Color: OLE_COLOR read Get_Color write Set_Color;
    property Font: IFontDisp read Get_Font write Set_Font;
    property Text: IStrings read Get_Text write Set_Text;
  end;
```

*continues* ▶

**Listing 4.5**   *continued*

```
// ********************************************************************//
// DispIntf:  IMemoIntfDisp
// Flags:     (4416) Dual OleAutomation Dispatchable
// GUID:      {A1E420C8-F75F-11D2-B3B9-0040F67455FE}
// ********************************************************************//
  IMemoIntfDisp = dispinterface
    ['{A1E420C8-F75F-11D2-B3B9-0040F67455FE}']
    property Color: OLE_COLOR dispid 2;
    property Font: IFontDisp dispid 1;
    property Text: IStrings dispid 3;
  end;

  CoMemoIntf = class
    class function Create: IMemoIntf;
    class function CreateRemote(const MachineName: string): IMemoIntf;
  end;

implementation

uses ComObj;

class function CoMemoIntf.Create: IMemoIntf;
begin
  Result := CreateComObject(CLASS_MemoIntf) as IMemoIntf;
end;

class function CoMemoIntf.CreateRemote(const MachineName: string): IMemoIntf;
begin
  Result := CreateRemoteComObject(MachineName, CLASS_MemoIntf) as IMemoIntf;
end;

end.
```

Add MemoSrv_TLB to the uses clause of your main form, and compile to make sure that Delphi found the import unit. If you get a compile error when trying to compile MemoSrv_TLB, check your Environment Options to make sure that $(Delphi)\Imports is in the library path (see Figure 4.10).

**Figure 4.10**   *Make sure $(DELPHI)\Imports is in your list of library paths.*

Now we can write the code that interfaces to the MemoSrv Automation server. Because we're using interfaces, the code to connect to and disconnect from the server is old hat.

```
procedure TForm1.btnConnectClick(Sender: TObject);
begin
  FMemo := CoMemoIntf.Create;
end;

procedure TForm1.btnDisconnectClick(Sender: TObject);
begin
  FMemo := nil;
end;
```

We'll also add three buttons to the main form for setting the font, color, and text of the remote memo. As I indicated earlier in the section "Marshaling and Automation Types," Delphi provides support for marshaling fonts, string lists, and pictures. This makes the amount of code we have to write trivial.

```
procedure TForm1.btnSetFontClick(Sender: TObject);
var
  FontDisp: IFontDisp;
begin
  if FontDialog1.Execute then begin
    Memo1.Font.Assign(FontDialog1.Font);

    GetOleFont(FontDialog1.Font, FontDisp);
    FMemo.Set_Font(FontDisp);
  end;
end;
```

GetOleFont is a Delphi procedure that "converts" a TFont object into an IFontDisp interface, suitable for passing across process boundaries. Similarly, GetOleStrings can create an IStrings interface from a TStrings object.

Listing 4.6 shows the complete source code for the client application.

---

**Listing 4.6**   *MemoCli Application—MainForm.pas*

```
unit MainForm;

interface

uses
  Windows, Messages, SysUtils, Classes, Graphics, Controls, Forms, Dialogs,
  StdCtrls, MemoSrv_TLB;

type
  TForm1 = class(TForm)
    btnSetColor: TButton;
```

*continues* ▶

**Listing 4.6**   *continued*

```
    btnConnect: TButton;
    btnSetFont: TButton;
    btnSetText: TButton;
    btnDisconnect: TButton;
    btnGetColor: TButton;
    btnGetFont: TButton;
    btnGetText: TButton;
    Memo1: TMemo;
    FontDialog1: TFontDialog;
    ColorDialog1: TColorDialog;
    procedure btnConnectClick(Sender: TObject);
    procedure btnDisconnectClick(Sender: TObject);
    procedure btnSetColorClick(Sender: TObject);
    procedure btnSetFontClick(Sender: TObject);
    procedure btnSetTextClick(Sender: TObject);
    procedure btnGetColorClick(Sender: TObject);
    procedure btnGetFontClick(Sender: TObject);
    procedure btnGetTextClick(Sender: TObject);
  private
    { Private declarations }
    FMemo: IMemoIntf;
  public
    { Public declarations }
  end;

var
  Form1: TForm1;

implementation

uses
  ActiveX, AXCtrls, StdVCL;

{$R *.DFM}

procedure TForm1.btnConnectClick(Sender: TObject);
begin
  FMemo := CoMemoIntf.Create;
end;

procedure TForm1.btnDisconnectClick(Sender: TObject);
begin
  FMemo := nil;
end;

procedure TForm1.btnSetColorClick(Sender: TObject);
begin
```

```
  if ColorDialog1.Execute then begin
    Memo1.Color := ColorDialog1.Color;
    FMemo.Set_Color(ColorToRGB(ColorDialog1.Color));
  end;
end;

procedure TForm1.btnSetFontClick(Sender: TObject);
var
  FontDisp: IFontDisp;
begin
  if FontDialog1.Execute then begin
    Memo1.Font.Assign(FontDialog1.Font);

    GetOleFont(FontDialog1.Font, FontDisp);
    FMemo.Set_Font(FontDisp);
  end;
end;

procedure TForm1.btnSetTextClick(Sender: TObject);
var
  Strings: IStrings;
begin
  GetOleStrings(Memo1.Lines, Strings);
  FMemo.Set_Text(Strings);
end;

procedure TForm1.btnGetColorClick(Sender: TObject);
begin
  Memo1.Color := FMemo.Get_Color;
end;

procedure TForm1.btnGetFontClick(Sender: TObject);
var
  FontDisp: IFontDisp;
begin
  FontDisp := FMemo.Get_Font;
  SetOleFont(Memo1.Font, FontDisp);
end;

procedure TForm1.btnGetTextClick(Sender: TObject);
var
  Strings: IStrings;
begin
  Strings := FMemo.Get_Text;
  SetOleStrings(Memo1.Lines, Strings);
end;

end.
```

Figure 4.11 shows the MemoCli application connected to MemoSrv.

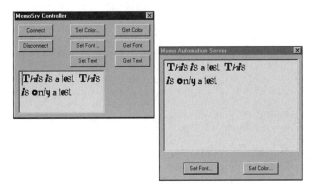

**Figure 4.11**    *MemoCli controls the MemoSrv Automation server.*

To recap this example, we performed the following steps to create an automation client:

- Create a new application.
- Import the automation server's type library.
- Add the import file to the client application's uses clause.
- Make method calls to the automation server.

At this point, we've covered the basics of automation. You now know how to create an Automation server, and how you can control that server using interfaces, dispinterfaces, and variants. In the next section, I'll discuss a more advanced feature of automation: COM events and callbacks.

# COM Events and Callbacks

Delphi programmers take events for granted in their everyday programming tasks. So far, I haven't shown you any automation controllers that fire events. Even though this is not really an advanced feature, you're going to have to do just a little bit of work in Delphi to support events. It certainly is less work than what you would expect to do in other languages, but nonetheless, Delphi does not make COM events completely seamless. (Of course, we can always look forward to future versions of Delphi!)

You can use either dispinterfaces or interfaces for implementing a mechanism in which the server calls back into the client application. Both have their advantages and disadvantages. Delphi provides better support for events through dispinterfaces, and you must use dispinterfaces if you intend for your code to be compatible with Visual Basic. Interfaces are slightly faster than dispinterfaces, but they are not compatible with Visual Basic, and you will have to write more code to support them. The following two sections discuss each method in detail.

Regardless of the method used, the end result is the same. The client application provides the server with an interface that the server uses to call the client back.

## Dispinterfaces

Delphi provides some automatic support for dispinterface events, so we'll take a look at creating a server and client that make use of dispinterface events first.

### Creating the Automation Server

For illustrative purposes, let's create an Automation server that lets multiple connected clients send text back and forth. In other words, a simple chat server.

Delphi can automatically handle the creation of Automation servers that support dispinterface-based events. Create a new application, and then run the Automation Object Wizard by selecting Automation Object from the Object Repository.

Figure 4.12 shows the Automation Object Wizard filled out to support event handling. Click OK to generate the source code for this object and display the Type Library Editor.

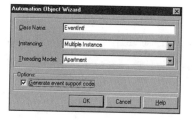

**Figure 4.12**    *Adding event handling to a dispinterface.*

You'll notice that this time, Delphi creates two interfaces: one for the COM object and one for the events that will be fired by the object.

Add a method to the IEventIntf interface named SendText. Give it a parameter named Text, of type WideString. Next, add an event to the IEventIntfEvents dispinterface named OnText. Add a WideString parameter named Text.

Click the Refresh Implementation button in the Type Library Editor and then close the Type Library Editor. Save the file as EventIntf.pas. At this point, the source code for the Automation server will look like the code in Listing 4.7.

**Listing 4.7**    *EventSrv Automation Server—EventIntf.pas*

```
unit EventIntf;

interface

uses
  ComObj, ActiveX, AxCtrls, Project1_TLB;

type
  TEventIntf = class(TAutoObject, IConnectionPointContainer, IEventIntf)
  private
    { Private declarations }
    FConnectionPoints: TConnectionPoints;
    FEvents: IEventIntfEvents;
  public
    procedure Initialize; override;
  protected
    { Protected declarations }
    property ConnectionPoints: TConnectionPoints read FConnectionPoints
      implements IConnectionPointContainer;
    procedure EventSinkChanged(const EventSink: IUnknown); override;
    procedure SendText(const Text: WideString); safecall;
  end;

implementation

uses ComServ;

procedure TEventIntf.EventSinkChanged(const EventSink: IUnknown);
begin
  FEvents := EventSink as IEventIntfEvents;
end;

procedure TEventIntf.Initialize;
begin
  inherited Initialize;
  FConnectionPoints := TConnectionPoints.Create(Self);
  if AutoFactory.EventTypeInfo <> nil then
    FConnectionPoints.CreateConnectionPoint(AutoFactory.EventIID,
      ckSingle, EventConnect);
end;

procedure TEventIntf.SendText(const Text: WideString);
begin

end;
```

```
initialization
  TAutoObjectFactory.Create(ComServer, TEventIntf, Class_EventIntf,
    ciMultiInstance, tmApartment);
end.
```

All we need to do is flesh out the SendText method, so add the following code to the unit:

```
procedure TEventIntf.SendText(const Text: WideString);
begin
  FEvents.OnText(Text);
end;
```

Compile this server, and register it by running it once.

The source code for the automatically generated EventSrv_TLB.pas file is shown in Listing 4.8.

**Listing 4.8**   *EventSrv Automation Server—EventSrv_TLB.pas*

```
unit EventSrv_TLB;

// ********************************************************************** //
// WARNING                                                              //
// -------                                                              //
// The types declared in this file were generated from data read from a //
// Type Library. If this type library is explicitly or indirectly (via  //
// another type library referring to this type library) re-imported, or the //
// 'Refresh' command of the Type Library Editor activated while editing the //
// Type Library, the contents of this file will be regenerated and all  //
// manual modifications will be lost.                                   //
// ********************************************************************** //

// PASTLWTR : $Revision:   1.11.1.75  $
// File generated on 7/31/99 2:22:22 PM from Type Library described below.

// ********************************************************************** //
// Type Lib: J:\Book\samples\Chap04\EventSrv\EventSrv.tlb
// IID\LCID: {34FB8111-476E-11D3-B83E-0040F67455FE}\0
// Helpfile:
// HelpString: Project1 Library
// Version:     1.0
// ********************************************************************** //

interface

uses Windows, ActiveX, Classes, Graphics, OleCtrls, StdVCL;

// ********************************************************************** //
// GUIDS declared in the TypeLibrary. Following prefixes are used:      //
//    Type Libraries     : LIBID_xxxx                                    //
//    CoClasses          : CLASS_xxxx                                    //
```

*continues* ▶

**Listing 4.8**   *continued*

```
//   DISPInterfaces    : DIID_xxxx                                         //
//   Non-DISP interfaces: IID_xxxx                                         //
// *********************************************************************//
const
  LIBID_EventSrv: TGUID = '{34FB8111-476E-11D3-B83E-0040F67455FE}';
  IID_IEventIntf: TGUID = '{34FB8112-476E-11D3-B83E-0040F67455FE}';
  DIID_IEventIntfEvents: TGUID = '{34FB8114-476E-11D3-B83E-0040F67455FE}';
  CLASS_EventIntf: TGUID = '{34FB8116-476E-11D3-B83E-0040F67455FE}';
type

// *********************************************************************//
// Forward declaration of interfaces defined in Type Library          //
// *********************************************************************//
  IEventIntf = interface;
  IEventIntfDisp = dispinterface;
  IEventIntfEvents = dispinterface;

// *********************************************************************//
// Declaration of CoClasses defined in Type Library                   //
// (NOTE: Here we map each CoClass to its Default Interface)           //
// *********************************************************************//
  EventIntf = IEventIntf;


// *********************************************************************//
// Interface: IEventIntf
// Flags:     (4416) Dual OleAutomation Dispatchable
// GUID:      {34FB8112-476E-11D3-B83E-0040F67455FE}
// *********************************************************************//
  IEventIntf = interface(IDispatch)
    ['{34FB8112-476E-11D3-B83E-0040F67455FE}']
    procedure SendText(const Text: WideString); safecall;
  end;

// *********************************************************************//
// DispIntf:  IEventIntfDisp
// Flags:     (4416) Dual OleAutomation Dispatchable
// GUID:      {34FB8112-476E-11D3-B83E-0040F67455FE}
// *********************************************************************//
  IEventIntfDisp = dispinterface
    ['{34FB8112-476E-11D3-B83E-0040F67455FE}']
    procedure SendText(const Text: WideString); dispid 1;
  end;

// *********************************************************************//
// DispIntf:  IEventIntfEvents
// Flags:     (0)
// GUID:      {34FB8114-476E-11D3-B83E-0040F67455FE}
// *********************************************************************//
  IEventIntfEvents = dispinterface
    ['{34FB8114-476E-11D3-B83E-0040F67455FE}']
```

```
  procedure OnText(const Text: WideString); dispid 3;
end;

CoEventIntf = class
  class function Create: IEventIntf;
  class function CreateRemote(const MachineName: string): IEventIntf;
end;

implementation

uses ComObj;

class function CoEventIntf.Create: IEventIntf;
begin
  Result := CreateComObject(CLASS_EventIntf) as IEventIntf;
end;

class function CoEventIntf.CreateRemote(const MachineName: string): IEventIntf;
begin
  Result := CreateRemoteComObject(MachineName, CLASS_EventIntf) as IEventIntf;
end;

end.
```

## Creating the Client Application with Delphi 3 or Delphi 4

Whereas Delphi takes care of all the dirty work on the server side for us, we need to put a little bit of effort into the client side of the equation.

> ### Note
>
> *Delphi 5 introduced new support for COM event handling that renders this section obsolete. I'm including this section for the benefit of readers using Delphi versions 3 and 4. If you're using Delphi 5, you can skip ahead to the section titled "Creating the Client Application with Delphi 5."* ◆

### The TEventSink Component

> ### Note
>
> *This isn't a book about writing Delphi components, but the functionality required for receiving events from a COM server is fairly boilerplate. For that reason, I have written a component named TEventSink. I'm not going to explain the steps of writing a component in this book. If you do not understand component development, you can check out any of the fine books listed in Appendix A, "Suggested Readings and Resources," of this book. Of course, you do not need to understand component development in order to use an existing component in your applications.* ◆

A short discussion of terminology would be useful here. An *event sink* implements an interface's events. An *event source* is responsible for calling the events defined by the interface. For the application we're currently writing, the server is the event source, and the client is the event sink. The server will call the events defined by the interface, and the events will be executed in the context of the client.

The code for the TEventSink component looks lengthy, but most of the methods are simply stubs for functionality that we do not need to implement. The important methods are QueryInterface, Invoke, Connect, and Disconnect.

QueryInterface first checks to see whether the caller is requesting an interface that we implement, which from the declaration of TAbstractEventSink we can see includes IUnknown and IDispatch. If the requested interface is not one of those two interfaces, then the code checks to see if the caller is requesting the events interface (FDispIntfIID). If that's the case, the IDispatch interface is returned.

```
function TAbstractEventSink.QueryInterface(const IID: TGUID; out Obj): HRESULT;
begin
  // We need to return the event interface when it's asked for
  Result := E_NOINTERFACE;
  if GetInterface(IID, Obj) then
    Result := S_OK;
  if IsEqualGUID(IID, FDispIntfIID) and GetInterface(IDispatch, Obj) then
    Result := S_OK;
end;
```

The Invoke method simply passes its parameters to the containing TEventSink component. The owner of the TEventSink component can respond to the event in any desirable fashion.

```
function TAbstractEventSink.Invoke(DispID: Integer; const IID: TGUID;
  LocaleID: Integer; Flags: Word; var Params; VarResult, ExcepInfo,
  ArgErr: Pointer): HRESULT;
begin
  (FOwner as TEventSink).DoInvoke(DispID, IID, LocaleID, Flags,
    Params, VarResult, ExcepInfo, ArgErr);

  Result := S_OK;
end;
```

The Connect and Disconnect methods simply take care of connecting and disconnecting the event sink to and from the server. They perform this magic by calling the predefined Delphi methods InterfaceConnect and InterfaceDisconnect.

The source code for the TEventSink component is shown in Listing 4.9.

## Listing 4.9    *EventSink Component*

```
unit EventSink;

interface

uses
  Windows, Messages, SysUtils, Classes, Graphics, Controls, Forms, Dialogs,
  ActiveX;

type
  TInvokeEvent = procedure(Sender: TObject; DispID: Integer;
    const IID: TGUID; LocaleID: Integer; Flags: Word;
    Params: TDispParams; VarResult, ExcepInfo, ArgErr: Pointer) of object;

  TAbstractEventSink = class(TInterfacedObject, IUnknown, IDispatch)
  private
    FDispatch: IDispatch;
    FDispIntfIID: TGUID;
    FConnection: Integer;
    FOwner: TComponent;
  protected
    { IUnknown }
    function QueryInterface(const IID: TGUID; out Obj): HRESULT; stdcall;
    function _AddRef: Integer; stdcall;
    function _Release: Integer; stdcall;
    { IDispatch }
    function GetTypeInfoCount(out Count: Integer): HRESULT; stdcall;
    function GetTypeInfo(Index, LocaleID: Integer; out TypeInfo): HRESULT; stdcall;
    function GetIDsOfNames(const IID: TGUID; Names: Pointer;
      NameCount, LocaleID: Integer; DispIDs: Pointer): HRESULT; stdcall;
    function Invoke(DispID: Integer; const IID: TGUID; LocaleID: Integer;
      Flags: Word; var Params; VarResult, ExcepInfo, ArgErr: Pointer): HRESULT; stdcall;
  public
    constructor Create(AOwner: TComponent);
    destructor Destroy; override;
    procedure Connect(AnAppDispatch: IDispatch; const AnAppDispIntfIID: TGUID);
    procedure Disconnect;
  end;

  TEventSink = class(TComponent)
  private
    { Private declarations }
    FSink: TAbstractEventSink;
    FOnInvoke: TInvokeEvent;
  protected
    { Protected declarations }
    procedure DoInvoke(DispID: Integer; const IID: TGUID;
      LocaleID: Integer; Flags: Word; var Params;
      VarResult, ExcepInfo, ArgErr: Pointer); virtual;
  public
    { Public declarations }
    constructor Create(AOwner: TComponent); override;
    destructor Destroy; override;
```

*continues* ▶

**Listing 4.9** *continued*

```
    procedure Connect(AnAppDispatch: IDispatch; const AnAppDispIntfIID: TGUID);
  published
    { Published declarations }
    property OnInvoke: TInvokeEvent read FOnInvoke write FOnInvoke;
  end;

procedure Register;

implementation

uses
  ComObj;

procedure Register;
begin
  RegisterComponents('DCP', [TEventSink]);
end;

{$IFDEF VER100}
procedure InterfaceConnect(const Source: IUnknown; const IID: TIID;
  const Sink: IUnknown; var Connection: Longint);
var
  CPC: IConnectionPointContainer;
  CP: IConnectionPoint;
begin
  Connection := 0;
  if Succeeded(Source.QueryInterface(IConnectionPointContainer, CPC)) then
    if Succeeded(CPC.FindConnectionPoint(IID, CP)) then
      CP.Advise(Sink, Connection);
end;

procedure InterfaceDisconnect(const Source: IUnknown; const IID: TIID;
  var Connection: Longint);
var
  CPC: IConnectionPointContainer;
  CP: IConnectionPoint;
begin
  if Connection <> 0 then
    if Succeeded(Source.QueryInterface(IConnectionPointContainer, CPC)) then
      if Succeeded(CPC.FindConnectionPoint(IID, CP)) then
        if Succeeded(CP.Unadvise(Connection)) then Connection := 0;
end;
{$ENDIF}

{ TAbstractEventSink }

function TAbstractEventSink._AddRef: Integer;
begin
  Result := -1;
end;

function TAbstractEventSink._Release: Integer;
begin
```

```
    Result := -1;
end;

constructor TAbstractEventSink.Create(AOwner: TComponent);
begin
  inherited Create;

  FOwner := AOwner;
end;

destructor TAbstractEventSink.Destroy;
begin
  Disconnect;

  inherited Destroy;
end;

function TAbstractEventSink.GetIDsOfNames(const IID: TGUID; Names: Pointer;
  NameCount, LocaleID: Integer; DispIDs: Pointer): HRESULT;
begin
  Result := E_NOTIMPL;
end;

function TAbstractEventSink.GetTypeInfo(Index, LocaleID: Integer;
  out TypeInfo): HRESULT;
begin
  Result := E_NOTIMPL;
end;

function TAbstractEventSink.GetTypeInfoCount(out Count: Integer): HRESULT;
begin
  Count := 0;
  Result := S_OK;
end;

function TAbstractEventSink.Invoke(DispID: Integer; const IID: TGUID;
  LocaleID: Integer; Flags: Word; var Params; VarResult, ExcepInfo,
  ArgErr: Pointer): HRESULT;
begin
  (FOwner as TEventSink).DoInvoke(DispID, IID, LocaleID, Flags,
    Params, VarResult, ExcepInfo, ArgErr);

  Result := S_OK;
end;

function TAbstractEventSink.QueryInterface(const IID: TGUID; out Obj): HRESULT;
begin
  // We need to return the event interface when it's asked for
  Result := E_NOINTERFACE;
  if GetInterface(IID,Obj) then
    Result := S_OK;
  if IsEqualGUID(IID, FDispIntfIID) and GetInterface(IDispatch,Obj) then
    Result := S_OK;
end;
```

*continues* ▶

**Listing 4.9**    *continued*

```
procedure TAbstractEventSink.Connect(AnAppDispatch: IDispatch;
  const AnAppDispIntfIID: TGUID);
begin
  FDispIntfIID := AnAppDispIntfIID;
  FDispatch := AnAppDispatch;

  // Hook the sink up to the automation server
  InterfaceConnect(FDispatch, FDispIntfIID, Self, FConnection);
end;

procedure TAbstractEventSink.Disconnect;
begin
  if Assigned(FDispatch) then begin
    // Unhook the sink from the automation server
    InterfaceDisconnect(FDispatch, FDispIntfIID, FConnection);
    FDispatch := nil;
    FConnection := 0;
  end;
end;

{ TEventSink }

procedure TEventSink.Connect(AnAppDispatch: IDispatch;
  const AnAppDispIntfIID: TGUID);
begin
  FSink.Connect(AnAppDispatch, AnAppDispIntfIID);
end;

constructor TEventSink.Create(AOwner: TComponent);
begin
  inherited Create(AOwner);

  FSink := TAbstractEventSink.Create(self);
end;

destructor TEventSink.Destroy;
begin
  FSink.Free;

  inherited Destroy;
end;

procedure TEventSink.DoInvoke(DispID: Integer; const IID: TGUID;
  LocaleID: Integer; Flags: Word; var Params; VarResult, ExcepInfo,
  ArgErr: Pointer);
begin
  if Assigned(FOnInvoke) then
    FOnInvoke(self, DispID, IID, LocaleID, Flags, TDispParams(Params),
      VarResult, ExcepInfo, ArgErr);
end;

end.
```

*The Client Application*
With the TEventSink component behind us, the client program is fairly simple to write, and is shown in Listing 4.10.

**Listing 4.10**    *EventCli—MainForm.pas*

```
unit MainForm;

interface

uses
  Windows, Messages, SysUtils, Classes, Graphics, Controls, Forms, Dialogs,
  StdCtrls, EventSrv_TLB, ActiveX, ComObj, EventSink, ExtCtrls;

type
  TForm1 = class(TForm)
    EventSink1: TEventSink;
    Panel1: TPanel;
    Panel2: TPanel;
    btnSend: TButton;
    Memo1: TMemo;
    Edit1: TEdit;
    procedure FormCreate(Sender: TObject);
    procedure btnSendClick(Sender: TObject);
    procedure EventSink1Invoke(Sender: TObject; DispID: Integer;
      const IID: TGUID; LocaleID: Integer; Flags: Word;
      Params: tagDISPPARAMS; VarResult, ExcepInfo, ArgErr: Pointer);
  private
    { Private declarations }
    F: IEventIntf;
  public
    { Public declarations }
  end;

var
  Form1: TForm1;

implementation

{$R *.DFM}

procedure TForm1.FormCreate(Sender: TObject);
begin
  F := CoEventIntf.Create;
  EventSink1.Connect(F, IEventIntfEvents);
end;

procedure TForm1.btnSendClick(Sender: TObject);
begin
  F.SendText(Edit1.Text);
end;
```

*continues* ▶

**Listing 4.10**    *continued*

```
procedure TForm1.EventSink1Invoke(Sender: TObject; DispID: Integer;
  const IID: TGUID; LocaleID: Integer; Flags: Word; Params: tagDISPPARAMS;
  VarResult, ExcepInfo, ArgErr: Pointer);
var
  vText: OleVariant;
begin
  case DispID of
    1: begin
      vText := OleVariant(Params.rgvarg^[0]);
      Memo1.Lines.Add(vText);
    end;
  end;
end;

end.
```

The biggest headache with this method is that you have to decipher the parameters for yourself in EventSink1Invoke. The EventSink1Invoke method shown in Listing 4.10 shows how to do that.

```
procedure TForm1.EventSink1Invoke(Sender: TObject; DispID: Integer;
  const IID: TGUID; LocaleID: Integer; Flags: Word; Params: tagDISPPARAMS;
  VarResult, ExcepInfo, ArgErr: Pointer);
var
  vText: OleVariant;
begin
  case DispID of
    1: begin
      vText := OleVariant(Params.rgvarg^[0]);
      Memo1.Lines.Add(vText);
    end;
  end;
end;
```

Notice that this code knows the number and types of arguments pertaining to each DispID. Argument numbers start at zero, and dispid 1 (OnText) takes a single argument of type WideString. It is possible to write code that detects the number and types of arguments at runtime, but that is beyond the scope of this book.

### Creating the Client Application with Delphi 5

With the introduction of Delphi 5, creating the client application is even easier than creating the server. Create a new application in Delphi, and then select Project, Import Type Library from the Delphi main menu. The Import Type Library dialog box appears, as shown in Figure 4.13.

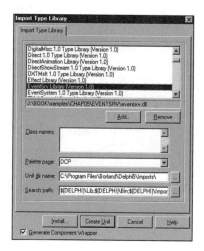

**Figure 4.13**   *Delphi 5 can automatically generate a
component wrapper for the COM server.*

Notice that Delphi 5's Import Type Library dialog box features an additional checkbox titled Generate Component Wrapper. Select EventSrv Library (Version 1.0) in the list box, and select DCP in the Palette page combo. If you prefer, you can install the component onto another page, such as ActiveX. Make sure you check the Generate Component Wrapper checkbox, and then click the Install...button.

Delphi will ask you what package to install the component into. You can accept the default and click OK. (Re)build the package when prompted to do so. If all goes well, Delphi will inform you that it has successfully installed the component onto the palette.

Create a new application, and drop a TEventIntf component onto the main form from the DCP page (or wherever you elected to install the component). TEventIntf publishes three properties that are of interest to us.

AutoConnect determines whether the application attempts to connect to the server automatically at startup. If AutoConnect is set to False, you must call EventIntf1.Connect to connect to the server. Set this property to True for this example.

ConnectKind tells the component how to connect to the server. Valid values for the ConnectKind property are shown in Table 4.1.

*Table 4.1    Valid Values for ConnectKind*

| Connection Option | Description |
|---|---|
| ckAttachToInterface | This is an advanced option, which will not be discussed in this book. |
| ckNewInstance | The client always creates and connects to a new instance of the server. |
| ckRemote | The server is running on a remote machine. This option is discussed in Chapter 6. |
| ckRunningInstance | The client only connects to a currently running instance of the server. |
| ckRunningOrNew | The client attempts to connect to a currently running instance of the server. If the server is not running, the client starts a new instance of the server. |

For this example, set this property to ckRunningOrNew.

The RemoteMachineName property only comes into play when connecting to a remote server. We'll explore this property in Chapter 6.

The TEventIntf component also publishes a single event named OnText. This corresponds to the event of the same name that we added to the IEventIntfEvents dispinterface.

The source code for the client application is shown in Listing 4.11.

**Listing 4.11**    *EventCli5—MainForm.pas*

```
unit MainForm;

interface

uses
  Windows, Messages, SysUtils, Classes, Graphics, Controls, Forms, Dialogs,
  OleServer, EventSrv_TLB, StdCtrls, ExtCtrls;

type
  TForm1 = class(TForm)
    EventIntf1: TEventIntf;
    Panel1: TPanel;
    Panel2: TPanel;
    Memo1: TMemo;
    Edit1: TEdit;
    Button1: TButton;
    procedure Button1Click(Sender: TObject);
    procedure EventIntf1Text(Sender: TObject; var Text: OleVariant);
  private
    { Private declarations }
  public
    { Public declarations }
  end;
```

```
var
  Form1: TForm1;

implementation

{$R *.DFM}

procedure TForm1.Button1Click(Sender: TObject);
begin
  EventIntf1.SendText(Edit1.Text);
end;

procedure TForm1.EventIntf1Text(Sender: TObject; var Text: OleVariant);
begin
  Memo1.Lines.Add(Text);
end;

end.
```

## Running the Client Application

Regardless of whether you used Delphi 3, 4, or 5 to create the client application, when you run it, it will look like Figure 4.14.

**Figure 4.14**    *The EventCli/EventCli5 applications allow you to send lines of text to other connected clients.*

## Connecting Multiple Clients to the Server

There is one small problem with the server code as it stands. Although a single server will be started to service all clients, the server will only fire events to the first connected client. For this application, that is not what we want.

You'll need to make minor modifications to both the server and the client to fix this problem. Fortunately, the changes to both sides are minimal.

> **Note**
>
> *If you're using Delphi 5, you can skip the changes to the client program. The TEventIntf component created automatically by Delphi 5 already takes care of this for you.*♦

First, modify the server's Initialize method to look as follows:

```
procedure TEventIntf.Initialize;
begin
  inherited Initialize;
  FConnectionPoints := TConnectionPoints.Create(Self);
  if AutoFactory.EventTypeInfo <> nil then
    FConnectionPoints.CreateConnectionPoint(AutoFactory.EventIID,
      ckMulti, EventConnect);
end;
```

Notice that I changed the next-to-last parameter of the CreateConnectionPoint call from ckSingle to ckMulti. This is all you must do to make the server remember multiple client connections.

Now that the server tracks multiple connections, we need some way to iterate through all active connections to the server. The IConnectionPointContainer interface provides us with an enumerator that can be used to iterate through the connections. The following method can be used to obtain an enumerator on the connection:

```
function TEventIntf.GetEnumerator: IEnumConnections;
var
  Container: IConnectionPointContainer;
  ConnectionPoint: IConnectionPoint;
begin
  OleCheck(QueryInterface(IConnectionPointContainer, Container));
  OleCheck(Container.FindConnectionPoint(AutoFactory.EventIID, ConnectionPoint));
  ConnectionPoint.EnumConnections(Result);
end;
```

After you have an enumerator for the connection, you simply need to iterate through the connections, firing the event on each one. The following code shows how to modify the Trigger event to support multiple connections:

```
procedure TEventIntf.SendText(const Text: WideString);
var
  Enum: IEnumConnections;
  ConnectData: TConnectData;
  Fetched: Cardinal;
begin
  Enum := GetEnumerator;
  if Enum <> nil then begin
    while Enum.Next(1, ConnectData, @Fetched) = S_OK do
      if ConnectData.pUnk <> nil then
        (ConnectData.pUnk as IEventIntfEvents).OnText(Text);
  end;
end;
```

The final code change you need to make to the server is to register the server in Windows' running object table. To do this, simply add the following line of code to the end of the Initialize function:

```
RegisterActiveObject(self as IUnknown, CLASS_EventIntf, ACTIVEOBJECT_WEAK, FObjectID);
```

To remove the server from the running object table, create a Destroy method and add the following line of code to it:

```
RevokeActiveObject(FObjectID, nil);
```

Listing 4.12 shows the source code for the modified server.

---

**Listing 4.12**    *EventMultSrv—EventIntf.pas*

```
unit EventIntf;

interface

uses
  ComObj, ActiveX, AxCtrls, EventSrv_TLB;

type
  TEventIntf = class(TAutoObject, IConnectionPointContainer, IEventIntf)
  private
    { Private declarations }
    FConnectionPoints: TConnectionPoints;
    FEvents: IEventIntfEvents;
    FObjectID: Integer;
  public
    procedure Initialize; override;
    destructor Destroy; override;
  protected
    { Protected declarations }
    property ConnectionPoints: TConnectionPoints read FConnectionPoints
      implements IConnectionPointContainer;
    procedure EventSinkChanged(const EventSink: IUnknown); override;
    procedure SendText(const Text: WideString); safecall;
    function GetEnumerator: IEnumConnections;
  end;

implementation

uses Windows, ComServ;

procedure TEventIntf.EventSinkChanged(const EventSink: IUnknown);
begin
  FEvents := EventSink as IEventIntfEvents;
end;

procedure TEventIntf.Initialize;
begin
  inherited Initialize;
```

*continues* ▶

**Listing 4.12**   *continued*

```
  FConnectionPoints := TConnectionPoints.Create(Self);
  if AutoFactory.EventTypeInfo <> nil then
    FConnectionPoints.CreateConnectionPoint(AutoFactory.EventIID,
      ckMulti, EventConnect);

  RegisterActiveObject(self as IUnknown, CLASS_EventIntf,
    ACTIVEOBJECT_WEAK, FObjectID);
end;

procedure TEventIntf.SendText(const Text: WideString);
var
  Enum: IEnumConnections;
  ConnectData: TConnectData;
  Fetched: Cardinal;
begin
  Enum := GetEnumerator;
  if Enum <> nil then begin
    while Enum.Next(1, ConnectData, @Fetched) = S_OK do
      if ConnectData.pUnk <> nil then
        (ConnectData.pUnk as IEventIntfEvents).OnText(Text);
  end;
end;

function TEventIntf.GetEnumerator: IEnumConnections;
var
  Container: IConnectionPointContainer;
  ConnectionPoint: IConnectionPoint;
begin
  OleCheck(QueryInterface(IConnectionPointContainer, Container));
  OleCheck(Container.FindConnectionPoint(AutoFactory.EventIID, ConnectionPoint));
  ConnectionPoint.EnumConnections(Result);
end;

destructor TEventIntf.Destroy;
begin
  RevokeActiveObject(FObjectID, nil);

  inherited Destroy;
end;

initialization
  TAutoObjectFactory.Create(ComServer, TEventIntf, Class_EventIntf,
    ciMultiInstance, tmApartment);
end.
```

On the client side, you need to modify the FormCreate method as follows:

```
procedure TForm1.FormCreate(Sender: TObject);
var
  Obj: IUnknown;
begin
  GetActiveObject(CLASS_EventIntf, nil, Obj);
```

```
if Obj <> nil then
  F := Obj as IEventIntf
else
  F := CoEventIntf.Create;

EventSink1.Connect(F, IEventIntfEvents);
end;
```

GetActiveObject looks for a running instance of the EventMultSrv Automation server. If it finds one, that instance is used. If there is no active instance of the server, CoEventIntf.Create starts a new one running.

Figure 4.15 shows two clients simultaneously accessing the chat server.

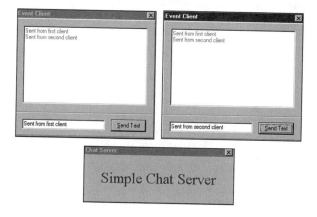

**Figure 4.15**    *The server can send events to multiple connected clients.*

## Callback Interfaces

The next method I will show you requires you to do a considerable amount of work on the server side, but not much work on the client side.

Rather than use dispinterfaces to send events back to the client application, you can create an interface in which you define callback methods. The callback interface is defined in the server, but implemented in the client.

In this section, we'll create a test client and server that illustrate the process of using a custom interface to call back from the server to the client.

### Creating the Server

To create the server application, you'll create a new project and add an automation object to it, as you've done before. Select File, New Application from the Delphi main menu. Then select File, New... to display the Object Repository. On the ActiveX page, select Automation Object and click OK. The Automation Object Wizard is displayed.

Fill out the Automation Object Wizard to look like Figure 4.16.

**Figure 4.16**    *The completed Automation Object Wizard.*

The Type Library Editor is displayed. The first thing you need to do is create an interface that you'll use to call back into the client. Use the Type Library Editor to add a new interface named IIntfCallbackEvents. Then add a single method to the interface named OnText. OnText is defined in the following code snippet:

```
procedure OnText(Text: WideString); safecall;
```

You should be familiar enough with the Type Library Editor by now that you can add this method on your own.

Now add three methods to the IIntfCallback interface, named Connect, Disconnect, and SendText. Their declarations are shown in the following code:

```
function Connect(const Callback: ITestEvents): Integer;
function Disconnect(UserID: Integer): Boolean;
procedure SendText(Text: WideString);
```

Those are the only methods we'll define for this example. Click the Refresh Implementation button in the Type Library Editor, and then close the Type Library Editor.

**Note**

*It should be apparent that I'm creating the same basic chat server as I did in the last section, although I am using a callback interface instead of COM events.* ◆

The IIntfCallbackEvents interface will be implemented in the client application, so I will not discuss how to implement OnText at this point. Rather, we'll concentrate on the three IIntfCallback methods Connect, Disconnect, and SendText.

*Initializing the Server*

When the server is requested by a client, the server's Initialize method is called. TIntfCallback.Initialize is coded as follows:

```
procedure TIntfCallback.Initialize;
begin
  inherited Initialize;

  // Add one to the global number of connections
  Inc(NumConnections);

  // Update the form to show # of connections
  if NumConnections = 1 then
    Form1.Label2.Caption := '(1 active connection)'
  else
    Form1.Label2.Caption := '(' + IntToStr(NumConnections) + ' active connections)';
end;
```

First, of course, we call the inherited Initialize procedure. After that, we increment the number of connections to the server. NumConnections is a global variable. It needs to be global because Initialize will be called when a client connects to the server. We want to keep track, in a centralized location, of the number of current connections to the server.

After the number of connections has been updated, the main form is updated to reflect the current number of connections.

*Handling Client Connections*

The client application will call the server's Connect method to establish a connection between the client and server.

**Note**

*There's nothing magical about the name Connect. I could have just as easily named it RegisterClient or something else that made sense.* ◆

You'll typically want to allow multiple clients to connect to the server, so the Connect method adds the connecting client to an internal list of clients. In order to achieve this, I've created two helper classes named TConn and TConns. Refer to Listing 4.13 for the implementation of these classes.

TConn represents a single client connection. Each client must provide an implementation of the IIntfCallbackEvents interface for the server to use when calling the client. Also, each client is assigned a unique ID that is used to identify the client.

TConns contains a list of TConn objects, and also remembers the unique ID assigned to the most recently connected client. When the next client connects to the server, the unique ID is incremented, and so on.

You might notice that TConns contains three methods named Connect, Disconnect, and SendText. TIntfCallback (which implements the IIntfCallback interface) simply passes control to the TConns method with the same name.

### Calling from the Server to the Clients

It's a simple matter to make calls from the server to all connected clients. The TConns list contains a list of all connected clients, along with a reference to their IIntfCallbackEvents interface, so you can simply walk the list of clients, calling a method of the IIntfCallbackEvents interface for each client. The following code shows how this is done:

```
procedure TConns.SendText(Text: WideString);
var
  Index: Integer;
  C: TConn;
begin
  for Index := 0 to FConns.Count - 1 do begin
    C := TConn(FConns[Index]);
    C.FCallback.OnText(Text);
  end;
end;
```

This simple procedure calls the OnText method on the IIntfCallbackEvents interface of all connected clients.

### The Completed Server Application

I've discussed the most important sections of code in the server application. Listing 4.13 shows the complete source code for IntfUnit.pas.

**Listing 4.13**    *IntfSrv Automation Server—IntfUnit.pas*

```
unit IntfUnit;

interface

uses
  Windows, classes, sysutils, ComObj, ActiveX, IntfSrv_TLB;

type
  // Class to handle a single connection
  TConn = class
  public
    FUserID: Integer;
    FCallback: IIntfCallbackEvents;
    destructor Destroy; override;
```

```
      end;

      // Class to handle the list of current connections
      TConns = class
      private
        FConns: TList;
        FLastUserID: Integer;
      public
        constructor Create;
        destructor Destroy; override;
        function Connect(const Callback: IIntfCallbackEvents): Integer;
        function Disconnect(UserID: Integer): Boolean;
        procedure SendText(Text: WideString);
      end;

      // COM Object that the client actually "talks" to
      TIntfCallback = class(TAutoObject, IIntfCallback)
      protected
        function Connect(const Callback: IIntfCallbackEvents): Integer; safecall;
        function Disconnect(UserID: Integer): WordBool; safecall;
        procedure SendText(const Text: WideString); safecall;
      public
        procedure Initialize; override;
        destructor Destroy; override;
        function Connections: TConns;
      end;

// These two variables are global so there will only be a single
// instance in the server app.
const
  NumConnections: Integer = 0;

var
  GlobalConnections: TConns;

implementation

uses ComServ, MainForm;

{ TIntfCallback }

procedure TIntfCallback.SendText(const Text: WideString);
begin
  // Pass the text on to the list of connections
  Connections.SendText(Text);
end;

function TIntfCallback.Connect(const Callback: IIntfCallbackEvents): Integer;
// Tell the list of connections to add a new connection
begin
  Result := Connections.Connect(Callback);
end;
```

*continues* ▶

**Listing 4.13**    *continued*

```
destructor TIntfCallback.Destroy;
begin
  // Decrement the number of connections
  Dec(NumConnections);

  // If there are no connections left, dispose of the connection list
  // This isn't required - you could hang on to the empty list.
  if NumConnections = 0 then begin
    GlobalConnections.Free;
    GlobalConnections := nil;
  end;

  // Update the main form to show # of current connections
  if NumConnections = 1 then
    Form1.Label2.Caption := '(1 active connection)'
  else
    Form1.Label2.Caption := '(' + IntToStr(NumConnections) + ' active connections)';

  inherited Destroy;
end;

// Initialize of a member of TAutoObject.  We override it here.
// It functions much like a constructor.  Use this function instead
// of a constructor.
procedure TIntfCallback.Initialize;
begin
  inherited Initialize;

  // Add one to the global number of connections
  Inc(NumConnections);

  // Update the form to show # of connections
  if NumConnections = 1 then
    Form1.Label2.Caption := '(1 active connection)'
  else
    Form1.Label2.Caption := '(' + IntToStr(NumConnections) + ' active connections)';
end;

function TIntfCallback.Disconnect(UserID: Integer): WordBool;
begin
  // Handle a disconnect request from the client
  Result := Connections.Disconnect(UserID);
end;

function TIntfCallback.Connections: TConns;
begin
  // Connections function returns a global connection list
  if GlobalConnections = nil then
    GlobalConnections := TConns.Create;

  Result := GlobalConnections;
end;
```

```
{ TConn }

destructor TConn.Destroy;
begin
  // Explicitly free the event interface
  FCallback := nil;

  inherited Destroy;
end;

{ TConns }

function TConns.Connect(const Callback: IIntfCallbackEvents): Integer;
var
  C: TConn;
begin
  // Assign each connection a unique user ID
  Inc(FLastUserID);

  // Create a new connection
  C := TConn.Create;

  // Remember the event interface
  C.FCallback := Callback;

  // Set the user ID
  C.FUserID := FLastUserID;

  // Add the user to the list
  FConns.Add(C);

  // Return the assigned user ID
  Result := FLastUserID;
end;

constructor TConns.Create;
begin
  FLastUserID := 0;
  FConns := TList.Create;
end;

destructor TConns.Destroy;
var
  Index: Integer;
  C: TConn;
begin
  for Index := 0 to FConns.Count - 1 do begin
    C := TConn(FConns[Index]);
    C.Free;
  end;
  FConns.Free;
end;
```

*continues* ▶

**Listing 4.13**   *continued*

```
function TConns.Disconnect(UserID: Integer): Boolean;
var
  Index: Integer;
  C: TConn;
begin
  Result := False;

  for Index := 0 to FConns.Count - 1 do begin
    C := TConn(FConns[Index]);
    if C.FUserID = UserID then begin
      C.Free;
      FConns.Delete(Index);
      Result := True;
      exit;
    end;
  end;
end;

procedure TConns.SendText(Text: WideString);
var
  Index: Integer;
  C: TConn;
begin
  for Index := 0 to FConns.Count - 1 do begin
    C := TConn(FConns[Index]);
    C.FCallback.OnText(Text);
  end;
end;

initialization
  // Change this to ciSingleInstance, and each copy of the client
  // will start its own copy of the server.
  TAutoObjectFactory.Create(ComServer, TIntfCallback, Class_IntfCallback,
    ciMultiInstance, tmApartment);
end.
```

Listing 4.14 shows the source code for the server's main form. Figure 4.17 shows the server at runtime.

**Figure 4.17**   *The IntfSrv application at runtime.*

**Listing 4.14**    *IntfSrv Automation Server—MainForm.pas*

```
unit MainForm;

interface

uses
  Windows, Messages, SysUtils, Classes, Graphics, Controls, Forms, Dialogs,
  StdCtrls, IntfUnit;

type
  TForm1 = class(TForm)
    Label1: TLabel;
    Label2: TLabel;
  private
    { Private declarations }
  public
    { Public declarations }
  end;

var
  Form1: TForm1;

implementation

{$R *.DFM}

end.
```

Listing 4.15 shows the Delphi-generated type library for the server.

**Listing 4.15**    *IntfSrv Automation Server—IntfSrv_TLB.pas*

```
unit IntfSrv_TLB;

// **************************************************************************** //
// WARNING                                                                      //
// -------                                                                      //
// The types declared in this file were generated from data read from a         //
// Type Library. If this type library is explicitly or indirectly (via          //
// another type library referring to this type library) re-imported, or the //
// 'Refresh' command of the Type Library Editor activated while editing the //
// Type Library, the contents of this file will be regenerated and all          //
// manual modifications will be lost.                                           //
// **************************************************************************** //

// PASTLWTR : $Revision:  1.11.1.75  $
// File generated on 7/31/99 2:59:14 PM from Type Library described below.

// **************************************************************************** //
```

*continues* ▶

## Listing 4.15    *continued*

```
// Type Lib: J:\Book\samples\Chap04\IntfSrv\IntfSrv.tlb
// IID\LCID: {E9D7678E-F7E3-11D2-909B-0040F6741DE2}\0
// Helpfile:
// HelpString: IntfSrv Library
// Version:    1.0
// ******************************************************************* //

interface

uses Windows, ActiveX, Classes, Graphics, OleCtrls, StdVCL;

// *****************************************************************//
// GUIDS declared in the TypeLibrary. Following prefixes are used:  //
//   Type Libraries    : LIBID_xxxx                                //
//   CoClasses         : CLASS_xxxx                                //
//   DISPInterfaces    : DIID_xxxx                                 //
//   Non-DISP interfaces: IID_xxxx                                 //
// *****************************************************************//
const
  LIBID_IntfSrv: TGUID = '{E9D7678E-F7E3-11D2-909B-0040F6741DE2}';
  IID_IIntfCallback: TGUID = '{E9D7678F-F7E3-11D2-909B-0040F6741DE2}';
  CLASS_IntfCallback: TGUID = '{E9D76791-F7E3-11D2-909B-0040F6741DE2}';
  IID_IIntfCallbackEvents: TGUID = '{E9D76793-F7E3-11D2-909B-0040F6741DE2}';
type

// *****************************************************************//
// Forward declaration of interfaces defined in Type Library      //
// *****************************************************************//
  IIntfCallback = interface;
  IIntfCallbackDisp = dispinterface;
  IIntfCallbackEvents = interface;
  IIntfCallbackEventsDisp = dispinterface;

// *****************************************************************//
// Declaration of CoClasses defined in Type Library               //
// (NOTE: Here we map each CoClass to its Default Interface)       //
// *****************************************************************//
  IntfCallback = IIntfCallback;


// *****************************************************************//
// Interface: IIntfCallback
// Flags:     (4416) Dual OleAutomation Dispatchable
// GUID:      {E9D7678F-F7E3-11D2-909B-0040F6741DE2}
// *****************************************************************//
  IIntfCallback = interface(IDispatch)
    ['{E9D7678F-F7E3-11D2-909B-0040F6741DE2}']
    procedure SendText(const Text: WideString); safecall;
    function Connect(const Callback: IIntfCallbackEvents): Integer; safecall;
    function Disconnect(UserID: Integer): WordBool; safecall;
  end;
```

```
// ***********************************************************************//
// DispIntf:  IIntfCallbackDisp
// Flags:     (4416) Dual OleAutomation Dispatchable
// GUID:      {E9D7678F-F7E3-11D2-909B-0040F6741DE2}
// ***********************************************************************//
  IIntfCallbackDisp = dispinterface
    ['{E9D7678F-F7E3-11D2-909B-0040F6741DE2}']
    procedure SendText(const Text: WideString); dispid 1;
    function Connect(const Callback: IIntfCallbackEvents): Integer; dispid 2;
    function Disconnect(UserID: Integer): WordBool; dispid 3;
  end;

// ***********************************************************************//
// Interface: IIntfCallbackEvents
// Flags:     (4416) Dual OleAutomation Dispatchable
// GUID:      {E9D76793-F7E3-11D2-909B-0040F6741DE2}
// ***********************************************************************//
  IIntfCallbackEvents = interface(IDispatch)
    ['{E9D76793-F7E3-11D2-909B-0040F6741DE2}']
    procedure OnText(const Text: WideString); safecall;
  end;

// ***********************************************************************//
// DispIntf:  IIntfCallbackEventsDisp
// Flags:     (4416) Dual OleAutomation Dispatchable
// GUID:      {E9D76793-F7E3-11D2-909B-0040F6741DE2}
// ***********************************************************************//
  IIntfCallbackEventsDisp = dispinterface
    ['{E9D76793-F7E3-11D2-909B-0040F6741DE2}']
    procedure OnText(const Text: WideString); dispid 1;
  end;

  CoIntfCallback = class
    class function Create: IIntfCallback;
    class function CreateRemote(const MachineName: string): IIntfCallback;
  end;

implementation

uses ComObj;

class function CoIntfCallback.Create: IIntfCallback;
begin
  Result := CreateComObject(CLASS_IntfCallback) as IIntfCallback;
end;

class function CoIntfCallback.CreateRemote(const MachineName: string): IIntfCallback;
begin
  Result := CreateRemoteComObject(MachineName, CLASS_IntfCallback) as IIntfCallback;
end;

end.
```

**Creating the Client**
After the server is complete, it's a straightforward task to create the client application that will connect to the server.

Start a new application in Delphi. Either add the server's copy of IntfSrv_TLB.pas to the **uses** clause of this application, or import the server's type library into Delphi using the technique described earlier in this chapter.

*Implementing the Callback Interface*
The client application is where we'll implement the ITestEvents interface that we defined in the server's type library. Because there is only one method on the  interface, the declaration is simple.

```
type
  TEventHandler = class(TAutoIntfObject, IIntfCallbackEvents)
    procedure OnText(const Text: WideString); safecall;
  end;
```

There is one point of interest about this declaration. TEventHandler derives from TAutoIntfObject. TAutoIntfObject is a lightweight automation-compatible class that you can use when you want to implement an interface that should not be advertised in Windows. In other words, IIntfCallbackEvents is a private interface that only this particular server and client know about. You don't want another application to be able to create an instance of IIntfCallbackEvents, because it makes no sense outside of this context.

---
**Note**

*You might remember that TInterfacedObject is also a lightweight COM class. TAutoIntfObject differs from TInterfacedObject in that TAutoIntfObject requires a type library, supports late binding via IDispatch, and can be called from out-of-process COM clients. TInterface supports none of this functionality, and is intended for use strictly within a single application.* ◆

---

IIntfCallbackEvents only contains one method, DoIt, and I've provided a very simple implementation that displays the passed-in string on the main form.

*Constructing the Callback Object*
When the client application starts, it creates the TEventHandler object. This process, although straightforward, is unlike anything you've seen so far. In order to create the class, the code calls LoadRegTypeLib, passing in the

GUID and version number of the type library. LoadRegTypeLib returns a reference to the ITypeLib interface. TEventHandler.Create uses this reference to construct an instance of TEventHandler.

```
procedure TForm1.FormCreate(Sender: TObject);
var
  TypeLib : ITypeLib;
begin
  OleCheck(LoadRegTypeLib(LIBID_IntfSrv, 1, 0, 0, TypeLib));

  FCallback := TEventHandler.Create(TypeLib, IIntfCallbackEvents);
end;
```

### Connecting to the Server

The rest of the code is similar to code you've seen previously. When the user presses the Connect button, the code calls CoTest.Create to create an instance of the server. Then, it calls Connect on the server, passing in a reference to the IIntfCallbackEvents interface implemented by TEventHandler. Actually, it passes in the TEventHandler itself, Delphi automatically converts it to an IIntfCallbackEvents interface.

When the user clicks the Trigger button, the code simply calls the server's Trigger method, which in turn calls the DoIt method for all connected clients.

Listing 4.16 shows the source code for the client application.

---

**Listing 4.16**   *IntfCli—MainForm.pas*

```
unit MainForm;

interface

uses
  Windows, Messages, SysUtils, Classes, Graphics, Controls, Forms,
  Dialogs, ComObj, ActiveX, IntfSrv_TLB, StdCtrls, ExtCtrls;

type
  TEventHandler = class(TAutoIntfObject, IIntfCallbackEvents)
    procedure OnText(const Text: WideString); safecall;
  end;

  TForm1 = class(TForm)
    Panel1: TPanel;
    Panel2: TPanel;
    btnSend: TButton;
    Memo1: TMemo;
    btnConnect: TButton;
    btnDisconnect: TButton;
    Edit1: TEdit;
```

*continues* ▶

**Listing 4.16** *continued*

```
    procedure FormCreate(Sender: TObject);
    procedure FormDestroy(Sender: TObject);
    procedure btnConnectClick(Sender: TObject);
    procedure btnDisconnectClick(Sender: TObject);
    procedure btnSendClick(Sender: TObject);
  private
    { Private declarations }
    FCallback: TEventHandler;
    FServer: IIntfCallback;
    FID: Integer;
  public
    { Public declarations }
  end;

var
  Form1: TForm1;

implementation

{$R *.DFM}

{ TEventHandler }

procedure TEventHandler.OnText(const Text: WideString);
begin
  Form1.Memo1.Lines.Add(Text);
end;

procedure TForm1.FormCreate(Sender: TObject);
var
  TypeLib : ITypeLib;
begin
  // Have to LoadRegTypeLib to get at the event interface
  OleCheck(LoadRegTypeLib(LIBID_IntfSrv, 1, 0, 0, TypeLib));

  FCallback := TEventHandler.Create(TypeLib, IIntfCallbackEvents);
end;

procedure TForm1.FormDestroy(Sender: TObject);
begin
  // Don't free FCallback here - the server will kill it for us
end;

procedure TForm1.btnConnectClick(Sender: TObject);
begin
  // Connect to the server
  FServer := CoIntfCallback.Create;
  FID := FServer.Connect(FCallback);

  btnConnect.Enabled := False;
  btnDisconnect.Enabled := True;
```

```
  btnSend.Enabled := True;
  Edit1.Enabled := True;
end;

procedure TForm1.btnDisconnectClick(Sender: TObject);
begin
  FServer.Disconnect(FID);

  btnConnect.Enabled := True;
  btnDisconnect.Enabled := False;
  btnSend.Enabled := False;
  Edit1.Enabled := False;
end;

procedure TForm1.btnSendClick(Sender: TObject);
begin
  FServer.SendText(Edit1.Text);
end;

end.
```

As you've seen, you can handle server callbacks through either dispinterfaces or interfaces. Both methods have their advantages and disadvantages. Dispinterfaces are required if you want your code to work with Visual Basic, for example. Also, Delphi provides better support for dispinterfaces through the Automation Object Wizard. However, you still need to write some code if you want multiple clients to connect to a single instance of the server.

Interfaces provide some benefits in terms of speed, and they also shield you from the hassles of having to implement IDispatch's Invoke method and manually decipher the parameters that are passed into your event handler.

My goal here was simply to familiarize you with the different mechanisms you can use to handle COM callbacks and let you decide which one best serves your needs. That said, I would say that, especially if you're using Delphi 5, unless you have an overwhelming reason to use a callback interface, you should stick with dispinterfaces and COM events.

In Chapter 6, I'll show you a real-world situation in which implementing COM events can be extremely beneficial. In the following section, I'll discuss a common automation server (Microsoft ADO), and show you how to write a COM client in Delphi that accesses it.

## Automating Microsoft ADO

Almost all the new technology coming out of Redmond is COM-based, and Microsoft's latest database technology is no exception. ActiveX Data Objects (ADO) is Microsoft's latest database technology designed to allow access to any type of data. This section isn't meant to be an exhaustive tutorial on ADO. Rather, I want to show you how you can use Delphi to quickly and easily take advantage of new Windows COM-based technologies.

### Note

*In Delphi versions 5 and later, Borland provides components for ADO development. As such, this section will mostly be of interest to Delphi 3 and Delphi 4 users, although the general concept of how to implement Microsoft COM-based technologies in your applications will apply to everyone.* ♦

ADO is one of a set of components in Microsoft's *Universal Data Access* strategy. ADO is the API that programmers can (and should) write to in order to access any type of data, from relational SQL databases to ISAM file formats to non-relational data, such as email messages. Microsoft ADO is essentially a wrapper around OLE DB. OLE DB is very powerful, but difficult to program. ADO goes a long way toward removing the complexity of OLE DB.

Note that because ADO is a Microsoft technology, you can rest assured that most of their efforts have been concentrated on providing the best possible performance with Microsoft Access and Microsoft SQL Server. If performance is of the utmost concern to your application, you might want to evaluate one of these two databases first. However, as time progresses, you can expect to see OLE DB providers appear from other database vendors that will provide optimal performance with their own databases.

ADO is a dual-interface automation server. The latest ADO version available at this time is version 2.1. However, because ADO 1.1 is installed with Internet Explorer 4.0 and Windows 98, most readers will already have ADO 1.1 installed on their machine. For that reason, this section does not discuss new features specific to ADO 2.1.

## The ADO Philosophy

Figure 4.18 shows a conceptual diagram of how ADO fits in with OLE DB and ODBC.

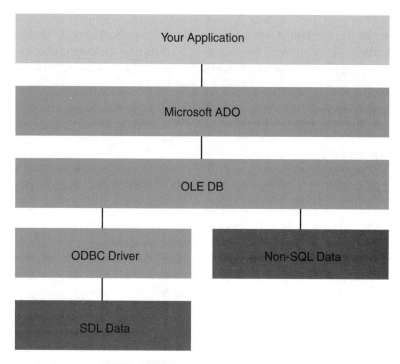

**Figure 4.18**   *The ADO architecture.*

As you can see, ADO can obtain data directly through an OLE DB provider, or indirectly through ODBC. You might argue that ADO adds yet another layer on top of the existing database architecture. Rest assured, the ADO layer is very thin, and performance is excellent.

ADO uses the concept of a *provider* to provide access to the data itself. If you're familiar with ODBC, you can think of a provider as the equivalent of an ODBC driver. The provider must expose (at least) a minimal set of interfaces so that ADO can access different types of data in a consistent manner. A provider for an advanced data store will necessarily provide more capability than a provider for a flat-file database, for example.

ADO already provides access to most common database formats, but what do you do if you are dealing with a unique file format? Perhaps you're the developer of a brand new, technologically advanced database system. If you have an ODBC driver for your data, you can use that. However, you can also write an OLE DB provider for your data. Writing an OLE DB provider is an advanced subject in and of itself, so I will not get into the details here. However, Microsoft's documentation covers this subject, and their download even includes a sample OLE DB provider that you can study.

The main components of ADO are the Connection, Recordset, and Command. The Connection object is responsible for connecting to a local or remote database. The Recordset object provides a connection to a set of records. The Command object is useful for issuing commands to the underlying database that do not return result sets, such as an UPDATE SQL statement. These objects will be discussed in detail later.

## Obtaining ADO

ADO is freely available for download. Simply visit www.microsoft.com/data/download.htm and select the link to the latest download available. You can either redistribute this file (MDAC_TYP.EXE) with your setup program, or you can direct your users to download the file from Microsoft's Web site. The good news is that future versions of Microsoft Windows will ship with ADO. Windows 98 and Microsoft Internet Explorer 4.0 both include ADO 1.1, which will work fine for your applications if you do not take advantage of ADO 2.1-specific features, such as asynchronous database connections and remote datasets.

After you've downloaded the appropriate file from Microsoft's Web site, simply execute it to install ADO, along with an OLE DB driver for the Microsoft Jet Engine, and ODBC drivers for SQL Server, Oracle, and Paradox.

## Installing ADO into Delphi

Now that ADO is installed on your machine, you will want to install it into Delphi so you can start writing ADO applications. From the Delphi main menu, select Project, Import Type Library. The dialog box shown in Figure 4.19 appears.

Select Microsoft ActiveX Data Objects 2.1 Library (Version 2.1) and click OK. Delphi will generate the Pascal import unit ADODB_TLB.PAS for you. Open the Import Type Library dialog box again and import Microsoft ActiveX Data Objects Recordset 2.1 Library (Version 2.1). Delphi will generate another import unit, ADOR_TLB.PAS. You should include these units in any ADO applications you write with Delphi.

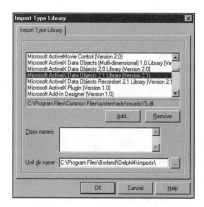

**Figure 4.19**   *Installing ADO into Delphi.*

## Connecting to a Database

In ADO terminology, a connection is roughly the equivalent of a Delphi
TDatabase. Like the Delphi TDatabase and TTable components, ADO is
flexible enough that you can either explicitly establish a connection to a
database, or you can let the recordset do it implicitly for you. In most serious applications, you will want to have total control over your database
connections, so we're going to establish a connection ourselves.

Depending on what provider you use, you can connect to the database in
a number of ways. I'll show you two typical scenarios here. First, you might
have an ODBC datasource set up for your database. If that's the case, then
you can connect to the database with the following code:

```
Connection.Open('Data Source=MyDataSourceName', 'UserID', 'Password', -1);
```

The first three parameters should be obvious from the code snippet. You
pass the DSN, the User ID, and the password. For an unsecured Access
database, you can leave the User ID and password blank. The last parameter represents the options to use when opening the connection. You will
typically set this to -1 to use the default options.

*Table 4.2   Valid Flags for Connection.Open*

| Connection Option | Description |
|---|---|
| CONNECTUNSPECIFIED | Unspecified connection type. |
| ASYNCCONNECT | Open the connection asynchronously. When the connection is established, the ConnectComplete event will be fired. (ADO 2.0 only) |

The following code is an example of how to connect to a Microsoft Jet database. Note that rather than going through an ODBC driver, this example connects directly through the Microsoft Jet OLE DB provider.

```
Connection.Open('Data Source=C:\MyData.mdb;Provider=Microsoft.Jet.OLEDB.3.51',
  'admin', '', -1);
```

## Opening a Recordset

After we have established a connection to the database, we can open a recordset. A recordset is the conceptual equivalent of a TQuery or a TTable. For instance, the following code opens the table named Customers in the database referred to by Connection:

```
Recordset.Open('Customers', Connection, adOpenForwardOnly, adLockReadOnly,
adCmdTable);
```

Alternately, we can specify an SQL statement to select a subset of the rows from the Customer table, like this:

```
Recordset.Open('SELECT * FROM Customers WHERE Balance> 1000',
  Connection, adOpenForwardOnly, adLockReadOnly, adCmdText);
```

Recordset.Open takes five parameters. The first is used to determine what information to pull into the recordset. In the first example in the previous code, we simply provided the name of a table in the database. In the second example, we provided an SQL statement instead.

The second parameter specifies the connection to use. Because we already explicitly created a connection, we can simply pass the connection as the parameter. If we hadn't created a connection, we could pass the connection information here instead, as follows:

```
Recordset.Open('Customers', 'Data
➥Source=C:\MyData.mdb;Provider=Microsoft.Jet.OLEDB.3.51',
  adOpenForwardOnly, adLockReadOnly, adCmdTable);
```

The third parameter specifies the type of cursor to use with the connection. Possible values are listed in Table 4.3.

*Table 4.3    Valid Cursor Types for Recordset.Open*

| Cursor Type | Description |
| --- | --- |
| adOpenUnspecified | Unspecified cursor type. |
| adOpenForwardOnly | Same as a static cursor, except you can only move forward through the recordset. This can improve performance. |
| adOpenKeyset | Changes and deletions by other users are visible to this recordset. Additions by other users are not visible. |

| Cursor Type | Description |
|---|---|
| adOpenDynamic | Additions, changes, and deletions by other users are visible to this recordset. |
| adOpenStatic | Additions, changes, and deletions by other users are not visible to this recordset. |

The fourth parameter specifies the lock type. Possible values are listed in Table 4.4.

*Table 4.4    Valid Lock Types for Recordset.Open*

| Lock Type | Description |
|---|---|
| adLockUnspecified | Unspecified lock type. |
| adLockReadOnly | Read only—The data may not be modified. |
| adLockPessimistic | The provider typically locks the record as soon as editing begins. |
| adLockOptimistic | The provider typically locks the record only when the Update method is called. |
| adLockBatchOptimistic | Same as adLockOptimistic, but required for batch updates. |

The fifth and final parameter specifies the type of command passed by the first parameter. Table 4.5 lists possible values for this parameter.

*Table 4.5    Valid Command Types for Recordset.Open*

| Command Type | Description |
|---|---|
| adCmdUnspecified | Unspecified command type. |
| adCmdUnknown | The type of the command is not known. |
| adCmdText | The command refers to a textual description—most likely an SQL command. |
| adCmdTable | The command refers to a table name where all columns are returned by an internally created SQL command. |
| adCmdStoredProc | The command refers to a stored procedure name. |
| adCmdFile | The command refers to the file name of a persistent recordset. |
| adCmdTableDirect | The command refers to a table name where all columns are returned. |
| adExecuteNoRecords | The command refers to a command or stored procedure that does not return a result set. This value is always logically ORed with either adCmdText or adCmdStoredProc. |

## Executing a Command

If you need to execute an action against the database that does not return a result set, you should use a Command object instead of a Recordset object. The Command object works hand in hand with the Parameter object, so I will discuss them together here. The following code snippet shows one way of giving everybody in the Employee table a ten percent raise:

```
Parameter := Command.CreateParameter('Raise', adDouble, adParamInput, sizeof(Double),
➥1.10);
Command.CommandText := 'UPDATE Employee SET Salary = Salary * ?';
Command.Execute(RecsAffected, Parameter, -1);
```

The first parameter is the name of the Parameter object. You can give this any name that sounds reasonable to you. The second parameter is the data type of the parameter. There are too many possible data types to list them all here. Refer either to the Microsoft documentation or to the Delphi-generated import files for a list of possible values.

The third parameter is the parameter type. Possible values are listed in Table 4.6.

*Table 4.6    Valid Parameter Types for Command.CreateParameter*

| Parameter Type | Description |
| --- | --- |
| adParamUnknown | The direction of the parameter is unknown. |
| adParamInput | The parameter is an input parameter. |
| adParamOutput | The parameter is an output parameter. |
| adParamInputOutput | The parameter is both an input and an output parameter. |
| adParamReturnValue | The parameter is a return value. |

The fourth parameter specifies the maximum length of the parameter, in either characters or bytes, depending on the parameter type. The fifth and final parameter is a variant that specifies the value of the parameter.

## Accessing Field Values

ADO creates a Field object for each column in the recordset. To retrieve data from a recordset or modify the value of a field, you must access the value of the corresponding Field object(s), as follows:

```
Recordset.Fields.Item[FieldNo].Value
```

You can also obtain the field name by using the Name property.

```
Recordset.Fields.Item[FieldNo].Name
```

The Field object contains a number of useful properties. Some of the ones you will use most often are listed in Table 4.7.

*Table 4.7*  *Common Properties of the Field Object*

| Property | Description |
|----------|-------------|
| Name | The name of the underlying database field. |
| Precision | The maximum number of digits used to represent numeric values. |
| Type | The data type of the field. See the Microsoft documentation for a list of supported data types. |
| Value | The value of the field. |

## Handling Database Errors

In all database programming, you should be prepared to handle errors as they arise, and ADO is no exception. ADO provides an Errors object that provides a detailed explanation of any and all errors that come up. Thanks to Delphi's exception handling mechanism, handling ADO errors is a breeze. The following code snippet illustrates how to trap and respond to an ADO error.

```
try
  FRecordset.MoveNext;
except
  E := FConnection.Errors[0];

  // Do something with the error here, such as log it to a file

  raise;  // Re-raise the exception
end;
```

As you can probably surmise from the previous code snippet, it's possible for ADO to generate multiple errors simultaneously. In order to relate all error information to the user, you should examine the FConnection.Errors.Count property to determine the number of errors generated. Then you should implement a mechanism to allow the user to scroll through the list of errors, which would be contained in FConnection.Errors[0] through FConnection.Errors[Count - 1]. Listing 4.17 contains a procedure called ShowADOErrors that demonstrates one (very simple) method of doing this.

## Example: A Microsoft ADO Application

This sample application does not really do anything useful within itself; rather, it's more of a collection of routines to perform common ADO functions.

**Listing 4.17**    *ADOTest—MainForm.pas*

```pascal
unit MainForm;

interface

uses
  Windows, Messages, SysUtils, Classes, Graphics, Controls, Forms,
  Dialogs, StdCtrls, ADODB_TLB, Grids;

const
  ConnectionString =
    'Data Source=c:\Program Files\Common Files\Borland Shared\Data\DBDemos.mdb;' +
    'Provider=Microsoft.Jet.OLEDB.3.51';

type
  TForm1 = class(TForm)
    StringGrid1: TStringGrid;
    btnLoadGrid: TButton;
    btnAdd: TButton;
    btnAddDuplicate: TButton;
    btnDelete: TButton;
    btnSearch: TButton;
    btnSort: TButton;
    procedure FormCreate(Sender: TObject);
    procedure btnLoadGridClick(Sender: TObject);
    procedure btnAddClick(Sender: TObject);
    procedure btnAddDuplicateClick(Sender: TObject);
    procedure btnDeleteClick(Sender: TObject);
    procedure btnSearchClick(Sender: TObject);
    procedure btnSortClick(Sender: TObject);
  private
    { Private declarations }
    FConnection: _Connection;
    FRecordset: _Recordset;
    FByOrder: Boolean;
  public
    { Public declarations }
  end;

var
  Form1: TForm1;

implementation

{$R *.DFM}

procedure ShowADOErrors(ErrorList: Errors);
var
  I: Integer;
  E: Error;
  S: String;
begin
```

```
    for I := 0 to ErrorList.Count - 1 do begin
      E := ErrorList[I];
      S := Format('ADO Error %d of %d:'#13#13'%s',
        [I + 1, ErrorList.Count, E.Description]);
      ShowMessage(S);
    end;
  end;

  procedure TForm1.FormCreate(Sender: TObject);
  begin
    FConnection := CoConnection.Create;
    FConnection.Open(ConnectionString, 'admin', '', -1);

    FRecordset := CoRecordset.Create;
    FRecordset.Open('SELECT * FROM Orders ORDER BY OrderNo',
      FConnection, adOpenKeyset, adLockOptimistic, adCmdText);

    FByOrder := True;

    btnLoadGridClick(Sender);
  end;

  procedure TForm1.btnLoadGridClick(Sender: TObject);
  var
    V: OleVariant;
    S: String;
    Row, Col: Integer;
  begin
    try
      FRecordset.MoveFirst;

      StringGrid1.ColCount := FRecordset.Fields.Count;
      StringGrid1.RowCount := FRecordset.RecordCount + 1;

      for Col := 0 to FRecordset.Fields.Count - 1 do
        StringGrid1.Cells[Col, 0] := FRecordset.Fields.Item[Col].Name;

      Row := 1;
      while not FRecordset.EOF do begin
        for Col := 0 to FRecordset.Fields.Count - 1 do begin
          V := FRecordset.Fields.Item[Col].Value;
          if VarType(V) <> varNull then
            S := V
          else
            S := '';
          StringGrid1.Cells[Col, Row] := S;
        end;
        Inc(Row);
        FRecordset.MoveNext;
      end;
    except
      ShowADOErrors(FConnection.Errors);
    end;
  end;
```

*continues* ▶

**Listing 4.17**    *continued*

```
procedure TForm1.btnAddClick(Sender: TObject);
var
  Fields: OleVariant;
  Values: OleVariant;
begin
  Fields := VarArrayCreate([1, 3], varVariant);
  Values := VarArrayCreate([1, 3], varVariant);

  try
    Fields[1] := 'OrderNo';
    Fields[2] := 'CustNo';
    Fields[3] := 'EmpNo';
    Values[1] := 99999;
    Values[2] := 3615;
    Values[3] := 2;
    FRecordset.AddNew(Fields, Values);
    btnLoadGridClick(Sender);
    ShowMessage('OrderNo 99999 was added');
  except
    ShowADOErrors(FConnection.Errors);
  end;
end;

procedure TForm1.btnAddDuplicateClick(Sender: TObject);
var
  Fields: OleVariant;
  Values: OleVariant;
begin
  Fields := VarArrayCreate([1, 3], varVariant);
  Values := VarArrayCreate([1, 3], varVariant);

  try
    Fields[1] := 'OrderNo';
    Fields[2] := 'CustNo';
    Fields[3] := 'EmpNo';
    Values[1] := 1035;
    Values[2] := 1645;
    Values[3] := 2;
    FRecordset.AddNew(Fields, Values);
  except
    ShowADOErrors(FConnection.Errors);
  end;
end;

procedure TForm1.btnDeleteClick(Sender: TObject);
begin
  FRecordset.MoveFirst;
  FRecordset.Find('OrderNo=99999', 0, adSearchForward, 0);
  if not FRecordset.EOF then begin
    FRecordset.Delete(adAffectCurrent);
    btnLoadGridClick(Sender);
```

```
    ShowMessage('OrderNo 99999 was deleted.');
  end else
    ShowMessage('OrderNo 99999 was not found.');
end;

procedure TForm1.btnSearchClick(Sender: TObject);
begin
  FRecordset.MoveFirst;
  FRecordset.Find('OrderNo=1070', 0, adSearchForward, 0);
  if not FRecordset.EOF then
    ShowMessage('OrderNo 1070 was found.')
  else
    ShowMessage('OrderNo 1070 was not found.')
end;

procedure TForm1.btnSortClick(Sender: TObject);
begin
  FByOrder := not FByOrder;

  FRecordset.Close;
  if FByOrder then
    FRecordset.Open('SELECT * FROM Orders ORDER BY OrderNo',
      FConnection, adOpenKeyset, adLockOptimistic, adCmdText)
  else
    FRecordset.Open('SELECT * FROM Orders ORDER BY CustNo, OrderNo',
      FConnection, adOpenKeyset, adLockOptimistic, adCmdText);

  btnLoadGridClick(Sender);
end;

end.
```

When you run ADOTest, you'll see the screen shown in Figure 4.20.

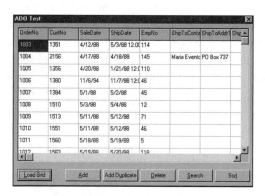

**Figure 4.20**    *ADOTest shows how to perform several common database tasks.*

The application's form has a string grid and six buttons on it. From left to right, the buttons perform the following operations:

- **Load Grid**: Forces the application to reload all data from the recordset
- **Add**: Adds a new order to the orders table. The order number is set to 99999, the customer number to 3615, and the employee number to 2. This record does not already exist in the database, so this routine demonstrates a successful add to the database.
- **Add Duplicate**: Attempts to add a new record with a duplicate order number 1035. This routine demonstrates a key violation.
- **Delete**: Attempts to find and delete order number 99999. If you have already added order 99999, this routine demonstrates how to successfully locate and delete the record.
- **Search**: Uses the Find method to search for order number 1070.
- **Sort**: Toggles between sorting by order number and sorting by customer number.

## Summary

In this chapter, I showed you how to create in-process and out-of-process COM automation servers. You saw how the type library plays an integral part in creating automation servers. This chapter pulled together all the topics we studied in earlier chapters into one cohesive unit.

I also discussed the role that variants play in COM automation, and how they are used to permit late binding to an automation object.

After showing you the basics of automation servers, I showed you how to implement COM events and callbacks in two different ways. You learned that implementing events through dispinterfaces is the most compatible method to use, but creating callback interfaces can be more efficient if you know that both the server and client provide interface support. Delphi 5 improvements to COM event handling make parts of this section obsolete.

Finally, I wrapped up the chapter with a section on Microsoft ADO. The goal of that section was not to make you a proficient ADO programmer, but rather to show you how you can use Delphi to relatively easily take advantage of emerging COM-based technologies. Delphi 5 provides a number of ADO components that you should use when writing applications that make use of ADO, but the general concept of importing type libraries into Delphi applies to automation servers in general.

After reading this chapter you should know the difference between interfaces, dispinterfaces, and variants. You should be armed with the knowledge you need to determine which of the three access methods is best for a particular programming situation.

In the next chapter, I'll discuss ActiveX controls and ActiveForms. You'll learn how to convert a VCL control to an ActiveX control. I'll also show you how to create a small application and distribute it as an ActiveForm.

# 5

# *ActiveX Controls and ActiveForms*

This chapter discusses ActiveX controls and ActiveForms, teaching you how to use existing ActiveX controls in your Delphi applications, and how to create your own ActiveX controls and ActiveForms.

## Using Existing ActiveX Controls in Delphi

There are a huge number of ActiveX controls available on the market today. ActiveX controls exist for almost any purpose you can imagine, and probably a lot of purposes you've never even thought of.

In this section, I'll introduce you to a freely available Microsoft ActiveX control that you may never have heard of—Microsoft Agent.

## Microsoft Agent

Microsoft Agent is a suite of DLLs that you can install into Windows 9x or Windows NT. The DLLs house a set of ActiveX controls that manage cartoon-like characters, called *agents*. Agents have motion, speech, and listening capabilities. They can be used for almost anything you can dream up, although possibly the most useful application of Microsoft Agent is in a tutorial or help-style context within your application.

### Obtaining Microsoft Agent

Obtaining a copy of Microsoft Agent is easy. Simply visit the Web page `http://msdn.microsoft.com/msagent`.

Click on the **Download Microsoft Agent** link. There are several "components" to Microsoft Agent. You will need to **Download the Microsoft Agent**

**Core Components** first. After that, download one or more **Microsoft Agent character files.** Finally, you should **Download the Speech Control Panel,** as this allows you to change speech settings, such as speed, volume, and so on. Microsoft provides four agents:

- Genie (a genie)
- Merlin (a wizard)
- Robbie (a robot)
- Peedy (a parrot)

I expect that over time Microsoft might create additional agents, and you might also see offerings from third-party companies. I will be using the genie for the sample applications in this chapter, so be sure to download at least the genie.

If you want to be able to hear the agent speak through your sound card, download the **Lernout & Hauspie TruVoice Text-To-Speech Engine.**

I also strongly recommend that you follow the link to **Go to the Microsoft Agent Downloads for Developers page,** and download the complete set of Microsoft Agent documentation. The documentation contains a complete reference to all aspects of programming with Microsoft Agent.

After you've downloaded the appropriate files, run MSAGENT.EXE to install Microsoft Agent. This setup program will install the core files into C:\Program Files\Microsoft Agent. Then run TV_ENUA.EXE, which will install the speech engine. Run GENIE.EXE to install the Genie agent, and lastly, run SPCHCPL.EXE to install the Speech Control Panel applet.

> ### Note
>
> *You may also create your own agents, if you are so inclined. To do so, you will need to download the **Microsoft Agent Character Editor** and the **Microsoft Agent Linguistic Information Sound Editing Tool.** This process requires a significant amount of time and effort, as well as artistic talent.* ♦

### Installing Microsoft Agent into Delphi

To install Microsoft Agent into Delphi, follow these steps:

1. Select Component, Import ActiveX Control from the Delphi main menu.

2. Click Microsoft Agent Control 2.0 (Version 2.0) in the list box, and click the Install... button (see Figure 5.1).

3. Select **Into new package,** enter a filename for the new package (such as MSAgent.dpk), type in a description, and click OK.

The Microsoft Agent ActiveX control is now installed into Delphi.

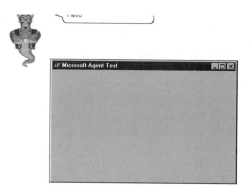

**Figure 5.1** *Installing the Microsoft Agent ActiveX Control into Delphi.*

### Programming with Microsoft Agent

Listings 5.1 and 5.2 contain source code for a very basic program that uses Microsoft Agent. When you run this application, if you have everything installed correctly, you'll see the genie appear in the upper-left corner of your screen in a puff of smoke and hear it say hello. You will also see the word "Hello" appear in a *balloon* over the genie's head. When you close the application, the genie goes away. Not very exciting, but it's a start.

Figure 5.2 shows the AgentTest application at runtime.

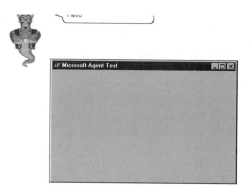

**Figure 5.2** *Testing Microsoft Agent.*

**Listing 5.1**    *AgentTest—AgentTest.dpr*

```
program AgentTest;

uses
  Forms,
  MainForm in 'MainForm.pas' {Form1};

{$R *.RES}

begin
  Application.Initialize;
  Application.CreateForm(TForm1, Form1);
  Application.Run;
end.
```

**Listing 5.2**    *AgentTest—MainForm.pas*

```
unit MainForm;

interface

uses
  Windows, Messages, SysUtils, Classes, Graphics, Controls, Forms, Dialogs,
  OleCtrls, AgentObjects_TLB;

type
  TForm1 = class(TForm)
    Agent1: TAgent;
    procedure FormCreate(Sender: TObject);
  private
    procedure WaitFor(Request: IAgentCtlRequest);
    { Private declarations }
  public
    { Public declarations }
  end;

var
  Form1: TForm1;

implementation

{$R *.DFM}

const
  AGENT = 'genie';
  AGENTPATH = 'C:\WinNT\MSAgent\Chars\genie.acs';

procedure TForm1.WaitFor(Request: IAgentCtlRequest);
var
  Status: LongInt;
begin
  repeat
    Application.ProcessMessages;
```

```
    Status := Request.Get_Status;
  until (Status <> 2) and (Status <> 4);
end;

procedure TForm1.FormCreate(Sender: TObject);
var
  Character: IAgentCtlCharacter;
  Request: IAgentCtlRequest;
begin
  Agent1.Connected := True;

  Request := Agent1.Characters.Load(AGENT, AGENTPATH);
  Character := Agent1.Characters.Character(AGENT);

  Request := Character.Show(False);
  WaitFor(Request);

  Request := Character.Speak('Hello', EmptyParam);
end;

end.
```

Note that because of space considerations, I have not shown the code for
AgentObjects_TLB.pas. Delphi generated this file for you automatically
when you installed the Agent ActiveX control into Delphi.

*User Controls*

In addition to what you, the programmer, can do, there are a number of
end-user interactions possible with Microsoft Agent. If you installed the
Speech Control Panel applet, you'll see a new Speech icon in the control
panel. Double-click this icon to display the Speech Properties dialog box
(Figure 5.3).

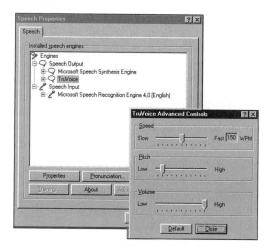

Figure 5.3    *The Speech Properties dialog box.*

This dialog box allows the user to control the speed, pitch and volume at which the agent speaks.

The user can also move an agent around the screen by clicking and dragging. This is important because agents appear in front of all other running programs. The user may need to move the agent out of the way in order to see what's behind it.

These user controls mean that you need to be aware not only of what your program is doing, but you also need to somehow track the user's direct interaction with the agent. Fortunately, Microsoft Agent provides a number of events that are triggered when the user interacts with the agent. I'll discuss these events later in this chapter, in the section titled "Event Notifications."

*Agent Requests*

Microsoft Agent makes extensive use of a feature known as *requests*. A request is a synchronization technique that allows your program to determine when a given command has finished. Most Agent commands are asynchronous (that is, they return control to the calling program before the command has completed), so the application must have a way of knowing when the command has been carried out. Let's say you want the agent to move to a specific point on the screen, point to a button, and inform the user that he should press this button to carry out a specific action. You might not want the agent to speak until after he has arrived at his destination on the screen. By using a request, you can wait until the agent has finished the move command before executing the speak command.

There are two ways you can use requests. The first, and simplest from a coding point of view, is to wait until the operation has finished before continuing with your program's flow of execution. I call this a *WaitFor* operation, and you can implement it as follows:

```
procedure TForm.WaitFor(RequestL IAgentCtlRequest)
var
  Status: LongInt;
begin
  repeat
    Application.ProcessMessages;
    Request.Get_Status(Status);
  until (Status <> 2) and (Status <> 4);
end;
```

The following pseudocode illustrates how this technique is used:

```
MoveTo location on screen
WaitFor request to complete
Speak
```

Although this is easy to implement, it does not make the most effective use of the system. The program just sits there while waiting for the request to complete. However, it might be adequate in some applications, so I demonstrated its use in Listing 5.2.

The second, more robust, method of tracking requests is to handle an event that Microsoft Agent fires when requests are complete. In this case, Microsoft Agent will trigger the OnRequestComplete event, indicating that the agent has finished moving. When your program receives the event, it instructs the agent to begin speaking. I'll discuss this event, along with several others, in the "Event Notifications" section later in this chapter.

If you are going to use the latter method, you must not declare your request variables locally. You need to make sure that the Request ID is readily available to the event handler when it is triggered. I like to declare request variables in the form declaration, so that they are available for the life of the form.

Requests are also critical when you are attempting to synchronize two agents together, such as when they're having a conversation. If you don't want one agent to constantly interrupt another, you'll need to wait for the first agent to finish speaking before telling the second agent to begin.

Let's go back to our example and examine the code we typed into the FormCreate event handler. First, we set Agent1.Connected := True. This initializes the Microsoft Agent ActiveX control for our application. Then, we set up a variant to hold the path to the agent "characters" on our computer. In a real application, you would probably allow the user to specify a path for the characters, or you might install your own custom character into your program directory.

Next, we load the genie, and obtain a reference to it, which we place into the variable Character. That's all the initialization required to begin using the agent. At this point, the program shows the genie, waits for the genie to be fully displayed, and instructs it to speak. The Show command takes two parameters. The parameters indicate whether the agent is to be displayed immediately, or whether it should display in an animated fashion. I set the parameter to False in the example, so the genie "slowly" appears in a puff of smoke. If I were to say

```
Request := Character.Show(True);
```

then the genie would have been displayed immediately, without any fanfare. It's faster, but much less exciting.

*Common Agent Commands*

Microsoft Agent understands a number of commands. Table 5.1 lists some of the commands you will frequently use.

*Table 5.1   Frequently Used Microsoft Agent Commands*

| Command | Description |
|---------|-------------|
| GestureAt | Points to a location on the screen |
| Hide | Hides the agent |
| MoveTo | Moves to a location on the screen |
| Play | Plays an animation |
| Show | Shows the agent |
| Speak | Speaks |
| Stop | Stops an ongoing animation |

Show and Hide are used to display the agent and remove it from view. Remember that the user can also show and hide the agent directly through the context menu associated with the tray icon, so you need to track the visibility state of the agent closely.

I discussed the Show command already. Hide simply hides the agent from view. It does not destroy the agent or shut down Microsoft Agent. It takes two parameters, an immediate flag and a request ID, and its usage corresponds directly to the Show command.

The MoveTo command is used to (what else?) move the agent around the screen. MoveTo takes three arguments. Its syntax is

```
function MoveTo(x: Smallint; y: Smallint; Speed: OleVariant): IAgentCtlRequest;
safecall;
```

The arguments x and y specify the position on the screen to move the agent to. Speed determines, in milliseconds, how quickly the agent is moved to the new location. While moving, the Moving animation is automatically played. A speed of zero causes the agent to arrive at its destination immediately, without playing any animation. Higher values for Speed cause the agent to move slower. Attempting to move the agent in an animated manner, or performing any other type of animation while the agent is not displayed, is an error. Animations are discussed in detail later in this chapter, in the section titled "Animation."

GestureAt instructs the agent to point to a location on the screen. It takes three parameters: an x and y location, and a request ID.

Note that for MoveTo and GestureAt, as well as other positional commands, the x and y values are specified in screen coordinates. This means you can instruct the agent to point at or move to locations on the screen that are not occupied by your application.

## Agent Speech Capabilities

One of the most basic, and most fun, features of Microsoft Agent is the ability to talk to the user by way of the Speak command. The following code snippet demonstrates how to use the Speak command.

```
Request := Character.Speak('Hello', nil);
```

The first argument is a variant, which specifies the text to be spoken. The second argument is also a variant, and is a specification for an audio file to be used for speech output. It can be either a URL or a filename. Both the first and second parameters are considered optional, but you must specify a value for at least one of them. Typically, you will use the first parameter only. It will provide the text string to be spoken and also displayed in the balloon. If you specify a value for both parameters, then the first one will be displayed in the balloon, while the second one will specify the audio file to be played in lieu of synthesized speech.

Don't forget that the users of your application can configure Microsoft Agent to their liking. They may have balloon text turned off, they may not have installed the text-to-speech driver, or they may be deaf. Your program should always provide for both spoken text and balloon text. Let the user decide which one, or both, he wants to enable.

The first argument may contain one or more *tags*. A tag is an indicator that instructs the agent to do something special during speech. Tags are inserted directly into the speech string using a backslash character, much like an escape sequence. For example, the Chr tag allows you to set the *character* of the speech to normal, monotone, or whispered. The string

```
\Chr="Whisper"\I am whispering
```

will be spoken as a whisper. Table 5.2 lists some common tags and their usage.

*Table 5.2*    *Common Microsoft Agent Speech Tags*

| Tag | Description | Example |
|-----|-------------|---------|
| Chr | Controls the "character" of the voice to normal, monotone, or whisper. Usage is \Chr= "string"\. | `\Chr="Whisper"\This is a whisper` |
| Emp | Emphasizes the next word. Usage is \Emp\. | `This is a \Emp\button` |
| Map | Maps spoken text to balloon text. This allows the agent to say one thing, while another is shown in the balloon. Usage is \Map="Spoken Text"="BalloonText"\. | `This is \Map="spoken"=" displayed"\` |

*continues* ▶

*Table 5.2    continued*

| Tag | Description | Example |
|-----|-------------|---------|
| Mrk | Sets a bookmark in the text. The bookmark will trigger an OnBookmark event when that point in the spoken text is reached. Usage is \Mrk=number\. | `Let me know when we get` `\Mrk=1\here` |
| Pau | Pauses for a specified number of milliseconds. Usage is \Pau=number\. | `Pause for \Pau=50\50` `milliseconds` |
| Rst | Resets all tags to their defaults. Usage is \Rst\. | `I'm going to reset now\Rst\` |

*Animation*

Each agent can perform a number of *animations*. An animation is exactly what it sounds like: It instructs the agent to perform a given gesture. The Play command is used to play an animation, as follows:

```
Request := Character.Play('Greet');
```

In this way, new animations can be added to agents without the need to change the API. Table 5.3 lists some of the most frequently used animations. A typical agent can perform over 100 animations, so you should see the Microsoft documentation for a complete list for each agent.

The following descriptions pertain to the genie. Other agents support these animations also, but the exact movements may vary slightly.

*Table 5.3    Common Microsoft Agent Animations*

| Animation | Description |
|-----------|-------------|
| Announce | Raises hand |
| GestureDown | Gestures down |
| GestureLeft | Gestures left |
| GestureRight | Gestures right |
| GestureUp | Gestures up |
| GetAttention | Waves hands |
| Greet | Bows |
| LookDown | Looks down |
| LookLeft | Looks left |
| LookRight | Looks right |
| LookUp | Looks up |
| Processing | Spins around continuously |

| Animation | Description |
|-----------|-------------|
| Read | Pulls a scroll out of vest and reads it |
| Think | Scratches head |
| Wave | Waves hand |
| Write | Pulls a scroll out of vest and writes on it |

Many animations also have a corresponding "return" command. For example, Read has a matching animation called ReadReturn, which causes the agent to put away what it's reading.

In addition, the Processing animation causes the genie to spin around continuously. You must use the Stop command to halt the Processing animation before you can play any other animations. The bottom line is, read the official documentation for any and all commands or animations you use, because some of them have caveats.

*Event Notifications*

As I mentioned earlier, Microsoft Agent notifies your program when certain events occur. Delphi makes it simple to respond to these events. Click the agent control on your project's main form, and then select the Events tab in the Object Inspector. You will see a list of possible events you can respond to. Table 5.4 lists some of the more commonly used events you will want to become familiar with. The sample application AgentDemo demonstrates the use of several of these events.

*Table 5.4   Commonly Used Microsoft Agent Events*

| Event | Description |
|-------|-------------|
| OnBookmark | A bookmark tag has been reached during the Speak command. |
| OnClick | The user clicked on the agent. |
| OnDblClick | The user double-clicked on the agent. |
| OnDragComplete | The user finished dragging the agent. |
| OnDragStart | The user started to drag the agent. |
| OnHide | The agent has been hidden. |
| OnMove | The agent has moved. |
| OnRequestComplete | A request has completed. |
| OnRequestStart | A request has started. |
| OnShow | The agent has been shown. |
| OnShutdown | The user shut down Microsoft Agent. |

## An Example Microsoft Agent Application

To help you get up to speed with Microsoft Agent, I have written a sample application called TestDriv, which allows you to experiment with speech output, play different animations, and move the genie around on the screen. In addition, it demonstrates the use of requests and events to notify the application of user interaction with the genie.

When you run AgentDemo, you will see the screen shown in Figure 5.4.

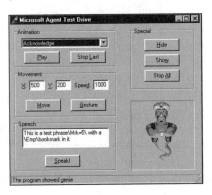

**Figure 5.4**    *The Microsoft Agent demo application.*

The AgentDemo application form is divided into four sections: Animation, Movement, Speech, and Special. There is also a box in the lower right-hand corner of the form that the genie is displayed in.

The Animation section contains a combo box that lists the animations the genie can perform. To play an animation, simply select the animation in the combo box and click Play. To stop a continuous animation, such as Processing, click Stop Last.

*Note*

*Note that this sample is tied very closely to the genie. If you want to use it to play with Merlin, for example, you will need to adjust the list of animations to reflect Merlin's capabilities.* ◆

The Movement section allows you to enter an X and Y position (in screen-relative coordinates) to move the genie to, as well as a speed. Click Move to move the genie, or click Gesture to command the genie to point to the location on the screen.

To make the genie speak, type the text into the edit control, and click Speak!. You can also embed tags into the speech, as Figure 5.4 illustrates.

The final area of interest is the Special section. This section gives you the ability to hide and show the genie, and you can also stop all pending and executing animations and speech.

I have also provided very basic event handlers for OnBookmark, OnDblClick, OnDragComplete, OnHide, and OnShow. By examining these event handlers, you will get a good idea of how to handle some of the most common Agent notification events.

If you experiment with TestDriv for a few minutes, you will become better acquainted with many Microsoft Agent basics. Listings 5.3 and 5.4 contain the complete source code for the Microsoft Agent test drive application.

**Listing 5.3**   *AgentDemo—AgentDemo.dpr*

```
program AgentDemo;

uses
  Forms,
  MainForm in 'MainForm.pas' {Form1};

{$R *.RES}

begin
  Application.Initialize;
  Application.CreateForm(TForm1, Form1);
  Application.Run;
end.
```

**Listing 5.4**   *AgentDemo—MainForm.pas*

```
unit MainForm;

interface

uses
  Windows, Messages, SysUtils, Classes, Graphics, Controls, Forms, Dialog boxes,
  ComCtrls, ExtCtrls, StdCtrls, OleCtrls, ActiveX, AgentObjects_TLB;

const
  WM_SHOWAGENT = WM_USER + 1;
  AGENT = 'genie';
  AGENTPATH = 'C:\WinNT\MSAgent\Chars\genie.acs';

  RequestCompleted = 0;
  RequestFailed = 1;
  RequestPending = 2;
  RequestInterrupted = 3;
  RequestInProgress = 4;
```

*continues* ▶

**Listing 5.4**    *continued*

```
  NeverShown = 0;
  UserHidSpeech = 1;
  UserShowed = 2;
  ProgramHid = 3;
  ProgramShowed = 4;
  OtherProgramHid = 5;
  OtherProgramShowed = 6;
  UserHidMenu = 7;

  LeftButton = 1;
  RightButton = 2;
  MiddleButton = 4;

type
  TForm1 = class(TForm)
    Agent1: TAgent;
    grpAnimation: TGroupBox;
    cbAnimations: TComboBox;
    btnPlay: TButton;
    btnStopLast: TButton;
    grpMovement: TGroupBox;
    Label2: TLabel;
    Label3: TLabel;
    Label4: TLabel;
    XPos: TEdit;
    YPos: TEdit;
    btnMove: TButton;
    btnGesture: TButton;
    Speed: TEdit;
    grpSpeech: TGroupBox;
    Memo1: TMemo;
    btnSpeak: TButton;
    grpSpecial: TGroupBox;
    btnHide: TButton;
    btnShow: TButton;
    btnStopAll: TButton;
    Bevel1: TBevel;
    StatusBar1: TStatusBar;
    procedure FormCreate(Sender: TObject);
    procedure FormDestroy(Sender: TObject);
    procedure FormShow(Sender: TObject);
    procedure btnPlayClick(Sender: TObject);
    procedure btnStopLastClick(Sender: TObject);
    procedure btnSpeakClick(Sender: TObject);
    procedure btnMoveClick(Sender: TObject);
    procedure btnGestureClick(Sender: TObject);
    procedure btnHideClick(Sender: TObject);
    procedure btnShowClick(Sender: TObject);
    procedure btnStopAllClick(Sender: TObject);
    procedure Agent1Bookmark(Sender: TObject; BookmarkID: Integer);
    procedure Agent1DblClick(Sender: TObject;
```

```
      const CharacterID: WideString; Button, Shift, x, y: Smallint);
    procedure Agent1DragComplete(Sender: TObject;
      const CharacterID: WideString; Button, Shift, x, y: Smallint);
    procedure Agent1HideShow(Sender: TObject; const CharacterID: WideString;
      Cause: Smallint);
  private
    { Private declarations }
    Character: IAgentCtlCharacterEx;
    FRequest: IAgentCtlRequest;
    procedure WaitFor(Request: IAgentCtlRequest);
    procedure WMShowAgent(var Message: TMessage); message WM_SHOWAGENT;
  public
    { Public declarations }
  end;

var
  Form1: TForm1;

implementation

{$R *.DFM}

procedure TForm1.WaitFor(Request: IAgentCtlRequest);
var
  Status: LongInt;
begin
  repeat
    Application.ProcessMessages;
    Status := Request.Get_Status;
  until (Status <> RequestPending) and (Status <> RequestInProgress);
end;

procedure TForm1.FormCreate(Sender: TObject);
var
  Animations: IAgentCtlAnimationNames;
  Enum: IEnumVariant;
  V: OleVariant;
  Fetched: Cardinal;
begin
  Character := nil;
  FRequest := nil;

  Agent1.Connected := True;

  Agent1.Characters.Load(AGENT, AGENTPATH);
  Character := Agent1.Characters.Character(AGENT);

  Animations := Character.AnimationNames;
  Enum := Animations.Enum as IEnumVariant;
  while Enum.Next(1, V, Fetched) = S_OK do
    cbAnimations.Items.Add(V);
```

*continues* ▶

**Listing 5.4**    *continued*

```
  cbAnimations.ItemIndex := 0;
end;

procedure TForm1.FormDestroy(Sender: TObject);
var
  Request: IAgentCtlRequest;
begin
  if Character <> nil then begin
    Character.StopAll('');

    Request := Character.Hide(False);
    WaitFor(Request);

    Agent1.Characters.Unload(AGENT);
  end;

  Agent1.Connected := False;
end;

procedure TForm1.WMShowAgent(var Message: TMessage);
var
  pt: TPoint;
begin
  pt.x := Bevel1.Left;
  pt.y := Bevel1.Top;
  pt := ClientToScreen(pt);
  Character.MoveTo(pt.x, pt.y, 0);

  Character.Show(False);
  Character.Play('Announce');
  Character.Speak('Hello.  I am an agent.', '');
  Character.Play('RestPose');
end;

procedure TForm1.FormShow(Sender: TObject);
begin
  PostMessage(Handle, WM_SHOWAGENT, 0, 0);
end;

// Animation

procedure TForm1.btnPlayClick(Sender: TObject);
var
  Status: LongInt;
begin
  // If we're already playing something, stop it
  if FRequest <> nil then begin
    Status := FRequest.Get_Status;
    if (Status = 2) or (Status = 4) then
      Character.Stop(FRequest);
  end;
```

```delphi
  FRequest := Character.Play(cbAnimations.Text);
end;

procedure TForm1.btnStopLastClick(Sender: TObject);
begin
  if FRequest <> nil then
    Character.Stop(FRequest);
end;

// Speech

procedure TForm1.btnSpeakClick(Sender: TObject);
begin
  Character.Speak(Memo1.Text, '');
end;

// Movement

procedure TForm1.btnMoveClick(Sender: TObject);
begin
  Character.MoveTo(StrToInt(XPos.Text), StrToInt(YPos.Text), StrToInt(Speed.Text));
end;

procedure TForm1.btnGestureClick(Sender: TObject);
begin
  Character.GestureAt(StrToInt(XPos.Text), StrToInt(YPos.Text));
end;

// Special

procedure TForm1.btnHideClick(Sender: TObject);
begin
  Character.Hide(False);
end;

procedure TForm1.btnShowClick(Sender: TObject);
begin
  Character.Show(False);
end;

procedure TForm1.btnStopAllClick(Sender: TObject);
begin
  Character.StopAll('');
end;

// Event handlers

procedure TForm1.Agent1Bookmark(Sender: TObject; BookmarkID: Integer);
begin
  StatusBar1.SimpleText := 'Triggered bookmark ' + IntToStr(BookmarkID);
end;
```

*continues* ▶

**Listing 5.4** *continued*

```
procedure TForm1.Agent1DblClick(Sender: TObject;
  const CharacterID: WideString; Button, Shift, x, y: Smallint);
begin
  if Button = LeftButton then
    StatusBar1.SimpleText := 'The user double-clicked on ' + CharacterID;
end;

procedure TForm1.Agent1DragComplete(Sender: TObject;
  const CharacterID: WideString; Button, Shift, x, y: Smallint);
begin
  StatusBar1.SimpleText := Format('The user moved %s to %d, %d', [CharacterID, x, y]);
end;

procedure TForm1.Agent1HideShow(Sender: TObject; const CharacterID: WideString;
  Cause: Smallint);
begin
  case Cause of
    NeverShown:
      StatusBar1.SimpleText := 'Nobody ever showed ' + CharacterID;
    UserHidSpeech:
      StatusBar1.SimpleText := 'The user hid ' + CharacterID + ' via spoken command';
    UserShowed:
      StatusBar1.SimpleText := 'The user showed ' + CharacterID;
    ProgramHid:
      StatusBar1.SimpleText := 'The program hid ' + CharacterID;
    ProgramShowed:
      StatusBar1.SimpleText := 'The program showed ' + CharacterID;
    OtherProgramHid:
      StatusBar1.SimpleText := 'Another program hid ' + CharacterID;
    OtherProgramShowed:
      StatusBar1.SimpleText := 'Another program showed ' + CharacterID;
    UserHidMenu:
      StatusBar1.SimpleText := 'The user hid ' + CharacterID + ' via menu';
    else
      StatusBar1.SimpleText := 'Unknown show/hide status for ' + CharacterID;
  end;
end;

end.
```

In this section, I showed you how to install an existing ActiveX control into Delphi, and I acquainted you with the Microsoft Agent ActiveX control in particular. In the next section, I'll show you how you can create your own ActiveX controls using Delphi.

# Creating ActiveX Controls

In this section, I'll show you how to create an ActiveX control from an existing Delphi component. In Delphi, you take an existing visual control (derived from TWinControl) and turn it into an ActiveX control. This means that you can write and test a VCL component completely in Delphi before taking the plunge and creating the ActiveX control.

## Reasons to Create ActiveX Controls

With all the capability of the VCL, why should you create an ActiveX control? For one very good reason: You want your control to be usable by all the developers out there who aren't using Delphi. By far, the largest market for ActiveX controls is the Visual Basic market.

### ActiveX One-Step Capability?

*One of the biggest marketing pitches for Delphi 3 was how it had one-step ActiveX capability. In other words, in just one step, you can turn a visual component into an ActiveX control. While this is technically true, the resulting ActiveX control isn't always acceptable. You can definitely create an ActiveX control in just one step, but it doesn't always have all the capability of the VCL component that it was created from. ◆*

## Converting a VCL Component to an ActiveX Control

For purposes of illustration, let's convert the TCheckListBox component into an ActiveX control. To do this, execute the following steps:

1. From the Delphi main menu, select File, New. The Object Repository is displayed.

2. On the ActiveX page, select ActiveX Library and click OK.

3. Select File, New again, and select the ActiveX Control icon from the ActiveX page of the Object Repository. The ActiveX Control Wizard appears, shown in Figure 5.5.

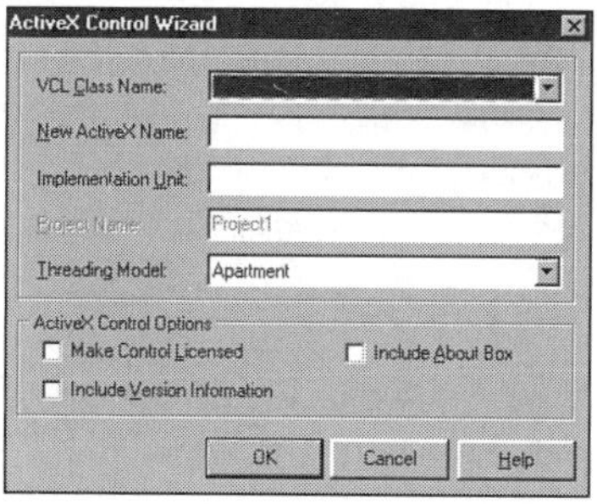

**Figure 5.5**  *The ActiveX Control Wizard Converts a VCL component to an ActiveX control.*

4. From the VCL Class Name combo box, select the VCL component to convert to an ActiveX control. You'll notice that a number of installed VCL components are missing from this list. In particular, the following types of components are not included in the list:

   - Components that are not derived from TWinControl

   - Components that have been registered through the RegisterNonActiveX procedure. Among others, these components include data-aware components, such as TDBEdit, and components that include collections, such as TListView.

   When you select TCheckListBox in the combo box, the ActiveX Control Wizard automatically generates default values for the ActiveX control name, Implementation unit, Project name, and Threading model.

> **Note**
>
> *You should always leave the threading model set to tmApartment, as it is required for ActiveX controls used by Visual Basic. Also, the VCL doesn't support any other model for ActiveX controls that contain VCL visual components. ♦*

The ActiveX Control Wizard also contains three checkboxes:

- Check the **Make Control Licensed** option if you want to enforce design-time licensing of your ActiveX control. When this option is checked, Delphi will automatically generate a license file, with the extension .LIC, for use with this ActiveX control. When you distribute the resulting ActiveX control to another developer for design-time use, you will provide him with the license file. This ActiveX control checks for the license file at design time. If the license file is missing or invalid, design-time use of the control is prohibited.

  When the developer redistributes your ActiveX control to his end users, he will not redistribute the license file. His end users will be able to use the ActiveX control at runtime, but they will not be able to develop an application using your ActiveX control.

- Unless you have a good reason not to, you should always check the **Include Version Information** checkbox. Using this option adds a version information resource to the ActiveX control. It is important to note that some products cannot load an ActiveX control that doesn't contain version information. Visual Basic 4 is an excellent example of such a product. When you check this option, make sure you also fill in the version info fields in the project options.

- If you check the **Include About Box** checkbox, Delphi will generate a dialog box that you can use to display information about the ActiveX control, your company, or any other information you would like to display to the user of your ActiveX control. Again, you will usually want to check this option.

When you have completely filled out the ActiveX Control Wizard, it will look like Figure 5.6.

**Figure 5.6**   *The completed ActiveX Control Wizard.*

5. Press OK to generate the ActiveX control and associated files. Listings 5.5 through 5.8 show the code generated for the ActiveX control.

---

**Listing 5.5**   *Main Project File for the ButtonX ActiveX Control*

```
library Project1;

uses
  ComServ,
  Project1_TLB in 'Project1_TLB.pas',
  CheckListBoxImpl1 in 'CheckListBoxImpl1.pas' {CheckListBoxX: CoClass},
  About1 in 'About1.pas' {CheckListBoxXAbout};

{$E ocx}

exports
  DllGetClassObject,
  DllCanUnloadNow,
  DllRegisterServer,
  DllUnregisterServer;

{$R *.TLB}

{$R *.RES}

begin
end.
```

**Listing 5.6**    *CheckListBoxImpl1.pas*

```
unit CheckListBoxImpl1;

interface

uses
  Windows, ActiveX, Classes, Controls, Graphics, Menus, Forms, StdCtrls,
  ComServ, StdVCL, AXCtrls, Project1_TLB, CheckLst;

type
  TCheckListBoxX = class(TActiveXControl, ICheckListBoxX)
  private
    { Private declarations }
    FDelphiControl: TCheckListBox;
    FEvents: ICheckListBoxXEvents;
    procedure ClickCheckEvent(Sender: TObject);
    procedure ClickEvent(Sender: TObject);
    procedure DblClickEvent(Sender: TObject);
    procedure KeyPressEvent(Sender: TObject; var Key: Char);
  protected
    { Protected declarations }
    procedure DefinePropertyPages(DefinePropertyPage: TDefinePropertyPage); override;
    procedure EventSinkChanged(const EventSink: IUnknown); override;
    procedure InitializeControl; override;
    function Get_AllowGrayed: WordBool; safecall;
    function Get_BorderStyle: TxBorderStyle; safecall;
    function Get_Color: OLE_COLOR; safecall;
    function Get_Columns: Integer; safecall;
    function Get_Ctl3D: WordBool; safecall;
    function Get_Cursor: Smallint; safecall;
    function Get_DoubleBuffered: WordBool; safecall;
    function Get_DragCursor: Smallint; safecall;
    function Get_DragMode: TxDragMode; safecall;
    function Get_Enabled: WordBool; safecall;
    function Get_Flat: WordBool; safecall;
    function Get_Font: IFontDisp; safecall;
    function Get_ImeMode: TxImeMode; safecall;
    function Get_ImeName: WideString; safecall;
    function Get_IntegralHeight: WordBool; safecall;
    function Get_ItemHeight: Integer; safecall;
    function Get_ItemIndex: Integer; safecall;
    function Get_Items: IStrings; safecall;
    function Get_ParentColor: WordBool; safecall;
    function Get_ParentCtl3D: WordBool; safecall;
    function Get_SelCount: Integer; safecall;
    function Get_Sorted: WordBool; safecall;
    function Get_Style: TxListBoxStyle; safecall;
    function Get_TabWidth: Integer; safecall;
    function Get_TopIndex: Integer; safecall;
    function Get_Visible: WordBool; safecall;
    function Get_VisibleDockClientCount: Integer; safecall;
    procedure _Set_Font(const Value: IFontDisp); safecall;
```

```
      procedure AboutBox; safecall;
      procedure Set_AllowGrayed(Value: WordBool); safecall;
      procedure Set_BorderStyle(Value: TxBorderStyle); safecall;
      procedure Set_Color(Value: OLE_COLOR); safecall;
      procedure Set_Columns(Value: Integer); safecall;
      procedure Set_Ctl3D(Value: WordBool); safecall;
      procedure Set_Cursor(Value: Smallint); safecall;
      procedure Set_DoubleBuffered(Value: WordBool); safecall;
      procedure Set_DragCursor(Value: Smallint); safecall;
      procedure Set_DragMode(Value: TxDragMode); safecall;
      procedure Set_Enabled(Value: WordBool); safecall;
      procedure Set_Flat(Value: WordBool); safecall;
      procedure Set_Font(var Value: IFontDisp); safecall;
      procedure Set_ImeMode(Value: TxImeMode); safecall;
      procedure Set_ImeName(const Value: WideString); safecall;
      procedure Set_IntegralHeight(Value: WordBool); safecall;
      procedure Set_ItemHeight(Value: Integer); safecall;
      procedure Set_ItemIndex(Value: Integer); safecall;
      procedure Set_Items(const Value: IStrings); safecall;
      procedure Set_ParentColor(Value: WordBool); safecall;
      procedure Set_ParentCtl3D(Value: WordBool); safecall;
      procedure Set_Sorted(Value: WordBool); safecall;
      procedure Set_Style(Value: TxListBoxStyle); safecall;
      procedure Set_TabWidth(Value: Integer); safecall;
      procedure Set_TopIndex(Value: Integer); safecall;
      procedure Set_Visible(Value: WordBool); safecall;
    end;

implementation

uses ComObj, About1;

{ TCheckListBoxX }

procedure TCheckListBoxX.DefinePropertyPages(DefinePropertyPage: TDefinePropertyPage);
begin
  {TODO: Define property pages here.  Property pages are defined by calling
    DefinePropertyPage with the class id of the page.  For example,
      DefinePropertyPage(Class_CheckListBoxXPage); }
end;

procedure TCheckListBoxX.EventSinkChanged(const EventSink: IUnknown);
begin
  FEvents := EventSink as ICheckListBoxXEvents;
end;

procedure TCheckListBoxX.InitializeControl;
begin
  FDelphiControl := Control as TCheckListBox;
  FDelphiControl.OnClick := ClickEvent;
  FDelphiControl.OnClickCheck := ClickCheckEvent;
  FDelphiControl.OnDblClick := DblClickEvent;
  FDelphiControl.OnKeyPress := KeyPressEvent;
end;
```

*continues* ▶

**Listing 5.6**   *continued*

```
function TCheckListBoxX.Get_AllowGrayed: WordBool;
begin
  Result := FDelphiControl.AllowGrayed;
end;

function TCheckListBoxX.Get_BorderStyle: TxBorderStyle;
begin
  Result := Ord(FDelphiControl.BorderStyle);
end;

function TCheckListBoxX.Get_Color: OLE_COLOR;
begin
  Result := OLE_COLOR(FDelphiControl.Color);
end;

function TCheckListBoxX.Get_Columns: Integer;
begin
  Result := FDelphiControl.Columns;
end;

function TCheckListBoxX.Get_Ctl3D: WordBool;
begin
  Result := FDelphiControl.Ctl3D;
end;

function TCheckListBoxX.Get_Cursor: Smallint;
begin
  Result := Smallint(FDelphiControl.Cursor);
end;

function TCheckListBoxX.Get_DoubleBuffered: WordBool;
begin
  Result := FDelphiControl.DoubleBuffered;
end;

function TCheckListBoxX.Get_DragCursor: Smallint;
begin
  Result := Smallint(FDelphiControl.DragCursor);
end;

function TCheckListBoxX.Get_DragMode: TxDragMode;
begin
  Result := Ord(FDelphiControl.DragMode);
end;

function TCheckListBoxX.Get_Enabled: WordBool;
begin
  Result := FDelphiControl.Enabled;
end;

function TCheckListBoxX.Get_Flat: WordBool;
```

```
begin
  Result := FDelphiControl.Flat;
end;

function TCheckListBoxX.Get_Font: IFontDisp;
begin
  GetOleFont(FDelphiControl.Font, Result);
end;

function TCheckListBoxX.Get_ImeMode: TxImeMode;
begin
  Result := Ord(FDelphiControl.ImeMode);
end;

function TCheckListBoxX.Get_ImeName: WideString;
begin
  Result := WideString(FDelphiControl.ImeName);
end;

function TCheckListBoxX.Get_IntegralHeight: WordBool;
begin
  Result := FDelphiControl.IntegralHeight;
end;

function TCheckListBoxX.Get_ItemHeight: Integer;
begin
  Result := FDelphiControl.ItemHeight;
end;

function TCheckListBoxX.Get_ItemIndex: Integer;
begin
  Result := FDelphiControl.ItemIndex;
end;

function TCheckListBoxX.Get_Items: IStrings;
begin
  GetOleStrings(FDelphiControl.Items, Result);
end;

function TCheckListBoxX.Get_ParentColor: WordBool;
begin
  Result := FDelphiControl.ParentColor;
end;

function TCheckListBoxX.Get_ParentCtl3D: WordBool;
begin
  Result := FDelphiControl.ParentCtl3D;
end;

function TCheckListBoxX.Get_SelCount: Integer;
begin
  Result := FDelphiControl.SelCount;
end;
```

*continues* ▶

**Listing 5.6**  *continued*

```
function TCheckListBoxX.Get_Sorted: WordBool;
begin
  Result := FDelphiControl.Sorted;
end;

function TCheckListBoxX.Get_Style: TxListBoxStyle;
begin
  Result := Ord(FDelphiControl.Style);
end;

function TCheckListBoxX.Get_TabWidth: Integer;
begin
  Result := FDelphiControl.TabWidth;
end;

function TCheckListBoxX.Get_TopIndex: Integer;
begin
  Result := FDelphiControl.TopIndex;
end;

function TCheckListBoxX.Get_Visible: WordBool;
begin
  Result := FDelphiControl.Visible;
end;

function TCheckListBoxX.Get_VisibleDockClientCount: Integer;
begin
  Result := FDelphiControl.VisibleDockClientCount;
end;

procedure TCheckListBoxX._Set_Font(const Value: IFontDisp);
begin
  SetOleFont(FDelphiControl.Font, Value);
end;

procedure TCheckListBoxX.AboutBox;
begin
  ShowCheckListBoxXAbout;
end;

procedure TCheckListBoxX.ClickCheckEvent(Sender: TObject);
begin
  if FEvents <> nil then FEvents.OnClickCheck;
end;

procedure TCheckListBoxX.ClickEvent(Sender: TObject);
begin
  if FEvents <> nil then FEvents.OnClick;
end;

procedure TCheckListBoxX.DblClickEvent(Sender: TObject);
```

```
begin
  if FEvents <> nil then FEvents.OnDblClick;
end;

procedure TCheckListBoxX.KeyPressEvent(Sender: TObject; var Key: Char);
var
  TempKey: Smallint;
begin
  TempKey := Smallint(Key);
  if FEvents <> nil then FEvents.OnKeyPress(TempKey);
  Key := Char(TempKey);
end;

procedure TCheckListBoxX.Set_AllowGrayed(Value: WordBool);
begin
  FDelphiControl.AllowGrayed := Value;
end;

procedure TCheckListBoxX.Set_BorderStyle(Value: TxBorderStyle);
begin
  FDelphiControl.BorderStyle := TBorderStyle(Value);
end;

procedure TCheckListBoxX.Set_Color(Value: OLE_COLOR);
begin
  FDelphiControl.Color := TColor(Value);
end;

procedure TCheckListBoxX.Set_Columns(Value: Integer);
begin
  FDelphiControl.Columns := Value;
end;

procedure TCheckListBoxX.Set_Ctl3D(Value: WordBool);
begin
  FDelphiControl.Ctl3D := Value;
end;

procedure TCheckListBoxX.Set_Cursor(Value: Smallint);
begin
  FDelphiControl.Cursor := TCursor(Value);
end;

procedure TCheckListBoxX.Set_DoubleBuffered(Value: WordBool);
begin
  FDelphiControl.DoubleBuffered := Value;
end;

procedure TCheckListBoxX.Set_DragCursor(Value: Smallint);
begin
  FDelphiControl.DragCursor := TCursor(Value);
end;
```

*continues* ▶

**Listing 5.6** *continued*

```
procedure TCheckListBoxX.Set_DragMode(Value: TxDragMode);
begin
  FDelphiControl.DragMode := TDragMode(Value);
end;

procedure TCheckListBoxX.Set_Enabled(Value: WordBool);
begin
  FDelphiControl.Enabled := Value;
end;

procedure TCheckListBoxX.Set_Flat(Value: WordBool);
begin
  FDelphiControl.Flat := Value;
end;

procedure TCheckListBoxX.Set_Font(var Value: IFontDisp);
begin
  SetOleFont(FDelphiControl.Font, Value);
end;

procedure TCheckListBoxX.Set_ImeMode(Value: TxImeMode);
begin
  FDelphiControl.ImeMode := TImeMode(Value);
end;

procedure TCheckListBoxX.Set_ImeName(const Value: WideString);
begin
  FDelphiControl.ImeName := TImeName(Value);
end;

procedure TCheckListBoxX.Set_IntegralHeight(Value: WordBool);
begin
  FDelphiControl.IntegralHeight := Value;
end;

procedure TCheckListBoxX.Set_ItemHeight(Value: Integer);
begin
  FDelphiControl.ItemHeight := Value;
end;

procedure TCheckListBoxX.Set_ItemIndex(Value: Integer);
begin
  FDelphiControl.ItemIndex := Value;
end;

procedure TCheckListBoxX.Set_Items(const Value: IStrings);
begin
  SetOleStrings(FDelphiControl.Items, Value);
end;

procedure TCheckListBoxX.Set_ParentColor(Value: WordBool);
```

```
begin
  FDelphiControl.ParentColor := Value;
end;

procedure TCheckListBoxX.Set_ParentCtl3D(Value: WordBool);
begin
  FDelphiControl.ParentCtl3D := Value;
end;

procedure TCheckListBoxX.Set_Sorted(Value: WordBool);
begin
  FDelphiControl.Sorted := Value;
end;

procedure TCheckListBoxX.Set_Style(Value: TxListBoxStyle);
begin
  FDelphiControl.Style := TListBoxStyle(Value);
end;

procedure TCheckListBoxX.Set_TabWidth(Value: Integer);
begin
  FDelphiControl.TabWidth := Value;
end;

procedure TCheckListBoxX.Set_TopIndex(Value: Integer);
begin
  FDelphiControl.TopIndex := Value;
end;

procedure TCheckListBoxX.Set_Visible(Value: WordBool);
begin
  FDelphiControl.Visible := Value;
end;

initialization
  TActiveXControlFactory.Create(
    ComServer,
    TCheckListBoxX,
    TCheckListBox,
    Class_CheckListBoxX,
    1,
    '{DEA0225E-5B44-11D3-B86D-0040F67455FE}',
    0,
    tmApartment);
end.
```

---

**Listing 5.7**    *Project1_TLB.pas*

```
unit Project1_TLB;

// ********************************************************************* //
// WARNING
// -------
// The types declared in this file were generated from data read from a
// Type Library. If this type library is explicitly or indirectly (via
// another type library referring to this type library) re-imported, or the
// 'Refresh' command of the Type Library Editor activated while editing the
// Type Library, the contents of this file will be regenerated and all
// manual modifications will be lost.
// ********************************************************************* //

// PASTLWTR : $Revision:   1.88  $
// File generated on 8/25/1999 7:29:09 PM from Type Library described below.

// *********************************************************************//
// NOTE:
// Items guarded by $IFDEF_LIVE_SERVER_AT_DESIGN_TIME are used by properties
// which return objects that may need to be explicitly created via a function
// call prior to any access via the property. These items have been disabled
// in order to prevent accidental use from within the object inspector. You
// may enable them by defining LIVE_SERVER_AT_DESIGN_TIME or by selectively
// removing them from the $IFDEF blocks. However, such items must still be
// programmatically created via a method of the appropriate CoClass before
// they can be used.
// ********************************************************************* //
// Type Lib: C:\Program Files\Borland\Delphi5\Projects\Project1.tlb (1)
// IID\LCID: {DEA02250-5B44-11D3-B86D-0040F67455FE}\0
// Helpfile:
// DepndLst:
//   (1) v2.0 stdole, (C:\WINNT\System32\STDOLE2.TLB)
//   (2) v4.0 StdVCL, (C:\WINNT\System32\STDVCL40.DLL)
// ********************************************************************* //
{$TYPEDADDRESS OFF} // Unit must be compiled without type-checked pointers.
interface

uses Windows, ActiveX, Classes, Graphics, OleServer, OleCtrls, StdVCL;

// *********************************************************************//
// GUIDS declared in the TypeLibrary. Following prefixes are used:
//   Type Libraries     : LIBID_xxxx
//   CoClasses          : CLASS_xxxx
//   DISPInterfaces     : DIID_xxxx
//   Non-DISP interfaces: IID_xxxx
// *********************************************************************//
const
  // TypeLibrary Major and minor versions
  Project1MajorVersion = 1;
  Project1MinorVersion = 0;
```

```
  LIBID_Project1: TGUID = '{DEA02250-5B44-11D3-B86D-0040F67455FE}';

  IID_ICheckListBoxX: TGUID = '{DEA02251-5B44-11D3-B86D-0040F67455FE}';
  DIID_ICheckListBoxXEvents: TGUID = '{DEA02253-5B44-11D3-B86D-0040F67455FE}';
  CLASS_CheckListBoxX: TGUID = '{DEA02255-5B44-11D3-B86D-0040F67455FE}';

// **********************************************************************//
// Declaration of Enumerations defined in Type Library
// **********************************************************************//
// Constants for enum TxBorderStyle
type
  TxBorderStyle = TOleEnum;
const
  bsNone = $00000000;
  bsSingle = $00000001;

// Constants for enum TxDragMode
type
  TxDragMode = TOleEnum;
const
  dmManual = $00000000;
  dmAutomatic = $00000001;

// Constants for enum TxImeMode
type
  TxImeMode = TOleEnum;
const
  imDisable = $00000000;
  imClose = $00000001;
  imOpen = $00000002;
  imDontCare = $00000003;
  imSAlpha = $00000004;
  imAlpha = $00000005;
  imHira = $00000006;
  imSKata = $00000007;
  imKata = $00000008;
  imChinese = $00000009;
  imSHanguel = $0000000A;
  imHanguel = $0000000B;

// Constants for enum TxListBoxStyle
type
  TxListBoxStyle = TOleEnum;
const
  lbStandard = $00000000;
  lbOwnerDrawFixed = $00000001;
  lbOwnerDrawVariable = $00000002;

// Constants for enum TxMouseButton
type
  TxMouseButton = TOleEnum;
const
  mbLeft = $00000000;
```

*continues* ▶

**Listing 5.7**  *continued*

```
  mbRight = $00000001;
  mbMiddle = $00000002;

type

// ********************************************************************//
// Forward declaration of types defined in TypeLibrary
// ********************************************************************//
  ICheckListBoxX = interface;
  ICheckListBoxXDisp = dispinterface;
  ICheckListBoxXEvents = dispinterface;

// ********************************************************************//
// Declaration of CoClasses defined in Type Library
// (NOTE: Here we map each CoClass to its Default Interface)
// ********************************************************************//
  CheckListBoxX = ICheckListBoxX;


// ********************************************************************//
// Declaration of structures, unions and aliases.
// ********************************************************************//
  PPUserType1 = ^IFontDisp; {*}


// ********************************************************************//
// Interface: ICheckListBoxX
// Flags:     (4416) Dual OleAutomation Dispatchable
// GUID:      {DEA02251-5B44-11D3-B86D-0040F67455FE}
// ********************************************************************//
  ICheckListBoxX = interface(IDispatch)
    ['{DEA02251-5B44-11D3-B86D-0040F67455FE}']
    function  Get_AllowGrayed: WordBool; safecall;
    procedure Set_AllowGrayed(Value: WordBool); safecall;
    function  Get_BorderStyle: TxBorderStyle; safecall;
    procedure Set_BorderStyle(Value: TxBorderStyle); safecall;
    function  Get_Color: OLE_COLOR; safecall;
    procedure Set_Color(Value: OLE_COLOR); safecall;
    function  Get_Columns: Integer; safecall;
    procedure Set_Columns(Value: Integer); safecall;
    function  Get_Ctl3D: WordBool; safecall;
    procedure Set_Ctl3D(Value: WordBool); safecall;
    function  Get_DragCursor: Smallint; safecall;
    procedure Set_DragCursor(Value: Smallint); safecall;
    function  Get_DragMode: TxDragMode; safecall;
    procedure Set_DragMode(Value: TxDragMode); safecall;
    function  Get_Enabled: WordBool; safecall;
    procedure Set_Enabled(Value: WordBool); safecall;
    function  Get_Flat: WordBool; safecall;
    procedure Set_Flat(Value: WordBool); safecall;
    function  Get_Font: IFontDisp; safecall;
```

```
procedure _Set_Font(const Value: IFontDisp); safecall;
procedure Set_Font(var Value: IFontDisp); safecall;
function  Get_ImeMode: TxImeMode; safecall;
procedure Set_ImeMode(Value: TxImeMode); safecall;
function  Get_ImeName: WideString; safecall;
procedure Set_ImeName(const Value: WideString); safecall;
function  Get_IntegralHeight: WordBool; safecall;
procedure Set_IntegralHeight(Value: WordBool); safecall;
function  Get_ItemHeight: Integer; safecall;
procedure Set_ItemHeight(Value: Integer); safecall;
function  Get_Items: IStrings; safecall;
procedure Set_Items(const Value: IStrings); safecall;
function  Get_ParentColor: WordBool; safecall;
procedure Set_ParentColor(Value: WordBool); safecall;
function  Get_ParentCtl3D: WordBool; safecall;
procedure Set_ParentCtl3D(Value: WordBool); safecall;
function  Get_Sorted: WordBool; safecall;
procedure Set_Sorted(Value: WordBool); safecall;
function  Get_Style: TxListBoxStyle; safecall;
procedure Set_Style(Value: TxListBoxStyle); safecall;
function  Get_TabWidth: Integer; safecall;
procedure Set_TabWidth(Value: Integer); safecall;
function  Get_Visible: WordBool; safecall;
procedure Set_Visible(Value: WordBool); safecall;
function  Get_ItemIndex: Integer; safecall;
procedure Set_ItemIndex(Value: Integer); safecall;
function  Get_SelCount: Integer; safecall;
function  Get_TopIndex: Integer; safecall;
procedure Set_TopIndex(Value: Integer); safecall;
function  Get_DoubleBuffered: WordBool; safecall;
procedure Set_DoubleBuffered(Value: WordBool); safecall;
function  Get_VisibleDockClientCount: Integer; safecall;
function  Get_Cursor: Smallint; safecall;
procedure Set_Cursor(Value: Smallint); safecall;
procedure AboutBox; safecall;
property AllowGrayed: WordBool read Get_AllowGrayed write Set_AllowGrayed;
property BorderStyle: TxBorderStyle read Get_BorderStyle write Set_BorderStyle;
property Color: OLE_COLOR read Get_Color write Set_Color;
property Columns: Integer read Get_Columns write Set_Columns;
property Ctl3D: WordBool read Get_Ctl3D write Set_Ctl3D;
property DragCursor: Smallint read Get_DragCursor write Set_DragCursor;
property DragMode: TxDragMode read Get_DragMode write Set_DragMode;
property Enabled: WordBool read Get_Enabled write Set_Enabled;
property Flat: WordBool read Get_Flat write Set_Flat;
property Font: IFontDisp read Get_Font write _Set_Font;
property ImeMode: TxImeMode read Get_ImeMode write Set_ImeMode;
property ImeName: WideString read Get_ImeName write Set_ImeName;
property IntegralHeight: WordBool read Get_IntegralHeight write Set_IntegralHeight;
property ItemHeight: Integer read Get_ItemHeight write Set_ItemHeight;
property Items: IStrings read Get_Items write Set_Items;
property ParentColor: WordBool read Get_ParentColor write Set_ParentColor;
property ParentCtl3D: WordBool read Get_ParentCtl3D write Set_ParentCtl3D;
property Sorted: WordBool read Get_Sorted write Set_Sorted;
```

*continues* ▶

**Listing 5.7** *continued*

```
    property Style: TxListBoxStyle read Get_Style write Set_Style;
    property TabWidth: Integer read Get_TabWidth write Set_TabWidth;
    property Visible: WordBool read Get_Visible write Set_Visible;
    property ItemIndex: Integer read Get_ItemIndex write Set_ItemIndex;
    property SelCount: Integer read Get_SelCount;
    property TopIndex: Integer read Get_TopIndex write Set_TopIndex;
    property DoubleBuffered: WordBool read Get_DoubleBuffered write Set_DoubleBuffered;
    property VisibleDockClientCount: Integer read Get_VisibleDockClientCount;
    property Cursor: Smallint read Get_Cursor write Set_Cursor;
  end;

// ***********************************************************************//
// DispIntf:  ICheckListBoxXDisp
// Flags:     (4416) Dual OleAutomation Dispatchable
// GUID:      {DEA02251-5B44-11D3-B86D-0040F67455FE}
// ***********************************************************************//
  ICheckListBoxXDisp = dispinterface
    ['{DEA02251-5B44-11D3-B86D-0040F67455FE}']
    property AllowGrayed: WordBool dispid 1;
    property BorderStyle: TxBorderStyle dispid 2;
    property Color: OLE_COLOR dispid -501;
    property Columns: Integer dispid 3;
    property Ctl3D: WordBool dispid 4;
    property DragCursor: Smallint dispid 5;
    property DragMode: TxDragMode dispid 6;
    property Enabled: WordBool dispid -514;
    property Flat: WordBool dispid 7;
    property Font: IFontDisp dispid -512;
    property ImeMode: TxImeMode dispid 8;
    property ImeName: WideString dispid 9;
    property IntegralHeight: WordBool dispid 10;
    property ItemHeight: Integer dispid 11;
    property Items: IStrings dispid 12;
    property ParentColor: WordBool dispid 13;
    property ParentCtl3D: WordBool dispid 14;
    property Sorted: WordBool dispid 15;
    property Style: TxListBoxStyle dispid 16;
    property TabWidth: Integer dispid 17;
    property Visible: WordBool dispid 18;
    property ItemIndex: Integer dispid 21;
    property SelCount: Integer readonly dispid 22;
    property TopIndex: Integer dispid 23;
    property DoubleBuffered: WordBool dispid 24;
    property VisibleDockClientCount: Integer readonly dispid 25;
    property Cursor: Smallint dispid 34;
    procedure AboutBox; dispid -552;
  end;

// ***********************************************************************//
// DispIntf:  ICheckListBoxXEvents
// Flags:     (0)
// GUID:      {DEA02253-5B44-11D3-B86D-0040F67455FE}
```

```
// *************************************************************************//
  ICheckListBoxXEvents = dispinterface
    ['{DEA02253-5B44-11D3-B86D-0040F67455FE}']
    procedure OnClickCheck; dispid 1;
    procedure OnClick; dispid 2;
    procedure OnDblClick; dispid 4;
    procedure OnKeyPress(var Key: Smallint); dispid 11;
  end;


// *************************************************************************//
// OLE Control Proxy class declaration
// Control Name     : TCheckListBoxX
// Help String      : CheckListBoxX Control
// Default Interface: ICheckListBoxX
// Def. Intf. DISP? : No
// Event   Interface: ICheckListBoxXEvents
// TypeFlags        : (38) CanCreate Licensed Control
// *************************************************************************//
  TCheckListBoxXOnKeyPress = procedure(Sender: TObject; var Key: Smallint) of object;

  TCheckListBoxX = class(TOleControl)
  private
    FOnClickCheck: TNotifyEvent;
    FOnClick: TNotifyEvent;
    FOnDblClick: TNotifyEvent;
    FOnKeyPress: TCheckListBoxXOnKeyPress;
    FIntf: ICheckListBoxX;
    function  GetControlInterface: ICheckListBoxX;
  protected
    procedure CreateControl;
    procedure InitControlData; override;
    function  Get_Items: IStrings;
    procedure Set_Items(const Value: IStrings);
  public
    procedure AboutBox;
    property  ControlInterface: ICheckListBoxX read GetControlInterface;
    property  DefaultInterface: ICheckListBoxX read GetControlInterface;
    property ItemIndex: Integer index 21 read GetIntegerProp write SetIntegerProp;
    property SelCount: Integer index 22 read GetIntegerProp;
    property TopIndex: Integer index 23 read GetIntegerProp write SetIntegerProp;
    property DoubleBuffered: WordBool index 24 read GetWordBoolProp write SetWordBoolProp;
    property VisibleDockClientCount: Integer index 25 read GetIntegerProp;
  published
    property AllowGrayed: WordBool index 1 read GetWordBoolProp write SetWordBoolProp
stored False;
    property BorderStyle: TOleEnum index 2 read GetTOleEnumProp write SetTOleEnumProp
stored False;
    property Color: TColor index -501 read GetTColorProp write SetTColorProp stored False;
    property Columns: Integer index 3 read GetIntegerProp write SetIntegerProp stored
False;
    property Ctl3D: WordBool index 4 read GetWordBoolProp write SetWordBoolProp stored
```

*continues* ▶

**Listing 5.7** *continued*

```
False;
    property DragCursor: Smallint index 5 read GetSmallintProp write SetSmallintProp
stored False;
    property DragMode: TOleEnum index 6 read GetTOleEnumProp write SetTOleEnumProp stored
False;
    property Enabled: WordBool index -514 read GetWordBoolProp write SetWordBoolProp
stored False;
    property Flat: WordBool index 7 read GetWordBoolProp write SetWordBoolProp stored
False;
    property Font: TFont index -512 read GetTFontProp write SetTFontProp stored False;
    property ImeMode: TOleEnum index 8 read GetTOleEnumProp write SetTOleEnumProp stored
False;
    property ImeName: WideString index 9 read GetWideStringProp write SetWideStringProp
stored False;
    property IntegralHeight: WordBool index 10 read GetWordBoolProp write SetWordBoolProp
stored False;
    property ItemHeight: Integer index 11 read GetIntegerProp write SetIntegerProp stored
False;
    property Items: IStrings read Get_Items write Set_Items stored False;
    property ParentColor: WordBool index 13 read GetWordBoolProp write SetWordBoolProp
stored False;
    property ParentCtl3D: WordBool index 14 read GetWordBoolProp write SetWordBoolProp
stored False;
    property Sorted: WordBool index 15 read GetWordBoolProp write SetWordBoolProp stored
False;
    property Style: TOleEnum index 16 read GetTOleEnumProp write SetTOleEnumProp stored
False;
    property TabWidth: Integer index 17 read GetIntegerProp write SetIntegerProp stored
False;
    property Visible: WordBool index 18 read GetWordBoolProp write SetWordBoolProp stored
False;
    property Cursor: Smallint index 34 read GetSmallintProp write SetSmallintProp stored
False;
    property OnClickCheck: TNotifyEvent read FOnClickCheck write FOnClickCheck;
    property OnClick: TNotifyEvent read FOnClick write FOnClick;
    property OnDblClick: TNotifyEvent read FOnDblClick write FOnDblClick;
    property OnKeyPress: TCheckListBoxXOnKeyPress read FOnKeyPress write FOnKeyPress;
  end;

procedure Register;

implementation

uses ComObj;

procedure TCheckListBoxX.InitControlData;
const
  CEventDispIDs: array [0..3] of DWORD = (
    $00000001, $00000002, $00000004, $0000000B);
  CTFontIDs: array [0..0] of DWORD = (
    $FFFFFE00);
```

```
  CControlData: TControlData2 = (
    ClassID: '{DEA02255-5B44-11D3-B86D-0040F67455FE}';
    EventIID: '{DEA02253-5B44-11D3-B86D-0040F67455FE}';
    EventCount: 4;
    EventDispIDs: @CEventDispIDs;
    LicenseKey: nil (*HR:$80040154*);
    Flags: $0000000D;
    Version: 401;
    FontCount: 1;
    FontIDs: @CTFontIDs);
begin
  ControlData := @CControlData;
  TControlData2(CControlData).FirstEventOfs := Cardinal(@@FOnClickCheck) - Cardinal(Self);
end;

procedure TCheckListBoxX.CreateControl;

  procedure DoCreate;
  begin
    FIntf := IUnknown(OleObject) as ICheckListBoxX;
  end;

begin
  if FIntf = nil then DoCreate;
end;

function TCheckListBoxX.GetControlInterface: ICheckListBoxX;
begin
  CreateControl;
  Result := FIntf;
end;

function  TCheckListBoxX.Get_Items: IStrings;
begin
  Result := DefaultInterface.Get_Items;
end;

procedure TCheckListBoxX.Set_Items(const Value: IStrings);
begin
  DefaultInterface.Set_Items(Value);
end;

procedure TCheckListBoxX.AboutBox;
begin
  DefaultInterface.AboutBox;
end;

procedure Register;
begin
  RegisterComponents('ActiveX',[TCheckListBoxX]);
end;

end.
```

**Listing 5.8**    *About1.pas*

```
unit About1;

interface

uses
  Windows, Messages, SysUtils, Classes, Graphics, Controls, Forms, Dialogs,
  StdCtrls, ExtCtrls;

type
  TCheckListBoxXAbout = class(TForm)
    CtlImage: TSpeedButton;
    NameLbl: TLabel;
    OkBtn: TButton;
    CopyrightLbl: TLabel;
    DescLbl: TLabel;
  end;

procedure ShowCheckListBoxXAbout;

implementation

{$R *.DFM}

procedure ShowCheckListBoxXAbout;
begin
  with TCheckListBoxXAbout.Create(nil) do
    try
      ShowModal;
    finally
      Free;
    end;
end;

end.
```

Select Project, Build Project1 from the Delphi main menu to compile the ActiveX control.

## Registering an ActiveX Control

After the ActiveX control is built, you need to register it with Windows in order to use it. From the Delphi main menu, select Run, Register ActiveX Server. Delphi will register the ActiveX control and display a message indicating that the control was registered successfully.

It's worth noting that you now have a fully functional ActiveX control.

## Testing the ActiveX Control in Visual Basic

Now that the ActiveX control is built and registered with Windows, we can test it to make sure it works properly. If at all possible, you should test with a copy of Visual Basic, because as I indicated earlier, Visual Basic users are by far the largest market available today for ActiveX controls.

---

### Note

*To ensure correct operation with a wide variety of hosting applications, you should test with as many ActiveX containers as you possibly can. ActiveX containers behave differently, so testing with a number of different applications, such as Explorer, Word, and so on will guarantee that your ActiveX control is as robust as possible.* ◆

Figure 5.7 shows a Visual Basic project using the CheckListBox ActiveX control just developed.

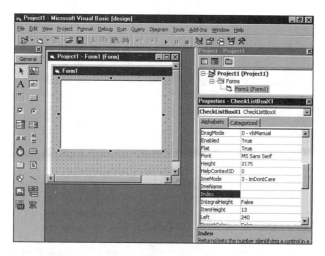

**Figure 5.7** *The TCheckListBoxX ActiveX control in Visual Basic.*

## Adding Property Pages to an ActiveX Control

You'll notice from Figure 5.7 that not all the properties of the VCL control show up in Visual Basic. In particular, there appears to be no way to modify the Items property of the component. However, by adding a property page to the ActiveX control, it's easy to provide access to the Items property at design time.

## Adding Predefined Delphi Property Pages

Delphi provides four predefined property pages that you can use to edit certain properties of your ActiveX control. The predefined property pages are listed in Table 5.5.

*Table 5.5    Predefined ActiveX Control Property Pages*

| CLSID | Description |
| --- | --- |
| Class_DColorPropPage | Used to edit TColor properties |
| Class_DFontPropPage | Used to edit TFont properties |
| Class_DPicturePropPage | Used to edit TPicture properties |
| Class_DStringPropPage | Used to edit TStrings properties |

To add one or more of the predefined property pages to your ActiveX control, you must add some code to the control's DefinePropertyPages method, as follows:

```
procedure TCheckListBoxX.DefinePropertyPages(DefinePropertyPage: TDefinePropertyPage);
begin
  {TODO: Define property pages here.  Property pages are defined by calling
    DefinePropertyPage with the class id of the page.  For example,
      DefinePropertyPage(Class_CheckListBoxXPage); }
  DefinePropertyPage(Class_DStringPropPage);
end;
```

## Adding Your Own Property Pages

It's also straightforward to create your own property page to edit other control data. Select File, New from Delphi's main menu. In the Object Inspector, select the ActiveX tab and double-click the Property Page item. Delphi generates a standard Delphi form that you can use to provide access to whatever properties of your ActiveX control that you like. It also creates a unique CLSID (which is simply a GUID) that you can use to add the property page to the ActiveX control, again by adding code to the control's DefinePropertyPages method.

```
procedure TCheckListBoxX.DefinePropertyPages(DefinePropertyPage: TDefinePropertyPage);
begin
  {TODO: Define property pages here.  Property pages are defined by calling
    DefinePropertyPage with the class id of the page.  For example,
      DefinePropertyPage(Class_CheckListBoxXPage); }
  DefinePropertyPage(Class_ppgGeneral);
  DefinePropertyPage(Class_DStringPropPage);
end;
```

## Distributing ActiveX Controls

After your ActiveX control has been built and thoroughly tested, it's time to package it up for distribution. At a minimum, you need to distribute the .OCX file that houses the ActiveX control. During installation of the ActiveX control, you must ensure that it gets registered with Windows. Any installation software worth its salt will provide an option to register the control during installation. You should also redistribute (and register) STD-VCL32.DLL, which contains the predefined Delphi property pages listed in Table 5.5, as well as certain predefined types such as IStrings.

If you enable the licensing option when creating the ActiveX control, you will also need to distribute the .LIC file to provide developers with a design-time license for your control.

Now that you know how to create an ActiveX control from a VCL component, I'll show you how to create an ActiveX control based on a Delphi form.

# ActiveForms

An ActiveForm is nothing more than an ActiveX control based on a Delphi form. Rather than converting an individual component to an ActiveX control, you can create an ActiveForm as easily as you can create a normal Delphi form.

## Creating an ActiveForm

Figure 5.8 shows the ActiveForm that we're going to create. As you can see, it allows the user to enter his name and email address. The procedure for creating a complicated ActiveForm is the same as the procedure for creating a simple one, so there is no need to get bogged down in the details of a complex form for this example. Suffice it to say that you can use any Delphi component on an ActiveForm, including data access and data-aware components.

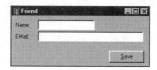

**Figure 5.8**   *A sample ActiveForm.*

To create an ActiveForm in an in-process COM server, execute the following steps:

1. First, create a new ActiveX library by selecting File, New from the Delphi main menu.

2. On the ActiveX page of the Object Repository, double-click the ActiveX Library icon.

3. Next, select File, New from the Delphi menu again, and this time, double-click the ActiveForm icon on the ActiveX page of the Object Repository.

4. The ActiveForm Wizard appears. Fill out the wizard so it looks like Figure 5.9 and click OK.

**Figure 5.9**    *Delphi's ActiveForm Wizard.*

5. Click the Save Project icon on Delphi's toolbar. Save unit About1 as AboutForm.pas, FriendFormImpl1 as FriendFormImpl.pas, and Project1 as FriendX.dpr.

   You should notice that Delphi creates a blank form for you. You use Delphi's familiar form designer to design an ActiveForm exactly the same way that you design a standard Delphi form. For this example, I've added two edit controls (for name and email address), and a Save button. I also added some code to the Save button's OnClick event that writes the name and email address to a text file.

Listings 5.9 through 5.12 show the complete source code for this application.

**Listing 5.9**    *FriendX—FriendX.dpr*

```
library FriendX;

uses
  ComServ,
  FriendX_TLB in 'FriendX_TLB.pas',
  FriendFormImpl in 'FriendFormImpl.pas' {FriendFormX: TActiveForm} {FriendFormX:
CoClass},
```

```
    AboutForm in 'AboutForm.pas' {FriendFormXAbout};

  {$E ocx}

  exports
    DllGetClassObject,
    DllCanUnloadNow,
    DllRegisterServer,
    DllUnregisterServer;

  {$R *.TLB}

  {$R *.RES}

  begin
  end.
```

---

## Listing 5.10    *FriendX—AboutForm.pas*

```
unit AboutForm;

interface

uses
  Windows, Messages, SysUtils, Classes, Graphics, Controls, Forms, Dialog boxes,
  StdCtrls, ExtCtrls, Buttons;

type
  TFriendFormXAbout = class(TForm)
    CtlImage: TSpeedButton;
    NameLbl: TLabel;
    OkBtn: TButton;
    CopyrightLbl: TLabel;
    DescLbl: TLabel;
  end;

procedure ShowFriendFormXAbout;

implementation

{$R *.DFM}

procedure ShowFriendFormXAbout;
begin
  with TFriendFormXAbout.Create(nil) do
    try
      ShowModal;
    finally
      Free;
    end;
end;

end.
```

**Listing 5.11**    *FriendX—FriendX_TLB.pas*

```
unit FriendX_TLB;

// *********************************************************************** //
// WARNING
// -------
// The types declared in this file were generated from data read from a
// Type Library. If this type library is explicitly or indirectly (via
// another type library referring to this type library) re-imported, or the
// 'Refresh' command of the Type Library Editor activated while editing the
// Type Library, the contents of this file will be regenerated and all
// manual modifications will be lost.
// *********************************************************************** //

// PASTLWTR : $Revision:   1.88  $
// File generated on 8/28/1999 1:48:21 PM from Type Library described below.

// ***********************************************************************//
// NOTE:
// Items guarded by $IFDEF_LIVE_SERVER_AT_DESIGN_TIME are used by properties
// which return objects that may need to be explicitly created via a function
// call prior to any access via the property. These items have been disabled
// in order to prevent accidental use from within the object inspector. You
// may enable them by defining LIVE_SERVER_AT_DESIGN_TIME or by selectively
// removing them from the $IFDEF blocks. However, such items must still be
// programmatically created via a method of the appropriate CoClass before
// they can be used.
// *********************************************************************** //
// Type Lib: J:\Book\samples\Chap06\ActiveForm\FriendX.tlb (1)
// IID\LCID: {9EC8AF31-5D6D-11D3-B872-0040F67455FE}\0
// Helpfile:
// DepndLst:
//   (1) v2.0 stdole, (C:\WINNT\System32\StdOle2.tlb)
//   (2) v4.0 StdVCL, (C:\WINNT\System32\STDVCL40.DLL)
// *********************************************************************** //
{$TYPEDADDRESS OFF} // Unit must be compiled without type-checked pointers.
interface

uses Windows, ActiveX, Classes, Graphics, OleServer, OleCtrls, StdVCL;

// ***********************************************************************//
// GUIDS declared in the TypeLibrary. Following prefixes are used:
//   Type Libraries     : LIBID_xxxx
//   CoClasses          : CLASS_xxxx
//   DISPInterfaces     : DIID_xxxx
//   Non-DISP interfaces: IID_xxxx
// ***********************************************************************//
const
  // TypeLibrary Major and minor versions
  FriendXMajorVersion = 1;
  FriendXMinorVersion = 0;
```

```
  LIBID_FriendX: TGUID = '{9EC8AF31-5D6D-11D3-B872-0040F67455FE}';

  IID_IFriendFormX: TGUID = '{9EC8AF32-5D6D-11D3-B872-0040F67455FE}';
  DIID_IFriendFormXEvents: TGUID = '{9EC8AF34-5D6D-11D3-B872-0040F67455FE}';
  CLASS_FriendFormX: TGUID = '{9EC8AF36-5D6D-11D3-B872-0040F67455FE}';

// **********************************************************************//
// Declaration of Enumerations defined in Type Library
// **********************************************************************//
// Constants for enum TxActiveFormBorderStyle
type
  TxActiveFormBorderStyle = TOleEnum;
const
  afbNone = $00000000;
  afbSingle = $00000001;
  afbSunken = $00000002;
  afbRaised = $00000003;

// Constants for enum TxPrintScale
type
  TxPrintScale = TOleEnum;
const
  poNone = $00000000;
  poProportional = $00000001;
  poPrintToFit = $00000002;

// Constants for enum TxMouseButton
type
  TxMouseButton = TOleEnum;
const
  mbLeft = $00000000;
  mbRight = $00000001;
  mbMiddle = $00000002;

type

// **********************************************************************//
// Forward declaration of types defined in TypeLibrary
// **********************************************************************//
  IFriendFormX = interface;
  IFriendFormXDisp = dispinterface;
  IFriendFormXEvents = dispinterface;

// **********************************************************************//
// Declaration of CoClasses defined in Type Library
// (NOTE: Here we map each CoClass to its Default Interface)
// **********************************************************************//
  FriendFormX = IFriendFormX;


// **********************************************************************//
// Declaration of structures, unions and aliases.
// **********************************************************************//
```

*continues* ▶

**Listing 5.11**    *continued*

```
  PPUserType1 = ^IFontDisp; {*}


// ********************************************************************//
// Interface: IFriendFormX
// Flags:     (4416) Dual OleAutomation Dispatchable
// GUID:      {9EC8AF32-5D6D-11D3-B872-0040F67455FE}
// ********************************************************************//
  IFriendFormX = interface(IDispatch)
    ['{9EC8AF32-5D6D-11D3-B872-0040F67455FE}']
    function  Get_Visible: WordBool; safecall;
    procedure Set_Visible(Value: WordBool); safecall;
    function  Get_AutoScroll: WordBool; safecall;
    procedure Set_AutoScroll(Value: WordBool); safecall;
    function  Get_AutoSize: WordBool; safecall;
    procedure Set_AutoSize(Value: WordBool); safecall;
    function  Get_AxBorderStyle: TxActiveFormBorderStyle; safecall;
    procedure Set_AxBorderStyle(Value: TxActiveFormBorderStyle); safecall;
    function  Get_Caption: WideString; safecall;
    procedure Set_Caption(const Value: WideString); safecall;
    function  Get_Color: OLE_COLOR; safecall;
    procedure Set_Color(Value: OLE_COLOR); safecall;
    function  Get_Font: IFontDisp; safecall;
    procedure _Set_Font(const Value: IFontDisp); safecall;
    procedure Set_Font(var Value: IFontDisp); safecall;
    function  Get_KeyPreview: WordBool; safecall;
    procedure Set_KeyPreview(Value: WordBool); safecall;
    function  Get_PixelsPerInch: Integer; safecall;
    procedure Set_PixelsPerInch(Value: Integer); safecall;
    function  Get_PrintScale: TxPrintScale; safecall;
    procedure Set_PrintScale(Value: TxPrintScale); safecall;
    function  Get_Scaled: WordBool; safecall;
    procedure Set_Scaled(Value: WordBool); safecall;
    function  Get_Active: WordBool; safecall;
    function  Get_DropTarget: WordBool; safecall;
    procedure Set_DropTarget(Value: WordBool); safecall;
    function  Get_HelpFile: WideString; safecall;
    procedure Set_HelpFile(const Value: WideString); safecall;
    function  Get_DoubleBuffered: WordBool; safecall;
    procedure Set_DoubleBuffered(Value: WordBool); safecall;
    function  Get_VisibleDockClientCount: Integer; safecall;
    function  Get_Enabled: WordBool; safecall;
    procedure Set_Enabled(Value: WordBool); safecall;
    function  Get_Cursor: Smallint; safecall;
    procedure Set_Cursor(Value: Smallint); safecall;
    procedure AboutBox; safecall;
    property Visible: WordBool read Get_Visible write Set_Visible;
    property AutoScroll: WordBool read Get_AutoScroll write Set_AutoScroll;
    property AutoSize: WordBool read Get_AutoSize write Set_AutoSize;
    property AxBorderStyle: TxActiveFormBorderStyle read Get_AxBorderStyle write
Set_AxBorderStyle;
```

```
    property Caption: WideString read Get_Caption write Set_Caption;
    property Color: OLE_COLOR read Get_Color write Set_Color;
    property Font: IFontDisp read Get_Font write _Set_Font;
    property KeyPreview: WordBool read Get_KeyPreview write Set_KeyPreview;
    property PixelsPerInch: Integer read Get_PixelsPerInch write Set_PixelsPerInch;
    property PrintScale: TxPrintScale read Get_PrintScale write Set_PrintScale;
    property Scaled: WordBool read Get_Scaled write Set_Scaled;
    property Active: WordBool read Get_Active;
    property DropTarget: WordBool read Get_DropTarget write Set_DropTarget;
    property HelpFile: WideString read Get_HelpFile write Set_HelpFile;
    property DoubleBuffered: WordBool read Get_DoubleBuffered write Set_DoubleBuffered;
    property VisibleDockClientCount: Integer read Get_VisibleDockClientCount;
    property Enabled: WordBool read Get_Enabled write Set_Enabled;
    property Cursor: Smallint read Get_Cursor write Set_Cursor;
  end;

// ***********************************************************************//
// DispIntf:  IFriendFormXDisp
// Flags:     (4416) Dual OleAutomation Dispatchable
// GUID:      {9EC8AF32-5D6D-11D3-B872-0040F67455FE}
// ***********************************************************************//
  IFriendFormXDisp = dispinterface
    ['{9EC8AF32-5D6D-11D3-B872-0040F67455FE}']
    property Visible: WordBool dispid 1;
    property AutoScroll: WordBool dispid 2;
    property AutoSize: WordBool dispid 3;
    property AxBorderStyle: TxActiveFormBorderStyle dispid 4;
    property Caption: WideString dispid -518;
    property Color: OLE_COLOR dispid -501;
    property Font: IFontDisp dispid -512;
    property KeyPreview: WordBool dispid 5;
    property PixelsPerInch: Integer dispid 6;
    property PrintScale: TxPrintScale dispid 7;
    property Scaled: WordBool dispid 8;
    property Active: WordBool readonly dispid 9;
    property DropTarget: WordBool dispid 10;
    property HelpFile: WideString dispid 11;
    property DoubleBuffered: WordBool dispid 12;
    property VisibleDockClientCount: Integer readonly dispid 13;
    property Enabled: WordBool dispid -514;
    property Cursor: Smallint dispid 14;
    procedure AboutBox; dispid -552;
  end;

// ***********************************************************************//
// DispIntf:  IFriendFormXEvents
// Flags:     (0)
// GUID:      {9EC8AF34-5D6D-11D3-B872-0040F67455FE}
// ***********************************************************************//
  IFriendFormXEvents = dispinterface
    ['{9EC8AF34-5D6D-11D3-B872-0040F67455FE}']
    procedure OnActivate; dispid 1;
    procedure OnClick; dispid 2;
```

*continues* ▶

**Listing 5.11** *continued*

```
  procedure OnCreate; dispid 3;
  procedure OnDblClick; dispid 5;
  procedure OnDestroy; dispid 6;
  procedure OnDeactivate; dispid 7;
  procedure OnKeyPress(var Key: Smallint); dispid 11;
  procedure OnPaint; dispid 16;
end;


// **********************************************************************//
// OLE Control Proxy class declaration
// Control Name      : TFriendFormX
// Help String       : FriendFormX Control
// Default Interface: IFriendFormX
// Def. Intf. DISP? : No
// Event   Interface: IFriendFormXEvents
// TypeFlags         : (38) CanCreate Licensed Control
// **********************************************************************//
  TFriendFormXOnKeyPress = procedure(Sender: TObject; var Key: Smallint) of object;

  TFriendFormX = class(TOleControl)
  private
    FOnActivate: TNotifyEvent;
    FOnClick: TNotifyEvent;
    FOnCreate: TNotifyEvent;
    FOnDblClick: TNotifyEvent;
    FOnDestroy: TNotifyEvent;
    FOnDeactivate: TNotifyEvent;
    FOnKeyPress: TFriendFormXOnKeyPress;
    FOnPaint: TNotifyEvent;
    FIntf: IFriendFormX;
    function  GetControlInterface: IFriendFormX;
  protected
    procedure CreateControl;
    procedure InitControlData; override;
  public
    procedure AboutBox;
    property  ControlInterface: IFriendFormX read GetControlInterface;
    property  DefaultInterface: IFriendFormX read GetControlInterface;
    property Visible: WordBool index 1 read GetWordBoolProp write SetWordBoolProp;
    property Active: WordBool index 9 read GetWordBoolProp;
    property DropTarget: WordBool index 10 read GetWordBoolProp write SetWordBoolProp;
    property HelpFile: WideString index 11 read GetWideStringProp write SetWideStringProp;
    property DoubleBuffered: WordBool index 12 read GetWordBoolProp write SetWordBoolProp;
    property VisibleDockClientCount: Integer index 13 read GetIntegerProp;
    property Enabled: WordBool index -514 read GetWordBoolProp write SetWordBoolProp;
  published
    property AutoScroll: WordBool index 2 read GetWordBoolProp write SetWordBoolProp
stored False;
    property AutoSize: WordBool index 3 read GetWordBoolProp write SetWordBoolProp stored
False;
```

```
      property AxBorderStyle: TOleEnum index 4 read GetTOleEnumProp write SetTOleEnumProp
  stored False;
      property Caption: WideString index -518 read GetWideStringProp write SetWideStringProp
  stored False;
      property Color: TColor index -501 read GetTColorProp write SetTColorProp stored False;
      property Font: TFont index -512 read GetTFontProp write SetTFontProp stored False;
      property KeyPreview: WordBool index 5 read GetWordBoolProp write SetWordBoolProp
  stored False;
      property PixelsPerInch: Integer index 6 read GetIntegerProp write SetIntegerProp
  stored False;
      property PrintScale: TOleEnum index 7 read GetTOleEnumProp write SetTOleEnumProp
  stored False;
      property Scaled: WordBool index 8 read GetWordBoolProp write SetWordBoolProp stored
  False;
      property Cursor: Smallint index 14 read GetSmallintProp write SetSmallintProp stored
  False;
    property OnActivate: TNotifyEvent read FOnActivate write FOnActivate;
    property OnClick: TNotifyEvent read FOnClick write FOnClick;
    property OnCreate: TNotifyEvent read FOnCreate write FOnCreate;
    property OnDblClick: TNotifyEvent read FOnDblClick write FOnDblClick;
    property OnDestroy: TNotifyEvent read FOnDestroy write FOnDestroy;
    property OnDeactivate: TNotifyEvent read FOnDeactivate write FOnDeactivate;
    property OnKeyPress: TFriendFormXOnKeyPress read FOnKeyPress write FOnKeyPress;
    property OnPaint: TNotifyEvent read FOnPaint write FOnPaint;
  end;

procedure Register;

implementation

uses ComObj;

procedure TFriendFormX.InitControlData;
const
  CEventDispIDs: array [0..7] of DWORD = (
    $00000001, $00000002, $00000003, $00000005, $00000006, $00000007,
    $0000000B, $00000010);
  CTFontIDs: array [0..0] of DWORD = (
    $FFFFFE00);
  CControlData: TControlData2 = (
    ClassID: '{9EC8AF36-5D6D-11D3-B872-0040F67455FE}';
    EventIID: '{9EC8AF34-5D6D-11D3-B872-0040F67455FE}';
    EventCount: 8;
    EventDispIDs: @CEventDispIDs;
    LicenseKey: nil (*HR:$80040154*);
    Flags: $0000001D;
    Version: 401;
    FontCount: 1;
    FontIDs: @CTFontIDs);
begin
  ControlData := @CControlData;
  TControlData2(CControlData).FirstEventOfs := Cardinal(@@FOnActivate) - Cardinal(Self);
end;
```

*continues* ▶

**Listing 5.11**    *continued*

```
procedure TFriendFormX.CreateControl;

  procedure DoCreate;
  begin
    FIntf := IUnknown(OleObject) as IFriendFormX;
  end;

begin
  if FIntf = nil then DoCreate;
end;

function TFriendFormX.GetControlInterface: IFriendFormX;
begin
  CreateControl;
  Result := FIntf;
end;

procedure TFriendFormX.AboutBox;
begin
  DefaultInterface.AboutBox;
end;

procedure Register;
begin
  RegisterComponents('ActiveX',[TFriendFormX]);
end;

end.
```

**Listing 5.12**    *FriendX—FriendFormImpl.pas*

```
unit FriendFormImpl;

interface

uses
  Windows, Messages, SysUtils, Classes, Graphics, Controls, Forms, Dialogs,
  ActiveX, AxCtrls, FriendX_TLB, StdVcl, StdCtrls;

type
  TFriendFormX = class(TActiveForm, IFriendFormX)
    Label1: TLabel;
    ecName: TEdit;
    ecEMail: TEdit;
    Label2: TLabel;
    btnSave: TButton;
    procedure btnSaveClick(Sender: TObject);
  private
    { Private declarations }
    FEvents: IFriendFormXEvents;
```

```
    procedure ActivateEvent(Sender: TObject);
    procedure ClickEvent(Sender: TObject);
    procedure CreateEvent(Sender: TObject);
    procedure DblClickEvent(Sender: TObject);
    procedure DeactivateEvent(Sender: TObject);
    procedure DestroyEvent(Sender: TObject);
    procedure KeyPressEvent(Sender: TObject; var Key: Char);
    procedure PaintEvent(Sender: TObject);
  protected
    { Protected declarations }
    procedure DefinePropertyPages(DefinePropertyPage: TDefinePropertyPage); override;
    procedure EventSinkChanged(const EventSink: IUnknown); override;
    function Get_Active: WordBool; safecall;
    function Get_AutoScroll: WordBool; safecall;
    function Get_AutoSize: WordBool; safecall;
    function Get_AxBorderStyle: TxActiveFormBorderStyle; safecall;
    function Get_Caption: WideString; safecall;
    function Get_Color: OLE_COLOR; safecall;
    function Get_Cursor: Smallint; safecall;
    function Get_DoubleBuffered: WordBool; safecall;
    function Get_DropTarget: WordBool; safecall;
    function Get_Enabled: WordBool; safecall;
    function Get_Font: IFontDisp; safecall;
    function Get_HelpFile: WideString; safecall;
    function Get_KeyPreview: WordBool; safecall;
    function Get_PixelsPerInch: Integer; safecall;
    function Get_PrintScale: TxPrintScale; safecall;
    function Get_Scaled: WordBool; safecall;
    function Get_Visible: WordBool; safecall;
    function Get_VisibleDockClientCount: Integer; safecall;
    procedure _Set_Font(const Value: IFontDisp); safecall;
    procedure AboutBox; safecall;
    procedure Set_AutoScroll(Value: WordBool); safecall;
    procedure Set_AutoSize(Value: WordBool); safecall;
    procedure Set_AxBorderStyle(Value: TxActiveFormBorderStyle); safecall;
    procedure Set_Caption(const Value: WideString); safecall;
    procedure Set_Color(Value: OLE_COLOR); safecall;
    procedure Set_Cursor(Value: Smallint); safecall;
    procedure Set_DoubleBuffered(Value: WordBool); safecall;
    procedure Set_DropTarget(Value: WordBool); safecall;
    procedure Set_Enabled(Value: WordBool); safecall;
    procedure Set_Font(var Value: IFontDisp); safecall;
    procedure Set_HelpFile(const Value: WideString); safecall;
    procedure Set_KeyPreview(Value: WordBool); safecall;
    procedure Set_PixelsPerInch(Value: Integer); safecall;
    procedure Set_PrintScale(Value: TxPrintScale); safecall;
    procedure Set_Scaled(Value: WordBool); safecall;
    procedure Set_Visible(Value: WordBool); safecall;
public
  { Public declarations }
  procedure Initialize; override;
end;
```

*continues* ▶

**Listing 5.12**   *continued*

```
implementation

uses ComObj, ComServ, AboutForm;

{$R *.DFM}

{ TFriendFormX }

procedure TFriendFormX.DefinePropertyPages(DefinePropertyPage: TDefinePropertyPage);
begin
  { Define property pages here.  Property pages are defined by calling
    DefinePropertyPage with the class id of the page.  For example,
      DefinePropertyPage(Class_FriendFormXPage); }
end;

procedure TFriendFormX.EventSinkChanged(const EventSink: IUnknown);
begin
  FEvents := EventSink as IFriendFormXEvents;
end;

procedure TFriendFormX.Initialize;
begin
  inherited Initialize;
  OnActivate := ActivateEvent;
  OnClick := ClickEvent;
  OnCreate := CreateEvent;
  OnDblClick := DblClickEvent;
  OnDeactivate := DeactivateEvent;
  OnDestroy := DestroyEvent;
  OnKeyPress := KeyPressEvent;
  OnPaint := PaintEvent;
end;

function TFriendFormX.Get_Active: WordBool;
begin
  Result := Active;
end;

function TFriendFormX.Get_AutoScroll: WordBool;
begin
  Result := AutoScroll;
end;

function TFriendFormX.Get_AutoSize: WordBool;
begin
  Result := AutoSize;
end;

function TFriendFormX.Get_AxBorderStyle: TxActiveFormBorderStyle;
begin
  Result := Ord(AxBorderStyle);
end;
```

```
function TFriendFormX.Get_Caption: WideString;
begin
  Result := WideString(Caption);
end;

function TFriendFormX.Get_Color: OLE_COLOR;
begin
  Result := OLE_COLOR(Color);
end;

function TFriendFormX.Get_Cursor: Smallint;
begin
  Result := Smallint(Cursor);
end;

function TFriendFormX.Get_DoubleBuffered: WordBool;
begin
  Result := DoubleBuffered;
end;

function TFriendFormX.Get_DropTarget: WordBool;
begin
  Result := DropTarget;
end;

function TFriendFormX.Get_Enabled: WordBool;
begin
  Result := Enabled;
end;

function TFriendFormX.Get_Font: IFontDisp;
begin
  GetOleFont(Font, Result);
end;

function TFriendFormX.Get_HelpFile: WideString;
begin
  Result := WideString(HelpFile);
end;

function TFriendFormX.Get_KeyPreview: WordBool;
begin
  Result := KeyPreview;
end;

function TFriendFormX.Get_PixelsPerInch: Integer;
begin
  Result := PixelsPerInch;
end;

function TFriendFormX.Get_PrintScale: TxPrintScale;
```

*continues* ▶

**Listing 5.12** *continued*

```
begin
  Result := Ord(PrintScale);
end;

function TFriendFormX.Get_Scaled: WordBool;
begin
  Result := Scaled;
end;

function TFriendFormX.Get_Visible: WordBool;
begin
  Result := Visible;
end;

function TFriendFormX.Get_VisibleDockClientCount: Integer;
begin
  Result := VisibleDockClientCount;
end;

procedure TFriendFormX._Set_Font(const Value: IFontDisp);
begin
  SetOleFont(Font, Value);
end;

procedure TFriendFormX.AboutBox;
begin
  ShowFriendFormXAbout;
end;

procedure TFriendFormX.ActivateEvent(Sender: TObject);
begin
  if FEvents <> nil then FEvents.OnActivate;
end;

procedure TFriendFormX.ClickEvent(Sender: TObject);
begin
  if FEvents <> nil then FEvents.OnClick;
end;

procedure TFriendFormX.CreateEvent(Sender: TObject);
begin
  if FEvents <> nil then FEvents.OnCreate;
end;

procedure TFriendFormX.DblClickEvent(Sender: TObject);
begin
  if FEvents <> nil then FEvents.OnDblClick;
end;

procedure TFriendFormX.DeactivateEvent(Sender: TObject);
```

```
begin
  if FEvents <> nil then FEvents.OnDeactivate;
end;

procedure TFriendFormX.DestroyEvent(Sender: TObject);
begin
  if FEvents <> nil then FEvents.OnDestroy;
end;

procedure TFriendFormX.KeyPressEvent(Sender: TObject; var Key: Char);
var
  TempKey: Smallint;
begin
  TempKey := Smallint(Key);
  if FEvents <> nil then FEvents.OnKeyPress(TempKey);
  Key := Char(TempKey);
end;

procedure TFriendFormX.PaintEvent(Sender: TObject);
begin
  if FEvents <> nil then FEvents.OnPaint;
end;

procedure TFriendFormX.Set_AutoScroll(Value: WordBool);
begin
  AutoScroll := Value;
end;

procedure TFriendFormX.Set_AutoSize(Value: WordBool);
begin
  AutoSize := Value;
end;

procedure TFriendFormX.Set_AxBorderStyle(Value: TxActiveFormBorderStyle);
begin
  AxBorderStyle := TActiveFormBorderStyle(Value);
end;

procedure TFriendFormX.Set_Caption(const Value: WideString);
begin
  Caption := TCaption(Value);
end;

procedure TFriendFormX.Set_Color(Value: OLE_COLOR);
begin
  Color := TColor(Value);
end;

procedure TFriendFormX.Set_Cursor(Value: Smallint);
begin
  Cursor := TCursor(Value);
end;
```

*continues* ▶

**Listing 5.12** *continued*

```
procedure TFriendFormX.Set_DoubleBuffered(Value: WordBool);
begin
  DoubleBuffered := Value;
end;

procedure TFriendFormX.Set_DropTarget(Value: WordBool);
begin
  DropTarget := Value;
end;

procedure TFriendFormX.Set_Enabled(Value: WordBool);
begin
  Enabled := Value;
end;

procedure TFriendFormX.Set_Font(var Value: IFontDisp);
begin
  SetOleFont(Font, Value);
end;

procedure TFriendFormX.Set_HelpFile(const Value: WideString);
begin
  HelpFile := String(Value);
end;

procedure TFriendFormX.Set_KeyPreview(Value: WordBool);
begin
  KeyPreview := Value;
end;

procedure TFriendFormX.Set_PixelsPerInch(Value: Integer);
begin
  PixelsPerInch := Value;
end;

procedure TFriendFormX.Set_PrintScale(Value: TxPrintScale);
begin
  PrintScale := TPrintScale(Value);
end;

procedure TFriendFormX.Set_Scaled(Value: WordBool);
begin
  Scaled := Value;
end;

procedure TFriendFormX.Set_Visible(Value: WordBool);
begin
  Visible := Value;
end;
```

```
procedure TFriendFormX.btnSaveClick(Sender: TObject);
var
  F: TextFile;
begin
  AssignFile(F, 'C:\FRIENDS.TXT');
  try
    Append(F);
  except
    Rewrite(F);
  end;
  Writeln(F, ecName.Text, ': ', ecEMail.Text);
  CloseFile(F);
end;

initialization
  TActiveFormFactory.Create(
    ComServer,
    TActiveFormControl,
    TFriendFormX,
    Class_FriendFormX,
    1,
    '{9EC8AF3C-5D6D-11D3-B872-0040F67455FE}',
    OLEMISC_SIMPLEFRAME or OLEMISC_ACTSLIKELABEL,
    tmApartment);
end.
```

## Testing an ActiveForm

Now that you've got an operational ActiveForm, you need to test it. Fortunately, Delphi helps us out a lot in that respect. To generate a test wrapper for the ActiveForm, select Project, Web Deployment Options... from the Delphi menu. Delphi presents you with a dialog box that you can use to specify where the ActiveForm's OCX file will be deployed, as well as a test directory in which to place an HTML file that you can use to try out your ActiveForm.

Fill out the Web Deployment Options dialog box to look like Figure 5.10 and click OK.

After you've set the Web deployment options, all that's left to do is generate the test files. Select Project, Web Deploy from the Delphi main menu. Delphi will generate your project's OCX file, along with the test HTML file. Now start your Web browser, and view the HTML file that Delphi generated. In this example, I placed the test files in the C:\TEST directory. Figure 5.11 shows Microsoft Internet Explorer viewing the test HTML file.

Figure 5.10    *Web Deployment Options.*

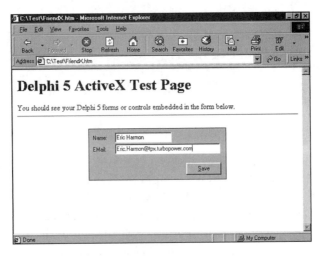

Figure 5.11    *Testing the ActiveForm.*

Enter your name and email address, and click the Save button. You'll have a new file named FRIENDS.TXT in the root directory on drive C:, with the information that you entered in it.

## Summary

In this chapter, I showed you how to take advantage of ActiveX controls in your Delphi applications. As a Delphi programmer, you will usually want to opt for a VCL component if one exists, but there are numerous ActiveX controls available today that might not have a VCL counterpart.

Next, I showed you how you can convert an existing VCL component to an ActiveX control for others to use. If you're a component developer, this opens up a huge additional market for you, in the form of Visual Basic programmers, who represent the largest market for ActiveX controls.

I showed you how you can manually implement functionality that Delphi does not automatically provide when creating an ActiveX control from a VCL component. You also learned how to add property pages to ActiveX controls to aid the user of those controls.

Finally, I discussed ActiveForms, and explained how you can create an ActiveX control from a Delphi form, which can then be displayed in Visual Basic or Internet Explorer, for example.

In the next chapter, we'll take a look at DCOM, which allows you to deploy COM servers and clients on machines connected across a network.

# 6

## DCOM

Up to this point, all the COM work we've done has been on a single
machine. This chapter discusses distributed COM (DCOM) which is really
nothing more than accessing a COM server across a network. After cover-
ing DCOM basics, this chapter will walk you through programming with
DCOM on the client and server side, as well as implementing remote
datasets with DCOM.

## DCOM Basics

DCOM is a technology that allows you to take everything you've learned
about COM and apply it across a network. In this way, you can deploy a
COM server on one machine, and a client that accesses that server on
another machine.

One of the nicest aspects of DCOM is that after you understand COM,
you know almost everything you need to know in order to use DCOM.
There is nothing to relearn.

Chances are, you've already got DCOM installed on your machine.
Windows NT and Windows 98 include DCOM as part of the operating sys-
tem. If you're running Windows 95, you'll need to visit the Web site
http://www.microsoft.com/com/dcom/dcom95/download.asp and download
DCOM95 for Windows 95. You should also download DCOM95 for
Windows 95 configuration utility.

If you're running Windows 98, you can get the latest version of DCOM
at http://www.microsoft.com/com/dcom/dcom98/dcom1_3.asp.

## Programming with DCOM

At this point, DCOM is installed on your machines, and you're ready to create your first DCOM server and client. Using Delphi, writing a DCOM client or server is no more difficult than writing a standard COM client or server. This section will lead you through the steps of creating a simple DCOM server and client, so you can verify that things are operating smoothly.

### Creating a DCOM Server

The first steps in creating a DCOM server are identical to creating a COM server. Start a new Delphi application. Then select File, New from the Delphi main menu, and click the ActiveX tab of the Object Repository. Select Automation Object and click OK.

At this point, Delphi displays the Automation Object Wizard. Fill it out to look like Figure 6.1 and click OK.

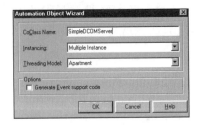

**Figure 6.1**   *Delphi provides the Automation*
*Object Wizard to assist you in creating DCOM servers.*

At this point, save your project. Save unit1 as MainForm.pas, unit2 as SimpleServer.pas, and project1 as DCOMServer.dpr.

Notice that we've done nothing to tell Delphi that we're creating a DCOM server, as opposed to a standard COM server. The only thing we've done is make sure we've created an out-of-process server, instead of an in-process server. After all, the server will be running on a remote machine, which is about as out-of-process as you can get!

Delphi should have automatically started the Type Library Editor after you filled out the Automation Object Wizard. If it didn't, select View, Type Library from the Delphi main menu.

Click the ISimpleDCOMServer node in the Object List of the Type Library Editor, and click the New Method button on the toolbar. Name the new method AreYouThere. Select the Parameters tab and add a parameter named Result, of type VARIANT_BOOL *, and with a modifier of [out, ret-val]. If you're using Delphi 3 or Delphi 4, instead of adding a parameter, you can simply set the Return Type of the AreYouThere method to WordBool.

*Don't forget the discussion in previous chapters on out-of-process servers, marshaling, and Automation-compatible types. That discussion is relevant to this chapter, and you must make sure you only use Automation-compatible types in the methods that you add to DCOM servers. If you're using Delphi 4 or higher, the Type Library Editor will enforce that rule for you. ◆*

Click the Refresh Implementation button in the Type Library Editor, and then close the Type Library Editor. Delphi has written skeletal code for the TSimpleDCOMServer.AreYouThere function. Modify the function so it looks like the following:

```
function TSimpleDCOMServer.AreYouThere: WordBool;
begin
  Result := True;
end;
```

As you can see, this function doesn't do much. It simply replies "Yes, I'm here." We'll use this simple example in the following sections to verify that DCOM is set up correctly on your computer(s).

Listings 6.1 through 6.4 show the complete source code for the DCOMServer server.

**Listing 6.1**  *DCOMServer—DCOMServer.dpr*

```
program DCOMServer;

uses
  Forms,
  MainForm in 'MainForm.pas' {frmMain},
  DCOMServer_TLB in 'DCOMServer_TLB.pas',
  SimpleServer in 'SimpleServer.pas' {SimpleDCOMServer: CoClass};

{$R *.TLB}

{$R *.RES}

begin
  Application.Initialize;
  Application.CreateForm(TfrmMain, frmMain);
  Application.Run;
end.
```

**Listing 6.2**    *DCOMServer—SimpleServer.pas*

```
unit SimpleServer;

interface

uses
  ComObj, ActiveX, DCOMServer_TLB;

type
  TSimpleDCOMServer = class(TAutoObject, ISimpleDCOMServer)
  protected
    function AreYouThere: WordBool; safecall;
    { Protected declarations }
  end;

implementation

uses ComServ;

function TSimpleDCOMServer.AreYouThere: WordBool;
begin
  Result := True;
end;

initialization
  TAutoObjectFactory.Create(ComServer, TSimpleDCOMServer, Class_SimpleDCOMServer,
    ciMultiInstance, tmApartment);
end.
```

**Listing 6.3**    *DCOMServer—DCOMServer_TLB.pas*

```
unit DCOMServer_TLB;

// ************************************************************************ //
// WARNING                                                                 //
// -------                                                                 //
// The types declared in this file were generated from data read from a    //
// Type Library. If this type library is explicitly or indirectly (via     //
// another type library referring to this type library) re-imported, or the //
// 'Refresh' command of the Type Library Editor activated while editing the //
// Type Library, the contents of this file will be regenerated and all      //
// manual modifications will be lost.                                       //
// ************************************************************************ //

// PASTLWTR : $Revision:   1.11.1.75  $
// File generated on 6/22/99 1:48:02 PM from Type Library described below.

// ************************************************************************ //
// Type Lib: J:\Book\samples\Chap06\DCOMServer\DCOMServer.tlb
// IID\LCID: {682C7F20-28C9-11D3-B802-0040F67455FE}\0
// Helpfile:
```

```
// HelpString: Project1 Library
// Version:    1.0
// *********************************************************************** //

interface

uses Windows, ActiveX, Classes, Graphics, OleCtrls, StdVCL;

// *********************************************************************** //
// GUIDS declared in the TypeLibrary. Following prefixes are used:      //
//   Type Libraries     : LIBID_xxxx                                   //
//   CoClasses          : CLASS_xxxx                                   //
//   DISPInterfaces     : DIID_xxxx                                    //
//   Non-DISP interfaces: IID_xxxx                                     //
// *********************************************************************** //
const
  LIBID_DCOMServer: TGUID = '{682C7F20-28C9-11D3-B802-0040F67455FE}';
  IID_ISimpleDCOMServer: TGUID = '{682C7F21-28C9-11D3-B802-0040F67455FE}';
  CLASS_SimpleDCOMServer: TGUID = '{682C7F23-28C9-11D3-B802-0040F67455FE}';
type

// *********************************************************************** //
// Forward declaration of interfaces defined in Type Library           //
// *********************************************************************** //
  ISimpleDCOMServer = interface;
  ISimpleDCOMServerDisp = dispinterface;

// *********************************************************************** //
// Declaration of CoClasses defined in Type Library                    //
// (NOTE: Here we map each CoClass to its Default Interface)            //
// *********************************************************************** //
  SimpleDCOMServer = ISimpleDCOMServer;


// *********************************************************************** //
// Interface: ISimpleDCOMServer
// Flags:     (4416) Dual OleAutomation Dispatchable
// GUID:      {682C7F21-28C9-11D3-B802-0040F67455FE}
// *********************************************************************** //
  ISimpleDCOMServer = interface(IDispatch)
    ['{682C7F21-28C9-11D3-B802-0040F67455FE}']
    function AreYouThere: WordBool; safecall;
  end;

// *********************************************************************** //
// DispIntf:  ISimpleDCOMServerDisp
// Flags:     (4416) Dual OleAutomation Dispatchable
// GUID:      {682C7F21-28C9-11D3-B802-0040F67455FE}
// *********************************************************************** //
  ISimpleDCOMServerDisp = dispinterface
    ['{682C7F21-28C9-11D3-B802-0040F67455FE}']
    function AreYouThere: WordBool; dispid 1;
  end;
```

*continues* ▶

Listing 6.3    *continued*

```
CoSimpleDCOMServer = class
    class function Create: ISimpleDCOMServer;
    class function CreateRemote(const MachineName: string): ISimpleDCOMServer;
  end;

implementation

uses ComObj;

class function CoSimpleDCOMServer.Create: ISimpleDCOMServer;
begin
  Result := CreateComObject(CLASS_SimpleDCOMServer) as ISimpleDCOMServer;
end;

class function CoSimpleDCOMServer.CreateRemote(const MachineName: string):
ISimpleDCOMServer;
begin
  Result := CreateRemoteComObject(MachineName, CLASS_SimpleDCOMServer) as
ISimpleDCOMServer;
end;

end.
```

Listing 6.4    *DCOMServer—MainForm.pas*

```
unit MainForm;

interface

uses
  Windows, Messages, SysUtils, Classes, Graphics, Controls, Forms, Dialogs,
  StdCtrls;

type
  TfrmMain = class(TForm)
    Label1: TLabel;
  private
    { Private declarations }
  public
    { Public declarations }
  end;

var
  frmMain: TfrmMain;

implementation

{$R *.DFM}

end.
```

## Installing the DCOM Server

You now have a functional COM (and DCOM) server. Installing and registering a DCOM server is an involved process, mostly due to Windows security issues. This section will show you what you need to do to install the COM server on a Windows NT Server machine.

### Installing on Windows NT Server

After you've compiled the DCOM server into an executable, you need to install it onto the server machine. This section assumes that you're using Windows NT Server as the DCOM server, set up as a Domain server (which is the recommended configuration).

> **Note**
>
> *It is possible to use a Windows NT machine as the DCOM server if it is not set up as a domain server. In order to do so, the client must have an account on the NT machine. In addition, for simplicity, the account on the server should have the same password as the client's login id.* ◆

The following steps will lead you through the process of setting up the DCOM server on the server machine.

1. Copy DCOMServer.exe to the server machine and run it once to register it with Windows. After the program starts, you can immediately exit the application.

2. On the server machine, run Programs, Administrative Tools (Common), User Manager for Domains from the Start menu. The User Manager is displayed, as shown in Figure 6.2.

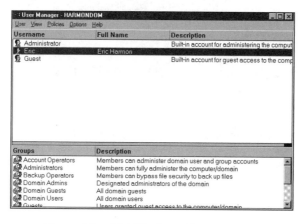

**Figure 6.2** *The Windows User Manager allows you to define new users and groups.*

Assuming your network is operational, you should already have a user account set up for the machine that will run the DCOM client. On my network, that account name is Eric.

3. Select User | New Local Group from the User Manager main menu. The dialog box shown in Figure 6.3 appears.

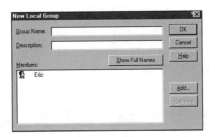

**Figure 6.3**    *Creating a new group with the ability to access DCOM servers.*

4. Enter a group name of DCP DCOM Servers (and a description, if you like), and press the Add... button. Windows displays the Add Users and Groups dialog box, shown in Figure 6.4.

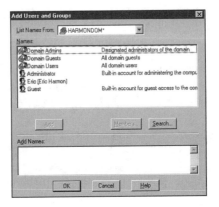

**Figure 6.4**    *Adding users to the new group.*

5. Double-click each user that you want to be included in the group (in other words, each user that you want to give access to the DCOM server). When you're finished, the screen will look something like Figure 6.5.

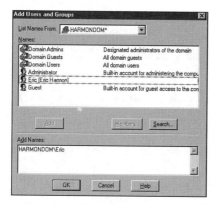

**Figure 6.5**  *New group with users defined.*

6. Click OK in both of the open dialog boxes to finish creating the new group. The User Manager will now display the new group name in the bottom pane of its main windows (see Figure 6.6).

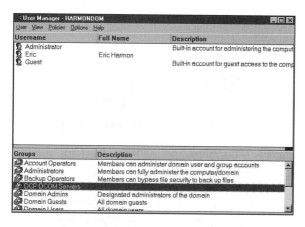

**Figure 6.6**  *The User Manager reflects newly added groups.*

7. Close the User Manager and run DCOMCNFG.EXE. DCOMCNFG.EXE is located in the Windows system32 directory. The newly created DCOM server, SimpleDCOMServer Object, will appear in the list of available servers, as shown in Figure 6.7.

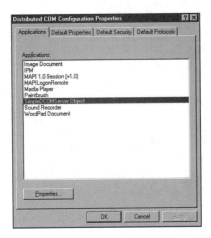

**Figure 6.7**   *DCOMCNFG displays*
*our new DCOM server.*

8. Highlight SimpleDCOMServer and click the Properties... button. The
   properties dialog box for the DCOM server is displayed. Select the
   Location tab and make sure the server is set up to run on this computer (Figure 6.8).

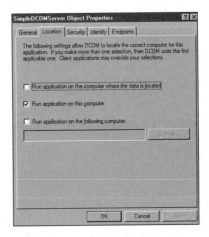

**Figure 6.8**   *DCOMCNFG can tell Windows*
*what machine to run the server on.*

9. Select the Security tab. Select the radio buttons for Use custom access permissions, Use custom launch permissions, and Use default configuration permissions. Click the Edit... button near the top of the dialog box to define the users who can access this DCOM server. The dialog box shown in Figure 6.9 appears.

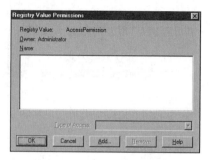

**Figure 6.9**   *Defining the users who have access to the DCOM server.*

10. Click the Add... button. Windows displays a list of groups defined on this domain (Figure 6.10).

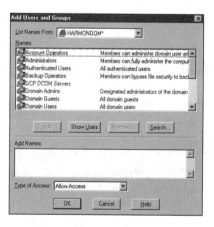

**Figure 6.10**   *Group names defined for the current domain.*

11. Double-click the DCP DCOM Servers group to add it to the list of groups that have access to this DCOM server. Click the OK button to close the Add Users and Groups dialog box. Then click the OK button again to close the Registry Value Permissions dialog box.

12. Click the Edit... button about halfway down the SimpleDCOMServer
Object Properties dialog box to define the users that have permission to
remotely launch the DCOM server on this machine. Repeat the same
sequence of steps we just used to define the users who have access to
the DCOM server. When you're finished, your screen will look like
Figure 6.11.

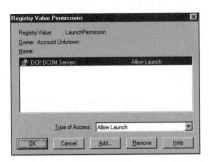

**Figure 6.11**   *The SimpleDCOMServer Object Properties
dialog box after defining users with access and launch permission.*

13. Click OK in all open dialog boxes to finish setting up the DCOM
server.

**Installing on Windows 95/98**

As I stated near the beginning of this chapter, DCOM servers can run on
both Windows 95/98 and Windows NT. In order to use DCOM effectively,
however, you'll want to use Windows NT as the DCOM server. If you're
determined to use Windows 9x to host your DCOM server, there are several
issues that you need to keep in mind.

- It is not possible to automatically start a DCOM server running on a
remote Windows 95/98 computer. In order for that machine to function as a DCOM server, the server application must be loaded into
memory before any clients attempt to connect to it.

- You will need to change the Registry entry HKEY_LOCAL_MACHINE\
Software\Microsoft\OLE\EnableRemoteConnect to Y on the Windows
95/98 machine in order for DCOM to operate correctly.

- You will also need to change the Registry entry HKEY_LOCAL_MACHINE\Software\Microsoft\OLE\LegacyAuthentic ationLevel to 1 on the Windows 95/98 machine. If the key doesn't exist, add it as a new key of type DWORD.

- You may need to run RPCSS.EXE on the Windows 95/98 machine, although this should not be necessary with DCOM versions 1.1 or later.

You should also check out the Microsoft technical article #Q165101 (HOWTO: Use Windows 95 or Windows 98 as a DCOM Server), located at http://support.microsoft.com/support/kb/articles/q165/1/01.asp.

Note that Windows 95/98 has no such limitations when running a DCOM client. The only limitations are when acting as a DCOM server.

After you have configured the Registry on the Windows 9x DCOM server, you must run DCOMServer.exe on the computer to register it with Windows. Leave the server running, as you cannot connect to a DCOM server on a Windows 9x machine unless it is already loaded in memory.

## Creating a DCOM Client

Now we've got a functional (although practically useless) DCOM server installed on a server machine. Please keep in mind that we've done nothing special in the source code to differentiate this server from a standard COM server. As a matter of fact, DCOMServer is a perfectly valid COM server, and can be used as such.

Let's go ahead, then, and create a client program to test this server. Start a new Delphi application. From the Delphi menu, select Project, Import Type Library. If DCOMServer (Version 1.0) is not listed in the list of servers, click the Add... button and import the DCOMServer.tlb type library. Click the OK button, and Delphi will generate the import file DCOMServer_TLB.pas.

> **Note**
>
> *We just finished writing the DCOM server, so you could have simply used DCOMServer_TLB.pas from that directory instead of importing the type library. However, in many cases you'll be accessing a server created by somebody else. I want to make sure you fully grasp the process of importing a type library.* ◆

Listings 6.5 and 6.6 contain the source code for a simple DCOM client.

**Listing 6.5**    *DCOMClient—DCOMClient.dpr*

```
program DCOMClient;

uses
  Forms,
  MainForm in 'MainForm.pas' {frmMain},
  DCOMServer_TLB in '..\DCOMServer\DCOMServer_TLB.pas';

{$R *.RES}

begin
  Application.Initialize;
  Application.CreateForm(TfrmMain, frmMain);
  Application.Run;
end.
```

**Listing 6.6**    *DCOMClient—MainForm.pas*

```
unit MainForm;

interface

uses
  Windows, Messages, SysUtils, Classes, Graphics, Controls, Forms, Dialogs,
  StdCtrls, DCOMServer_TLB, ExtCtrls;

type
  TfrmMain = class(TForm)
    pnlBottom: TPanel;
    btnTest: TButton;
    pnlClient: TPanel;
    Label1: TLabel;
    ecServer: TEdit;
    procedure btnTestClick(Sender: TObject);
  private
    { Private declarations }
  public
    { Public declarations }
  end;

var
  frmMain: TfrmMain;

implementation

{$R *.DFM}

procedure TfrmMain.btnTestClick(Sender: TObject);
var
```

```
  FServer: ISimpleDCOMServer;
begin
  FServer := CoSimpleDCOMServer.CreateRemote(ecServer.Text);
  if FServer.AreYouThere then
    ShowMessage('I am here.')
  else
    ShowMessage('Where''d I go?');
end;

end.
```

This code is almost identical to the code we wrote in previous chapters when creating COM clients. In fact, the only difference is that here we're using CoSimpleDCOMServer.CreateRemote instead of CoSimpleDCOMServer.Create. However, if you'll look at the source code for DCOMServer_TLB.pas, you'll see that the function CoSimpleDCOMServer.Create is still defined. This means that you can use this server as either a local (out-of-process) server or a remote (DCOM) server by changing a single line of code in the client!

## Tip

*You can launch a local COM server by calling CreateRemote and passing \\. or the local machine name as the parameter. This way, you don't need to change any code at all—you can simply change the machine name in the call to CreateRemote. ◆*

There is one "gotcha" that you need to be aware of before you can run the client application. You must register the type library for the DCOM server on the client machine. The easiest way to do this is by using TREGSVR, as follows:

```
TRegSvr DCOMServer.tlb
```

After you've registered the type library, you can run the client application. Figure 6.12 shows the client at runtime.

Enter the name of the server (in my case, it's SERVER) and click the Test button. If all goes well, you'll see a message box appear that reads "I am here." If you get a message indicating that access to the server was denied, then you probably didn't set something up correctly through the DCOMC-NFG utility.

Well, that was remarkably simple. Now you've seen that you already know everything you need to know about DCOM in order to use it in your Delphi apps. In the next section, I'll show you how to use DCOM to implement a remote dataset.

**Figure 6.12**    *DCOMClient allows the user
to select the DCOM server at runtime.*

*Everything that you learned about COM out-of-process servers pertains to
DCOM servers as well. For example, you can use the same methods you learned
in Chapter 4, "Automation," to implement COM events and callbacks in a
DCOM server. As a matter of fact, in the next section we'll create an application
that does just that. ◆*

# Implementing Remote Datasets with DCOM

A remote dataset, as you might imagine, is simply a dataset that resides on a
remote machine. Typically, when you write database applications with
Delphi, you can take one of two routes. You can use an inexpensive file
server solution, such as Paradox or dBase; or you can purchase the
Client/Server version of Delphi and use the BDE along with a client server
database, or MIDAS.

What I'm going to show you here is a third option: You can use DCOM
to place the database server on one machine, while placing the client application on another machine.

This application was developed using Delphi 5, in order to take advantage of the new COM Server components introduced in Delphi 5. If you're
using an older version of Delphi, the application won't compile as-is.
However, using the techniques described in Chapter 4 to support dispinterface events, you could modify the code to work in older versions of Delphi.

## Defining the Application

Before we jump into a coding frenzy, let's take a few moments to define the
problem that we're going to solve. We're going to create a database that
contains a single table for a simple parts inventory application. The table
structure is shown in Table 6.1.

*Table 6.1    Structure of the Parts Table*

| Field | Type |
| --- | --- |
| PartNo | 10-character alphanumeric. Primary Key |
| Description | 25-character alphanumeric |
| UnitPrice | Currency |
| OnHand | Integer |
| Reorder | Integer |

As you can see, this is a fairly straightforward table structure. It stores the part number and description, along with the unit price, the quantity on hand, and the "low-water" quantity, at which point an order is automatically placed for more of this item.

The application itself consists of three programs. The DCOM server handles the interface to the database itself. Nobody talks to the database without going through the DCOM server.

In addition to the DCOM server, there is an administrative application, which allows the user to add and delete parts, or update the price of a particular part.

The last application is a point-of-sale application, which would typically sit on a cashier's desk. This application allows the user to query the price of a part and relieve inventory when a part is sold.

## Creating the Server

The server will contain all the code necessary to interface with the database. For this example, I'm going to use a dBase database. The BDE won't be installed on the client machine, so the server must contain all database-related functionality that will be required by the application. Taking just a few moments to ponder this, we can come up with the following basic requirements:

- Obtain a list of some or all parts in the table
- Add a new part to the table
- Delete a part from the table
- Modify the description or unit price of a part
- Query the information on a part, such as description and unit price
- Deduct a quantity from inventory

There's probably more that this application could do, but that's a good enough list to get us started. Note that I didn't include a function in this list to place an order for more parts. The ordering process is not done by the client application—the server will automatically issue a new order when the quantity on hand drops too low. (At least in theory. I'm not going to include code in this server that physically places the order, but I'll show you the way to implement that feature yourself.)

**Marshaling Record Structures**

Because the database is only resident on the server machine, we're going to need some way to marshal the data from server to client. To meet that need, we'll use a variant array. Recall that I discussed variant arrays in Chapter 4, and I indicated that variant arrays can be used to transfer complex structures, such as records, across process boundaries.

We can take one of two approaches in the way we marshal the data. First, we can define a record structure in memory, and then pass that record structure as an array of bytes. For example,

```
TPartRecord = packed record
  PartNumber: string[10];
  Description: string[25];
  UnitPrice: Double;
  OnHand: Integer;
end;
```

Note that I left out the Reorder field. The client application doesn't need to know anything about this field, so we can save a small amount of time and space by not marshaling that information.

Now, after the server reads the data from the table and fills out the fields of the TPartRecord structure, it can stuff that data into a variant array, as follows:

```
function RecordToVariant(Part: TPartRecord): OleVariant;
var
  P: Pointer;
begin
  Result := VarArrayCreate([0, sizeof(TPartRecord)], varByte);
  P := VarArrayLock(Result);
  Move(Part, P^, sizeof(Part));
  VarArrayUnlock(Result);
end;
```

After the variant array is marshaled to the client, the client can convert it back into a TPartRecord, as follows:

```
function VariantToRecord(V: OleVariant): TPartRecord;
var
  P: Pointer;
begin
  P := VarArrayLock(V);
  Move(P^, Result, sizeof(TPartRecord));
  VarArrayUnlovk(V);
end;
```

Although this process works, there is one thing I don't like about it: If the record structure changes, both server and client need to be updated to use the new record structure.

Instead, I'm going to use two variant arrays to marshal the data. The first array is sent from the client to the server, and contains a list of fields that the client is interested in. The second array is returned from the server to the client, and contains a list of field values in the same order as the fields in the first array. For example, if the client is only interested in the part number and description, it sends a variant array to the server, as follows:

**Field**

PARTNO

DESCRIPTION

If we add another field to the table (perhaps ExpectedDate, which indicates when another batch or parts is expected to arrive), the marshaling code can simply add another field to the end of this list.

After the server reads the data from the database, it returns a variant array of variant arrays to the client, and the response looks like the following:

**Rows**

Row 1

Row 2

...

Each row is composed of a number of fields, as follows:

**Field Values**

P123

Widget

### The Server Application

With the previous discussion in mind, take a look at Listings 6.7 through 6.12. They contain the source code for the server side of this application. Listing 6.7 shows the main program file for the server.

---

**Listing 6.7**    *PartSrv—PartSrv.dpr*

```
program PartSrv;

uses
  Forms,
  MainForm in 'MainForm.pas' {Form1},
  PartSrv_TLB in 'PartSrv_TLB.pas',
  PartServerImpl in 'PartServerImpl.pas' {PartServer: CoClass},
  Parts in 'Parts.pas',
  DataModule in 'DataModule.pas' {PartDM: TDataModule};

{$R *.TLB}

{$R *.RES}

begin
  Application.Initialize;
  Application.CreateForm(TForm1, Form1);
  Application.CreateForm(TPartDM, PartDM);
  Application.Run;
end.
```

---

Listing 6.8 shows the Delphi-generated type library import file for the server.

---

**Listing 6.8**    *PartSrv—PartSrv_TLB.pas*

```
unit PartSrv_TLB;

// ******************************************************************* //
// WARNING                                                            //
// -------                                                            //
// The types declared in this file were generated from data read from a  //
// Type Library. If this type library is explicitly or indirectly (via   //
// another type library referring to this type library) re-imported, or the //
// 'Refresh' command of the Type Library Editor activated while editing the //
// Type Library, the contents of this file will be regenerated and all    //
// manual modifications will be lost.                                 //
// ******************************************************************* //

// PASTLWTR : $Revision:   1.11.1.75  $
// File generated on 8/1/99 11:26:35 AM from Type Library described below.
```

```
// ********************************************************************* //
// Type Lib: J:\Book\samples\Chap06\PartServer2\PartSrv.tlb
// IID\LCID: {046CB030-4824-11D3-B83F-0040F67455FE}\0
// Helpfile:
// HelpString: PartSrv Library
// Version:    1.0
// ********************************************************************* //

interface

uses Windows, ActiveX, Classes, Graphics, OleCtrls, StdVCL;

// *********************************************************************//
// GUIDS declared in the TypeLibrary. Following prefixes are used:    //
//    Type Libraries     : LIBID_xxxx                                 //
//    CoClasses          : CLASS_xxxx                                 //
//    DISPInterfaces     : DIID_xxxx                                  //
//    Non-DISP interfaces: IID_xxxx                                   //
// *********************************************************************//
const
  LIBID_PartSrv: TGUID = '{046CB030-4824-11D3-B83F-0040F67455FE}';
  IID_IPartServer: TGUID = '{046CB031-4824-11D3-B83F-0040F67455FE}';
  DIID_IPartServerEvents: TGUID = '{046CB033-4824-11D3-B83F-0040F67455FE}';
  CLASS_PartServer: TGUID = '{046CB035-4824-11D3-B83F-0040F67455FE}';

// *********************************************************************//
// Declaration of Enumerations defined in Type Library                //
// *********************************************************************//
// FieldNumbers constants
type
  FieldNumbers = TOleEnum;
const
  fnPartNumber = $00000000;
  fnDescription = $00000001;
  fnUnitPrice = $00000002;
  fnOnHand = $00000003;
  fnReorder = $00000004;

type

// *********************************************************************//
// Forward declaration of interfaces defined in Type Library          //
// *********************************************************************//
  IPartServer = interface;
  IPartServerDisp = dispinterface;
  IPartServerEvents = dispinterface;

// *********************************************************************//
// Declaration of CoClasses defined in Type Library                   //
// (NOTE: Here we map each CoClass to its Default Interface)           //
// *********************************************************************//
```

*continues* ▶

**Listing 6.8** *continued*

```
  PartServer = IPartServer;


// ***********************************************************//
// Interface: IPartServer
// Flags:      (4416) Dual OleAutomation Dispatchable
// GUID:       {046CB031-4824-11D3-B83F-0040F67455FE}
// ***********************************************************//
  IPartServer = interface(IDispatch)
    ['{046CB031-4824-11D3-B83F-0040F67455FE}']
    function GetAll(varFields: OleVariant): OleVariant; safecall;
    function GetPart(const PartNumber: WideString; varFields: OleVariant): OleVariant;
safecall;
    procedure AddPart(varFields: OleVariant; varValues: OleVariant); safecall;
    procedure DeletePart(const PartNumber: WideString); safecall;
    procedure ModifyPart(const PartNumber: WideString; varFields: OleVariant; varValues:
OleVariant); safecall;
    procedure UsePart(const PartNumber: WideString; Quantity: Integer); safecall;
  end;

// ***********************************************************//
// DispIntf:   IPartServerDisp
// Flags:      (4416) Dual OleAutomation Dispatchable
// GUID:       {046CB031-4824-11D3-B83F-0040F67455FE}
// ***********************************************************//
  IPartServerDisp = dispinterface
    ['{046CB031-4824-11D3-B83F-0040F67455FE}']
    function GetAll(varFields: OleVariant): OleVariant; dispid 1;
    function GetPart(const PartNumber: WideString; varFields: OleVariant): OleVariant;
dispid 2;
    procedure AddPart(varFields: OleVariant; varValues: OleVariant); dispid 3;
    procedure DeletePart(const PartNumber: WideString); dispid 4;
    procedure ModifyPart(const PartNumber: WideString; varFields: OleVariant; varValues:
OleVariant); dispid 5;
    procedure UsePart(const PartNumber: WideString; Quantity: Integer); dispid 6;
  end;

// ***********************************************************//
// DispIntf:   IPartServerEvents
// Flags:      (0)
// GUID:       {046CB033-4824-11D3-B83F-0040F67455FE}
// ***********************************************************//
  IPartServerEvents = dispinterface
    ['{046CB033-4824-11D3-B83F-0040F67455FE}']
    procedure OnAdd(varFields: OleVariant; varValues: OleVariant); dispid 1;
    procedure OnDelete(const PartNumber: WideString); dispid 2;
    procedure OnModify(const PartNumber: WideString; varFields: OleVariant; varValues:
OleVariant); dispid 3;
  end;
```

```
CoPartServer = class
  class function Create: IPartServer;
  class function CreateRemote(const MachineName: string): IPartServer;
end;

implementation

uses ComObj;

class function CoPartServer.Create: IPartServer;
begin
  Result := CreateComObject(CLASS_PartServer) as IPartServer;
end;

class function CoPartServer.CreateRemote(const MachineName: string): IPartServer;
begin
  Result := CreateRemoteComObject(MachineName, CLASS_PartServer) as IPartServer;
end;

end.
```

Listing 6.9 defines a helper class that is used to copy data to and from a dataset, and to and from a variant array.

**Listing 6.9**    *PartSrv—Parts.pas*
```
unit Parts;

interface

uses
  DB, PartSrv_TLB;

type
  TPart = class
    PartNumber: string;
    Description: string;
    UnitPrice: Double;
    OnHand: Integer;
    Reorder: Integer;
  public
    function ToVariant(varFields: OleVariant): OleVariant;
    procedure FromVariant(varFields: OleVariant; varValues: OleVariant);
    procedure CreateFromDataSet(DataSet: TDataSet);
  end;

implementation

{ TPartRecord }

procedure TPart.CreateFromDataSet(DataSet: TDataSet);
begin
  PartNumber := DataSet.FieldByName('PARTNO').AsString;
```

```
  Description := DataSet.FieldByName('DESC').AsString;
  UnitPrice := DataSet.FieldByName('UNITPRICE').AsFloat;
  OnHand := DataSet.FieldByName('ONHAND').AsInteger;
  Reorder := DataSet.FieldByName('REORDER').AsInteger;
end;

procedure TPart.FromVariant(varFields: OleVariant; varValues: OleVariant);
var
  Index: Integer;
  FieldNumber: Integer;
begin
  for Index := VarArrayLowBound(varFields, 1) to VarArrayHighBound(varFields, 1) do begin
    FieldNumber := varFields[Index];
    case FieldNumber of
      fnPartNumber: PartNumber := varValues[Index];
      fnDescription: Description := varValues[Index];
      fnUnitPrice: UnitPrice := varValues[Index];
      fnOnHand: OnHand := varValues[Index];
      fnReorder: Reorder := varValues[Index];
    end;
  end;
end;

function TPart.ToVariant(varFields: OleVariant): OleVariant;
var
  Index: Integer;
  FieldNumber: Integer;
begin
  Result := VarArrayCreate([VarArrayLowBound(varFields, 1), VarArrayHighBound(varFields,
1)], varVariant);

  for Index := VarArrayLowBound(varFields, 1) to VarArrayHighBound(varFields, 1) do begin
    FieldNumber := varFields[Index];

    case FieldNumber of
      fnPartNumber: Result[Index] := PartNumber;
      fnDescription: Result[Index] := Description;
      fnUnitPrice: Result[Index] := UnitPrice;
      fnOnHand: Result[Index] := OnHand;
      fnReorder: Result[Index] := Reorder;
    end;
  end;
end;

end.
```

Listing 6.10 shows the data module for the COM server. The data module
contains code to add a part to the database, delete a part from the database,
and update an existing part. For simplicity's sake, I've used a dBase database and a TTable to access the part table. In a real-life situation, you might
want to use a TQuery instead, because with a TQuery, you can restrict the
number of rows returned to the client application.

**Listing 6.10**   *PartSrv—DataModule.pas*

```
unit DataModule;

interface

uses
  Windows, Messages, SysUtils, Classes, Graphics, Controls, Forms, Dialogs,
  Db, DBTables;

type
  TPartDM = class(TDataModule)
    dbParts: TDatabase;
    tblParts: TTable;
    tblPartsPARTNO: TStringField;
    tblPartsDESC: TStringField;
    tblPartsUNITPRICE: TFloatField;
    tblPartsONHAND: TFloatField;
    tblPartsREORDER: TFloatField;
  private
    { Private declarations }
  public
    { Public declarations }
    procedure GetAllParts(varFields: OleVariant; var varValues: OleVariant);
    procedure GetPart(PartNumber: string; varFields: OleVariant; var varValues:
OleVariant);
    function UsePart(PartNumber: string; Quantity: Integer): Integer;
    function AddPart(varFields: OleVariant; varValues: OleVariant): string;
    function DeletePart(PartNo: string): Boolean;
    function ModifyPart(PartNo: string; varFields: OleVariant; varValues: OleVariant):
Boolean;
  end;

var
  PartDM: TPartDM;

implementation

uses
  Parts, PartSrv_TLB;

{$R *.DFM}

{ TPartDM }

function TPartDM.AddPart(varFields: OleVariant; varValues: OleVariant): string;
var
  Part: TPart;
begin
  Part := TPart.Create;
  try
    Part.FromVariant(varFields, varValues);
    with tblParts do begin
```

*continues* ▶

**Listing 6.10**  *continued*

```
      Append;
      tblPartsPARTNO.AsString := Part.PartNumber;
      tblPartsDESC.AsString := Part.Description;
      tblPartsUNITPRICE.AsFloat := Part.UnitPrice;
      tblPartsONHAND.AsInteger := Part.OnHand;
      tblPartsREORDER.AsInteger := Part.Reorder;
      Post;

      Result := Part.PartNumber;
    end;
  finally
    Part.Free;
  end;
end;

function TPartDM.DeletePart(PartNo: string): Boolean;
begin
  Result := tblParts.Locate('PARTNO', PartNo, []);
  if Result then
    tblParts.Delete;
end;

procedure TPartDM.GetAllParts(varFields: OleVariant; var varValues: OleVariant);
var
  Part: TPart;
  Index: Integer;
begin
  Part := TPart.Create;
  try
    with tblParts do begin
      varValues := VarArrayCreate([0, RecordCount - 1], varVariant);

      Index := 0;
      First;
      while not EOF do begin
        Part.CreateFromDataSet(tblParts);
        varValues[Index] := Part.ToVariant(varFields);
        Inc(Index);
        Next;
      end;
    end;
  finally
    Part.Free;
  end;
end;

procedure TPartDM.GetPart(PartNumber: string; varFields: OleVariant;
  var varValues: OleVariant);
var
  Part: TPart;
```

```
begin
  if tblParts.Locate('PARTNO', PartNumber, []) then begin
    Part := TPart.Create;
    try
      Part.CreateFromDataSet(tblParts);
      varValues := Part.ToVariant(varFields);
    finally
      Part.Free;
    end;
  end;
end;

function TPartDM.ModifyPart(PartNo: string; varFields: OleVariant; varValues: OleVariant):
Boolean;
var
  Index: Integer;
begin
  Result := False;

  if tblParts.Locate('PARTNO', PartNo, []) then begin
    with tblParts do begin
      Edit;
      try
        for Index := VarArrayLowBound(varFields, 1) to varArrayHighBound(varFields, 1) do
begin
          case varFields[Index] of
            fnPartNumber: tblPartsPARTNO.AsString := varValues[Index];
            fnDescription: tblPartsDESC.AsString := varValues[Index];
            fnUnitPrice: tblPartsUNITPRICE.AsFloat := varValues[Index];
            fnOnHand: tblPartsONHAND.AsInteger := varValues[Index];
            fnReorder: tblPartsREORDER.AsInteger := varValues[Index];
          end;
        end;
        Post;

        Result := True;
      except
        Cancel;
      end;
    end;
  end;
end;

function TPartDM.UsePart(PartNumber: string; Quantity: Integer): Integer;
begin
  if tblParts.Locate('PARTNO', PartNumber, []) then begin
    if Quantity > tblPartsONHAND.AsInteger then
      raise Exception.CreateFmt('You requested %d of part %s.  ' +
        'That part currently has an onhand quantity of %d.',
        [Quantity, PartNumber, tblPartsONHAND.AsInteger]);
```

*continues* ▶

**Listing 6.10**  *continued*

```
    tblParts.Edit;
    Result := tblPartsONHAND.AsInteger - Quantity;
    tblPartsONHAND.AsInteger := Result;
    tblParts.Post;

    // Check remaining inventory here.  If Result < tblPartsREORDER.AsInteger,
    // then trigger a routine to order more parts automatically.
  end else
    raise Exception.CreateFmt('Unknown part number %s.',
      [PartNumber]);
end;

end.
```

Listing 6.11 defines the class that implements the COM interface
IPartServer. Because this server will send notification to all connected clients
whenever someone adds, deletes, or modifies a part, I've used the dispinterface techniques described in Chapter 4 to implement COM events.

**Listing 6.11**  *PartSrv—PartServerImpl*

```
unit PartServerImpl;

interface

uses
  ComObj, ActiveX, AxCtrls, PartSrv_TLB;

type
  TPartServer = class(TAutoObject, IConnectionPointContainer, IPartServer)
  private
    { Private declarations }
    FConnectionPoints: TConnectionPoints;
    FEvents: IPartServerEvents;
    FObjectID: Integer;
  public
    procedure Initialize; override;
    destructor Destroy; override;
  protected
    { Protected declarations }
    property ConnectionPoints: TConnectionPoints read FConnectionPoints
      implements IConnectionPointContainer;
    procedure EventSinkChanged(const EventSink: IUnknown); override;
    function GetAll(varFields: OleVariant): OleVariant; safecall;
    function GetPart(const PartNumber: WideString;
      varFields: OleVariant): OleVariant; safecall;
    procedure AddPart(varFields, varValues: OleVariant); safecall;
    procedure DeletePart(const PartNumber: WideString); safecall;
    procedure ModifyPart(const PartNumber: WideString; varFields,
      varValues: OleVariant); safecall;
```

```
    procedure UsePart(const PartNumber: WideString; Quantity: Integer);
      safecall;
    function GetEnumerator: IEnumConnections;
  end;

implementation

uses Windows, ComServ, DataModule;

procedure TPartServer.EventSinkChanged(const EventSink: IUnknown);
begin
  FEvents := EventSink as IPartServerEvents;
end;

procedure TPartServer.Initialize;
begin
  inherited Initialize;
  FConnectionPoints := TConnectionPoints.Create(Self);
  if AutoFactory.EventTypeInfo <> nil then
    FConnectionPoints.CreateConnectionPoint(AutoFactory.EventIID,
      ckMulti, EventConnect);

  RegisterActiveObject(self as IUnknown, CLASS_PartServer,
    ACTIVEOBJECT_WEAK, FObjectID);
end;

destructor TPartServer.Destroy;
begin
  RevokeActiveObject(FObjectID, nil);

  inherited Destroy;
end;

function TPartServer.GetAll(varFields: OleVariant): OleVariant;
begin
  PartDM.GetAllParts(varFields, Result);
end;

function TPartServer.GetPart(const PartNumber: WideString;
  varFields: OleVariant): OleVariant;
begin
  PartDM.GetPart(PartNumber, varFields, Result);
end;

procedure TPartServer.AddPart(varFields, varValues: OleVariant);
var
  Enum: IEnumConnections;
  ConnectData: TConnectData;
  Fetched: Cardinal;
begin
  PartDM.AddPart(varFields, varValues);
```

*continues* ▶

**Listing 6.11**    *continued*

```
  Enum := GetEnumerator;
  if Enum <> nil then begin
    while Enum.Next(1, ConnectData, @Fetched) = S_OK do
      if ConnectData.pUnk <> nil then
        (ConnectData.pUnk as IPartServerEvents).OnAdd(varFields, varValues);
  end;
end;

procedure TPartServer.DeletePart(const PartNumber: WideString);
var
  Enum: IEnumConnections;
  ConnectData: TConnectData;
  Fetched: Cardinal;
begin
  if PartDM.DeletePart(PartNumber) then begin
    Enum := GetEnumerator;
    if Enum <> nil then begin
      while Enum.Next(1, ConnectData, @Fetched) = S_OK do
        if ConnectData.pUnk <> nil then
          (ConnectData.pUnk as IPartServerEvents).OnDelete(PartNumber);
    end;
  end;
end;

procedure TPartServer.ModifyPart(const PartNumber: WideString; varFields,
  varValues: OleVariant);
var
  Enum: IEnumConnections;
  ConnectData: TConnectData;
  Fetched: Cardinal;
begin
  PartDM.ModifyPart(PartNumber, varFields, varValues);

  Enum := GetEnumerator;
  if Enum <> nil then begin
    while Enum.Next(1, ConnectData, @Fetched) = S_OK do
      if ConnectData.pUnk <> nil then
        (ConnectData.pUnk as IPartServerEvents).OnModify(PartNumber, varFields,
varValues);
  end;
end;

procedure TPartServer.UsePart(const PartNumber: WideString;
  Quantity: Integer);
var
  NewQuantity: Integer;
  Enum: IEnumConnections;
  ConnectData: TConnectData;
  Fetched: Cardinal;
  varFields: OleVariant;
  varValues: OleVariant;
```

```
begin
  NewQuantity := PartDM.UsePart(PartNumber, Quantity);

  varFields := VarArrayCreate([0, 0], varVariant);
  varValues := VarArrayCreate([0, 0], varVariant);
  varFields[0] := fnOnHand;
  varValues[0] := NewQuantity;

  Enum := GetEnumerator;
  if Enum <> nil then begin
    while Enum.Next(1, ConnectData, @Fetched) = S_OK do
      if ConnectData.pUnk <> nil then
        (ConnectData.pUnk as IPartServerEvents).OnModify(PartNumber, varFields,
varValues);
  end;
end;

function TPartServer.GetEnumerator: IEnumConnections;
var
  Container: IConnectionPointContainer;
  ConnectionPoint: IConnectionPoint;
begin
  OleCheck(QueryInterface(IConnectionPointContainer, Container));
  OleCheck(Container.FindConnectionPoint(AutoFactory.EventIID, ConnectionPoint));
  ConnectionPoint.EnumConnections(Result);
end;

initialization
  TAutoObjectFactory.Create(ComServer, TPartServer, Class_PartServer,
    ciMultiInstance, tmApartment);
end.
```

Listing 6.12 shows the source code for the main form of the server. This is a simple form that displays a grid showing the contents of the parts database. I've done this so you can see the database being updated as the client applications interact with the server.

**Listing 6.12**  *PartSrv—MainForm.pas*

```
unit MainForm;

interface

uses
  Windows, Messages, SysUtils, Classes, Graphics, Controls, Forms, Dialogs,
  StdCtrls, Grids, DBGrids, ExtCtrls, Db;

type
  TForm1 = class(TForm)
    DataSource1: TDataSource;
    pnlBottom: TPanel;
    pnlClient: TPanel;
```

*continues* ▶

**Listing 6.12** *continued*

```
   DBGrid1: TDBGrid;
   btnClose: TButton;
   procedure btnCloseClick(Sender: TObject);
 private
   { Private declarations }
 public
   { Public declarations }
 end;

var
  Form1: TForm1;

implementation

uses DataModule;

{$R *.DFM}

procedure TForm1.btnCloseClick(Sender: TObject);
begin
  Close;
end;

end.
```

After the server is compiled, you must install it on the server machine and configure it, using the same technique discussed earlier in this chapter, in the section "Install the DCOM Server."

Figure 6.13 shows the parts server's user interface.

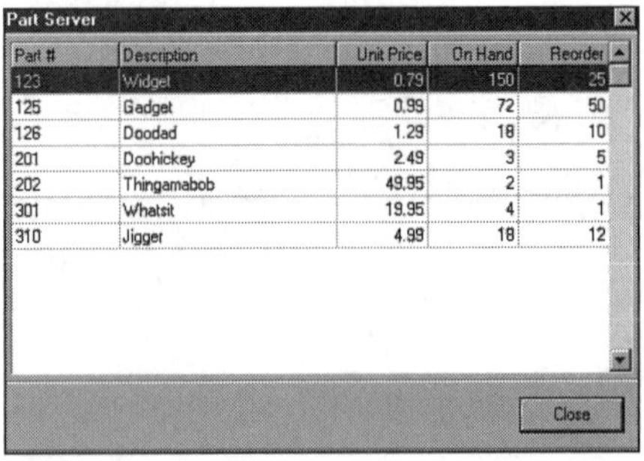

**Figure 6.13**   *Though PartSrv is a DCOM
server, it can also be run as a standalone application.*

## Creating the Administrative Client

Now that the parts server is created, installed, and configured, let's create the first of the two client applications that will access it.

The administrative client is used to add new parts, delete parts, and update the part information, such as unit price, quantity on hand, and reorder quantity.

Listings 6.13 through 6.15 show the source code for the administrative client. The main application code is contained in Listing 6.14.

**Listing 6.13**    *PartAdmin—PartAdmin.dpr*

```
program PartAdmin;

uses
  Forms,
  MainForm in 'MainForm.pas' {frmMain},
  PartForm in 'PartForm.pas' {frmPart},
  PartSrv_TLB in 'PartSrv_TLB.pas';

{$R *.RES}

begin
  Application.Initialize;
  Application.CreateForm(TfrmMain, frmMain);
  Application.Run;
end.
```

**Listing 6.14**    *PartAdmin—MainForm.pas*

```
unit MainForm;

interface

uses
  Windows, Messages, SysUtils, Classes, Graphics, Controls, Forms, Dialogs,
  Grids, ComObj, ActiveX, PartSrv_TLB, Menus, ExtCtrls, OleServer, StdCtrls;

type
  TfrmMain = class(TForm)
    MainMenu1: TMainMenu;
    pnlClient: TPanel;
    StringGrid1: TStringGrid;
    pnlBottom: TPanel;
    File1: TMenuItem;
    Exit1: TMenuItem;
    Edit1: TMenuItem;
    InsertPart1: TMenuItem;
    EditPart1: TMenuItem;
    DeletePart1: TMenuItem;
    PartServer1: TPartServer;
```

*continues* ▶

**Listing 6.14**    *continued*

```
  ecServer: TEdit;
  btnConnect: TButton;
  Label1: TLabel;
  procedure FormCreate(Sender: TObject);
  procedure Exit1Click(Sender: TObject);
  procedure InsertPart1Click(Sender: TObject);
  procedure DeletePart1Click(Sender: TObject);
  procedure EditPart1Click(Sender: TObject);
  procedure PartServer1Add(Sender: TObject; varFields,
    varValues: OleVariant);
  procedure PartServer1Delete(Sender: TObject;
    var PartNumber: OleVariant);
  procedure PartServer1Modify(Sender: TObject;
    var PartNumber: OleVariant; varFields, varValues: OleVariant);
  procedure btnConnectClick(Sender: TObject);
private
  { Private declarations }
  FFields: OleVariant;
  procedure LoadPartGrid;
  procedure LoadRow(Row: Integer; varFields, varValues: OleVariant);
public
  { Public declarations }
end;

var
  frmMain: TfrmMain;

implementation

uses PartForm;

{$R *.DFM}

procedure TfrmMain.FormCreate(Sender: TObject);
begin
  FFields := VarArrayCreate([0, 4], varInteger);
  FFields[0] := fnPartNumber;
  FFields[1] := fnDescription;
  FFields[2] := fnUnitPrice;
  FFields[3] := fnOnHand;
  FFields[4] := fnReorder;
end;

procedure TfrmMain.btnConnectClick(Sender: TObject);
begin
  // If no server was entered, we'll use the local machine
  if ecServer.Text <> '' then
    PartServer1.RemoteMachineName := ecServer.Text;

  PartServer1.Connect;
```

```
  // Load all parts from the database server
  LoadPartGrid;

  // Enable the edit menu
  Edit1.Enabled := True;
end;

procedure TfrmMain.LoadRow(Row: Integer; varFields, varValues: OleVariant);
var
  ValueIndex: Integer;
  ColIndex: Integer;
begin
  for ValueIndex := VarArrayLowBound(varValues, 1) to VarArrayHighBound(varValues, 1) do
    for ColIndex := VarArrayLowBound(FFields, 1) to VarArrayHighBound(FFields, 1) do
      if FFields[ColIndex] = varFields[ValueIndex] then
        StringGrid1.Cells[ColIndex, Row] := varValues[ValueIndex];
end;

procedure TfrmMain.LoadPartGrid;
var
  varValues: OleVariant;
  Index: Integer;
  FieldNumber: Integer;
  Row: Integer;
begin
  varValues := PartServer1.GetAll(FFields);

  StringGrid1.RowCount := VarArrayHighBound(varValues, 1) -
    VarArrayLowBound(varValues, 1) + 2;

  StringGrid1.ColCount := VarArrayHighBound(FFields, 1) -
    VarArrayLowBound(FFields, 1) + 1;

  for Index := VarArrayLowBound(FFields, 1) to VarArrayHighBound(FFields, 1) do begin
    FieldNumber := FFields[Index];
    case FieldNumber of
      fnPartNumber: StringGrid1.Cells[Index, 0] := 'Part #';
      fnDescription: StringGrid1.Cells[Index, 0] := 'Description';
      fnUnitPrice: StringGrid1.Cells[Index, 0] := 'Unit Price';
      fnOnHand: StringGrid1.Cells[Index, 0] := 'On Hand';
      fnReorder: StringGrid1.Cells[Index, 0] := 'Reorder';
    end;
  end;

  Row := 1;
  for Index := VarArrayLowBound(varValues, 1) to VarArrayHighBound(varValues, 1) do begin
    LoadRow(Row, FFields, varValues[Index]);
    Inc(Row);
  end;
end;

procedure TfrmMain.Exit1Click(Sender: TObject);
```

*continues* ▶

**Listing 6.14** *continued*

```
begin
  Close;
end;

procedure TfrmMain.InsertPart1Click(Sender: TObject);
var
  frmPart: TfrmPart;
  varValues: OleVariant;
begin
  frmPart := TfrmPart.Create(nil);
  try
    if frmPart.ShowModal = mrOk then begin
      varValues := VarArrayCreate([0, 4], varVariant);
      varValues[0] := frmPart.PartNumber;
      varValues[1] := frmPart.Description;
      varValues[2] := frmPart.UnitPrice;
      varValues[3] := frmPart.OnHand;
      varValues[4] := frmPart.Reorder;
      PartServer1.AddPart(FFields, varValues);
    end;
  finally
    frmPart.Free;
  end;
end;

procedure TfrmMain.DeletePart1Click(Sender: TObject);
begin
  if StringGrid1.Row > 0 then
    PartServer1.DeletePart(StringGrid1.Cells[0, StringGrid1.Row]);
end;

procedure TfrmMain.EditPart1Click(Sender: TObject);
var
  PartNumber: string;
  frmPart: TfrmPart;
  varValues: OleVariant;
begin
  if StringGrid1.Row > 0 then begin
    PartNumber := StringGrid1.Cells[0, StringGrid1.Row];
    varValues := PartServer1.GetPart(PartNumber, FFields);

    frmPart := TfrmPart.Create(nil);
    try
      frmPart.ecPartNumber.Text := varValues[0];
      frmPart.ecDescription.Text := varValues[1];
      frmPart.ecUnitPrice.Text := varValues[2];
      frmPart.ecOnHand.Text := varValues[3];
      frmPart.ecReorder.Text := varValues[4];
```

```
      if frmPart.ShowModal = mrOk then begin
        varValues := VarArrayCreate([0, 4], varVariant);
        varValues[0] := frmPart.PartNumber;
        varValues[1] := frmPart.Description;
        varValues[2] := frmPart.UnitPrice;
        varValues[3] := frmPart.OnHand;
        varValues[4] := frmPart.Reorder;
        PartServer1.ModifyPart(PartNumber, FFields, varValues);
      end;
    finally
      frmPart.Free;
    end;
  end;
end;

procedure TfrmMain.PartServer1Add(Sender: TObject; varFields,
  varValues: OleVariant);
begin
  // A new part was added - reload the whole grid
  LoadPartGrid;
end;

procedure TfrmMain.PartServer1Delete(Sender: TObject;
  var PartNumber: OleVariant);
begin
  // A part was deleted - reload the whole grid
  LoadPartGrid;
end;

procedure TfrmMain.PartServer1Modify(Sender: TObject;
  var PartNumber: OleVariant; varFields, varValues: OleVariant);
var
  Index: Integer;
  Found: Boolean;
begin
  Found := False;
  Index := 1;

  // If we can find the original part, just reload the row
  while (not Found) and (Index < StringGrid1.RowCount) do begin
    if StringGrid1.Cells[0, Index] = PartNumber then begin
      LoadRow(Index, varFields, varValues);
      Found := True;
    end else
      Inc(Index);
  end;

  // Couldn't find the part, so reload the whole grid
  if not Found then
    LoadPartGrid;
end;

end.
```

Listing 6.14 contains the meat of the administrative client program. The FormCreate method sets up a variant array to hold the fields that the administrative client is interested in. This client has access to all information in the database, so I load the FFields array with a list of all fields.

btnConnectClick is called when the user clicks the Connect button at the bottom of the main form (see Figure 6.14). If the user leaves the server field blank, then the client attempts to connect to a local server. Otherwise, the client tries to connect to the server on the machine indicated by the server field. If the connection succeeds, the code then calls LoadPartGrid, which retrieves all part records from the server and displays them in a string grid.

PartServer1Add, PartServer1Delete, and PartServer1Modify are methods of the IPartsEvents event interface. They are called from the server whenever any user (not just this instance of the administrative application) adds, modifies, or deletes a part from the parts database. Chapter 5, "ActiveX Controls and ActiveForms," discussed event interfaces in detail.

InsertPart1Click prompts the user to enter information for a new part, and then calls the part server's AddPart method to add the part to the database. As described at the beginning of this section, the client application sends both the list of fields to be added, along with their values.

DeletePart1Click deletes the current part in the string grid, and EditPart1Click allows the user to edit the data for the currently highlighted part. The edit method re-reads the current part from the server to make sure it has the latest data, and then posts the updated data using the two variant array approach.

PartForm.pas, shown in Listing 6.15, implements a dialog box that allows the user to add parts to or edit parts in the database.

**Listing 6.15**   *PartAdmin—PartForm.pas*

```
unit PartForm;

interface

uses
  Windows, Messages, SysUtils, Classes, Graphics, Controls, Forms, Dialogs,
  StdCtrls, ExtCtrls;

type
  TfrmPart = class(TForm)
    pnlClient: TPanel;
    pnlBottom: TPanel;
    Label1: TLabel;
    Label2: TLabel;
```

```
      Label3: TLabel;
      Label4: TLabel;
      Label5: TLabel;
      ecPartNumber: TEdit;
      ecDescription: TEdit;
      ecUnitPrice: TEdit;
      ecOnHand: TEdit;
      ecReorder: TEdit;
      btnOK: TButton;
      btnCancel: TButton;
      procedure btnOKClick(Sender: TObject);
    private
      { Private declarations }
      FUnitPrice: Double;
      FReorder: Integer;
      FOnHand: Integer;
      FDescription: string;
      FPartNumber: string;
    public
      { Public declarations }
      property PartNumber: string read FPartNumber;
      property Description: string read FDescription;
      property UnitPrice: Double read FUnitPrice;
      property OnHand: Integer read FOnHand;
      property Reorder: Integer read FReorder;
    end;

implementation

{$R *.DFM}

procedure TfrmPart.btnOKClick(Sender: TObject);
begin
  FPartNumber := ecPartNumber.Text;
  FDescription := ecDescription.Text;
  FUnitPrice := StrToFloat(ecUnitPrice.Text);
  FOnHand := StrToInt(ecOnHand.Text);
  FReorder := StrToInt(ecReorder.Text);
end;

end.
```

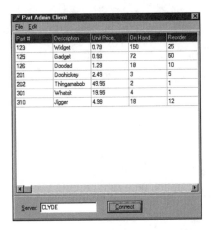

**Figure 6.14**    *The PartAdmin application lets
the user add, modify, and delete parts in inventory.*

## Creating the Point-of-Sale Client

The second client program in this application is a point-of-sale client. The point-of-sale client is situated at the front desk of the store that's running this application.

Listings 6.16 and 6.17 show the source code for the point-of-sale client.

**Listing 6.16**    *PartStock—PartStock.dpr*

```
program PartStock;

uses
  Forms,
  MainForm in 'MainForm.pas' {frmMain};

{$R *.RES}

begin
  Application.Initialize;
  Application.CreateForm(TfrmMain, frmMain);
  Application.Run;
end.
```

**Listing 6.17**   *PartStock—MainForm.pas*

```
unit MainForm;

interface

uses
  Windows, Messages, SysUtils, Classes, Graphics, Controls, Forms, Dialogs,
  Grids, ComObj, ActiveX, Menus, ExtCtrls, OleServer, PartSrv_TLB, StdCtrls;

type
  TfrmMain = class(TForm)
    MainMenu1: TMainMenu;
    pnlClient: TPanel;
    StringGrid1: TStringGrid;
    pnlBottom: TPanel;
    File1: TMenuItem;
    Exit1: TMenuItem;
    Edit1: TMenuItem;
    UsePart1: TMenuItem;
    PartServer1: TPartServer;
    ecServer: TEdit;
    btnConnect: TButton;
    Label1: TLabel;
    procedure FormCreate(Sender: TObject);
    procedure Exit1Click(Sender: TObject);
    procedure UsePart1Click(Sender: TObject);
    procedure PartServer1Add(Sender: TObject; varFields,
      varValues: OleVariant);
    procedure PartServer1Delete(Sender: TObject;
      var PartNumber: OleVariant);
    procedure PartServer1Modify(Sender: TObject;
      var PartNumber: OleVariant; varFields, varValues: OleVariant);
    procedure btnConnectClick(Sender: TObject);
  private
    { Private declarations }
    FFields: OleVariant;
    procedure LoadPartGrid;
    procedure LoadRow(Row: Integer; varFields, varValues: OleVariant);
  public
    { Public declarations }
  end;

var
  frmMain: TfrmMain;

implementation

{$R *.DFM}

procedure TfrmMain.FormCreate(Sender: TObject);
```

*continues* ▶

**Listing 6.17**    *continued*

```
begin
  FFields := VarArrayCreate([0, 3], varInteger);
  FFields[0] := fnPartNumber;
  FFields[1] := fnDescription;
  FFields[2] := fnUnitPrice;
  FFields[3] := fnOnHand;
end;

procedure TfrmMain.btnConnectClick(Sender: TObject);
begin
  // If no server was entered, we'll use the local machine
  if ecServer.Text <> '' then
    PartServer1.RemoteMachineName := ecServer.Text;

  PartServer1.Connect;

  // Load all parts from the database server
  LoadPartGrid;

  // Enable the edit menu
  Edit1.Enabled := True;
end;

procedure TfrmMain.LoadRow(Row: Integer; varFields, varValues: OleVariant);
var
  ValueIndex: Integer;
  ColIndex: Integer;
begin
  for ValueIndex := VarArrayLowBound(varValues, 1) to VarArrayHighBound(varValues, 1) do
    for ColIndex := VarArrayLowBound(FFields, 1) to VarArrayHighBound(FFields, 1) do
      if FFields[ColIndex] = varFields[ValueIndex] then
        StringGrid1.Cells[ColIndex, Row] := varValues[ValueIndex];
end;

procedure TfrmMain.LoadPartGrid;
var
  varValues: OleVariant;
  Index: Integer;
  FieldNumber: Integer;
  Row: Integer;
begin
  varValues := PartServer1.GetAll(FFields);

  StringGrid1.RowCount := VarArrayHighBound(varValues, 1) -
    VarArrayLowBound(varValues, 1) + 2;

  StringGrid1.ColCount := VarArrayHighBound(FFields, 1) -
    VarArrayLowBound(FFields, 1) + 1;

  for Index := VarArrayLowBound(FFields, 1) to VarArrayHighBound(FFields, 1) do begin
    FieldNumber := FFields[Index];
```

```
      case FieldNumber of
        fnPartNumber: StringGrid1.Cells[Index, 0] := 'Part #';
        fnDescription: StringGrid1.Cells[Index, 0] := 'Description';
        fnUnitPrice: StringGrid1.Cells[Index, 0] := 'Unit Price';
        fnOnHand: StringGrid1.Cells[Index, 0] := 'On Hand';
        fnReorder: StringGrid1.Cells[Index, 0] := 'Reorder';
      end;
    end;

  Row := 1;
  for Index := VarArrayLowBound(varValues, 1) to VarArrayHighBound(varValues, 1) do begin
    LoadRow(Row, FFields, varValues[Index]);
    Inc(Row);
  end;
end;

procedure TfrmMain.Exit1Click(Sender: TObject);
begin
  Close;
end;

procedure TfrmMain.UsePart1Click(Sender: TObject);
var
  Value: string;
  PartNumber: string;
begin
  if InputQuery('Use Part', 'How many would you like to relieve from stock?',
    Value) then begin
    PartNumber := StringGrid1.Cells[0, StringGrid1.Row];
    PartServer1.UsePart(PartNumber, StrToInt(Value));
  end;
end;

procedure TfrmMain.PartServer1Add(Sender: TObject; varFields,
  varValues: OleVariant);
begin
  // A new part was added - reload the whole grid
  LoadPartGrid;
end;

procedure TfrmMain.PartServer1Delete(Sender: TObject;
  var PartNumber: OleVariant);
begin
  // A part was deleted - reload the whole grid
  LoadPartGrid;
end;

procedure TfrmMain.PartServer1Modify(Sender: TObject;
  var PartNumber: OleVariant; varFields, varValues: OleVariant);
var
  Index: Integer;
  Found: Boolean;
```

*continues* ▶

**Listing 6.17**    *continued*

```
begin
  Found := False;
  Index := 1;

  // If we can find the original part, just reload the row
  while (not Found) and (Index < StringGrid1.RowCount) do begin
    if StringGrid1.Cells[0, Index] = PartNumber then begin
      LoadRow(Index, varFields, varValues);
      Found := True;
    end else
      Inc(Index);
  end;

  // Couldn't find the part, so reload the whole grid
  if not Found then
    LoadPartGrid;
end;

end.
```

Most of the code in this unit is the same as the code in the MainForm unit of the administrative client. The main difference in this program is that the POS client doesn't have access to the Reorder Quantity field in the database. Because the FFields array does not include the fnReorder constant, the reorder quantity will never be sent from the server to this client.

The UsePart1Click method runs when the user clicks on the Use button of the program. It asks the user how many of the currently highlighted parts to relieve from inventory, and calls the server's UsePart method to update the database. In this example, if there isn't enough quantity in stock to satisfy the request, an exception is raised in the server alerting the user to the "error". I did this to show you that the exception is actually displayed on the client machine, even though it is raised on a remote machine. (Obviously, if this were a production application, the program should allow for an override, because the parts are physically located on the showroom floor. If the database doesn't agree with reality, we can't arbitrarily alter reality.)

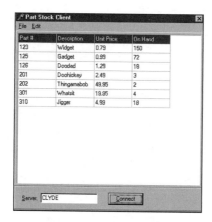

**Figure 6.15**  *The PartStock application is meant to be run from the parts floor. The user can view and relieve inventory, but cannot change prices.*

## Summary

In this chapter, I showed you how to create DCOM servers and clients. As you saw, a DCOM server is no different from a COM server—it just resides on a remote machine.

The most difficult part of installing a DCOM server is configuring the server machine correctly. If at all possible, you should use Windows NT Server (configured as a Domain Server) as your DCOM server.

After the DCOM server is operational, the client application simply calls the CreateRemote method of the CoClass, rather than Create.

In second half of this chapter, I showed you how you can use DCOM to implement remote datasets. We built a sample application that could be used as an inventory program in an auto parts store, for example.

In the next chapter, I'll introduce you to structured storage files.

# 7

## Structured Storage

In this chapter, I'm going to discuss structured storage. Like interfaces, structured storage is a technology that has both general-purpose application and predefined COM-related application. For that reason, this chapter discusses how you can take advantage of what structured storage has to offer in your own applications. Chapter 8, "Structured Storage and OLE," will discuss two specific COM-defined applications of structured storage: Property Sets and Compound Documents.

## Defining Structured Storage

Structured storage files (also known as DocFiles) provide a powerful, structured means of storing persistent information in files. I'll use the terms *structured storage* and *DocFile* interchangeably in this chapter. In a nutshell, structured storage is a complete file system within a single file.

Consider an application that needs to store a number of different types of data in its data files. For this discussion, let's say you're writing an application to track automobile expenditures. Assume the application tracks the following information:

- Gas costs
- Oil changes
- Service records

For gasoline, the application tracks the date, number of gallons of gas purchased, and mileage at the time of fillup. Oil changes track the date and mileage. Service records track the date, description of service performed, and cost of service.

Clearly these three parts of the program will use different data structures to store this information. Traditionally, this data might be stored in several different ways:

- In a database with three tables of differing structure. The problem with this approach is that it requires the overhead of a database engine. A small, single-user application might not need (or want) the additional overhead.

- In three separate data files named GAS.DAT, OIL.DAT, and SERVICE.DAT. The problem with this approach is that it creates numerous data files for the user to worry about.

- In a single data file, with the lists of data streamed out one after the other. The problem with this approach is that the application needs to read the entire file in order to gain access to the information stored at the end of the file.

Structured storage brings another alternative to the party. Using structured storage, it is possible to combine the second and third alternative listed above, while avoiding the problems associated with each.

Conceptually, a structured storage file resembles the directory structure on your hard drive. To continue with the hypothetical automobile example, take a look at Figure 7.1. This figure shows the structure of a DocFile that could be used to store this information.

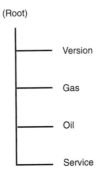

(Root)

Version

Gas

Oil

Service

**Figure 7.1**    *Structured storage files resemble directory structures.*

In structured storage parlance, the equivalent of a directory is a *storage*, and the equivalent of a file is a *stream*. You can see from Figure 7.1 that there is one (root) storage and four streams in this DocFile.

There is an additional benefit to this structure, which should not be underestimated. You can use a separate stream, as I've done in Figure 7.1, to store version information associated with the file. When a new version of your application is released (perhaps it allows you to track multiple vehicles), you can modify the structure of the file to resemble Figure 7.2. Your application can read the version stream from the file without having to access any other data. If the version number of the file doesn't match the version of the program, you can either update the file on-the-fly, or display an error message and exit.

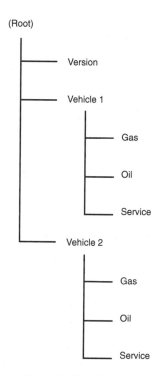

**Figure 7.2**  *Modified file structure.*

Structured storage files can easily be upgraded when you release a new version of your application. Now that you know what structured storage is, let's discuss what is required to use structured storage files in your Delphi applications.

# Programming with Structured Storage

This section will concentrate on the common tasks necessary to create, open, read from, and write to structured storage files in your programs.

## Creating a Structured Storage File

The function used to create a structured storage file is named StgCreateDocFile, and is defined in activex.pas with the following:

```
function StgCreateDocfile(pwcsName: POleStr; grfMode: Longint;
  reserved: Longint; out stgOpen: IStorage): HResult; stdcall;
```

pwcsName is the name of the file to create. grfMode specifies the access mode with which to open the file. It can be one of the values listed in Table 7.1. reserved is reserved by Microsoft for future use—it must be set to zero. StgOpen returns a reference to an IStorage interface, which you can then use to manipulate the file.

---

**Note**

*StgOpen actually refers to the root storage in the structured storage file. It doesn't refer to the structured storage file itself. The difference between the structured storage file and the root storage is analogous to the difference between a hard drive and the root directory on the drive.* ◆

---

*Table 7.1    Valid grfMode Values for StgCreateDocFile*

| Value | Description |
| --- | --- |
| STGM_DIRECT | Each modification to the file is written as soon as it occurs. |
| STGM_TRANSACTED | Modifications to the file are buffered in memory, and only written when an explicit Commit command is given. Modifications can be "rolled back" by sending a Revert command. |
| STGM_SIMPLE | Supports a simple form of structured storage. A number of limitations are enforced, but the operations on the file are much faster. This flag is discussed in the sidebar titled "Simple Structured Storage." |
| STGM_READ | Opens the file for read access. |
| STGM_WRITE | Opens the file for write access. |
| STGM_READWRITE | Opens the file for both read and write access. |
| STGM_SHARE_DENY_NONE | Does not deny others the ability to open the file. |

| Value | Description |
|---|---|
| STGM_SHARE_DENY_READ | Denies others the ability to open the file with read access. |
| STGM_SHARE_DENY_WRITE | Denies others the ability to open the file with write access. |
| STGM_SHARE_EXCLUSIVE | Denies others the ability to open the file with either read or write access. |
| STGM_PRIORITY | Prevents others from committing changes to the file while you have it open. You must also specify STGM_DIRECT and STGM_READ with this flag. |
| STGM_DELETEONRELEASE | The structured storage file is automatically deleted when the interface is released. This is used for creating temporary files. |
| STGM_CREATE | Deletes an existing file with the same name, if it exists. |
| STGM_CONVERT | Creates a new file, while preserving existing data in the CONTENTS stream of a file with the same name, if it exists. |
| STGM_FAILIFTHERE | Returns the error code STG_E_FILEAL-READYEXISTS if a file with the same name exists. |
| STGM_NOSCRATCH | When STGM_TRANSACTED is specified, Windows 95 usually creates a scratch file to save changes until a Commit command is executed. STGM_NOSCRATCH allows Windows 95 to use the unused area of the structured storage file as scratch space, providing a more efficient use of memory. |
| STGM_NOSNAPSHOT | Used only with STGM_TRANSACTED and without STGM_SHARE_EXCLUSIVE and STGM_SHARE_DENY_WRITE. STGM_NOSNAPSHOT prevents Windows from making a snapshot copy of the file. Changes to the file are written to the end of the file. When STGM_NOSNAPSHOT is specified, all concurrent users of the file must specify this flag. |

The following code snippet will create a structured storage file named MyFile.SS.

```
var
  stgRoot: IStorage;
begin
  OleCheck(StgCreateDocFile('C:\MyFile.SS', STGM_CREATE or STGM_READWRITE or
    STGM_SHARE_EXCLUSIVE, 0, stgRoot));
  ...
end;
```

## Simple Structured Storage

*STGM_SIMPLE is only applicable when combined with STGM_DIRECT, STGM_CREATE, STGM_READWRITE, and STGM_SHARE_EXCLUSIVE. It enforces the following restrictions on the application:*

- *No substorages are supported. You can only create streams in the root storage.*
- *After a stream has been closed, you cannot reopen it.*
- *Storages and streams cannot be marshaled.*
- *All streams are at least 4096 bytes long. Any streams you create that are less than 4096 bytes in length will automatically be extended to contain 4096 bytes.*
- *Only a subset of the methods of IStorage and IStream are supported. In particular, only the methods QueryInterface, AddRef, Release, CreateStream, Commit, and SetClass are supported for IStorage. Supported IStream methods include QueryInterface, AddRef, Release, Seek, and SetSize. ISequentialStream methods Read and Write are also supported. Any other method calls will result in a return value of STGM_E_INVALID-FUNCTION.* ◆

## Opening an Existing Structured Storage File

The API call to open an existing structured storage file is StgOpenStorage, defined with the following code:

```
function StgOpenStorage(pwcsName: POleStr; stgPriority: IStorage;
  grfMode: Longint; snbExclude: TSNB; reserved: Longint;
  out stgOpen: IStorage): HResult; stdcall;
```

Again, pwcsName is the name of the existing structured storage file to open. stgPriority is typically nil. If non-nil, it points to a previous opening of a root storage object. stgPriority will not be discussed in this book. grfMode specifies the access mode to use when opening the file. It can be any of the values listed in Table 7.1. snbExclude will also usually be nil. If non-nil, it points to an SNB structure that specifies which elements in the storage are to be excluded as the storage is opened. I will not discuss this parameter further in this book. reserved is reserved by Microsoft, and should be set to zero. stgOpen receives a reference to the IStorage interface on the opened structured storage file.

The following code snippet shows how to open an existing structured storage file.

```
var
  stgRoot: IStorage;
begin
  OleCheck(StgOpenStorage('C:\MyFile.SS', nil, STGM_READWRITE or
    STGM_SHARE_EXCLUSIVE, nil, 0, stgRoot));
  ...
end;
```

## Working with Streams

After you have obtained a reference to the root storage, you are free to create a stream in that storage. Recall that a storage is conceptually equivalent to a directory, and a stream is the rough equivalent of a file. Therefore, you need to create a stream before you can write data. The following sections will address creating, writing to, opening, and reading a stream.

### Creating a Stream

You'll use IStorage.CreateStream to create a new stream. CreateStream is defined with the following code:

```
function CreateStream(pwcsName: POleStr; grfMode: Longint; reserved1: Longint;
    reserved2: Longint; out stm: IStream): HResult; stdcall;
```

pwcsName is the name of the stream to create. grfMode is the access mode for the stream. reserved1 and reserved2 are, again, reserved, and should be set to zero. stm receives a reference to the IStream interface on the newly created stream.

The following code snippet shows how to create a stream:

```
var
  stgRoot: IStorage;
  stmData: IStream;
begin
  // Create a new structured storage file
  OleCheck(StgCreateDocFile('C:\MyFile.SS', STGM_CREATE or STGM_READWRITE or
    STGM_SHARE_EXCLUSIVE, 0, stgRoot));

  // Create a stream in the storage
  OleCheck(stgRoot.CreateStream('MyData', STGM_CREATE or STGM_READWRITE or
    STGM_SHARE_EXCLUSIVE, 0, 0, stmData));
  ...
end;
```

## Writing to a Stream

Now that you have created a stream, you'll want to save some data to it. The standard method of writing to a stream is through the IStream.Write method, like this:

```
var
  stgRoot: IStorage;
  stmData: IStream;
  MyIntValue: Integer;
  BytesWritten: LongInt;
begin
  // Create a new structured storage file
  OleCheck(StgCreateDocFile('C:\MyFile.SS', STGM_CREATE or STGM_READWRITE or
    STGM_SHARE_EXCLUSIVE, 0, stgRoot));

  // Create a stream in the storage
  OleCheck(stgRoot.CreateStream('MyData', STGM_CREATE or STGM_READWRITE or
    STGM_SHARE_EXCLUSIVE, 0, 0, stmData));

  MyIntValue := 100;

  // Write to the stream
  OleCheck(stmData.Write(@MyIntValue, sizeof(Integer), @BytesWritten));
  ...
end;
```

Delphi provides a class called TOleStream that makes this task even easier. TOleStream implements a wrapper around the IStream interface. That way, you can write to a structured storage stream using the same commands you use when writing to any standard Delphi stream.

For example, here is a code snippet that creates a structured storage file, creates a stream, and writes a bitmap to the stream using TOleStream.

```
var
  stgRoot: IStorage;
  stmData: IStream;
  OS: TOleStream;
begin
  // Create a new structured storage file
  OleCheck(StgCreateDocFile('C:\MyFile.SS', STGM_CREATE or STGM_READWRITE or
    STGM_SHARE_EXCLUSIVE, 0, stgRoot));

  // Create a stream in the storage
  OleCheck(stgRoot.CreateStream('MyData', STGM_CREATE or STGM_READWRITE or
    STGM_SHARE_EXCLUSIVE, 0, 0, stmData));

  // Wrap the stream with a TOleStream
  OS := TOleStream.Create(stmData);
  try
    Image1.Picture.Bitmap.SaveToStream(OS);
  finally
```

```
      OS.Free;
    end;
    ...
  end;
```

## Opening a Stream

Opening a stream is similar to creating a stream, except you use IStorage.OpenStream, defined with the following code:

```
function OpenStream(pwcsName: POleStr; reserved1: Pointer; grfMode: Longint;
    reserved2: Longint; out stm: IStream): HResult; stdcall;
```

pwcsName is the name of the (existing) stream to open. reserved1 is reserved, and should be set to zero. grfMode is the access mode used to open the stream. reserved2 is also reserved, and should be set to zero. stm receives a reference to the IStream interface on the opened stream.

Here is a code snippet that shows how to open an existing structured storage file and open a stream in that file.

```
var
  stgRoot: IStorage;
  stmData: IStream;
begin
  OleCheck(StgOpenStorage('C:\MyFile.SS', nil, STGM_READWRITE or
    STGM_SHARE_EXCLUSIVE, nil, 0, stgRoot));

  OleCheck(stgRoot.OpenStream('MyData', 0, STGM_READWRITE or
    STGM_SHARE_EXCLUSIVE, 0, stmData));
  ...
end;
```

## Reading from a Stream

Reading from a stream involves using the IStream.Read method, as shown in the following code:

```
var
  stgRoot: IStorage;
  stmData: IStream;
  MyIntValue: Integer;
  BytesRead: LongInt;
begin
  OleCheck(StgOpenStorage('C:\MyFile.SS', nil, STGM_READWRITE or
    STGM_SHARE_EXCLUSIVE, nil, 0, stgRoot));

  OleCheck(stgRoot.OpenStream('MyData', nil, STGM_READWRITE or
    STGM_SHARE_EXCLUSIVE, 0, stmData));

  OleCheck(stmData.Read(@MyIntValue, sizeof(Integer), @BytesRead));
  ...
end;
```

Similarly to writing to a stream, you'll typically want to use TOleStream when reading from a stream.

The following is a code snippet that shows how you can read an image from an existing stream using TOleStream:

```
var
  stgRoot: IStorage;
  stmData: IStream;
  OS: TOleStream;
begin
  OleCheck(StgOpenStorage('C:\MyFile.SS', nil, STGM_READWRITE or
    STGM_SHARE_EXCLUSIVE, nil, 0, stgRoot));

  OleCheck(stgRoot.OpenStream('MyData', nil, STGM_READWRITE or
    STGM_SHARE_EXCLUSIVE, 0, stmData));

  OS := TOleStream.Create(stmData);
  try
    Image1.Picture.Bitmap.LoadFromStream(OS);
  finally
    OS.Free;
  end;
  ...
end;
```

## Creating and Using Additional Storages

You are not limited to having only a single storage in your DocFiles, although typically that will be the case. To create an additional storage, use the IStorage method CreateStorage, defined with the following code:

```
function CreateStorage(pwcsName: POleStr; grfMode: Longint;
    dwStgFmt: Longint; reserved2: Longint; out stg: IStorage): HResult;
    stdcall;
```

pwcsName is, of course, the name of the storage to create. grfMode again specifies the access mode to use when creating the storage. dwStgFmt is typically set to zero. reserved2 is reserved, and should be set to zero. stg receives a reference to the IStorage interface on the newly created storage.

To open an existing storage (other than the root storage), use IStorage.OpenStorage:

```
function OpenStorage(pwcsName: POleStr; const stgPriority: IStorage;
    grfMode: Longint; snbExclude: TSNB; reserved: Longint;
    out stg: IStorage): HResult; stdcall;
```

pwcsName is the name of the storage to open. stgPriority must be set to nil, or the call to OpenStorage will return STG_E_INVALIDPARAMETER. grfMode specifies the access mode to use when opening the storage. snbExclude must also be set to nil. reserved is reserved and must be set to zero. stg receives a reference to the IStorage interface on the opened storage.

After you have created or opened an additional storage, you can use it exactly as you would use the root storage. In other words, you can create and access streams in the storage, and you can even create substorages under it.

## Iterating Through a Structured Storage File

When you use structured storage files in your own applications, you will obviously know the layout of the file. However, it can sometimes be useful to view the structure of a DocFile that was created by another application.

Because structured storage files are self-documenting, you can enumerate the storages and streams contained in the file. You'll use IStorage.EnumElements for this. EnumElements is defined as

```
function EnumElements(reserved1: Longint; reserved2: Pointer; reserved3: Longint;
    out enm: IEnumStatStg): HResult; stdcall;
```

reserved1, reserved2, and reserved3 are reserved, and should be set to zero. enm receives a reference to a IEnumStatStg interface. IEnumStatStg provides methods for enumerating the individual elements in the structured storage file. The only method we're interested in is Next, which is defined with the following code:

```
function Next(celt: Longint; out elt;
    pceltFetched: PLongint): HResult; stdcall;
```

celt specifies the number of elements to retrieve at once. elt points to an array that will receive the elements. pceltFetched is a pointer to a variable which will receive the number of elements actually retrieved. You may set it to nil if the number of elements requested is 1.

> **Note**
>
> *Even if you request more than one element at a time, the implementation of IEnumStatStg is not required to return more than one element at a time. Most COM enumerators (including IEnumStatStg) only return one element at a time, regardless of how many you request. Make sure you check the value of pceltFetched to see how many elements were actually returned.* ♦

pceltFetches actually points to an array of TStatStg records. TStatStg is defined as follows:

```
tagSTATSTG = record
  pwcsName: POleStr;
  dwType: Longint;
  cbSize: Largeint;
  mtime: TFileTime;
  ctime: TFileTime;
```

```
    atime: TFileTime;
    grfMode: Longint;
    grfLocksSupported: Longint;
    clsid: TCLSID;
    grfStateBits: Longint;
    reserved: Longint;
  end;
  TStatStg = tagSTATSTG;
```

Typically, you'll be most interested in the pwcsName field of the record. This field contains the name of the element in question.

Combining these two methods, we can write a procedure that does something with each element in the structured storage file, as follows:

```
procedure IterateSS(stg: IStorage);
var
  EnumStatStg: IEnumStatStg;
  StatStg: TStatStg;
begin
  OleCheck(stg.EnumElements(0, nil, 0, EnumStatStg));

  while EnumStatStg.Next(1, StatStg, nil) = S_OK do begin
    // Do something with StatStg here...
  end;
end;
```

Note that you can call IterateSS with a reference to any storage, including the root storage.

## Compressing a Structured Storage File

A structured storage file is in many ways similar to the directory structure on your hard drive, so it also suffers from one of the same problems— namely, fragmentation. It also has one problem that your hard drive does not—it cannot automatically reclaim wasted space. When you delete a file from your hard drive, the space previously occupied by the file is immediately released and available for other files to use. When you delete a stream from a structured storage file, the space is available for other streams to use, but the structured storage file does not shrink to close up any gaps left by the deleted stream.

Unfortunately, there is no simple method to optimize a structured storage file. That does not mean it cannot be done, however. To defragment the storages and streams in a structured storage file, as well as reclaim all wasted space, you must do the following:

1. Open the original file in exclusive mode.

2. Create a new, temporary file.

3. Copy all storages and streams from the original file to the temporary file.

4. Close the temporary file.

5. Close the original file.

6. Delete the original file.

7. Rename the temporary file so it has the same name as the original file.

The following procedure shows how to do this:

```
procedure CompressStructuredStorageFile(AFileName: WideString);
var
  stgOriginal: IStorage;
  stgTemp: IStorage;
  TempFileName: WideString;
begin
  // Step 1 - Open the original file
  OleCheck(StgOpenStorage(PWideChar(AFileName), nil, STGM_READ or
    STGM_SHARE_EXCLUSIVE, nil, 0, stgOriginal));

  // Step 2 - Create a new, temporary file
  TempFileName := ChangeFileExt(AFileName, '.$$$');
  OleCheck(StgCreateDocFile(PWideChar(TempFileName), STGM_WRITE or
    STGM_SHARE_EXCLUSIVE, 0, stgTemp));

  // Step 3 - Copy the old file to the new one
  stgOriginal.CopyTo(0, nil, nil, stgTemp);

  // Step 4 - Close the temporary file
  stgTemp := nil;

  // Step 5 - Close the original file
  stgOriginal := nil;

  // Step 6 - Delete the original file
  DeleteFile(AFileName);

  // Step 7 - Rename the temporary file
  RenameFile(TempFileName, AFileName);
end;
```

I've already discussed all the methods used in this code snippet, except CopyTo. IStorage.CopyTo is used to copy the contents of one storage to another storage, and is defined as follows:

```
function CopyTo(ciidExclude: Longint; rgiidExclude: PIID;
    snbExclude: TSNB; const stgDest: IStorage): HResult; stdcall;
```

ciidExclude contains the number of elements specified by rgiidExclude. If rgiidExclude is nil, then ciidExclude is ignored. snbExclude may also be set to nil. Together, these three parameters allow you to specify a set of storages and/or streams that will not be copied by CopyTo. This is a rather advanced feature, and one that you'll seldom use, so I won't discuss these parameters further in this chapter. stgDest specifies the IStorage interface on the destination storage object. A typical usage of this method, shown in the previous example, copies the entire storage, including substorages and streams, to the destination storage.

# Example: Using Structured Storage Files in Your Applications

Now that you know the basics of using structured storage, let's create an application that uses structured storage as its native file format. This application is somewhat lengthy compared to the other samples in this book, but it isn't difficult to understand.

At the beginning of this chapter, I talked a little about a hypothetical automobile application. Let's make this application a reality. For space considerations, I have only implemented the gas and oil portions of the program, and I only allow for a single vehicle to be tracked—you can easily expand on the code shown here to track service and anything else you like.

The CarDemo application stores all data in a single structured storage file named CARS.CAR. CARS.CAR contains a single storage (the root storage) and three streams: one for gas, one for oil, and one to store general information about the car, such as the description and model year.

The application is broken down into seven source files, shown in Listings 7.1 through 7.7. The vast majority of the code is self explanatory, although I did resort to a nifty trick in order to easily stream the gas and oil information to the file. I'll discuss each source file in turn.

Listing 7.2 contains the source code for the main form of the application.

FormCreate attempts to open the structured storage file CARS.CAR. If it is not successful, it creates a structured storage file of the same name. A more robust program would need to examine the error code returned by StgOpenStorage and only create the data file if is doesn't exist. FormCreate leaves the structured storage file open for the duration of the program.

I'll skip the rest of FormCreate for the moment, and instead concentrate on FormDestroy. FormDestroy opens the Info stream for writing. Recall that the car name and model year will be saved to this stream. Here, I've used a TWriter class to write the car name and model year. Using a Delphi-centric method like TWriter means that I won't easily be able to read this information from another programming environment such as Visual C++ or Visual Basic, but I'm not too concerned about that for this example.

> **Note**
>
> *Using TWriter is a bit of overkill in this situation, because I'm only writing out a string and an integer (so I could just use the stream class). However, if this were a real application, it could easily be expanded to include the purchase price of the car, purchase date, interest rate, and much more. TWriter includes a number of methods that make quick work of writing out various types of data.* ◆

Getting back to FormCreate, after the file is opened, the program tries to open the Info stream. If it is successful, it uses a TReader component to read the information stored out by the TWriter component in FormDestroy. If the stream cannot be opened, a new one is created, as shown in Listing 7.2.

**Listing 7.1**    *CarDemo—CarDemo.dpr*

```
program CarDemo;

uses
  Forms,
  MainForm in 'MainForm.pas' {frmMain},
  GasForm in 'GasForm.pas' {frmGas},
  OilForm in 'OilForm.pas' {frmOil},
  GasItemForm in 'GasItemForm.pas' {frmGasItem},
  CarInfoForm in 'CarInfoForm.pas' {frmCarInfo},
  OilItemForm in 'OilItemForm.pas' {frmOilItem};

{$R *.RES}

begin
  Application.Initialize;
  Application.CreateForm(TfrmMain, frmMain);
  Application.Run;
end.
```

**Listing 7.2**    *CarDemo—MainForm.pas*

```
unit MainForm;

interface

uses
  Windows, Messages, SysUtils, Classes, Graphics, Controls, Forms, Dialogs,
  Menus, ActiveX, AxCtrls, ComObj;

type
  TfrmMain = class(TForm)
    MainMenu1: TMainMenu;
    File1: TMenuItem;
    Exit1: TMenuItem;
```

*continues* ▶

**Listing 7.2**  *continued*

```
    N1: TMenuItem;
    Gas1: TMenuItem;
    Oil1: TMenuItem;
    Edit1: TMenuItem;
    CarInformation1: TMenuItem;
    procedure FormCreate(Sender: TObject);
    procedure FormDestroy(Sender: TObject);
    procedure Gas1Click(Sender: TObject);
    procedure Oil1Click(Sender: TObject);
    procedure CarInformation1Click(Sender: TObject);
  private
    FRootStorage: IStorage;
    FCarName: string;
    FYear: Integer;
    function ActivateForm(ACaption: string): Boolean;
    { Private declarations }
  public
    { Public declarations }
    property RootStorage: IStorage read FRootStorage;
  end;

var
  frmMain: TfrmMain;

implementation

uses GasForm, OilForm, CarInfoForm;

{$R *.DFM}

procedure TfrmMain.FormCreate(Sender: TObject);
var
  stm: IStream;
  OS: TOleStream;
  Reader: TReader;
begin
  if not SUCCEEDED(StgOpenStorage('CARS.CAR', nil,
    STGM_READWRITE or STGM_SHARE_EXCLUSIVE,
    nil, 0, FRootStorage)) then
    OleCheck(StgCreateDocFile('CARS.CAR',
      STGM_CREATE or STGM_READWRITE or STGM_SHARE_EXCLUSIVE,
      0, FRootStorage));

  if SUCCEEDED(FRootStorage.OpenStream('Info', nil,
    STGM_READ or STGM_SHARE_EXCLUSIVE, 0, stm)) then begin
    OS := TOleStream.Create(stm);
    try
      Reader := TReader.Create(OS, 1024);
      try
        FCarName := Reader.ReadString;
        FYear := Reader.ReadInteger;
```

```
      finally
        Reader.Free;
      end;
    finally
      OS.Free;
    end;
  end else begin
    OleCheck(FRootStorage.CreateStream('Info',
      STGM_CREATE or STGM_READ or STGM_SHARE_EXCLUSIVE, 0, 0, stm));
  end;
end;

procedure TfrmMain.FormDestroy(Sender: TObject);
var
  stm: IStream;
  OS: TOleStream;
  Writer: TWriter;
begin
  OleCheck(FRootStorage.OpenStream('Info', nil, STGM_WRITE or
    STGM_SHARE_EXCLUSIVE, 0, stm));

  OS := TOleStream.Create(stm);
  try
    Writer := TWriter.Create(OS, 1024);
    try
      Writer.WriteString(FCarName);
      Writer.WriteInteger(FYear);
    finally
      Writer.Free;
    end;
  finally
    OS.Free;
  end;
end;

function TfrmMain.ActivateForm(ACaption: string): Boolean;
var
  Index: Integer;
begin
  Result := False;

  for Index := 0 to MDIChildCount - 1 do
    if MDIChildren[Index].Caption = ACaption then begin
      if MDIChildren[Index].WindowState = wsMinimized then
        MDIChildren[Index].WindowState := wsNormal;
      MDIChildren[Index].SetFocus;
      Result := True;
      exit;
    end;
end;
```

*continues* ▶

**Listing 7.2**   *continued*

```
procedure TfrmMain.Gas1Click(Sender: TObject);
var
  frmGas: TfrmGas;
begin
  if not ActivateForm('Gas') then begin
    frmGas := TfrmGas.Create(self);
    frmGas.Show;
  end;
end;

procedure TfrmMain.Oil1Click(Sender: TObject);
var
  frmOil: TfrmOil;
begin
  if not ActivateForm('Oil') then begin
    frmOil := TfrmOil.Create(self);
    frmOil.Show;
  end;
end;

procedure TfrmMain.CarInformation1Click(Sender: TObject);
var
  frmCarInfo: TfrmCarInfo;
begin
  frmCarInfo := TfrmCarInfo.Create(nil);
  try
    frmCarInfo.ecDescription.Text := FCarName;
    frmCarInfo.ecYear.Text := IntToStr(FYear);

    if frmCarInfo.ShowModal = mrOk then begin
      FCarName := frmCarInfo.Description;
      FYear := frmCarInfo.Year;
    end;
  finally
    frmCarInfo.Free;
  end;
end;

end.
```

Listing 7.3 contains the source code for the car information dialog box. This dialog box allows the user to view and/or change the car name and model year.

**Listing 7.3**    *CarDemo—CarInfoForm.pas*

```
unit CarInfoForm;

interface

uses
  Windows, Messages, SysUtils, Classes, Graphics, Controls, Forms, Dialogs,
  StdCtrls, ExtCtrls;

type
  TfrmCarInfo = class(TForm)
    pnlBottom: TPanel;
    pnlClient: TPanel;
    btnOK: TButton;
    btnCancel: TButton;
    Label1: TLabel;
    Label2: TLabel;
    ecDescription: TEdit;
    ecYear: TEdit;
    procedure btnOKClick(Sender: TObject);
  private
    FYear: Integer;
    FDescription: string;
    { Private declarations }
  public
    { Public declarations }
    property Description: string read FDescription;
    property Year: Integer read FYear;
  end;

implementation

{$R *.DFM}

procedure TfrmCarInfo.btnOKClick(Sender: TObject);
begin
  FDescription := ecDescription.Text;

  try
    FYear := StrToInt(ecYear.Text);
  except
    ModalResult := mrNone;
    ActiveControl := ecYear;
    ShowMessage('Year is not a valid number.');
    exit;
  end;
end;

end.
```

Figure 7.3 shows the car information dialog box at runtime.

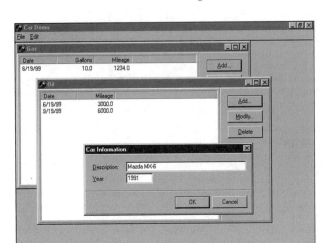

**Figure 7.3**    *Viewing my car information.*

Listing 7.4 implements TfrmGas. TfrmGas is used to enter the date and mileage when gasoline is purchased. It also defines the helper classes TGasItem and TGasItems. I elected to store the line items in a collection for two reasons. First, a collection is an ideal data structure to store homogenous data items. More importantly, however, with a little finesse, we can convince Delphi's streaming mechanism to read and write the whole collection to a stream with just a couple of lines of code.

Take a look at the FormDestroy method shown in Listing 7.4. It is repeated here for reference.

```
OleCheck(frmMain.RootStorage.CreateStream('Gas',
  STGM_CREATE or STGM_WRITE or STGM_SHARE_EXCLUSIVE, 0, 0, stm));

Dummy := TDummy.Create(nil);
Dummy.Items.Assign(FItems);
try
  OS := TOleStream.Create(stm);
  try
    OS.WriteComponent(Dummy);
  finally
    OS.Free;
  end;
finally
  Dummy.Free;
end;
```

After creating the Gas stream, the application creates a dummy component that is used to stream out the order items. Delphi doesn't directly support streaming collections by themselves. However, if a collection is a published property of a component, then Delphi will automatically stream the collection when streaming the component. So, I assign the collection to the TDummy component just long enough to stream it out, then dispose of the TDummy component.

FormCreate takes care of reading in the gasoline line items in an analogous manner.

**Listing 7.4**    *CarDemo—GasForm.pas*

```
unit GasForm;

interface

uses
  Windows, Messages, SysUtils, Classes, Graphics, Controls, Forms,
  Dialogs, ComObj, ActiveX, AxCtrls, ComCtrls, ExtCtrls, StdCtrls;

type
  TGasItem = class(TCollectionItem)
  private
    FDate: TDateTime;
    FGallons: Double;
    FMileage: Double;
  public
    procedure Assign(Source: TPersistent); override;
  published
    property Date: TDateTime read FDate write FDate;
    property Gallons: Double read FGallons write FGallons;
    property Mileage: Double read FMileage write FMileage;
  end;

  TGasItems = class(TCollection)
  public
    constructor Create;
    function Add: TGasItem;
    function GetItem(Index: Integer): TGasItem;
    procedure SetItem(Index: Integer; Value: TGasItem);
    property Items[Index: Integer]: TGasItem
      read GetItem write SetItem;
  end;

  TfrmGas = class(TForm)
    Panel1: TPanel;
    Panel2: TPanel;
    list: TListView;
    btnAdd: TButton;
```

*continues* ▶

**Listing 7.4**    *continued*

```
    btnModify: TButton;
    btnDelete: TButton;
    procedure FormCreate(Sender: TObject);
    procedure FormClose(Sender: TObject; var Action: TCloseAction);
    procedure FormDestroy(Sender: TObject);
    procedure btnAddClick(Sender: TObject);
    procedure btnModifyClick(Sender: TObject);
    procedure btnDeleteClick(Sender: TObject);
  private
    { Private declarations }
    FItems: TGasItems;
    procedure AddListItem(GasItem: TGasItem);
    procedure SetListItem(LI: TListItem; GasItem: TGasItem);
    procedure EnableButtons;
  public
    { Public declarations }
  end;

implementation

uses MainForm, GasItemForm;

{$R *.DFM}

type
  TDummy = class(TComponent)
  private
    FItems: TGasItems;
  public
    constructor Create(AOwner: TComponent); override;
    destructor Destroy; override;
  published
    property Items: TGasItems read FItems write FItems;
  end;

{ TfrmGas }

procedure TfrmGas.AddListItem(GasItem: TGasItem);
var
  LI: TListItem;
begin
  LI := list.Items.Add;
  LI.Caption := DateToStr(GasItem.Date);
  LI.SubItems.Add(FloatToStrF(GasItem.Gallons, ffFixed, 8, 1));
  LI.SubItems.Add(FloatToStrF(GasItem.Mileage, ffFixed, 8, 1));

  list.Selected := LI;
end;
```

```
procedure TfrmGas.SetListItem(LI: TListItem; GasItem: TGasItem);
begin
  LI.Caption := DateToStr(GasItem.Date);
  LI.SubItems[0] := FloatToStrF(GasItem.Gallons, ffFixed, 8, 1);
  LI.SubItems[1] := FloatToStrF(GasItem.Mileage, ffFixed, 8, 1);
end;

procedure TfrmGas.EnableButtons;
begin
  btnModify.Enabled := list.Selected <> nil;
  btnDelete.Enabled := list.Selected <> nil;
end;

procedure TfrmGas.FormCreate(Sender: TObject);
var
  stm: IStream;
  Dummy: TDummy;
  OS: TOleStream;
  Index: Integer;
  GasItem: TGasItem;
begin
  FItems := TGasItems.Create;

  if SUCCEEDED(frmMain.RootStorage.OpenStream('Gas', nil,
    STGM_READ or STGM_SHARE_EXCLUSIVE, 0, stm)) then begin
    Dummy := TDummy.Create(nil);
    try
      OS := TOleStream.Create(stm);
      try
        OS.ReadComponent(Dummy);
        FItems.Assign(Dummy.FItems);
      finally
        OS.Free;
      end;
    finally
      Dummy.Free;
    end;
  end else begin
    OleCheck(frmMain.RootStorage.CreateStream('Gas',
      STGM_CREATE or STGM_READ or STGM_SHARE_EXCLUSIVE, 0, 0, stm));
  end;

  for Index := 0 to FItems.Count - 1 do begin
    GasItem := FItems.Items[Index];
    AddListItem(GasItem);
  end;
end;

procedure TfrmGas.FormClose(Sender: TObject;
  var Action: TCloseAction);
begin
  Action := caFree;
end;
```

*continues* ▶

**Listing 7.4**    *continued*

```
procedure TfrmGas.FormDestroy(Sender: TObject);
var
  stm: IStream;
  OS: TOleStream;
  Dummy: TDummy;
begin
  OleCheck(frmMain.RootStorage.CreateStream('Gas',
    STGM_CREATE or STGM_WRITE or STGM_SHARE_EXCLUSIVE, 0, 0, stm));

  Dummy := TDummy.Create(nil);
try
    Dummy.Items.Assign(FItems);
    OS := TOleStream.Create(stm);
    try
      OS.WriteComponent(Dummy);
    finally
      OS.Free;
    end;
  finally
    Dummy.Free;
  end;

  FItems.Free;
end;

procedure TfrmGas.btnAddClick(Sender: TObject);
var
  frmGasItem: TfrmGasItem;
  GasItem: TGasItem;
begin
  frmGasItem := TfrmGasItem.Create(nil);
  try
    if frmGasItem.ShowModal = mrOk then begin
      GasItem := FItems.Add;
      GasItem.Date := frmGasItem.Date;
      GasItem.Gallons := frmGasItem.Gallons;
      GasItem.Mileage := frmGasItem.Mileage;

      AddListItem(GasItem);

      EnableButtons;
    end;
  finally
    frmGasItem.Free;
  end;
end;

procedure TfrmGas.btnModifyClick(Sender: TObject);
var
  frmGasItem: TfrmGasItem;
  GasItem: TGasItem;
```

```
begin
  frmGasItem := TfrmGasItem.Create(nil);
  try
    GasItem := FItems.Items[list.Selected.Index];
    frmGasItem.dtDate.Date := GasItem.Date;
    frmGasItem.ecGallons.Text := FloatToStr(GasItem.Gallons);
    frmGasItem.ecMileage.Text := FloatToStr(GasItem.Mileage);

    if frmGasItem.ShowModal = mrOk then begin
      GasItem.Date := frmGasItem.Date;
      GasItem.Gallons := frmGasItem.Gallons;
      GasItem.Mileage := frmGasItem.Mileage;

      SetListItem(list.Selected, GasItem);
    end;
  finally
    frmGasItem.Free;
  end;
end;

procedure TfrmGas.btnDeleteClick(Sender: TObject);
var
  Index: Integer;
  GasItem: TGasItem;
begin
  Index := list.Selected.Index;
  list.Items.Delete(Index);
  GasItem := FItems.Items[Index];
  GasItem.Free;

  EnableButtons;
end;

{ TGasItem }

procedure TGasItem.Assign(Source: TPersistent);
begin
  if Source is TGasItem then begin
    FDate := TGasItem(Source).FDate;
    FGallons := TGasItem(Source).FGallons;
    FMileage := TGasItem(Source).FMileage;
  end else
    inherited Assign(Source);
end;

{ TGasItems }

function TGasItems.Add: TGasItem;
begin
  Result := inherited Add as TGasItem;
end;
```

*continues* ▶

---

**Listing 7.4**    *continued*

```
constructor TGasItems.Create;
begin
  inherited Create(TGasItem);
end;

function TGasItems.GetItem(Index: Integer): TGasItem;
begin
  Result := inherited GetItem(Index) as TGasItem;
end;

procedure TGasItems.SetItem(Index: Integer; Value: TGasItem);
begin
  inherited SetItem(Index, Value);
end;

{ TDummy }

constructor TDummy.Create(AOwner: TComponent);
begin
  FItems := TGasItems.Create;
end;

destructor TDummy.Destroy;
begin
  FItems.Free;
end;

end.
```

---

Listing 7.5 shows the source code for the TfrmGasItem dialog box. The user will enter information for a single gas purchase (such as date, number of gallons, and car mileage) into this dialog box.

---

**Listing 7.5**    *CarDemo—GasItemForm.pas*

```
unit GasItemForm;

interface

uses
  Windows, Messages, SysUtils, Classes, Graphics, Controls, Forms, Dialogs,
  StdCtrls, ComCtrls, ExtCtrls;

type
  TfrmGasItem = class(TForm)
    pnlBottom: TPanel;
    pnlClient: TPanel;
    btnOK: TButton;
    btnCancel: TButton;
    Label1: TLabel;
    Label2: TLabel;
```

```
    Label3: TLabel;
    dtDate: TDateTimePicker;
    ecGallons: TEdit;
    ecMileage: TEdit;
    procedure btnOKClick(Sender: TObject);
  private
    FDate: TDateTime;
    FGallons: Double;
    FMileage: Double;
    { Private declarations }
  public
    { Public declarations }
    property Date: TDateTime read FDate;
    property Gallons: Double read FGallons;
    property Mileage: Double read FMileage;
  end;

implementation

{$R *.DFM}

procedure TfrmGasItem.btnOKClick(Sender: TObject);
begin
  FDate := dtDate.Date;

  try
    FGallons := StrToFloat(ecGallons.Text);
  except
    ModalResult := mrNone;
    ActiveControl := ecGallons;
    ShowMessage('Gallons is not a valid number.');
    exit;
  end;

  try
    FMileage := StrToFloat(ecMileage.Text);
  except
    ModalResult := mrNone;
    ActiveControl := ecMileage;
    ShowMessage('Mileage is not a valid number.');
    exit;
  end;
end;

end.
```

Listings 7.6 and 7.7 are almost identical to Listings 7.4 and 7.5, except they contain the code for tracking oil instead of gas.

**Listing 7.6**    *CarDemo—OilForm.pas*

```
unit OilForm;

interface

uses
  Windows, Messages, SysUtils, Classes, Graphics, Controls, Forms, Dialogs,
  ComCtrls, StdCtrls, ExtCtrls, ActiveX, AxCtrls, ComObj;

type
  TOilItem = class(TCollectionItem)
  private
    FDate: TDateTime;
    FMileage: Double;
  public
    procedure Assign(Source: TPersistent); override;
  published
    property Date: TDateTime read FDate write FDate;
    property Mileage: Double read FMileage write FMileage;
  end;

  TOilItems = class(TCollection)
  public
    constructor Create;
    function Add: TOilItem;
    function GetItem(Index: Integer): TOilItem;
    procedure SetItem(Index: Integer; Value: TOilItem);
    property Items[Index: Integer]: TOilItem
      read GetItem write SetItem;
  end;

  TfrmOil = class(TForm)
    Panel1: TPanel;
    btnAdd: TButton;
    btnModify: TButton;
    btnDelete: TButton;
    Panel2: TPanel;
    list: TListView;
    procedure FormCreate(Sender: TObject);
    procedure FormClose(Sender: TObject; var Action: TCloseAction);
    procedure FormDestroy(Sender: TObject);
    procedure btnAddClick(Sender: TObject);
    procedure btnModifyClick(Sender: TObject);
    procedure btnDeleteClick(Sender: TObject);
  private
    { Private declarations }
    FItems: TOilItems;
    procedure AddListItem(OilItem: TOilItem);
    procedure SetListItem(LI: TListItem; OilItem: TOilItem);
    procedure EnableButtons;
  public
    { Public declarations }
  end;
```

```
var
  frmOil: TfrmOil;

implementation

uses MainForm, OilItemForm;

{$R *.DFM}

type
  TDummy = class(TComponent)
  private
    FItems: TOilItems;
  public
    constructor Create(AOwner: TComponent); override;
    destructor Destroy; override;
  published
    property Items: TOilItems read FItems write FItems;
  end;

{ TfrmOil }

procedure TfrmOil.AddListItem(OilItem: TOilItem);
var
  LI: TListItem;
begin
  LI := list.Items.Add;
  LI.Caption := DateToStr(OilItem.Date);
  LI.SubItems.Add(FloatToStrF(OilItem.Mileage, ffFixed, 8, 1));

  list.Selected := LI;
end;

procedure TfrmOil.SetListItem(LI: TListItem; OilItem: TOilItem);
begin
  LI.Caption := DateToStr(OilItem.Date);
  LI.SubItems[0] := FloatToStrF(OilItem.Mileage, ffFixed, 8, 1);
end;

procedure TfrmOil.EnableButtons;
begin
  btnModify.Enabled := list.Selected <> nil;
  btnDelete.Enabled := list.Selected <> nil;
end;

procedure TfrmOil.FormCreate(Sender: TObject);
var
  stm: IStream;
  Dummy: TDummy;
  OS: TOleStream;
  Index: Integer;
  OilItem: TOilItem;
```

*continues* ▶

**Listing 7.6**  *continued*

```
begin
  FItems := TOilItems.Create;

  if SUCCEEDED(frmMain.RootStorage.OpenStream('Oil', nil,
    STGM_READ or STGM_SHARE_EXCLUSIVE, 0, stm)) then begin
    Dummy := TDummy.Create(nil);
    try
      OS := TOleStream.Create(stm);
      try
        OS.ReadComponent(Dummy);
        FItems.Assign(Dummy.FItems);
      finally
        OS.Free;
      end;
    finally
      Dummy.Free;
    end;
  end else begin
    OleCheck(frmMain.RootStorage.CreateStream('Oil',
      STGM_CREATE or STGM_READ or STGM_SHARE_EXCLUSIVE, 0, 0, stm));
  end;

  for Index := 0 to FItems.Count - 1 do begin
    OilItem := FItems.Items[Index];
    AddListItem(OilItem);
  end;
end;

procedure TfrmOil.FormClose(Sender: TObject; var Action: TCloseAction);
begin
  Action := caFree;
end;

procedure TfrmOil.FormDestroy(Sender: TObject);
var
  stm: IStream;
  OS: TOleStream;
  Dummy: TDummy;
begin
  OleCheck(frmMain.RootStorage.CreateStream('Oil',
    STGM_CREATE or STGM_WRITE or STGM_SHARE_EXCLUSIVE, 0, 0, stm));

  Dummy := TDummy.Create(nil);
  try
    Dummy.Items.Assign(FItems);
    OS := TOleStream.Create(stm);
    try
      OS.WriteComponent(Dummy);
    finally
      OS.Free;
    end;
```

```
    finally
      Dummy.Free;
    end;

  FItems.Free;
end;

procedure TfrmOil.btnAddClick(Sender: TObject);
var
  frmOilItem: TfrmOilItem;
  OilItem: TOilItem;
begin
  frmOilItem := TfrmOilItem.Create(nil);
  try
    if frmOilItem.ShowModal = mrOk then begin
      OilItem := FItems.Add;
      OilItem.Date := frmOilItem.Date;
      OilItem.Mileage := frmOilItem.Mileage;

      AddListItem(OilItem);

      EnableButtons;
    end;
  finally
    frmOilItem.Free;
  end;
end;

procedure TfrmOil.btnModifyClick(Sender: TObject);
var
  frmOilItem: TfrmOilItem;
  OilItem: TOilItem;
begin
  frmOilItem := TfrmOilItem.Create(nil);
  try
    OilItem := FItems.Items[list.Selected.Index];
    frmOilItem.dtDate.Date := OilItem.Date;
    frmOilItem.ecMileage.Text := FloatToStr(OilItem.Mileage);

    if frmOilItem.ShowModal = mrOk then begin
      OilItem.Date := frmOilItem.Date;
      OilItem.Mileage := frmOilItem.Mileage;

      SetListItem(list.Selected, OilItem);
    end;
  finally
    frmOilItem.Free;
  end;
end;
```

*continues* ▶

**Listing 7.6** *continued*

```pascal
procedure TfrmOil.btnDeleteClick(Sender: TObject);
var
  Index: Integer;
  OilItem: TOilItem;
begin
  Index := list.Selected.Index;
  list.Items.Delete(Index);
  OilItem := FItems.Items[Index];
  OilItem.Free;

  EnableButtons;
end;

{ TOilItem }

procedure TOilItem.Assign(Source: TPersistent);
begin
  if Source is TOilItem then begin
    FDate := TOilItem(Source).FDate;
    FMileage := TOilItem(Source).FMileage;
  end else
    inherited Assign(Source);
end;

{ TOilItems }

function TOilItems.Add: TOilItem;
begin
  Result := inherited Add as TOilItem;
end;

constructor TOilItems.Create;
begin
  inherited Create(TOilItem);
end;

function TOilItems.GetItem(Index: Integer): TOilItem;
begin
  Result := inherited GetItem(Index) as TOilItem;
end;

procedure TOilItems.SetItem(Index: Integer; Value: TOilItem);
begin
  inherited SetItem(Index, Value);
end;

{ TDummy }

constructor TDummy.Create(AOwner: TComponent);
begin
  FItems := TOilItems.Create;
end;
```

```
destructor TDummy.Destroy;
begin
  FItems.Free;
end;

end.
```

## Listing 7.7    CarDemo—OilItemForm.pas

```
unit OilItemForm;

interface

uses
  Windows, Messages, SysUtils, Classes, Graphics, Controls, Forms, Dialogs,
  StdCtrls, ComCtrls, ExtCtrls;

type
  TfrmOilItem = class(TForm)
    pnlBottom: TPanel;
    btnOK: TButton;
    btnCancel: TButton;
    pnlClient: TPanel;
    Label1: TLabel;
    Label3: TLabel;
    dtDate: TDateTimePicker;
    ecMileage: TEdit;
    procedure btnOKClick(Sender: TObject);
  private
    { Private declarations }
    FDate: TDateTime;
    FMileage: Double;
  public
    { Public declarations }
    property Date: TDateTime read FDate;
    property Mileage: Double read FMileage;
  end;

var
  frmOilItem: TfrmOilItem;

implementation

{$R *.DFM}

procedure TfrmOilItem.btnOKClick(Sender: TObject);
begin
  FDate := dtDate.Date;

  try
    FMileage := StrToFloat(ecMileage.Text);
  except
```

*continues* ▶

**Listing 7.7**  *continued*

```
    ModalResult := mrNone;
    ActiveControl := ecMileage;
    ShowMessage('Mileage is not a valid number.');
    exit;
  end;
end;

end.
```

When you run this application, you are presented with an empty main form.
Select File, Gas from the main menu to view historical gas purchases or
enter a new gas purchase. Select File, Oil from the menu to view or enter oil
change data.

Figure 7.4 shows the CarDemo application with both gasoline data and
oil change data displayed.

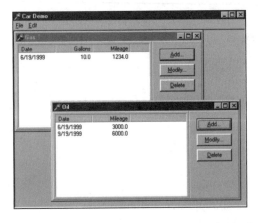

**Figure 7.4**    *CarDemo allows you to track gasoline
purchases and oil changes for your car.*

## Example: Viewing Structured Storage Files

Now that you've seen an example of an application that uses structured
storage as its native file format, let's take a look at an application that can
display the internal structure of any given structured storage file.

As an added bonus, SSView contains a Compress! menu item that allows
you to compress a structured storage file after you've viewed its contents.

Listings 7.8 and 7.9 contain the complete source code for the SSView
application.

**Listing 7.8**   *SSView—SSView.dpr*

```
program SSView;

uses
  Forms,
  MainForm in 'MainForm.pas' {Form1};

{$R *.RES}

begin
  Application.Initialize;
  Application.CreateForm(TForm1, Form1);
  Application.Run;
end.
```

**Listing 7.9**   *SSView—MainForm.pas*

```
unit MainForm;

interface

uses
  Windows, Messages, SysUtils, Classes, Graphics, Controls, Forms,
  Dialogs, Menus, ComCtrls, ExtCtrls, ActiveX, ComObj;

type
  TForm1 = class(TForm)
    MainMenu1: TMainMenu;
    File1: TMenuItem;
    FileExit1: TMenuItem;
    OpenDialog1: TOpenDialog;
    tree: TTreeView;
    FileOpen1: TMenuItem;
    N1: TMenuItem;
    pnlHeader: TPanel;
    Bevel1: TBevel;
    Compress1: TMenuItem;
    procedure FileExit1Click(Sender: TObject);
    procedure FileOpen1Click(Sender: TObject);
    procedure Compress1Click(Sender: TObject);
  private
    { Private declarations }
    FFileName: WideString;
    procedure DisplayFileStructure;
    procedure RecurseStorage(ParentNode: TTreeNode; stg: IStorage);
  public
    { Public declarations }
  end;
```

*continues* ▶

**Listing 7.9** *continued*

```
var
  Form1: TForm1;

implementation

{$R *.DFM}

procedure TForm1.FileExit1Click(Sender: TObject);
begin
  Close;
end;

procedure TForm1.RecurseStorage(ParentNode: TTreeNode; stg: IStorage);
var
  EnumStatStg: IEnumStatStg;
  StatStg: TStatStg;
  NodeName: string;
  ChildNode: TTreeNode;
  stgChild: IStorage;
begin
  OleCheck(stg.EnumElements(0, nil, 0, EnumStatStg));

  while EnumStatStg.Next(1, StatStg, nil) = S_OK do begin
    NodeName := StatStg.pwcsName;
    if Ord(NodeName[1]) < 32 then
      NodeName := '#' + IntToStr(Ord(NodeName[1])) +
        Copy(NodeName, 2, Length(NodeName) - 1);

{$IFDEF VER100}
    ChildNode := tree.Items.AddChild(ParentNode, NodeName +
      ' (' + FloatToStr(StatStg.cbSize) + ' bytes)');
{$ELSE}
    ChildNode := tree.Items.AddChild(ParentNode, NodeName +
      ' (' + IntToStr(StatStg.cbSize) + ' bytes)');
{$ENDIF}

    if StatStg.dwType = STGTY_STORAGE then begin
      // See if we can open the child storage
      OleCheck(stg.OpenStorage(StatStg.pwcsName, nil, STGM_READ or
        STGM_SHARE_EXCLUSIVE, nil, 0, stgChild));

      // Process the sub-storage
      RecurseStorage(ChildNode, stgChild);
    end;
  end;
end;

procedure TForm1.DisplayFileStructure;
var
  stgRoot: IStorage;
  Node: TTreeNode;
```

```
begin
  // First, check to see if it's a structured storage file
  if StgIsStorageFile(PWideChar(FFileName)) <> S_OK then begin
    ShowMessage(FFileName + ' is not a structured storage file.');
    exit;
  end;

  pnlHeader.Caption := FFileName;

  // Open the file
  OleCheck(StgOpenStorage(PWideChar(FFileName), nil, STGM_READ or
    STGM_SHARE_EXCLUSIVE, nil, 0, stgRoot));

  tree.Items.BeginUpdate;
  try
    tree.Items.Clear;
    Node := tree.Items.Add(nil, '<Root>');
    RecurseStorage(Node, stgRoot);
    Node.Expand(True);
  finally
    tree.Items.EndUpdate;
  end;

  Compress1.Enabled := True;
end;

procedure TForm1.FileOpen1Click(Sender: TObject);
begin
  if OpenDialog1.Execute then begin
    FFileName := OpenDialog1.FileName;
    DisplayFileStructure;
  end;
end;

procedure TForm1.Compress1Click(Sender: TObject);
var
  stgOriginal: IStorage;
  stgTemp: IStorage;
  TempFileName: WideString;
begin
  // Step 1 - Open the original file
  OleCheck(StgOpenStorage(PWideChar(FFileName), nil, STGM_READ or
    STGM_SHARE_EXCLUSIVE, nil, 0, stgOriginal));

  // Step 2 - Create a new, temporary file
  TempFileName := ChangeFileExt(FFileName, '.$$$');
  OleCheck(StgCreateDocFile(PWideChar(TempFileName),
    STGM_WRITE or STGM_SHARE_EXCLUSIVE, 0, stgTemp));

  // Step 3 - Copy the old file to the new one
  stgOriginal.CopyTo(0, nil, nil, stgTemp);
```

*continues* ▶

**Listing 7.9**     *continued*

```
// Step 4 - Close the temporary file
stgTemp := nil;

// Step 5 - Close the original file
stgOriginal := nil;

// Step 6 - Delete the original file
DeleteFile(FFileName);

// Step 7 - Rename the temporary file
  RenameFile(TempFileName, FFileName);
end;

end.
```

The guts of SSView are contained in the RecurseStorage procedure. When you select File, Open from the main menu, SSView first checks the file to make sure it's a valid structured storage file. If it is, it opens the file using StgOpenStorage, and then calls RecurseStorage, passing in the root storage as a parameter.

RecurseStorage uses the technique described in the section "Iterating Through a Structured Storage File" to walk through the substorages and streams contained in the storage. When a substorage is encountered, RecurseStorage recursively calls itself to process that substorage.

In the sidebar "Simple Structured Storage" near the beginning of this chapter, I discussed the features and limitations of opening a structured storage file in simple mode. It's interesting to use SSView to detect whether structured storage files were created in simple mode. For example, if you view a (small) Word document in SSView, you'll see streams of exactly 4096 bytes—a surefire indication that Word saves its documents using the STGM_SIMPLE flag.

On the other hand, in the CarDemo application, I don't specify the STGM_SIMPLE flag when creating the structured storage file. As a result, if you view a file created with that application, you'll see streams with fewer than 4096 bytes.

Figure 7.5 shows the structure of a Word document in SSView.

**Figure 7.5**   *Viewing the structure of a Word document.*

## Summary

In this chapter, I discussed structured storage. I explained what it is, why it is useful, and how you can take advantage of it in your own applications.

As you've seen, it's really not any more difficult to deal with structured storage files than it is to use standard files in your Delphi applications. After you've taken care of the additional few lines of code required to open the file and any necessary streams, you can simply use TOleStream to read and write to the file.

I would suggest that you try to familiarize yourself with structured storage as much as possible, and consider using it in new projects where it makes sense. Microsoft has indicated that in a future version of Windows, structured storage might become the standard file format. Incorporating it into your applications today gives you a leg up when that day arrives.

In the next chapter, I'll discuss structured storage and OLE. In particular, I'll cover OLE Containers and compound documents, and I'll explain OLE property sets.

# 8

# *Structured Storage and OLE*

In Chapter 7, "Structured Storage," I discussed structured storage, what it is, and how you can use it in your Delphi applications. Although structured storage is a very usable technology in and of itself, OLE adds a couple of layers on top of it. This chapter discusses those layers: OLE Property Sets and Compound Documents/OLE Containers.

## OLE Property Sets

Just as Microsoft has defined and published a number of standard COM interfaces, they have also defined a common stream format for saving document summary information in a structured storage file. If you've ever used Microsoft Word or another Microsoft Office application, you've seen that it stores certain information about the document, such as author name, subject, and total editing time, inside the document. This summary information can be viewed not only from inside Word, but also directly from the Windows Explorer. Figure 8.1 shows the summary information stored in the Word document for Chapter 1, "Using Interfaces in Delphi."

Prior to the release of Windows 95, Microsoft Word used a proprietary file format to save its documents. It still stored summary information, but that information was stored such that the only way you could get to it was to use Word to open the document. After Windows 95 was released, Microsoft decided to save summary information in a standard way, so that any program that understood the storage method could read the summary information.

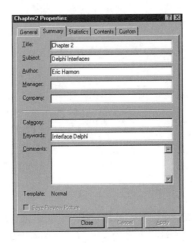

**Figure 8.1**    *Viewing summary information from Windows Explorer.*

Structured storage is the vehicle used, and OLE Property Sets are the method. Unfortunately, when OLE Property Sets were first introduced, the format was published, but Microsoft had not made an API publicly available to read (and write) OLE Property Sets, making it a hassle to incorporate OLE Property Sets into your applications.

Since then, Microsoft released the IPropertyStorageSet and IPropertyStorage interfaces, which make reading and writing OLE Property Sets much easier.

## OLE Property Set Conventions

OLE Property Sets are stored in streams. Stream names that begin with Chr(5) are reserved for property sets. In this book, I'll show these stream names as #5SummaryInformation, for example, where #5 refers to the single character Chr(5), and not the two characters '#' and '5'. The total length of a property set stream is limited to 256K.

As of the present time, Microsoft has published three standard property set names: #5SummaryInformation, #5DocumentSummaryInformation, and #5UserDefinedProperties.

## The IPropertySetStorage and IPropertyStorage Interfaces

As I indicated earlier, the IPropertySetStorage and IPropertyStorage interfaces provide the means necessary to read and write OLE Property Sets.

Delphi 4 and later versions include the definitions of these interfaces in the file activex.pas. If you're using Delphi 3, refer to Listing 8.1 for the definitions of the required interfaces and supporting structures required to read and write property sets.

**Listing 8.1**   *PropSets.pas—Interface Definitions for Delphi 3*

```
unit PropSets;

interface

uses
  Windows;

const
  // Property IDs for the SummaryInformation Property Set
  PIDSI_TITLE          = $00000002;  // VT_LPSTR
  PIDSI_SUBJECT        = $00000003;  // VT_LPSTR
  PIDSI_AUTHOR         = $00000004;  // VT_LPSTR
  PIDSI_KEYWORDS       = $00000005;  // VT_LPSTR
  PIDSI_COMMENTS       = $00000006;  // VT_LPSTR
  PIDSI_TEMPLATE       = $00000007;  // VT_LPSTR
  PIDSI_LASTAUTHOR     = $00000008;  // VT_LPSTR
  PIDSI_REVNUMBER      = $00000009;  // VT_LPSTR
  PIDSI_EDITTIME       = $0000000a;  // VT_FILETIME (UTC)
  PIDSI_LASTPRINTED    = $0000000b;  // VT_FILETIME (UTC)
  PIDSI_CREATE_DTM     = $0000000c;  // VT_FILETIME (UTC)
  PIDSI_LASTSAVE_DTM   = $0000000d;  // VT_FILETIME (UTC)
  PIDSI_PAGECOUNT      = $0000000e;  // VT_I4
  PIDSI_WORDCOUNT      = $0000000f;  // VT_I4
  PIDSI_CHARCOUNT      = $00000010;  // VT_I4
  PIDSI_THUMBNAIL      = $00000011;  // VT_CF
  PIDSI_APPNAME        = $00000012;  // VT_LPSTR
  PIDSI_DOC_SECURITY   = $00000013;  // VT_I4

  PRSPEC_INVALID       = $ffffffff;
  PRSPEC_LPWSTR        = 0;
  PRSPEC_PROPID        = 1;

type
  PShortInt = ^ShortInt;

  TOleDate = Double;
  POleDate = ^TOleDate;

  POleStr = PWideChar;
  PPOleStr = ^POleStr;

  PBStr = ^TBStr;
  TBStr = POleStr;

  TOleBool = WordBool;
  POleBool = ^TOleBool;

  PSCODE = ^Integer;
  SCODE = Integer;
```

*continues* ▶

**Listing 8.1**    *continued*

```
PLargeInteger = ^TLargeInteger;
_LARGE_INTEGER = record
  case Integer of
  0: (
    LowPart: DWORD;
    HighPart: Longint);
  1: (
    QuadPart: LONGLONG);
end;
TLargeInteger = _LARGE_INTEGER;
LARGE_INTEGER = _LARGE_INTEGER;

ULARGE_INTEGER = record
  case Integer of
  0: (
    LowPart: DWORD;
    HighPart: DWORD);
  1: (
    QuadPart: LONGLONG);
end;
PULargeInteger = ^TULargeInteger;
TULargeInteger = ULARGE_INTEGER;

PLPSTR = ^LPSTR;

PLPWSTR = ^LPWSTR;

PClipData = ^TClipData;
tagCLIPDATA = record
  cbSize: Longint;
  ulClipFmt: Longint;
  pClipData: Pointer;
end;
TClipData = tagCLIPDATA;
CLIPDATA = TClipData;

PCLSID = PGUID;
TCLSID = TGUID;

TVarType = Word;

PBlob = ^TBlob;
tagBLOB = record
  cbSize: Longint;
  pBlobData: Pointer;
end;
TBlob = tagBLOB;
BLOB = TBlob;

PROPID = ULONG;
PPropID = ^TPropID;
TPropID = PROPID;
```

```
FMTID = TGUID;
PFmtID = ^TFmtID;
TFmtID = TGUID;

{ IPropertyStorage / IPropertySetStorage }

PPropVariant = ^TPropVariant;

tagCAUB = packed record
  cElems: ULONG;
  pElems: PByte;
end;
CAUB = tagCAUB;
PCAUB = ^TCAUB;
TCAUB = tagCAUB;

tagCAI = packed record
  cElems: ULONG;
  pElems: PShortInt;
end;
CAI = tagCAI;
PCAI = ^TCAI;
TCAI = tagCAI;

tagCAUI = packed record
  cElems: ULONG;
  pElems: PWord;
end;
CAUI = tagCAUI;
PCAUI = ^TCAUI;
TCAUI = tagCAUI;

tagCAL = packed record
  cElems: ULONG;
  pElems: PLongint;
end;
CAL = tagCAL;
PCAL = ^TCAL;
TCAL = tagCAL;

tagCAUL = packed record
  cElems: ULONG;
  pElems: PULONG;
end;
CAUL = tagCAUL;
PCAUL = ^TCAUL;
TCAUL = tagCAUL;

tagCAFLT = packed record
  cElems: ULONG;
  pElems: PSingle;
end;
```

*continues* ▶

**Listing 8.1** *continued*

```
CAFLT = tagCAFLT;
PCAFLT = ^TCAFLT;
TCAFLT = tagCAFLT;

tagCADBL = packed record
  cElems: ULONG;
  pElems: PDouble;
end;
CADBL = tagCADBL;
PCADBL = ^TCADBL;
TCADBL = tagCADBL;

tagCACY = packed record
  cElems: ULONG;
  pElems: PCurrency;
end;
CACY = tagCACY;
PCACY = ^TCACY;
TCACY = tagCACY;

tagCADATE = packed record
  cElems: ULONG;
  pElems: POleDate;
end;
CADATE = tagCADATE;
PCADATE = ^TCADATE;
TCADATE = tagCADATE;

tagCABSTR = packed record
  cElems: ULONG;
  pElems: PBSTR;
end;
CABSTR = tagCABSTR;
PCABSTR = ^TCABSTR;
TCABSTR = tagCABSTR;

tagCABOOL = packed record
  cElems: ULONG;
  pElems: POleBool;
end;
CABOOL = tagCABOOL;
PCABOOL = ^TCABOOL;
TCABOOL = tagCABOOL;

tagCASCODE = packed record
  cElems: ULONG;
  pElems: PSCODE;
end;
CASCODE = tagCASCODE;
PCASCODE = ^TCASCODE;
TCASCODE = tagCASCODE;
```

```
tagCAPROPVARIANT = packed record
  cElems: ULONG;
  pElems: PPropVariant;
end;
CAPROPVARIANT = tagCAPROPVARIANT;
PCAPROPVARIANT = ^TCAPROPVARIANT;
TCAPROPVARIANT = tagCAPROPVARIANT;

tagCAH = packed record
  cElems: ULONG;
  pElems: PLargeInteger;
end;
CAH = tagCAH;
PCAH = ^TCAH;
TCAH = tagCAH;

tagCAUH = packed record
  cElems: ULONG;
  pElems: PULargeInteger;
end;
CAUH = tagCAUH;
PCAUH = ^TCAUH;
TCAUH = tagCAUH;

tagCALPSTR = packed record
  cElems: ULONG;
  pElems: PLPSTR;
end;
CALPSTR = tagCALPSTR;
PCALPSTR = ^TCALPSTR;
TCALPSTR = tagCALPSTR;

tagCALPWSTR = packed record
  cElems: ULONG;
  pElems: PLPWSTR;
end;
CALPWSTR = tagCALPWSTR;
PCALPWSTR = ^TCALPWSTR;
TCALPWSTR = tagCALPWSTR;

tagCAFILETIME = packed record
  cElems: ULONG;
  pElems: PFileTime;
end;
CAFILETIME = tagCAFILETIME;
PCAFILETIME = ^TCAFILETIME;
TCAFILETIME = tagCAFILETIME;

tagCACLIPDATA = packed record
  cElems: ULONG;
  pElems: PClipData;
end;
```

*continues* ▶

**Listing 8.1** *continued*

```
CACLIPDATA = tagCACLIPDATA;
PCACLIPDATA = ^TCACLIPDATA;
TCACLIPDATA = tagCACLIPDATA;

tagCACLSID = packed record
  cElems: ULONG;
  pElems: PCLSID;
end;
CACLSID = tagCACLSID;
PCACLSID = ^TCACLSID;
TCACLSID = tagCACLSID;

tagPROPVARIANT = packed record
  vt: TVarType;
  wReserved1: Word;
  wReserved2: Word;
  wReserved3: Word;
  case Integer of
    0: (bVal: Byte);
    1: (iVal: SmallInt);
    2: (uiVal: Word);
    3: (boolVal: TOleBool);
    4: (bool: TOleBool);
    5: (lVal: Longint);
    6: (ulVal: Cardinal);
    7: (fltVal: Single);
    8: (scode: SCODE);
    9: (hVal: LARGE_INTEGER);
   10: (uhVal: ULARGE_INTEGER);
   11: (dblVal: Double);
   12: (cyVal: Currency);
   13: (date: TOleDate);
   14: (filetime: TFileTime);
   15: (puuid: PGUID);
   16: (blob: TBlob);
   17: (pclipdata: PClipData);
   18: (pStream: Pointer{IStream});
   19: (pStorage: Pointer{IStorage});
   20: (bstrVal: TBStr);
   21: (pszVal: PAnsiChar);
   22: (pwszVal: PWideChar);
   23: (caub: TCAUB);
   24: (cai: TCAI);
   25: (caui: TCAUI);
   26: (cabool: TCABOOL);
   27: (cal: TCAL);
   28: (caul: TCAUL);
   29: (caflt: TCAFLT);
   30: (cascode: TCASCODE);
   31: (cah: TCAH);
   32: (cauh: TCAUH);
```

```
      33: (cadbl: TCADBL);
      34: (cacy: TCACY);
      35: (cadate: TCADATE);
      36: (cafiletime: TCAFILETIME);
      37: (cauuid: TCACLSID);
      38: (caclipdata: TCACLIPDATA);
      39: (cabstr: TCABSTR);
      40: (calpstr: TCALPSTR);
      41: (calpwstr: TCALPWSTR );
      42: (capropvar: TCAPROPVARIANT);
  end;
  PROPVARIANT = tagPROPVARIANT;
  TPropVariant = tagPROPVARIANT;

  tagPROPSPEC = packed record
    ulKind: ULONG;
    case Integer of
      0: (propid: TPropID);
      1: (lpwstr: POleStr);
  end;
  PROPSPEC = tagPROPSPEC;
  PPropSpec = ^TPropSpec;
  TPropSpec = tagPROPSPEC;

  tagSTATPROPSTG = packed record
    lpwstrName: POleStr;
    propid: TPropID;
    vt: TVarType;
  end;
  STATPROPSTG = tagSTATPROPSTG;
  PStatPropStg = ^TStatPropStg;
  TStatPropStg = tagSTATPROPSTG;

  tagSTATPROPSETSTG = packed record
    fmtid: TFmtID;
    clsid: TClsID;
    grfFlags: DWORD;
    mtime: TFileTime;
    ctime: TFileTime;
    atime: TFileTime;
    dwOSVersion: DWORD;
  end;
  STATPROPSETSTG = tagSTATPROPSETSTG;
  PStatPropSetStg = ^TStatPropSetStg;
  TStatPropSetStg = tagSTATPROPSETSTG;

  IPropertySetStorage = interface;
  IPropertyStorage = interface;
  IEnumSTATPROPSTG = interface;
  IEnumSTATPROPSETSTG = interface;
```

*continues* ▶

**Listing 8.1** *continued*

```
IPropertyStorage = interface(IUnknown)
  ['{00000138-0000-0000-C000-000000000046}']
  function ReadMultiple(cpspec: ULONG; rgpspec, rgpropvar: PPropSpec): HResult; stdcall;
  function WriteMultiple(cpspec: ULONG; rgpspec, rgpropvar: PPropSpec;
    propidNameFirst: TPropID): HResult; stdcall;
  function DeleteMultiple(cpspec: ULONG; rgpspec: PPropSpec): HResult; stdcall;
  function ReadPropertyNames(cpropid: ULONG; rgpropid: PPropID;
    rglpwstrName: PPOleStr): HResult; stdcall;
  function WritePropertyNames(cpropid: ULONG; rgpropid: PPropID;
    rglpwstrName: PPOleStr): HResult; stdcall;
  function DeletePropertyNames(cpropid: ULONG; rgpropid: PPropID): HResult; stdcall;
  function Commit(grfCommitFlags: DWORD): HResult; stdcall;
  function Revert: HResult; stdcall;
  function Enum(out ppenum: IEnumSTATPROPSTG): HResult; stdcall;
  function SetTimes(const pctime, patime, pmtime: TFileTime): HResult; stdcall;
  function SetClass(const clsid: TCLSID): HResult; stdcall;
  function Stat(pstatpsstg: PStatPropSetStg): HResult; stdcall;
end;

IPropertySetStorage = interface(IUnknown)
  ['{0000013A-0000-0000-C000-000000000046}']
  function Create(const rfmtid: TFmtID; const pclsid: TCLSID; grfFlags,
    grfMode: DWORD; out ppprstg: IPropertyStorage): HResult; stdcall;
  function Open(const rfmtid: TFmtID; grfMode: DWORD;
    out ppprstg: IPropertyStorage): HResult; stdcall;
  function Delete(const rfmtid: TFmtID): HResult; stdcall;
  function Enum(out ppenum: IEnumSTATPROPSETSTG): HResult; stdcall;
end;

IEnumSTATPROPSTG = interface(IUnknown)
  ['{00000139-0000-0000-C000-000000000046}']
  function Next(celt: ULONG; out rgelt; pceltFetched: PULONG): HResult; stdcall;
  function Skip(celt: ULONG): HResult; stdcall;
  function Reset: HResult; stdcall;
  function Clone(out ppenum: IEnumSTATPROPSTG): HResult; stdcall;
end;

IEnumSTATPROPSETSTG = interface(IUnknown)
  ['{0000013B-0000-0000-C000-000000000046}']
  function Next(celt: ULONG; out rgelt; pceltFetched: PULONG): HResult; stdcall;
  function Skip(celt: ULONG): HResult; stdcall;
  function Reset: HResult; stdcall;
  function Clone(out ppenum: IEnumSTATPROPSETSTG): HResult; stdcall;
end;

implementation

end.
```

## Reading Properties

To read known properties from a stream, you should call
IPropertyStorage.ReadMultiple, as follows:

```
const
  FMTID_SummaryInformation: TGUID = '{F29F85E0-4FF9-1068-AB91-08002B27B3D9}';

procedure TForm1.Button1Click(Sender: TObject);
type
  TPropSpecArray = array[0 .. 1000] of TPropSpec;
  PPropSpecArray = ^TPropSpecArray;
  TPropVariantArray = array[0 .. 1000] of TPropVariant;
  PPropVariantArray = ^TPropVariantArray;
var
  stgRoot: IStorage;
  stgPS: IPropertySetStorage;
  stgP: IPropertyStorage;
  ps: PPropSpecArray;
  pv: PPropVariantArray;
begin
  OleCheck(StgOpenStorage('J:\BOOK\CHAPTER2.DOC', nil,
    STGM_READ or STGM_SHARE_EXCLUSIVE, nil, 0, stgRoot));
  stgPS := stgRoot as IPropertySetStorage;
  OleCheck(stgPS.Open(FMTID_SummaryInformation,
    STGM_READ or STGM_SHARE_EXCLUSIVE, stgP));

  ps := nil;
  pv := nil;
  try
    GetMem(ps, sizeof(TPropSpec));
    GetMem(pv, sizeof(TPropVariant));

    ps[0].ulKind := PRSPEC_PROPID;
    ps[0].propid := PIDSI_TITLE;

    OleCheck(stgP.ReadMultiple(1, @ps[0], @pv[0]));

    // Do something with pv[0] here
  finally
    if ps <> nil then
      FreeMem(ps);
    if pv <> nil then
      FreeMem(pv);
  end;
end;
```

This code first opens the structured storage file J:\BOOK\CHAPTER2.DOC.
It then uses the **as** operator to obtain an IPropertySetStorage from IStorage.
I then call IPropertySetStorage.Open to obtain a reference to an
IPropertyStorage interface. Note that I pass FMTID_SummaryInformation
to this method. FMTID_SummaryInformation specifies the GUID of the
standard #5SummaryInformation property set stream.

Next, I use IPropertyStorage.ReadMultiple to read, in this case, only one property. I could just as easily read ten properties at once with this call by setting up an array of ten TPropSpec records. On return from IPropertyStorage.ReadMultiple, pv[0] contains the value of the Title property.

### Writing Properties

To write properties to a stream, you issue calls to IPropertyStorage.WriteMultiple, as follows:

```
const
  FMTID_SummaryInformation: TGUID = '{F29F85E0-4FF9-1068-AB91-08002B27B3D9}';

procedure TForm1.Button1Click(Sender: TObject);
type
  TPropSpecArray = array[0 .. 1000] of TPropSpec;
  PPropSpecArray = ^TPropSpecArray;
  TPropVariantArray = array[0 .. 1000] of TPropVariant;
  PPropVariantArray = ^TPropVariantArray;
var
  stgRoot: IStorage;
  stgPS: IPropertySetStorage;
  stgP: IPropertyStorage;
  ps: PPropSpecArray;
  pv: PPropVariantArray;
begin
  OleCheck(StgOpenStorage('J:\BOOK\CHAPTER2.DOC', nil,
    STGM_WRITE or STGM_SHARE_EXCLUSIVE, nil, 0, stgRoot));
  stgPS := stgRoot as IPropertySetStorage;
  OleCheck(stgPS.Open(FMTID_SummaryInformation,
    STGM_WRITE or STGM_SHARE_EXCLUSIVE, stgP));

  ps := nil;
  pv := nil;
  try
    GetMem(ps, sizeof(TPropSpec));
    GetMem(pv, sizeof(TPropVariant));

    ps[0].ulKind := PRSPEC_PROPID;
    ps[0].propid := PIDSI_TITLE;

    pv[0].vt := VT_LPSTR;
    pv[0].lpzstr := 'New title';

    OleCheck(stgP.WriteMultiple(1, @ps[0], @pv[0], 2));
  finally
    if ps <> nil then
      FreeMem(ps);
    if pv <> nil then
      FreeMem(pv);
  end;
end;
```

Similar to the previous code snippet, this code opens the structured storage file J:\BOOK\CHAPTER2.DOC and obtains a reference to an IPropertyStorage interface.

Next, I use IPropertyStorage.WriteMultiple to write one property. You can write more than one property at a time by setting up an array of more than one TPropSpec record.

### Deleting Properties

To delete one or more properties from a stream, call IPropertyStorage.DeleteMultiple, as follows:

```
const
  FMTID_SummaryInformation: TGUID = '{F29F85E0-4FF9-1068-AB91-08002B27B3D9}';

procedure TForm1.Button1Click(Sender: TObject);
type
  TPropSpecArray = array[0 .. 1000] of TPropSpec;
  PPropSpecArray = ^TPropSpecArray;
  TPropVariantArray = array[0 .. 1000] of TPropVariant;
  PPropVariantArray = ^TPropVariantArray;
var
  stgRoot: IStorage;
  stgPS: IPropertySetStorage;
  stgP: IPropertyStorage;
  ps: PPropSpecArray;
begin
  OleCheck(StgOpenStorage('J:\BOOK\CHAPTER2.DOC', nil,
    STGM_WRITE or STGM_SHARE_EXCLUSIVE, nil, 0, stgRoot));
  stgPS := stgRoot as IPropertySetStorage;
  OleCheck(stgPS.Open(FMTID_SummaryInformation,
    STGM_WRITE or STGM_SHARE_EXCLUSIVE, stgP));

  GetMem(ps, sizeof(TPropSpec));
  try
    ps[0].ulKind := PRSPEC_PROPID;
    ps[0].propid := PIDSI_TITLE;

    OleCheck(stgP.DeleteMultiple(1, @ps[0]));
  finally
    FreeMem(ps);
  end;
end;
```

Similar to the previous code snippet, this code opens the structured storage file J:\BOOK\CHAPTER2.DOC and obtains a reference to an IPropertyStorage interface.

I then use IPropertyStorage.DeleteMultiple to write one property. You can delete more than one property at a time by setting up an array of more than one TPropSpec record.

**Enumerating Properties**

ReadMultiple, WriteMultiple, and DeleteMultiple require you to know the name or ID of the property or properties in question. What if you don't know the properties that are present in the property stream? In addition to #5SummaryInformation and #5DocumentSummaryInformation property sets, which contain predefined properties, Microsoft has defined the #5UserDefinedProperties property set. The interesting thing about the #5UserDefinedProperties property set is that any Windows user can add properties to that property set by using the standard Windows Properties dialog box, as shown in Figure 8.2.

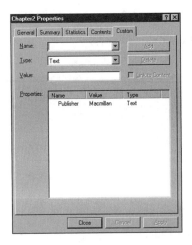

**Figure 8.2**    *Windows allows you to set properties in*
*the #5UserDefinedProperties property set.*

You can see that I've added a property named Publisher to this document. This property was not added from Word—it was added directly from this property sheet.

Because the #5UserDefinedProperties stream does not contain standard property names, there needs to be a way to obtain the names of properties stored in the stream. This is where IPropertyStorage.Enum comes in. Much like enumerating the storages and streams in a structured storage file, we can enumerate the properties in a property set. The following code snippet shows how it's done.

```
const
  FMTID_UserDefined Properties: TGUPD= {D5CDD505-2E9C-101B-9397-´08002B2CF9AE};


procedure TForm1.Button1Click(Sender: TObject);

type
  TPropSpecArray = array[0 .. 1000] of TPropSpec;
  PPropSpecArray = ^TPropSpecArray;
```

```
    TPropVariantArray = array[0 .. 1000] of TPropVariant;
    PPropVariantArray = ^TPropVariantArray;
    TStatPropStgArray = array[0 .. 1000] of TStatPropStg;
    PStatPropStgArray = ^TStatPropStgArray;

var
    stgRoot: IStorage;
    stgPS: IPropertySetStorage;
    stgP: IPropertyStorage;
    ps: PPropSpecArray;
    pv: PPropVariantArray;
    Enum: IEnumStatPropStg;
    sps: PStatPropStgArray;
    fetched: LongInt;
begin
    OleCheck(StgOpenStorage('J:\BOOK\SAMPLES\CHAP08\TEST.DOC', nil,
      STGM_READ or STGM_SHARE_EXCLUSIVE, nil, 0, stgRoot));
    stgPS := stgRoot as IPropertySetStorage;
    OleCheck(stgPS.Open(FMTID_UserDefinedProperties,
      STGM_READ or STGM_SHARE_EXCLUSIVE, stgP));

    ps := nil;
    pv := nil;
    sps := nil;
    try
      GetMem(ps, sizeof(TPropSpec));
      GetMem(pv, sizeof(TPropVariant));
      GetMem(sps, sizeof(TStatPropStg));

      OleCheck(stgP.Enum(Enum));
      while Enum.Next(1, sps[0], @fetched) = S_OK do begin
        ps[0].ulKind := PRSPEC_PROPID;
        ps[0].propid := sps[0].propid;
        OleCheck(stgP.ReadMultiple(NumIDs, @ps[0], @pv[0]));

        // Do something with pv here
      end;
    finally
      if ps <> nil then
        FreeMem(ps);
      if pv <> nil then
        FreeMem(pv);
      if sps <> nil then
        FreeMem(sps);
    end;
end;
```

This code snippet is much the same as the one for reading properties from the #5SummaryInformation stream, except I use IPropertyStorage to enumerate through the properties, reading them one by one from the stream.

## A Component for Reading and Writing Property Sets

As you can see, it's not very difficult to read and write properties using the
IPropertySetStorage and IPropertyStorage interfaces. However, it would be
handy to have a component to make things even easier.

Listing 8.2 shows the entire source code for a component that can read
from and write to any property set stream.

---

Listing 8.2    *The TPropertySet Component*

```
unit PropertySet;

interface

uses
  Windows, Messages, SysUtils, Classes, Graphics, Controls, Forms, Dialogs,
{$IFDEF VER100}
  PropSets, // For Delphi 3
{$ENDIF}
  ComObj, ActiveX;

const
  FMTID_SummaryInformation: TGUID = '{F29F85E0-4FF9-1068-AB91-08002B27B3D9}';
  FMTID_DocumentSummaryInformation: TGUID = '{D5CDD502-2E9C-101B-9397-08002B2CF9AE}';
  FMTID_UserDefinedProperties: TGUID = '{D5CDD505-2E9C-101B-9397-08002B2CF9AE}';

type
  TEnumPropertiesEvent = procedure(Sender: TObject; PropertyName: WideString;
    PropertyID: Integer; PropertyVariant: TPropVariant) of object;

  TPropertySet = class(TComponent)
  private
    FFileName: WideString;
    FActive: Boolean;
    FStorage: IStorage;
    FPropertySetStorage: IPropertySetStorage;
    FPropertyStorage: IPropertyStorage;
    FStreamGUID: TGUID;
    FOnEnumProperties: TEnumPropertiesEvent;
    procedure SetFileName(const Value: WideString);
    procedure SetActive(const Value: Boolean);
    procedure SetStreamGUID(const Value: TGUID);
    { Private declarations }
  protected
    { Protected declarations }
    procedure InternalOpen; dynamic;
    procedure InternalClose; dynamic;
    procedure DoEnumProperty(PropertyName: WideString; PropertyID: Integer;
      PropertyVariant: TPropVariant); dynamic;
  public
    { Public declarations }
    destructor Destroy; override;
    procedure Open;
```

```
    procedure Close;
    procedure Enumerate;
    function GetPropertyByName(APropertyName: WideString): TPropVariant;
    function GetPropertyByID(APropertyID: Integer): TPropVariant;
    procedure SetProperty(APropertyName: WideString; AValue: WideString);
    procedure DeleteProperty(APropertyName: WideString);
  published
    { Published declarations }
    property Active: Boolean read FActive write SetActive;
    property FileName: WideString read FFileName write SetFileName;
    property OnEnumProperties: TEnumPropertiesEvent read FOnEnumProperties write
FOnEnumProperties;
    property StreamGUID: TGUID read FStreamGUID write SetStreamGUID;
  end;

procedure Register;

implementation

type
  TPropSpecArray = array[0 .. 1000] of TPropSpec;
  PPropSpecArray = ^TPropSpecArray;
  TPropVariantArray = array[0 .. 1000] of TPropVariant;
  PPropVariantArray = ^TPropVariantArray;
  TStatPropStgArray = array[0 .. 1000] of TStatPropStg;
  PStatPropStgArray = ^TStatPropStgArray;

procedure Register;
begin
  RegisterComponents('DCP', [TPropertySet]);
end;

{ TPropertySet }

procedure TPropertySet.Close;
begin
  Active := False;
end;

procedure TPropertySet.DeleteProperty(APropertyName: WideString);
var
  ps: PPropSpecArray;
begin
  GetMem(ps, sizeof(TPropSpec));
  try
    ps[0].ulKind := PRSPEC_LPWSTR;
    ps[0].lpwstr := PWideChar(APropertyName);

    OleCheck(FPropertyStorage.DeleteMultiple(1, @ps[0]));
  finally
    FreeMem(ps);
  end;
end;
```

*continues* ▶

**Listing 8.2** *continued*

```
destructor TPropertySet.Destroy;
begin
  Close;
end;

procedure TPropertySet.DoEnumProperty(PropertyName: WideString;
  PropertyID: Integer; PropertyVariant: TPropVariant);
begin
  if Assigned(FOnEnumProperties) then
    FOnEnumProperties(self, PropertyName, PropertyID, PropertyVariant);
end;

procedure TPropertySet.Enumerate;
var
  ps: PPropSpecArray;
  pv: PPropVariantArray;
  sps: PStatPropStgArray;
  Enum: IEnumStatPropStg;
  Fetched: LongInt;
  Prop: TPropVariant;
begin
  ps := nil;
  pv := nil;
  sps := nil;
  try
    GetMem(ps, sizeof(TPropSpec));
    GetMem(pv, sizeof(TPropVariant));
    GetMem(sps, sizeof(TStatPropStg));

    OleCheck(FPropertyStorage.Enum(Enum));

    while Enum.Next(1, sps[0], @Fetched) = S_OK do begin
      Prop := GetPropertyByID(sps[0].propid);
      DoEnumProperty(sps[0].lpwstrName, sps[0].propid, Prop);
    end;
  finally
    if ps <> nil then
      FreeMem(ps);
    if pv <> nil then
      FreeMem(pv);
    if sps <> nil then
      FreeMem(sps);
  end;
end;

function TPropertySet.GetPropertyByID(APropertyID: Integer): TPropVariant;
var
  ps: PPropSpecArray;
  pv: PPropVariantArray;
begin
  ps := nil;
```

```
    pv := nil;
    try
      GetMem(ps, sizeof(TPropSpec));
      GetMem(pv, sizeof(TPropVariant));

      ps[0].ulKind := PRSPEC_PROPID;
      ps[0].propid := APropertyID;

      OleCheck(FPropertyStorage.ReadMultiple(1, @ps[0], @pv[0]));
      Result := pv[0];
    finally
      if ps <> nil then
        FreeMem(ps);
      if pv <> nil then
        FreeMem(pv);
    end;
end;

function TPropertySet.GetPropertyByName(
  APropertyName: WideString): TPropVariant;
var
  ps: PPropSpecArray;
  pv: PPropVariantArray;
begin
  ps := nil;
  pv := nil;
  try
    GetMem(ps, sizeof(TPropSpec));
    GetMem(pv, sizeof(TPropVariant));

    ps[0].ulKind := PRSPEC_LPWSTR;
    ps[0].lpwstr := PWideChar(APropertyName);

    OleCheck(FPropertyStorage.ReadMultiple(1, @ps[0], @pv[0]));
    Result := pv[0];
  finally
    if ps <> nil then
      FreeMem(ps);
    if pv <> nil then
      FreeMem(pv);
  end;
end;

procedure TPropertySet.InternalClose;
begin
  FPropertyStorage := nil;
  FPropertySetStorage := nil;
  FStorage := nil;
end;

procedure TPropertySet.InternalOpen;
begin
  FStorage := nil;
```

*continues* ▶

**Listing 8.2**    *continued*

```
  if FFileName = '' then
    raise Exception.Create('File name must be set.');

  if StgIsStorageFile(PWideChar(FFileName)) <> S_OK then
    raise Exception.Create('File ' + FFileName + ' is not a structured storage file.');

  OleCheck(StgOpenStorage(PWChar(FFileName), nil,
    STGM_READWRITE or STGM_SHARE_EXCLUSIVE, nil, 0, FStorage));

  FPropertySetStorage := FStorage as IPropertySetStorage;

  OleCheck(FPropertySetStorage.Open(FStreamGUID, STGM_READWRITE or STGM_SHARE_EXCLUSIVE,
    FPropertyStorage));
end;

procedure TPropertySet.Open;
begin
  Active := True;
end;

procedure TPropertySet.SetActive(const Value: Boolean);
begin
  if FActive <> Value then
    if Value then
      InternalOpen
    else
      InternalClose;
end;

procedure TPropertySet.SetFileName(const Value: WideString);
begin
  FFileName := Value;
end;

procedure TPropertySet.SetProperty(APropertyName: WideString; AValue: WideString);
var
  ps: PPropSpecArray;
  pv: PPropVariantArray;
begin
  ps := nil;
  pv := nil;
  try
    GetMem(ps, sizeof(TPropSpec));
    GetMem(pv, sizeof(TPropVariant));

    ps[0].ulKind := PRSPEC_LPWSTR;
    ps[0].lpwstr := PWideChar(APropertyName);

    pv[0].vt := VT_LPSTR;
    pv[0].pszval := PChar(AValue);
```

```
    OleCheck(FPropertyStorage.WriteMultiple(1, @ps[0], @pv[0], 2));
  finally
    if ps <> nil then
      FreeMem(ps);
    if pv <> nil then
      FreeMem(pv);
  end;
end;

procedure TPropertySet.SetStreamGUID(const Value: TGUID);
begin
  FStreamGUID := Value;
end;

end.
```

The TPropertySet component is actually pretty simple. It merely pulls together the code snippets I've already shown you for reading, writing, deleting, and enumerating properties in a stream. As it stands, this component can only work with a single property at a time. You could, of course, enhance it so that it can deal with whole arrays of properties at once.

## Example: Accessing User Defined Properties

Listings 8.3 and 8.4 show the complete source for a program that can read, write, and delete properties from the #5UserDefinedProperties property set stream.

**Listing 8.3**   *PropDemo—PropDemo.dpr*

```
program PropDemo;

uses
  Forms,
  MainForm in 'MainForm.pas' {frmMain};

{$R *.RES}

begin
  Application.Initialize;
  Application.CreateForm(TfrmMain, frmMain);
  Application.Run;
end.
```

**Listing 8.4**    *PropDemo—MainForm.pas*

```pascal
unit MainForm;

interface

uses
  Windows, Messages, SysUtils, Classes, Graphics, Controls, Forms, Dialogs,
  StdCtrls, ComCtrls, ExtCtrls,
{$IFDEF VER100}
  PropSets,  // For Delphi 3
{$ENDIF}
  PropertySet, ActiveX;

type
  TfrmMain = class(TForm)
    pnlBottom: TPanel;
    pnlClient: TPanel;
    Label1: TLabel;
    listProperties: TListView;
    btnClose: TButton;
    Label2: TLabel;
    Label3: TLabel;
    ecPropertyName: TEdit;
    ecValue: TEdit;
    btnDelete: TButton;
    btnSet: TButton;
    btnOpen: TButton;
    OpenDialog1: TOpenDialog;
    PropertySet1: TPropertySet;
    procedure btnOpenClick(Sender: TObject);
    procedure btnCloseClick(Sender: TObject);
    procedure btnSetClick(Sender: TObject);
    procedure btnDeleteClick(Sender: TObject);
    procedure PropertySet1EnumProperties(Sender: TObject;
      PropertyName: String; PropertyID: Integer;
      PropertyVariant: tagPROPVARIANT);
    procedure listPropertiesClick(Sender: TObject);
  private
    procedure LoadPropertyList;
    { Private declarations }
  public
    { Public declarations }
  end;

var
  frmMain: TfrmMain;

implementation

{$R *.DFM}

procedure TfrmMain.LoadPropertyList;
```

```
begin
  listProperties.Items.Clear;

  PropertySet1.Enumerate;
end;

procedure TfrmMain.btnOpenClick(Sender: TObject);
begin
  if OpenDialog1.Execute then begin
    PropertySet1.Close;

    PropertySet1.FileName := OpenDialog1.FileName;
    PropertySet1.StreamGUID := FMTID_UserDefinedProperties;
    PropertySet1.Open;

    listProperties.Enabled := True;
    ecPropertyName.Enabled := True;
    ecValue.Enabled := True;
    btnSet.Enabled := True;
    btnDelete.Enabled := True;

    LoadPropertyList;
  end;
end;

procedure TfrmMain.btnCloseClick(Sender: TObject);
begin
  Close;
end;

procedure TfrmMain.listPropertiesClick(Sender: TObject);
var
  LI: TListItem;
begin
  LI := listProperties.Selected;

  if LI <> nil then begin
    ecPropertyName.Text := LI.Caption;
    ecValue.Text := LI.SubItems[0];
  end;
end;

procedure TfrmMain.btnSetClick(Sender: TObject);
begin
  PropertySet1.SetProperty(ecPropertyName.Text, ecValue.Text);

  LoadPropertyList;
end;

procedure TfrmMain.btnDeleteClick(Sender: TObject);
begin
  PropertySet1.DeleteProperty(ecPropertyName.Text);
```

*continues* ▶

**Listing 8.4**    *continued*

```
  LoadPropertyList;
end;

procedure TfrmMain.PropertySet1EnumProperties(Sender: TObject;
  PropertyName: String; PropertyID: Integer;
  PropertyVariant: tagPROPVARIANT);
var
  LI: TListItem;
begin
  if PropertyVariant.vt = VT_LPSTR then begin
    LI := listProperties.Items.Add;
    LI.Caption := PropertyName;
    LI.SubItems.Add(PropertyVariant.pszVal);
  end;
end;

end.
```

Figure 8.3 shows PropDemo at runtime.

**Figure 8.3**    *PropDemo manages user-defined properties.*

When the application starts, no data file is open, so the edit controls and buttons are disabled. When the user opens a structured storage file, the list control is populated with the properties in the #5UserDefinedProperties stream. For this example, I've only listed the properties of type VT_LPSTR, although you could easily expand it to handle other property types as well.

As the user clicks properties in the list control, the two edit controls are updated to reflect the highlighted property. This makes it easy to enter a new value and press the Set button, or delete the property by pressing the Delete button.

The user can even add a new property to the file by entering a new property name and value and pressing the New button.

As you can see from the listing, the code for this example is very simple. The work for the Set and Delete buttons is handled by making a simple method call into the TPropertySet component.

## Example: Finding Files by Property

Here's another example program that illustrates another very useful feature of property sets: the ability to perform a cross-file search based on properties of the file. This example program will allow you to search the property sets of files on your hard drive to locate a file with a given property.

Figure 8.4 shows the user interface for the FindProp example program.

**Figure 8.4**    *FindProp allows the user to find files by property.*

Enter a file path to search in the File path edit control, and select a property stream in the Stream combo. If you select the SummaryInformation or DocumentSummaryInformation stream, you must select a predefined property from the Property name combo. If you select the UserDefinedProperties stream, you can enter a property name in the Property name combo.

Finally, enter a property value to search for and press the Find button. The program searches through the files that meet the specified file mask, and lists all matching files in the list box.

Note that in the interest of space, this example suffers from some minor limitations:

- It doesn't recurse subdirectories when performing the search.

- It only matches VT_LPSTR and VT_I4 property types.

- Property matches must be exact, with the exception that case-insensitive comparisons are performed. There is currently no way to search for integer properties that fall between two values, date/time properties, or substrings of a string property.

These limitations can be addressed fairly easily, but I'll leave the implementation of these features to you as an exercise.

Listings 8.5 and 8.6 contain the source code for the FindProp example application.

**Listing 8.5**  *FindProp—FindProp.dpr*

```
program FindProp;

uses
  Forms,
  MainForm in 'MainForm.pas' {frmMain};

{$R *.RES}

begin
  Application.Initialize;
  Application.CreateForm(TfrmMain, frmMain);
  Application.Run;
end.
```

**Listing 8.6**  *FindProp—MainForm.pas*

```
unit MainForm;

interface

uses
  Windows, Messages, SysUtils, Classes, Graphics, Controls, Forms, Dialogs,
  StdCtrls, ExtCtrls,
{$IFDEF VER100}
  PropSets,  // For Delphi 3
{$ENDIF}
  PropertySet, ActiveX;

type
  TfrmMain = class(TForm)
    pnlBottom: TPanel;
    pnlClient: TPanel;
    Label1: TLabel;
    cbStream: TComboBox;
    Label2: TLabel;
    cbPropertyName: TComboBox;
    Label3: TLabel;
    ecValue: TEdit;
```

```
    btnFind: TButton;
    btnClose: TButton;
    Label4: TLabel;
    lbFiles: TListBox;
    PropertySet1: TPropertySet;
    Label5: TLabel;
    ecFilePath: TEdit;
    procedure btnFindClick(Sender: TObject);
    procedure FormCreate(Sender: TObject);
    procedure btnCloseClick(Sender: TObject);
    procedure cbStreamClick(Sender: TObject);
  private
    function Matches(P: TPropVariant): Boolean;
    { Private declarations }
  public
    { Public declarations }
  end;

var
  frmMain: TfrmMain;

implementation

{$R *.DFM}

const
  StreamGUIDs: array[0 .. 2] of TGUID = (
    '{F29F85E0-4FF9-1068-AB91-08002B27B3D9}', // SummaryInformation
    '{D5CDD502-2E9C-101B-9397-08002B2CF9AE}', // DocumentSummaryInformation
    '{D5CDD505-2E9C-101B-9397-08002B2CF9AE}'  // UserDefinedProperties
  );

procedure TfrmMain.FormCreate(Sender: TObject);
begin
  cbStream.ItemIndex := 0;
  cbStreamClick(Sender);
end;

procedure TfrmMain.cbStreamClick(Sender: TObject);
begin
  cbPropertyName.Items.Clear;

  case cbStream.ItemIndex of
    0: begin
      cbPropertyName.Style := csDropDownList;
      cbPropertyName.Items.AddObject('Title', TObject(PIDSI_TITLE));
      cbPropertyName.Items.AddObject('Subject', TObject(PIDSI_SUBJECT));
      cbPropertyName.Items.AddObject('Author', TObject(PIDSI_AUTHOR));
      cbPropertyName.Items.AddObject('Keywords', TObject(PIDSI_KEYWORDS));
      cbPropertyName.Items.AddObject('Comments', TObject(PIDSI_COMMENTS));
      cbPropertyName.Items.AddObject('Template', TObject(PIDSI_TEMPLATE));
      cbPropertyName.Items.AddObject('Last Author', TObject(PIDSI_LASTAUTHOR));
```

*continues* ▶

**Listing 8.6**    *continued*

```
      cbPropertyName.Items.AddObject('Revision Number', TObject(PIDSI_REVNUMBER));
      cbPropertyName.Items.AddObject('Page Count', TObject(PIDSI_PAGECOUNT));
      cbPropertyName.Items.AddObject('Word Count', TObject(PIDSI_WORDCOUNT));
      cbPropertyName.Items.AddObject('Character Count', TObject(PIDSI_CHARCOUNT));
      cbPropertyName.Items.AddObject('Application Name', TObject(PIDSI_APPNAME));
      cbPropertyName.Items.AddObject('Document Security', TObject(PIDSI_DOC_SECURITY));
      cbPropertyName.ItemIndex := 0;
    end;

    1: begin
      cbPropertyName.Style := csDropDownList;
    end;

    2: begin
      cbPropertyName.Style := csDropDown;
    end;
  end;
end;

function TfrmMain.Matches(P: TPropVariant): Boolean;
begin
  case P.vt of
    VT_LPSTR:
      Result := UpperCase(P.pszVal) = UpperCase(ecValue.Text);

    VT_I4:
      Result := P.lVal = StrToInt(ecValue.Text);

    // Handle other property types here...

    else
      Result := False;
  end;
end;

procedure TfrmMain.btnFindClick(Sender: TObject);
var
  SR: TSearchRec;
  Res: Integer;
  P: TPropVariant;
  ID: Integer;
  FileName: WideString;
begin
  lbFiles.Items.Clear;

  Res := FindFirst(ecFilePath.Text, faReadOnly or faArchive, SR);
  try
    while Res = 0 do begin
      FileName := ExtractFilePath(ecFilePath.Text) + SR.Name;
      if StgIsStorageFile(PWideChar(FileName)) = S_OK then begin
        PropertySet1.FileName := FileName;
```

```
    PropertySet1.StreamGUID := StreamGuids[cbStream.ItemIndex];
    PropertySet1.Open;

    try
      if cbStream.ItemIndex = 2 then begin
        P := PropertySet1.GetPropertyByName(cbPropertyName.Text);
      end else begin
        ID := Integer(cbPropertyName.Items.Objects[cbPropertyName.ItemIndex]);
        P := PropertySet1.GetPropertyByID(ID);
      end;

      if Matches(P) then
        lbFiles.Items.Add(FileName);
    finally
      PropertySet1.Close;
    end;
  end;

  Res := FindNext(SR);
  end;
finally
  FindClose(SR);
end;

if lbFiles.Items.Count = 0 then
  ShowMessage('No matching files found.');
end;

procedure TfrmMain.btnCloseClick(Sender: TObject);
begin
  Close;
end;

end.
```

At this point, you've seen how you can read and write OLE Property Sets in your Delphi applications. You've seen that Microsoft Office applications (as well as others) use property sets to store document summary information. I also showed you a nifty example of searching for files on your hard drive based on the values stored in property sets.

In the following section, I'll explore another use of structured storage files—OLE containers.

# Compound Documents and OLE Containers

In this section I'll discuss compound documents and OLE containers. An OLE container is a program that lets you embed one or more visual COM servers within it. If you've ever used Microsoft Word, for example, and embedded a Paint picture inside the Word document, you've used an OLE container (see Figure 8.5). Compound documents contain data of different formats. The different pieces of data are typically stored in separate streams within a single file (in other words, structured storage files).

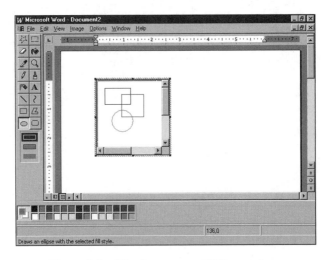

**Figure 8.5**    *Word acts as an OLE container.*

Creating an OLE container with Delphi is easy. Create a new application, and drop a TOleContainer component on the main form. The TOleContainer component can be found on the System page of the component palette.

At design time, you can right-click the component, and select "Insert Object" from the popup menu. The Insert Object dialog box appears, as shown in Figure 8.6.

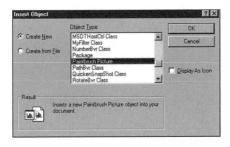

**Figure 8.6**    *Windows' Insert Object dialog box.*

If you select Paintbrush Picture in the list box and click OK, Windows will start up an instance of Paint in a separate window.

> **Note**
>
> *Delphi does not support in-place activation at design time. However, at runtime, Paint will appear in place as you would expect.* ◆

If you draw something in Paint, and then select File, Exit & Return to OleContainer1 from the Paint menu, you'll see the image appear in the TOleContainer component on your main form (Figure 8.7).

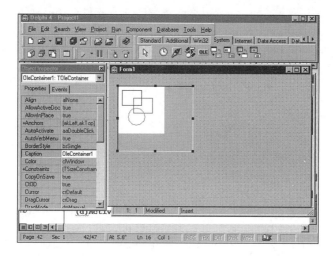

**Figure 8.7**  *A Delphi OLE container with a Paint bitmap.*

## Activating and Deactivating OLE Servers

The goal here is to provide a means for the user to embed objects at runtime, not at design time. The following code snippet shows how to do this:

```
if OleContainer1.InsertObjectDialog then
  OleContainer1.DoVerb(OleContainer1.PrimaryVerb);
```

InsertObjectDialog displays the Windows Insert Object dialog box. If the user selected an object type to insert, it returns True. Typically, when the user inserts an object, he wants to immediately act on that object, so I make a call to DoVerb to execute the default action on that object (usually, the default action is to activate the object).

Deactivating a server, which returns control to the container application, occurs automatically when the object loses focus. If you want to manually close a server application, you can simply call

```
OleContainer1.Close;
```

## Saving and Loading Objects to Files and Streams

Although the server application is responsible for operating on the embedded object, it is not responsible for saving that object to disk. That is the responsibility of your application. TOleContainer provides the capability of saving objects to either a stream or a file. For this example, I'll be saving the object to a file, although for a complex application, you might have several embedded objects in your application, so you would probably save them to a stream instead.

It should go without saying that since structured storage files support a number of streams, an obvious way to save multiple objects to a single file is to use structured storage, and assign a separate stream to each object!

Saving an object to disk is as easy as writing

```
OleContainer1.SaveToFile('C:\MyFile.Doc');
```

Reloading the object is just as easy:

```
OleContainer1.LoadFromFile('C:\MyFile.Doc');
```

## Merging Menus

As you might have noticed if you've ever used Microsoft Word (for example) as an OLE container, when you activate the server application, the server takes over the container's main menu. More accurately, the server merges its menu with the container's menu. Delphi supports this functionality through the use of TMenu.GroupIndex.

When assigning values to the GroupIndex property of the main menu, remember that menu items with even-numbered GroupIndex values are retained, while menu items with odd-numbered GroupIndex values are replaced by menu items of the server. For instance, in the example application OLECont, the File menu has a group index of 0 (which is considered even), so the File menu is kept. The Edit menu has a group index of 1, so it is replaced by the Edit menu of Paint. All remaining menu items from the Paint application are merged in following the Edit menu.

## Using the Clipboard

In addition to loading and saving objects to and from disk, you can also copy and paste to and from the clipboard. To copy an object to the clipboard so that it might be pasted into another OLE container, for example, you can simply call

```
OleContainer1.Copy;
```

If you're performing a Cut operation, you'll need to destroy the object after you copy it, as follows:

```
OleContainer1.Copy;
OleContainer1.DestroyObject;
```

Pasting from the clipboard is equally easy. However, you must check to make sure there's something on the clipboard that can be pasted. The following two lines of code show how you can handle this:

```
if OleContainer1.CanPaste then
  OleContainer1.PasteSpecialDialog;
```

PasteSpecialDialog brings up a dialog box, as shown in Figure 8.8, that allows the user to determine how to paste the object.

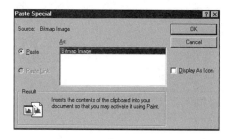

**Figure 8.8**    *Pasting an object into an OLE container.*

## Example: A Simple OLE Container

In this example, I'll basically pull all the pieces of the ongoing discussion together to create a simple OLE container application. This example contains very few lines of code, yet it supports creating a new object, loading and saving to disk, and cutting, copying, and pasting to the clipboard. Listings 8.7 and 8.8 contain the complete source code for the OLECont sample application.

**Listing 8.7**    *OLECont—OLECont.dpr*

```
program OLECont;

uses
  Forms,
  MainForm in 'MainForm.pas' {Form1};

{$R *.RES}

begin
  Application.Initialize;
  Application.CreateForm(TForm1, Form1);
  Application.Run;
end.
```

---

**Listing 8.8**   *OLECont—MainForm.pas*

```
unit MainForm;

interface

uses
  Windows, Messages, SysUtils, Classes, Graphics, Controls, Forms, Dialogs,
  Menus, OleCtnrs, StdCtrls, ExtCtrls;

type
  TForm1 = class(TForm)
    MainMenu1: TMainMenu;
    File1: TMenuItem;
    Exit1: TMenuItem;
    New1: TMenuItem;
    Open1: TMenuItem;
    Save1: TMenuItem;
    N1: TMenuItem;
    OpenDialog1: TOpenDialog;
    Panel1: TPanel;
    OleContainer1: TOleContainer;
    Edit1: TMenuItem;
    Cut1: TMenuItem;
    Copy1: TMenuItem;
    Paste1: TMenuItem;
    InsertObject1: TMenuItem;
    N2: TMenuItem;
    N3: TMenuItem;
    Return1: TMenuItem;
    SaveDialog1: TSaveDialog;
    procedure New1Click(Sender: TObject);
    procedure Open1Click(Sender: TObject);
    procedure Save1Click(Sender: TObject);
    procedure Return1Click(Sender: TObject);
    procedure Exit1Click(Sender: TObject);
    procedure InsertObject1Click(Sender: TObject);
    procedure Cut1Click(Sender: TObject);
    procedure Copy1Click(Sender: TObject);
    procedure Paste1Click(Sender: TObject);
    procedure OleContainer1Activate(Sender: TObject);
    procedure OleContainer1Deactivate(Sender: TObject);
  private
    { Private declarations }
    FFileName: string;
  public
    { Public declarations }
  end;

var
  Form1: TForm1;

implementation
```

```
{$R *.DFM}

procedure TForm1.Exit1Click(Sender: TObject);
begin
  Close;
end;

procedure TForm1.New1Click(Sender: TObject);
begin
  OleContainer1.DestroyObject;
end;

procedure TForm1.Open1Click(Sender: TObject);
begin
  if OpenDialog1.Execute then begin
    FFileName := OpenDialog1.FileName;
    OleContainer1.LoadFromFile(FFileName);
  end;
end;

procedure TForm1.Save1Click(Sender: TObject);
begin
  if FFileName = '' then begin
    if SaveDialog1.Execute then
      FFileName := SaveDialog1.FileName
    else
      exit;
  end;

  OleContainer1.SaveToFile(FFileName);
end;

procedure TForm1.Return1Click(Sender: TObject);
begin
  OleContainer1.Close;
end;

procedure TForm1.InsertObject1Click(Sender: TObject);
begin
  if OleContainer1.InsertObjectDialog then
    OleContainer1.DoVerb(OleContainer1.PrimaryVerb);
end;

procedure TForm1.Cut1Click(Sender: TObject);
begin
  OleContainer1.Copy;
  OleContainer1.DestroyObject;
end;

procedure TForm1.Copy1Click(Sender: TObject);
begin
  OleContainer1.Copy;
end;
```

*continues* ▶

**Listing 8.8** *continued*

```
procedure TForm1.Paste1Click(Sender: TObject);
begin
  if OleContainer1.CanPaste then
    OleContainer1.PasteSpecialDialog;
end;

procedure TForm1.OleContainer1Activate(Sender: TObject);
begin
  Return1.Enabled := True;
end;

procedure TForm1.OleContainer1Deactivate(Sender: TObject);
begin
  Return1.Enabled := False;
end;

end.
```

Figure 8.9 shows OLECont at runtime.

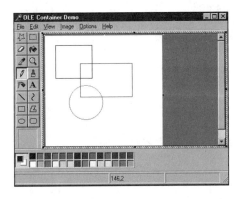

**Figure 8.9**    *A Delphi OLE container application at runtime.*

## Summary

I spent a considerable amount of time in this chapter discussing property sets. Property sets are very useful and powerful features that have not yet seen much appreciation outside of applications such as Microsoft Office.

By now, you should have all the ammunition you need to easily allow property sets to be stored with your own data files. Of course, you'll have to switch to structured storage files in order to do that.

In the second part of this chapter, I explained OLE containers. As you saw, it's remarkably easy to create an OLE container in Delphi, thanks to the TOleContainer component.

# 9

# *Programming the*
# *Windows Shell*

This final chapter will focus on writing Windows shell extensions. You extend the Windows shell by writing COM extensions that implement pre-defined COM interfaces.

In Chapter 2, "Interfaces and COM," I discussed in-process COM servers at length. In this chapter, you will see concrete, real-world uses of in-process COM servers, including the following:

- Context Menu Handlers
- Copy Hook Handlers
- Shell Links
- Tray Icons
- Property Sheet Handlers

In addition to reinforcing concepts discussed in early chapters in this book (namely, in-process COM servers and interface reference counting), this chapter will provide examples and results that are highly visible to you and, ultimately, your end users.

## Context Menu Handlers

Context menu handlers are one of the easiest shell extensions you can write. In this section, I'll show you how to create a context menu handler that adds a "View Type Library" menu item to the Windows menu when the user right-clicks a file with extension .EXE, .DLL, .TLB, or .OLB.

*Note*

*Most type libraries are contained in .EXE, .DLL, or .TLB files. Microsoft Office uses .OLB files for its type libraries.* ◆

The first task you need to perform when creating a context menu handler is creating the COM server. Select File, New from the Delphi main menu. Click the ActiveX tab, select the ActiveX Library icon, and click OK. Next, select File, New from the Delphi menu, and select COM Object from the ActiveX tab. Delphi displays the COM Object Wizard. Fill it out to look like Figure 9.1.

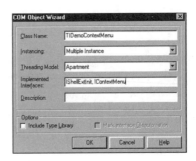

**Figure 9.1**    *COM Object Wizard for a Context Menu Handler.*

When you click OK, Delphi generates the code shown in Listing 9.1.

*Note*

*Remember that Delphi 3 does not provide the COM Object Wizard. If you're a Delphi 3 user, you'll need to enter the code shown in Listing 9.1 by hand.* ◆

**Listing 9.1**    *Template Code for a Context Menu Handler*

```
unit Unit1;

interface

uses
  Windows, ActiveX, ComObj;

type
  TTIDemoContextMenu = class(TComObject, IShellExtInit, IContextMenu)
  protected
    {Declare IShellExtInit methods here}
    {Declare IContextMenu methods here}
  end;
```

```
const
  Class_TIDemoContextMenu: TGUID = '{66DA0B20-098C-11D3-B3DC-0040F67455FE}';

implementation

uses ComServ;

initialization
  TComObjectFactory.Create(ComServer, TTIDemoContextMenu, Class_TIDemoContextMenu,
    'TIDemoContextMenu', '', ciMultiInstance, tmApartment);
end.
```

Save this file as TIViewImpl.pas. You should notice right away that this COM object implements two interfaces: IShellExtInit and IContextMenu. These interfaces are defined by Windows. Therefore, we don't have to declare the interfaces in this unit, because Windows already knows what they are. You only need to make sure you include ShlObj in the uses section of the unit.

## The IShellExtInit Interface

IShellExtInit is responsible, as you might guess, for initializing the context menu handler. The IShellExtInit interface is shown here:

```
SID_IShellExtInit     = '{000214E8-0000-0000-C000-000000000046}';

IShellExtInit = interface(IUnknown)
  [SID_IShellExtInit]
  function Initialize(pidlFolder: PItemIDList; lpdobj: IDataObject;
    hKeyProgID: HKEY): HResult; stdcall;
end;
```

As you can see, there isn't much to it. It only defines one method, Initialize, but as luck would have it, the method name clashes with a method of TComObject itself.

In Chapter 1, "Using Interfaces in Delphi," I discussed method resolution clauses. This is the exact situation that method resolution clauses were created to handle. Through a method resolution clause, we can map IShellExtInit.Initialize to a function named InitShellExtension.

IShellExtInit.Initialize takes three parameters (passed to you by Windows). The first parameter, pidlFolder, describes the folder, or directory, containing the file(s) for which the user invoked the context menu. lpdobj is used to reference the names of the file(s) themselves. The final parameter, hKeyProgID, contains a handle to the HKEY in the Windows Registry that describes the type of file that the user selected.

The following function, taken from Listing 9.4, is a typical implementation of IShellExtInit.Initialize:

```
function TTIDemoContextMenu.InitShellExtension(pidlFolder: PItemIDList; lpdobj:
➡IDataObject;
      hKeyProgID: HKEY): HResult; stdcall;
var
  Medium: TStgMedium;
  Format: TFormatEtc;
begin
  // Fail if no data object was provided
  if lpdobj = nil then begin
    Result := E_FAIL;
    exit;
  end;

  // Set up the TFormatEtc structure...
  with Format do begin
    cfFormat := CF_HDROP;
    ptd := nil;
    dwAspect := DVASPECT_CONTENT;
    lIndex := =1;
    tymed := TYMED_HGLOBAL;
  end;

  // Fail if we can't get to the data
  Result := lpdobj.GetData(Format, Medium);
  if Failed(Result) then
    exit;

  try
    // Make sure the user only selected one file
    if DragQueryFile(Medium.hGlobal, $FFFFFFFF, nil, 0) = 1 then begin
      SetLength(FFileName, MAX_PATH);
      DraqQueryFile(Medium.hGlobal, 0, PChar(FFileName), MAX_PATH);
      Result := NOERROR;
    end else
      Result := E_FAIL;
  finally
    ReleaseStgMedium(Medium);
  end;
end;
```

First, we must check to make sure that the lpdobj parameter in this function is valid. Then, a call is made to lpdobj.GetData to retrieve the data from lpdobj.

The call to GetData allocates memory for the Medium parameter, so the rest of the function is enclosed in a try/finally block that ensures memory is released. The first call to DragQueryFile, with a value of $FFFFFFFF, returns the number of files selected by the user before invoking the context menu. If the user didn't select exactly one file, the function returns a result of E_FAIL.

If the user *did* select exactly one file, another call is made to DragQueryFile (this time with a value of 0) to retrieve the filename in question. The filename is saved in the variable FFileName for future use.

## The IContextMenu Interface

The IContextMenu interface is responsible for setting up and responding to the context menu itself. IContextMenu is declared in shlobj.pas as follows:

```
SID_IContextMenu     = '{000214E4-0000-0000-C000-000000000046}';

IContextMenu = interface(IUnknown)
  [SID_IContextMenu]
  function QueryContextMenu(Menu: HMENU;
    indexMenu, idCmdFirst, idCmdLast, uFlags: UINT): HResult; stdcall;
  function InvokeCommand(var lpici: TCMInvokeCommandInfo): HResult; stdcall;
  function GetCommandString(idCmd, uType: UINT; pwReserved: PUINT;
    pszName: LPSTR; cchMax: UINT): HResult; stdcall;
end;
```

After the call to IShellExtInit.Initialize, Windows calls IContextMenu QueryContextMenu. This method is your opportunity to add menu items to the context menu. QueryContextMenu takes five parameters: a handle to the context menu, the index in the menu at which point you are to insert menu items, the lower and upper bounds of the IDs that may be assigned to the new menu items, and a bitmapped set of flags. Valid flags are listed in Table 9.1.

You should set the return value of QueryContextMenu equal to the number of menu items that you add.

*Table 9.1*    *Valid uFlags Values for QueryContextMenu*

| Value | Description |
| --- | --- |
| CMF_CANRENAME | Set if the application supports renaming. Context menu handlers should ignore this flag—it is only used by namespace extensions. |
| CMF_DEFAULTONLY | Specified when the user activates the default menu option by double-clicking it. Context menu handlers should not add any menu items if this flag is set. |
| CMF_EXPLORE | Set when the tree view is shown in Windows Explorer. Context menu handlers should ignore this value. |
| CMF_INCLUDESTATIC | Set when a static menu is being created. This flag is only used by the browser. |

*continues* ▶

*Table 9.1    continued*

| Value | Description |
|---|---|
| CMF_NODEFAULT | Set if there should not be a default menu item in the menu. Context menu handlers should ignore this flag. |
| CMF_NORMAL | Set for normal operation. A context menu handler should add any menu items that it supports if this flag is set. |
| CMF_NOVERBS | Set for items displayed in the Send To: menu. Context menu handlers should ignore this flag. |
| CMF_VERBSONLY | Set if the menu is for a shortcut. Context menu handlers should ignore this flag. |

As you can see from Table 9.1, most flags don't pertain to context menu handlers (the IContextMenu interface is also used in other situations).

Here is an implementation of QueryContextMenu that adds a single menu item to the context menu. The text of the menu item differs depending on the context in which QueryContextMenu is called.

```
function TTIDemoContextMenu.QueryContextMenu(Menu: HMENU; indexMenu,
  idCmdFirst, idCmdLast, uFlags: UINT): HResult;
begin
  Result := NOERROR;

  FViewMenuItem := indexMenu;

  if (uFlags and $000F) = CMF_NORMAL then begin
    InsertMenu(Menu, FViewMenuItem, MF_STRING or MF_BYPOSITION, idCmdFirst,
      'View TypeLib...');
    Result := 1;
  end else if (uFlags and CMF_EXPLORE) <> 0 then begin
    InsertMenu(Menu, FViewMenuItem, MF_STRING or MF_BYPOSITION, idCmdFirst,
      'View TypeLib from Explorer...');
    Result := 1;
  end else if (uFlags and CMF_VERBSONLY) <> 0 then begin
    InsertMenu(Menu, FViewMenuItem, MF_STRING or MF_BYPOSITION, idCmdFirst,
      'View TypeLib from Shortcut...');
    Result := 1;
  end;
end;
```

QueryContextMenu **ands** uFlags with $000F and compares the result to CMF_NORMAL. **Anding** with $000F strips off all flags except CMF_DEFAULTONLY, CMF_VERBSONLY, CMF_EXPLORE, and CMF_NOVERBS. CMF_NORMAL is defined in shlobj.pas as zero, so the CMF_NORMAL flag is implied by the absence of CMF_DEFAULTONLY, CMF_VERBSONLY, CMF_EXPLORE, and CMF_NOVERBS.

InsertMenu is a Windows API call that you might not be familiar with
unless you've had to work with the low-level Windows API using Delphi or
another language. It is defined in windows.pas as follows:

```
function InsertMenu(hMenu: HMENU; uPosition, uFlags, uIDNewItem: UINT;
  lpNewItem: PChar): BOOL; stdcall;
```

The first parameter, hMenu, is the handle to the menu. You can simply pass
in the first parameter from QueryContextMenu. uPosition is a 0-based
index into the menu, which indicates where to insert the new menu item.
You can pass in the indexMenu parameter from QueryContextMenu.

uFlags is a set of flags that determine how the new menu item is to be
inserted. You will typically set this parameter to MF_STRING or
MF_BYPOSITION. MF_STRING indicates that the final parameter to
InsertMenu is actually a string. MF_BYPOSITION indicates that the
uPosition parameter is the 0-based index into the menu. For a list of other
acceptable flags, see the Windows documentation for InsertMenu.

UIDNewItem is the numeric ID to assign to the menu item. The final
parameter, lpNewItem, designates the menu item itself. You'll typically pass
the text of the new menu item here.

The next method you'll want to deal with is GetCommandString.
GetCommandString is responsible for providing a help string (or hint, in
Delphi parlance) for the menu item(s) that you add to the context menu.

```
function TTIDemoContextMenu.GetCommandString(idCmd, uType: UINT;
  pwReserved: PUINT; pszName: LPSTR; cchMax: UINT): HResult;
begin
  Result := S_OK;

  if (idCmd = FViewMenuItem) and
     ((uType and GCS_HELPTEXT) <> 0) then
    StrLCopy(pszName, 'View selected type library', cchMax)
  else
    Result := E_INVALIDARG;
end;
```

GetCommandString provides four useful parameters for you to work with
(pwReserved is reserved for future use by Microsoft). The first parameter,
idCmd, indicates the 0-based index of the menu item for which you are to
provide a help string. uType indicates the type of information you are to
provide. Valid values for this parameter are shown in Table 9.2. pszName
points to a buffer to hold the string. The final parameter, cchMax, indicates
the maximum buffer size in bytes.

**Table 9.2**    *Valid uType Values for GetCommandString*

| Value | Description |
|---|---|
| GCS_HELPTEXT | Retrieves help text for the context menu item |
| GCS_VALIDATE | Verifies that the context menu item exists |
| GCS_VERB | Retrieves the command name for the context menu item |

Finally, when the user selects the context menu item, Windows calls IContextMenu.InvokeCommand. InvokeCommand takes a single parameter, lpici, of type TCMInvokeCommandInfo. TCMInvokeCommandInfo is declared in shlobj.pas as follows:

```
PCMInvokeCommandInfo = ^TCMInvokeCommandInfo;
{$EXTERNALSYM _CMINVOKECOMMANDINFO}
_CMINVOKECOMMANDINFO = record
  cbSize: DWORD;         { must be sizeof(CMINVOKECOMMANDINFO) }
  fMask: DWORD;          { any combination of CMIC_MASK_* }
  hwnd: HWND;            { might be NULL (indicating no owner window) }
  lpVerb: LPCSTR;        { either a string of MAKEINTRESOURCE(idOffset) }
  lpParameters: LPCSTR;  { might be NULL (indicating no parameter) }
  lpDirectory: LPCSTR;   { might be NULL (indicating no specific directory) }
  nShow: Integer;        { one of SW_ values for ShowWindow() API }
  dwHotKey: DWORD;
  hIcon: THandle;
end;
TCMInvokeCommandInfo = _CMINVOKECOMMANDINFO;
```

The main field in this structure that will be of interest to you is lpVerb. Contrary to what you might expect, lpVerb is actually an integer value with a low word that represents the 0-based index of the menu item that was selected. Conveniently, hwnd provides us with the owner window, which we can use to display error messages, as I do in InvokeCommand.

Note that in InvokeCommand, I naively assume that TIDemo.exe is located somewhere in the Windows path. In a shipping application, you might want to store the path to the application somewhere in the Windows registry, where the context menu handler can locate it.

```
function TTIDemoContextMenu.InvokeCommand(
  var lpici: TCMInvokeCommandInfo): HResult;
var
  MI: Integer;
begin
  Result := S_OK;

  MI := Integer(lpici.lpVerb);

  if HiWord(MI) <> 0 then begin
    // We were called by another application
```

```
  // not supported in this example.
  Result := E_FAIL;
  exit;
end;

if LoWord(MI) = FViewMenuItem then
  // Execute TIDemo
  ShellExecute(0, nil, 'TIDemo.exe', PChar(FFileName), nil, SW_SHOW)
else
  Result := E_INVALIDARG;
end;
```

## Registering the Context Menu Handler

After you've written a context menu handler, you must register it with Windows, so Windows knows it's available. Context menu handlers are located under the HKEY_CLASSES_ROOT\<extension>\shellex\ ContextMenuHandlers key in the Registry. The easiest way to register and unregister a context menu handler is by deriving a custom class factory from TComObjectFactory. You only need override the UpdateRegistry procedure to handle both registering and unregistering the context menu handler.

```
procedure TTIDemoFactory.UpdateRegistry(Register: Boolean);
begin
  inherited UpdateRegistry(Register);

  if Register then begin
    CreateRegKey('.tlb', '', 'TypeLibrary');
    CreateRegKey('TypeLibrary\shellex\ContextMenuHandlers\' +
      ClassName, '', GUIDToString(ClassID));
    CreateRegKey('exefiles\shellex\ContextMenuHandlers\' +
      ClassName, '', GUIDToString(ClassID));
  end else begin
    DeleteRegKey('.tlb');
    DeleteRegKey('TypeLibrary\shellex\ContextMenuHandlers\' +
      ClassName);
    DeleteRegKey('exefiles\shellex\ContextMenuHandlers\' +
      ClassName);
  end;
end;
```

The first task you need to perform in this method is call the inherited method, so that the COM server is registered or unregistered correctly. Next, add the context menu handler-specific Registry entries.

Listings 9.2 through 9.4 show the complete implementation of a context menu handler COM server, along with the associated class factory.

---

**Listing 9.2** *CtxDemo—CtxDemo.dpr*

```
library CtxDemo;

uses
  ComServ,
  TIViewImpl in 'TIViewImpl.pas',
  CtxDemo_TLB in 'CtxDemo_TLB.pas';

exports
  DllGetClassObject,
  DllCanUnloadNow,
  DllRegisterServer,
  DllUnregisterServer;

{$R *.TLB}

{$R *.RES}

begin
end.
```

---

**Listing 9.3** *CtxDemo—CtxDemo_TLB.pas*

```
unit CtxDemo_TLB;

// ************************************************************************ //
// WARNING                                                                  //
// -------                                                                  //
// The types declared in this file were generated from data read from a     //
// Type Library. If this type library is explicitly or indirectly (via      //
// another type library referring to this type library) re-imported, or the //
// 'Refresh' command of the Type Library Editor activated while editing the //
// Type Library, the contents of this file will be regenerated and all       //
// manual modifications will be lost.                                       //
// ************************************************************************ //

// PASTLWTR : $Revision:   1.11.1.75  $
// File generated on 5/14/99 8:00:37 PM from Type Library described below.

// ************************************************************************ //
// Type Lib: J:\Book\samples\Chap9\CtxDemo\CtxDemo.tlb
// IID\LCID: {3577B511-0A4F-11D3-B3DE-0040F67455FE}\0
// Helpfile:
// HelpString: CtxDemo Library
// Version:    1.0
// ************************************************************************ //

interface

uses Windows, ActiveX, Classes, Graphics, OleCtrls, StdVCL;
```

```
// **************************************************************//
// GUIDS declared in the TypeLibrary. Following prefixes are used:  //
//   Type Libraries    : LIBID_xxxx                             //
//   CoClasses         : CLASS_xxxx                             //
//   DISPInterfaces    : DIID_xxxx                              //
//   Non-DISP interfaces: IID_xxxx                              //
// **************************************************************//
const
  LIBID_CtxDemo: TGUID = '{3577B511-0A4F-11D3-B3DE-0040F67455FE}';

implementation

uses ComObj;

end.
```

---

## Listing 9.4    CtxDemo—TIViewImpl.pas

```pascal
unit TIViewImpl;

interface

uses
  Windows, ActiveX, ComObj, ShlObj;

type
  TTIDemoContextMenu = class(TComObject, IShellExtInit, IContextMenu)
  private
    FFileName: string;
    FViewMenuItem: UINT;

    function IShellExtInit.Initialize = InitShellExtension;
  protected
    {Declare IShellExtInit methods here}
    function InitShellExtension(pidlFolder: PItemIDList;
      lpdobj: IDataObject; hKeyProgID: HKEY): HResult; stdcall;

    {Declare IContextMenu methods here}
    function QueryContextMenu(Menu: HMENU;
      indexMenu, idCmdFirst, idCmdLast, uFlags: UINT): HResult; stdcall;
    function GetCommandString(idCmd, uType: UINT; pwReserved: PUINT;
      pszName: LPSTR; cchMax: UINT): HResult; stdcall;
    function InvokeCommand(var lpici: TCMInvokeCommandInfo): HResult; stdcall;
  end;

  TTIDemoFactory = class(TComObjectFactory)
  public
    procedure UpdateRegistry(Register: Boolean); override;
  end;
```

*continues* ▶

**Listing 9.4**   *continued*

```
const
  Class_TIDemoContextMenu: TGUID = '{66DA0B20-098C-11D3-B3DC-0040F67455FE}';

implementation

uses ComServ, ShellAPI, SysUtils;

function TTIDemoContextMenu.GetCommandString(idCmd, uType: UINT;
  pwReserved: PUINT; pszName: LPSTR; cchMax: UINT): HResult;
begin
  Result := S_OK;

  if (idCmd = FViewMenuItem) and
     ((uType and GCS_HELPTEXT) <> 0) then
    StrLCopy(pszName, 'View selected type library', cchMax)
  else
    Result := E_INVALIDARG;
end;

function TTIDemoContextMenu.InitShellExtension(pidlFolder: PItemIDList; lpdobj:
IDataObject;
      hKeyProgID: HKEY): HResult; stdcall;
var
  Medium: TStgMedium;
  Format: TFormatEtc;
begin
  // Fail if no data object was provided
  if lpdobj = nil then begin
    Result := E_FAIL;
    exit;
  end;

  // Set up the TFormatEtc structure...
  with Format do begin
    cfFormat := CF_HDROP;
    ptd := nil;
    dwAspect := DVASPECT_CONTENT;
    lIndex := -1;
    tymed := TYMED_HGLOBAL;
  end;

  // Fail if we can't get to the data
  Result := lpdobj.GetData(Format, Medium);
  if Failed(Result) then
    exit;

  try
    // Make sure the user only selected one file
    if DragQueryFile(Medium.hGlobal, $FFFFFFFF, nil, 0) = 1 then begin
      SetLength(FFileName, MAX_PATH);
      DragQueryFile(Medium.hGlobal, 0, PChar(FFileName), MAX_PATH);
```

```
      Result := NOERROR;
    end else
      Result := E_FAIL;
  finally
    ReleaseStgMedium(Medium);
  end;
end;

function TTIDemoContextMenu.InvokeCommand(
  var lpici: TCMInvokeCommandInfo): HResult;
var
  MI: Integer;
begin
  Result := S_OK;

  MI := Integer(lpici.lpVerb);

  if HiWord(MI) <> 0 then begin
    // We were called by another application
    // not supported in this example.
    Result := E_FAIL;
    exit;
  end;

  if LoWord(MI) = FViewMenuItem then
    // Execute TIDemo
    ShellExecute(0, nil, 'TIDemo.exe', PChar(FFileName), nil, SW_SHOW)
  else
    Result := E_INVALIDARG;
end;

function TTIDemoContextMenu.QueryContextMenu(Menu: HMENU; indexMenu,
  idCmdFirst, idCmdLast, uFlags: UINT): HResult;
begin
  Result := NOERROR;

  FViewMenuItem := indexMenu;

  if (uFlags and $000F) = CMF_NORMAL then begin
    InsertMenu(Menu, FViewMenuItem, MF_STRING or MF_BYPOSITION, idCmdFirst,
      'View TypeLib...');
    Result := 1;
  end else if (uFlags and CMF_EXPLORE) <> 0 then begin
    InsertMenu(Menu, FViewMenuItem, MF_STRING or MF_BYPOSITION, idCmdFirst,
      'View TypeLib from Explorer...');
    Result := 1;
  end else if (uFlags and CMF_VERBSONLY) <> 0 then begin
    InsertMenu(Menu, FViewMenuItem, MF_STRING or MF_BYPOSITION, idCmdFirst,
      'View TypeLib from Shortcut...');
    Result := 1;
  end;
end;
```

*continues* ▶

**Listing 9.4**  *continued*

```
{ TTIDemoFactory }

procedure TTIDemoFactory.UpdateRegistry(Register: Boolean);
begin
  inherited UpdateRegistry(Register);

  if Register then begin
    CreateRegKey('.tlb', '', 'TypeLibrary');
    CreateRegKey('TypeLibrary\shellex\ContextMenuHandlers\' +
      ClassName, '', GUIDToString(ClassID));
  end else begin
    DeleteRegKey('.tlb');
    DeleteRegKey('TypeLibrary\shellex\ContextMenuHandlers\' +
      ClassName);
  end;
end;

initialization
{$IFDEF VER100}
  TTIDemoFactory.Create(ComServer, TTIDemoContextMenu, Class_TIDemoContextMenu,
    'TIDemoContextMenu', '', ciMultiInstance);
{$ELSE}
  TTIDemoFactory.Create(ComServer, TTIDemoContextMenu, Class_TIDemoContextMenu,
    'TIDemoContextMenu', '', ciMultiInstance, tmApartment);
{$ENDIF}
end.
```

Figures 9.2 through 9.4 show three different scenarios in which a context menu can be invoked. Figure 9.2 shows a context menu invoked from the Windows explorer.

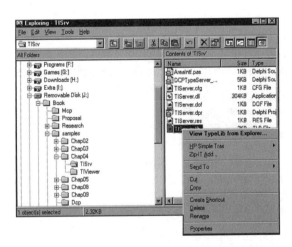

**Figure 9.2**  *Context Menu from the Windows Explorer.*

Figure 9.3 shows a context menu invoked from within Microsoft Word's File Open dialog box.

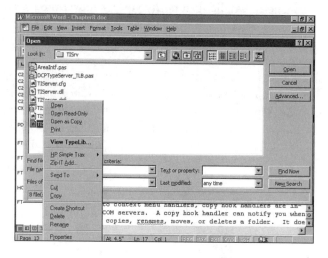

**Figure 9.3**   *Context menu from File Open.*

Figure 9.4 shows a context menu invoked from the Windows desktop.

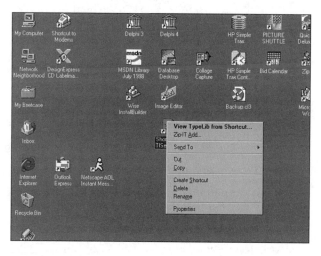

**Figure 9.4**   *Context menu from the Windows Desktop.*

You've seen how easy it is to create a context menu handler in Delphi. In the next section, we'll take a look at copy hook handlers.

## Copy Hook Handlers

Similar to context menu handlers, copy hook handlers are in-process COM servers. A copy hook handler can notify you whenever the user copies, renames, moves, or deletes a folder. It does not notify you for individual file operations. The copy hook handler has the option of preventing the operation, if it so chooses.

As with context menu handlers, the first step in building a copy hook handler is to create the COM server. Select File, New from the Delphi main menu. Click the ActiveX tab, select the ActiveX Library icon, and click OK. Next, select File, New from the Delphi menu, and select COM Object from the ActiveX tab. Delphi displays the COM Object Wizard. Fill it out to look like Figure 9.5.

**Figure 9.5**    *COM Object Wizard for a Copy Hook Handler.*

When you click OK, Delphi generates the code shown in Listing 9.5. (Enter this code manually if you're using Delphi 3.)

**Listing 9.5**    *Template Code for Copy Hook Handler*

```
unit Unit1;

interface

uses
  Windows, ActiveX, ComObj;

type
  TCopyHook = class(TComObject, ICopyHook)
  protected
    {Declare ICopyHook methods here}
  end;

const
  Class_CopyHook: TGUID = '{9090D650-0ACE-11D3-B3DF-0040F67455FE}';
```

```
implementation

uses ComServ;

initialization
  TComObjectFactory.Create(ComServer, TCopyHook, Class_CopyHook,
    'CopyHook', '', ciMultiInstance, tmApartment);
end.
```

Save this file as CopyHookImpl.pas. Copy hook handlers implement one simple interface: ICopyHook.

## The ICopyHook Interface

ICopyHook is defined in shlobj.pas as follows:

```
SID_IShellCopyHookA   = '{000214EF-0000-0000-C000-000000000046}';

ICopyHookA = interface(IUnknown) { sl }
  [SID_IShellCopyHookA]
  function CopyCallback(Wnd: HWND; wFunc, wFlags: UINT; pszSrcFile: PAnsiChar;
    dwSrcAttribs: DWORD; pszDestFile: PAnsiChar; dwDestAttribs: DWORD): UINT;
stdcall;
  end;
```

As you can see, it defines only one method. CopyCallback is the method that gets called when the user attempts one of the folder operations described previously.

CopyCallback takes seven parameters. The first parameter, Wnd, provides an owner window for error messages. wFunc indicates the operation that is being attempted. Valid values for wFunc are listed in Table 9.3.

> ### Note
>
> *Readers familiar with SHFileOperation will recognize the values listed in Tables 9.3 and 9.4.* ♦

*Table 9.3   Valid wFunc Values for CopyCallback*

| Value | Description |
|-------|-------------|
| FO_COPY | Copies files in the folder referenced by pszSrcFile to the folder referenced by pszDestFile |
| FO_DELETE | Deletes the files in the folder referenced by pszSrcFile |
| FO_MOVE | Moves files in the folder referenced by pszSrcFile to the folder referenced by pszDestFile |
| FO_RENAME | Renames the files in the folder referenced by pszSrcFile |

wFlags contains a bitmapped list of flags pertaining to the operation. Valid values for wFlags are listed in Table 9.4.

*Table 9.4    Valid wFlags Values for CopyCallback*

| Value | Description |
| --- | --- |
| FOF_ALLOWUNDO | Save information required to perform an undo operation. |
| FOF_CONFIRMMOUSE | Not yet implemented by Microsoft. |
| FOF_FILESONLY | Perform the selected operation only if a filename of *.* is specified. |
| FOF_MULTIDESTFILES | The pszDestFile parameter specifies multiple destinations. Instead of a single folder location, it contains one destination file for each source file. |
| FOF_NOCONFIRMATION | Don't confirm file operations. Assume the user selected Yes to All. |
| FOF_NOCONFIRMMKDIR | Don't confirm creating a new directory, for file operations that require a new directory to be created. |
| FOF_NOCOPYSECURITYATTRIBS | Don't copy security attributes associated with the source files. NT only. |
| FOF_NOERRORUI | Don't display an error message to the user if an error occurs. |
| FOF_RENAMEONCOLLISION | If a copy, move, or rename operation results in a duplicate file name, automatically give the file a new name. |
| FOF_SILENT | Don't display a progress dialog box during the file operation. |
| FOF_SIMPLEPROGRESS | Display a progress dialog box, but don't display individual file names in the dialog box. |

pszSrcFile contains the name of the folder that is being manipulated. The next parameter, dwSrcAttribs, contains the file attributes of the folder in question.

pszDestFile is the name of the destination folder, if any. The final parameter, dwDestAttribs, contains the file attributes of the destination folder.

The return value must be IDYES to allow the operation; IDNO to disallow the operation but continue processing other operations, if there are any; or IDCANCEL to disallow the operation and cancel any other operations.

Listing 9.6 shows the source code for a fully functional copy hook handler.

**Listing 9.6**    *Copy Hook Handler*

```
unit CopyHookImpl;

interface

uses
  Windows, ComObj, ShlObj, ShellApi;

type
  TCopyHook = class(TComObject, ICopyHook)
  protected
    {Declare ICopyHook methods here}
    function CopyCallback(Wnd: HWND; wFunc, wFlags: UINT;
      pszSrcFile: PAnsiChar; dwSrcAttribs: DWORD;
      pszDestFile: PAnsiChar; dwDestAttribs: DWORD): UINT; stdcall;
  end;

const
  Class_CopyHook: TGUID = '{9090D650-0ACE-11D3-B3DF-0040F67455FE}';

implementation

uses ComServ;

{ TCopyHook }

function TCopyHook.CopyCallback(Wnd: HWND; wFunc, wFlags: UINT;
  pszSrcFile: PAnsiChar; dwSrcAttribs: DWORD; pszDestFile: PAnsiChar;
  dwDestAttribs: DWORD): UINT;
var
  OpString: string;
begin
  case wFunc of
    FO_MOVE: OpString := ' move ';
    FO_COPY: OpString := ' copy ';
    FO_DELETE: OpString := ' delete ';
    FO_RENAME: OpString := ' rename ';
  end;

  Result := MessageBox(Wnd, PChar('Are you sure you want to ' + OpString +
    pszSrcFile + '?'), 'CopyHookDemo', MB_YESNOCANCEL);
end;
```

*continues* ▶

**Listing 9.6**    *continued*

```
initialization
{$IFDEF VER100}
  TComObjectFactory.Create(ComServer, TCopyHook, Class_CopyHook,
    'CopyHook', '', ciMultiInstance);
{$ELSE}
  TComObjectFactory.Create(ComServer, TCopyHook, Class_CopyHook,
    'CopyHook', '', ciMultiInstance, tmApartment);
{$ENDIF}
end.
```

As you can see, there isn't much source code involved. This implementation of CopyCallback simply verifies that the user knows what he's doing when he moves, copies, deletes, or renames a folder. You could use a copy hook handler to prevent the user from deleting, moving, or renaming hidden folders, for example.

## Registering the Copy Hook Handler

Similar to registering a context menu handler, registering a copy hook handler requires some additional entries in the Windows Registry.

Again, the easiest way to register and unregister a context menu handler is by deriving a custom class factory from TComObjectFactory. Listings 9.7 through 9.9 show the completed copy hook handler, along with the TCHClassFactory class, used to register it with Windows.

**Listing 9.7**    *CopyHookDemo—CopyHookDemo.dpr*

```
library CopyHookDemo;

uses
  ComServ,
  CopyHookImpl in 'CopyHookImpl.pas',
  CopyHookDemo_TLB in 'CopyHookDemo_TLB.pas';

exports
  DllGetClassObject,
  DllCanUnloadNow,
  DllRegisterServer,
  DllUnregisterServer;

{$R *.TLB}

{$R *.RES}

begin
end.
```

## Listing 9.8    *CopyHookDemo—CopyHookDemo_TLB.pas*

```
unit CopyHookDemo_TLB;

// *********************************************************************** //
// WARNING
// -------
// The types declared in this file were generated from data read from a
// Type Library. If this type library is explicitly or indirectly (via
// another type library referring to this type library) re-imported, or the
// 'Refresh' command of the Type Library Editor activated while editing the
// Type Library, the contents of this file will be regenerated and all
// manual modifications will be lost.
// *********************************************************************** //

// PASTLWTR : $Revision:   1.88  $
// File generated on 8/24/1999 7:51:50 PM from Type Library described below.


// ***********************************************************************//
// NOTE:
// Items guarded by $IFDEF_LIVE_SERVER_AT_DESIGN_TIME are used by properties
// which return objects that may need to be explicitly created via a function
// call prior to any access via the property. These items have been disabled
// in order to prevent accidental use from within the object inspector. You
// may enable them by defining LIVE_SERVER_AT_DESIGN_TIME or by selectively
// removing them from the $IFDEF blocks. However, such items must still be
// programmatically created via a method of the appropriate CoClass before
// they can be used.
// *********************************************************************** //
// Type Lib: J:\Book\samples\Chap9\CHDemo\CopyHookDemo.tlb (1)
// IID\LCID: {E025D8F0-5A7E-11D3-B86C-0040F67455FE}\0
// Helpfile:
// DepndLst:
//   (1) v2.0 stdole, (C:\WINNT\System32\STDOLE2.TLB)
//   (2) v4.0 StdVCL, (C:\WINNT\System32\STDVCL40.DLL)
// *********************************************************************** //
{$TYPEDADDRESS OFF} // Unit must be compiled without type-checked pointers.
interface

uses Windows, ActiveX, Classes, Graphics, OleServer, OleCtrls, StdVCL;

// ***********************************************************************//
// GUIDS declared in the TypeLibrary. Following prefixes are used:
//   Type Libraries     : LIBID_xxxx
//   CoClasses          : CLASS_xxxx
//   DISPInterfaces     : DIID_xxxx
//   Non-DISP interfaces: IID_xxxx
// ***********************************************************************//
const
  // TypeLibrary Major and minor versions
  CopyHookDemoMajorVersion = 1;
  CopyHookDemoMinorVersion = 0;
```

*continues* ▶

---

**Listing 9.8**    *continued*

```
LIBID_CopyHookDemo: TGUID = '{E025D8F0-5A7E-11D3-B86C-0040F67455FE}';


implementation

uses ComObj;

end.
```

---

**Listing 9.9**    *CopyHookDemo—CopyHookImpl.pas*

```
unit CopyHookImpl;

interface

uses
  Windows, ComObj, ShlObj, ShellApi;

type
  TCopyHook = class(TComObject, ICopyHook)
  protected
    {Declare ICopyHook methods here}
    function CopyCallback(Wnd: HWND; wFunc, wFlags: UINT;
      pszSrcFile: PAnsiChar; dwSrcAttribs: DWORD;
      pszDestFile: PAnsiChar; dwDestAttribs: DWORD): UINT; stdcall;
  end;

  TCHClassFactory = class(TComObjectFactory)
  public
    procedure UpdateRegistry(Register: Boolean); override;
  end;

const
  Class_CopyHook: TGUID = '{9090D650-0ACE-11D3-B3DF-0040F67455FE}';

implementation

uses ComServ;

{ TCopyHook }

function TCopyHook.CopyCallback(Wnd: HWND; wFunc, wFlags: UINT;
  pszSrcFile: PAnsiChar; dwSrcAttribs: DWORD; pszDestFile: PAnsiChar;
  dwDestAttribs: DWORD): UINT;
var
  OpString: string;
begin
  case wFunc of
    FO_MOVE: OpString := ' move ';
    FO_COPY: OpString := ' copy ';
    FO_DELETE: OpString := ' delete ';
```

```
   FO_RENAME: OpString := ' rename ';
  end;

  Result := MessageBox(Wnd, PChar('Are you sure you want to ' + OpString +
    pszSrcFile + '?'), 'CopyHookDemo', MB_YESNOCANCEL);
end;

{ TCHClassFactory }

procedure TCHClassFactory.UpdateRegistry(Register: Boolean);
begin
  inherited UpdateRegistry(Register);

  if Register then begin
    CreateRegKey('directory\shellex\CopyHookHandlers\' + ClassName,
      '', GUIDToString(ClassID));
  end else begin
    DeleteRegKey('directory\shellex\CopyHookHandlers\' + ClassName);
  end;
end;

initialization
{$IFDEF VER100}
  TCHClassFactory.Create(ComServer, TCopyHook, Class_CopyHook,
    'CopyHook', '', ciMultiInstance);
{$ELSE}
  TCHClassFactory.Create(ComServer, TCopyHook, Class_CopyHook,
    'CopyHook', '', ciMultiInstance, tmApartment);
{$ENDIF}
end.
```

TCHClassFactory simply creates or removes one entry in the Windows
Registry. Figure 9.6 shows the copy hook handler in action.

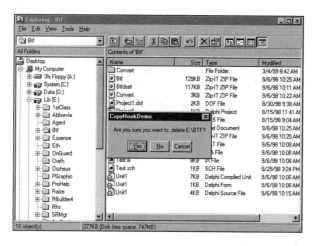

**Figure 9.6**  *Trying to delete the BTF Directory from my E: drive.*

In this section, we looked at copy hook handlers. The first two sections in this chapter concentrated on writing COM servers. In the next, we'll be writing a client program that uses some predefined Windows interfaces. In other words, the interfaces described in the following section are already completely implemented by Windows. All you need to do is make calls to the interfaces to get the work done.

## Shell Links

If you've ever installed a Windows software package, you've seen the effects of a shell link. Shell links are used to create the application's entries in the Start menu, and are also used to create the application's icon on the desktop.

Physically, a shell link is simply a file with a .LNK extension, stored in one of the standard Windows directories. For instance, to create a shortcut on the desktop for the Administrator of a Windows NT system, you place a .LNK file in the C:\WINNT\PROFILES\Administrator\DESKTOP directory. (The directory is different on a Windows 9x machine.) It would be a lot of work for you to go through and try to determine the correct location for a shortcut manually. Windows provides the SHGetSpecialFolderLocation function to retrieve this information for you.

SHGetSpecialFolderLocation is defined in shlobj.pas as follows:

```
function SHGetSpecialFolderLocation(hwndOwner: HWND; nFolder: Integer;
  var ppidl: PItemIDList): HResult; stdcall;
```

The first parameter, hwndOwner, contains the handler to an owner window that can be used if Windows needs to display an error dialog box. nFolder specifies the folder that you want to locate. Valid values for this parameter are listed in Table 9.5. The last parameter, ppidl, is a pointer to an item identifier list specifying the folder's location relative to the desktop. After you obtain this value, you'll use SHGetPathFromIDList to convert it to an absolute path, as shown in the following examples.

*Table 9.5    Valid nFolder Values for SHGetSpecialFolderLocation*

| Value | Description |
| --- | --- |
| CSIDL_ALTSTARTUP | Directory that corresponds to the user's nonlocalized Startup program group. |
| CSIDL_APPDATA | Directory that serves as a common repository for application-specific data. |
| CSIDL_BITBUCKET | Directory containing file objects in the user's Recycle Bin. The location of this directory is not in the Registry; it is marked with the hidden and system attributes to prevent the user from moving or deleting it. |

| Value | Description |
|---|---|
| CSIDL_COMMON_ALTSTARTUP | Directory that corresponds to the nonlocalized Startup program group for all users. |
| CSIDL_COMMON_DESKTOP DIRECTORY | Directory that contains files and folders that appear on the desktop for all users. |
| CSIDL_COMMON_FAVORITES | Directory that serves as a common repository for all users' favorite items. |
| CSIDL_COMMON_PROGRAMS | Directory that contains the directories for the common program groups that appear on the Start menu for all users. |
| CSIDL_COMMON_STARTMENU | Directory that contains the programs and folders that appear on the Start menu for all users. |
| CSIDL_COMMON_STARTUP | Directory that contains the programs that appear in the Startup folder for all users. |
| CSIDL_CONTROLS | Virtual folder containing icons for the Control Panel applications. |
| CSIDL_COOKIES | Directory that serves as a common repository for Internet cookies. |
| CSIDL_DESKTOP | Windows Desktop—virtual folder at the root of the namespace. |
| CSIDL_DESKTOPDIRECTORY | Directory used to physically store file objects on the desktop (not to be confused with the desktop folder itself). |
| CSIDL_DRIVES | My Computer—virtual folder containing everything on the local computer: storage devices, printers, and Control Panel. The folder may also contain mapped network drives. |
| CSIDL_FAVORITES | Directory that serves as a common repository for the user's favorite items. |
| CDISL_FONTS | Virtual folder containing fonts. |
| CSIDL_HISTORY | Directory that serves as a common repository for Internet history items. |
| CSIDL_INTERNET | Virtual folder representing the Internet. |
| CSIDL_INTERNET_CACHE | Directory that serves as a common repository for temporary Internet files. |
| CSIDL_NETHOOD | Directory containing objects that appear in the network neighborhood. |
| CSIDL_NETWORK | Network Neighborhood Folder—virtual folder representing the top level of the network hierarchy. |

*continues* ▶

*Table 9.5    continued*

| Value | Description |
|-------|-------------|
| CSIDL_PERSONAL | Directory that serves as a common repository for documents. |
| CSIDL_PRINTERS | Virtual folder containing installed printers. |
| CSIDL_PRINTHOOD | Directory that serves as a common repository for printer links. |
| CSIDL_PROGRAMS | Directory that contains the user's program groups (which are also directories). |
| CSIDL_RECENT | Directory that contains the user's most recently used documents. |
| CSIDL_SENDTO | Directory that contains Send To menu items. |
| CSIDL_STARTMENU | Directory containing Start menu items. |
| CSIDL_STARTUP | Directory that corresponds to the user's Startup program group. The system starts these programs whenever any user logs on to Windows NT or starts Windows 9x. |
| CSIDL_TEMPLATES | Directory that serves as a common repository for document templates. |

## Shell Link Interfaces

You'll use two COM interfaces when creating shell links: IShellLink and IPersistFile.

IShellLink is defined in shlobj.pas as follows:

```
SID_IShellLinkA      = '{000214EE-0000-0000-C000-000000000046}';

IShellLinkA = interface(IUnknown) { sl }
  [SID_IShellLinkA]
  function GetPath(pszFile: PAnsiChar; cchMaxPath: Integer;
    var pfd: TWin32FindData; fFlags: DWORD): HResult; stdcall;
  function GetIDList(var ppidl: PItemIDList): HResult; stdcall;
  function SetIDList(pidl: PItemIDList): HResult; stdcall;
  function GetDescription(pszName: PAnsiChar; cchMaxName: Integer): HResult;
stdcall;
  function SetDescription(pszName: PAnsiChar): HResult; stdcall;
  function GetWorkingDirectory(pszDir: PAnsiChar; cchMaxPath: Integer): HResult;
stdcall;
  function SetWorkingDirectory(pszDir: PAnsiChar): HResult; stdcall;
  function GetArguments(pszArgs: PAnsiChar; cchMaxPath: Integer): HResult; stdcall;
  function SetArguments(pszArgs: PAnsiChar): HResult; stdcall;
  function GetHotkey(var pwHotkey: Word): HResult; stdcall;
  function SetHotkey(wHotkey: Word): HResult; stdcall;
  function GetShowCmd(out piShowCmd: Integer): HResult; stdcall;
  function SetShowCmd(iShowCmd: Integer): HResult; stdcall;
  function GetIconLocation(pszIconPath: PAnsiChar; cchIconPath: Integer;
```

```
        out piIcon: Integer): HResult; stdcall;
      function SetIconLocation(pszIconPath: PAnsiChar; iIcon: Integer): HResult;
➡stdcall;
      function SetRelativePath(pszPathRel: PAnsiChar; dwReserved: DWORD): HResult;
➡stdcall;
      function Resolve(Wnd: HWND; fFlags: DWORD): HResult; stdcall;
      function SetPath(pszFile: PAnsiChar): HResult; stdcall;
    end;
```

IPersistFile is defined in activex.pas as follows:

```
    IPersistFile = interface(IPersist)
    ['{0000010B-0000-0000-C000-000000000046}']
      function IsDirty: HResult; stdcall;
      function Load(pszFileName: POleStr; dwMode: Longint): HResult;
        stdcall;
      function Save(pszFileName: POleStr; fRemember: BOOL): HResult;
        stdcall;
      function SaveCompleted(pszFileName: POleStr): HResult;
        stdcall;
      function GetCurFile(out pszFileName: POleStr): HResult;
        stdcall;
    end;
```

# Creating a Link

To place a link to Microsoft Paint in the Startup folder, you could write
code as follows:

```
procedure TForm1.Button1Click(Sender: TObject);
var
  ShellLink: IShellLink;
  PersistFile: IPersistFile;
  Dir: array[0 .. MAX_PATH] of char;
  ItemIDList : PItemIDList;
begin
  ShellLink := CreateComObject(CLSID_ShellLink) as IShellLink;
  PersistFile := ShellLink as IPersistFile;

  if GetSystemDirectory(Dir, MAX_PATH) = 0 then
    exit;
  OleCheck(ShellLink.SetPath(PChar(Dir + '\MsPaint.exe')));

  // Find the startup folder
  OleCheck(SHGetSpecialFolderLocation(0, CSIDL_STARTUP, ItemIDList));
  if SHGetPathFromIDList(ItemIDList, Dir) then

    OleCheck(PersistFile.Save(PWideChar(WideString(string(Dir) + '\MsPaint.lnk'),
➡False));
end;
```

Let's take a few moments to examine what's going on in this procedure. First, I'm calling CreateComObject to obtain a reference to the IShellLink interface. Next, I "convert" the IShellLink interface to an IPersistFile interface. Any implementation of IShellLink must also implement IPersistFile, so I know that I can safely obtain an IPersistFile interface from an IShellLink interface.

GetSystemDirectory is a Windows API call that retrieves the Windows system directory (typically C:\WINDOWS\SYSTEM for Windows 9x machines, and C:\WINNT\SYSTEM32 for Windows NT machines). This is the directory that you'll find MsPaint.exe in, assuming that it was installed in the default location when you installed Windows. IShellLink.SetPath tells the COM object where the target file resides.

Next, I call SHGetSpecialFolderLocation to retrieve the Windows startup folder. After I do, I append the link filename (MsPaint.lnk) to that folder. IPersistFile.Save takes a wide string as a parameter, so I typecast to a WideString and then a PWideChar when calling IPersistFile.Save.

There are a number of options that you can set when creating a shortcut, such as working directory, hotkey, description, and arguments. The sample program shown in Listings 9.10 through 9.12 shows how to use IShellLink to set the other attributes of the link.

Even though this code isn't conceptually difficult, sometimes it's difficult to remember the exact code sequences necessary for manipulating shortcuts. In the example that follows, I'll create a set of procedures that you can use to create, load, and save a shortcut. An even better alternative is to create a Delphi component that does the job for you. There are various third-party libraries available that provide components for creating shortcuts, along with other related components for adding tray icons to your application, and so on. The one that I am most familiar with is TurboPower's SysTools library (http://www.turbopower.com).

**Listing 9.10**    *LinkDemo—LinkDemo.dpr*

```
program LinkDemo;

uses
  Forms,
  MainForm in 'MainForm.pas' {frmMain},
  NewLinkForm in 'NewLinkForm.pas' {frmNewShortcut};

{$R *.RES}

begin
  Application.Initialize;
  Application.CreateForm(TfrmMain, frmMain);
  Application.Run;
end.
```

**Listing 9.11**  *LinkDemo—MainForm.pas*

```pascal
unit MainForm;

interface

uses
  SysUtils, Windows, Registry, Messages, Classes, Graphics, Controls,
  Forms, Dialogs, StdCtrls, ActiveX, ShlObj, ExtCtrls, Menus,
  ShellAPI, ComCtrls, CommCtrl;

type
  TfrmMain = class(TForm)
    Panel1: TPanel;
    Panel2: TPanel;
    btnNew: TButton;
    btnOpen: TButton;
    btnSave: TButton;
    Label1: TLabel;
    Label2: TLabel;
    ecTarget: TEdit;
    btnFindTarget: TButton;
    Label3: TLabel;
    ecStartIn: TEdit;
    Label4: TLabel;
    Label5: TLabel;
    btnChangeIcon: TButton;
    cbRun: TComboBox;
    OpenTarget: TOpenDialog;
    Label6: TLabel;
    Label7: TLabel;
    ecDescription: TEdit;
    ecArguments: TEdit;
    OpenIcon: TOpenDialog;
    hkShortcut: THotKey;
    ecLinkName: TEdit;
    GroupBox1: TGroupBox;
    imgIcon: TImage;
    UpDown1: TUpDown;
    procedure btnNewClick(Sender: TObject);
    procedure btnFindTargetClick(Sender: TObject);
    procedure btnChangeIconClick(Sender: TObject);
    procedure UpDown1Click(Sender: TObject; Button: TUDBtnType);
    procedure btnSaveClick(Sender: TObject);
    procedure btnOpenClick(Sender: TObject);
    procedure ecTargetChange(Sender: TObject);
  private
    { Private declarations }
    FLinkFile: string;
    FLocation: Integer;
    FTarget: string;
    FDescription: string;
    FArguments: string;
```

*continues* ▶

**Listing 9.11** *continued*

```
    FIconFile: string;
    FIconIndex: Integer;
    FStartIn: string;
    FShortcut: Word;
    FRun: Integer;
    FLoading: Boolean;
    procedure SetFields;
    procedure CreateShortcut(const ALinkFile: WideString; AFolder: Integer);
    procedure LoadShortcut(const ALinkFile: WideString);
    procedure SaveShortcut(const ALinkFile: WideString);
    procedure ShowIcon;
  public
    { Public declarations }
  end;

var
  frmMain: TfrmMain;

implementation

uses
  ComObj, NewLinkForm;

{$R *.DFM}

const
  RunCommands: array[0 .. 2] of Integer =
    (SW_SHOWNORMAL, SW_SHOWMINIMIZED, SW_SHOWMAXIMIZED);

procedure TfrmMain.CreateShortcut(const ALinkFile: WideString;
  AFolder: Integer);
var
  ShellLink: IShellLink;
  PersistFile: IPersistFile;
  ItemIDList : PItemIDList;
  Dir: array[0 .. MAX_PATH] of char;
begin
  ShellLink := CreateComObject(CLSID_ShellLink) as IShellLink;
  PersistFile := ShellLink as IPersistFile;

  // Find the startup folder
  OleCheck(SHGetSpecialFolderLocation(0, AFolder, ItemIDList));
  if SHGetPathFromIDList(ItemIDList, Dir) then begin
    FLinkFile := string(Dir) + '\' + ALinkFile + '.lnk';
    OleCheck(PersistFile.Save(PWideChar(WideString(FLinkFile)), True));
  end;
end;

procedure TfrmMain.LoadShortcut(const ALinkFile: WideString);
var
  ShellLink: IShellLink;
```

```
    PersistFile: IPersistFile;
    AStr: array[0 .. MAX_PATH] of char;
    FindData: TWin32FindData;
    ShowCmd: Integer;
  begin
    FLoading := True;
    try
      ShellLink := CreateComObject(CLSID_ShellLink) as IShellLink;
      PersistFile := ShellLink as IPersistFile;
      OleCheck(PersistFile.Load(PWideChar(ALinkFile), STGM_READ));

      // Gather information from shortcut
      FLinkFile := ALinkFile;
      OleCheck(ShellLink.GetPath(AStr, MAX_PATH, FindData, SLGP_SHORTPATH));
      FTarget := AStr;
      OleCheck(ShellLink.GetArguments(AStr, MAX_PATH));
      FArguments := AStr;
      OleCheck(ShellLink.GetDescription(AStr, MAX_PATH));
      FDescription := AStr;
      OleCheck(ShellLink.GetWorkingDirectory(AStr, MAX_PATH));
      FStartIn := AStr;
      OleCheck(ShellLink.GetIconLocation(AStr, MAX_PATH, FIconIndex));
      FIconFile := AStr;
      if FIconFile = '' then
        FIconFile := FTarget;
      OleCheck(ShellLink.GetShowCmd(ShowCmd));
      FRun := ShowCmd - 1;
      OleCheck(ShellLink.GetHotKey(FShortcut));

      // Display the information
      SetFields;
    finally
      FLoading := False;
    end;
  end;

procedure TfrmMain.SaveShortcut(const ALinkFile: WideString);
var
  ShellLink: IShellLink;
  PersistFile: IPersistFile;
  HotKey: Word;
  HKMod: Byte;
begin
  ShellLink := CreateComObject(CLSID_ShellLink) as IShellLink;
  PersistFile := ShellLink as IPersistFile;
  OleCheck(PersistFile.Load(PWideChar(ALinkFile), STGM_SHARE_DENY_WRITE));

  // Assign hotkey
  HotKey := hkShortcut.HotKey;
  HKMod := 0;
  if hkCtrl in hkShortcut.Modifiers then
    HKMod := HKMod or HOTKEYF_CONTROL;
```

*continues* ▶

**Listing 9.11**    *continued*

```
if hkShift in hkShortcut.Modifiers then
  HKMod := HKMod or HOTKEYF_SHIFT;
if hkAlt in hkShortcut.Modifiers then
  HKMod := HKMod or HOTKEYF_ALT;
if hkExt in hkShortcut.Modifiers then
  HKMod := HKMod or HOTKEYF_EXT;
HotKey := (HKMod shl 8) + HotKey;

// Set parameters
OleCheck(ShellLink.SetPath(PChar(ecTarget.Text)));
OleCheck(ShellLink.SetIconLocation(PChar(FIconFile), FIconIndex));
OleCheck(ShellLink.SetDescription(PChar(ecDescription.Text)));
OleCheck(ShellLink.SetWorkingDirectory(PChar(ecStartIn.Text)));
OleCheck(ShellLink.SetArguments(PChar(ecArguments.Text)));
OleCheck(ShellLink.SetHotkey(HotKey));
OleCheck(ShellLink.SetShowCmd(RunCommands[cbRun.ItemIndex]));

// Save shortcut
OleCheck(PersistFile.Save(PWideChar(ALinkFile), True));
end;

procedure TfrmMain.ShowIcon;
begin
  UpDown1.Max := ExtractIcon(hInstance, PChar(FIconFile),
    UINT(-1)) - 1;

  imgIcon.Picture.Icon.Handle := ExtractIcon(hInstance,
    PChar(FIconFile), FIconIndex);
end;

procedure TfrmMain.btnNewClick(Sender: TObject);
var
  frmNewShortcut: TfrmNewShortcut;
begin
  frmNewShortcut := TfrmNewShortcut.Create(nil);
  try
    if frmNewShortcut.ShowModal = mrOk then begin
      FLocation := frmNewShortcut.Folder;
      FLinkFile := frmNewShortcut.ecName.Text;
      CreateShortcut(FLinkFile, FLocation);

      // Enable fields and buttons
      UpDown1.Enabled := True;
      ecTarget.Enabled := True;
      ecDescription.Enabled := True;
      ecArguments.Enabled := True;
      ecStartIn.Enabled := True;
      hkShortcut.Enabled := True;
      cbRun.Enabled := True;
      btnFindTarget.Enabled := True;
      btnChangeIcon.Enabled := True;
      btnSave.Enabled := True;
```

```
        // Blank out fields
        FTarget := '';
        FDescription := '';
        FArguments := '';
        FIconFile := '';
        FIconIndex := 0;
        FStartIn := '';
        FShortcut := 0;
        FRun := 0;
        SetFields;
      end;
    finally
      frmNewShortcut.Free;
    end;
end;

procedure TfrmMain.SetFields;
var
  H: Byte;
  Modifier: THKModifiers;
begin
  ecLinkName.Text := FLinkFile;
  ecTarget.Text := FTarget;
  ecDescription.Text := FDescription;
  ecArguments.Text := FArguments;
  ecStartIn.Text := FStartIn;
  cbRun.ItemIndex := FRun;

  H := Hi(FShortcut);
  Modifier := [];
  if (H and HOTKEYF_ALT) = HOTKEYF_ALT then
    Include(Modifier, hkAlt);
  if (H and HOTKEYF_CONTROL) = HOTKEYF_CONTROL then
    Include(Modifier, hkCtrl);
  if (H and HOTKEYF_EXT) = HOTKEYF_EXT then
    Include(Modifier, hkExt);
  if (H and HOTKEYF_SHIFT) = HOTKEYF_SHIFT then
    Include(Modifier, hkShift);
  hkShortcut.HotKey := FShortcut;
  hkShortcut.Modifiers := Modifier;

  ShowIcon;
  ActiveControl := ecTarget;
end;

procedure TfrmMain.btnFindTargetClick(Sender: TObject);
begin
  if OpenTarget.Execute then begin
    ecTarget.Text := OpenTarget.FileName;
    FIconFile := ecTarget.Text;
    FIconIndex := 0;
```

*continues* ▶

## Listing 9.11    *continued*

```
    UpDown1.Max := ExtractIcon(hInstance, PChar(FIconFile),
      UINT(-1)) - 1;
    UpDown1.Position := 0;

    ShowIcon;
  end;
end;

procedure TfrmMain.btnChangeIconClick(Sender: TObject);
begin
  if OpenIcon.Execute then begin
    FIconFile := OpenIcon.FileName;
    FIconIndex := 0;
    UpDown1.Max := ExtractIcon(hInstance, PChar(FIconFile),
      UINT(-1)) - 1;
    UpDown1.Position := 0;

    ShowIcon;
  end;
end;

procedure TfrmMain.UpDown1Click(Sender: TObject; Button: TUDBtnType);
begin
  FIconIndex := UpDown1.Position;
  ShowIcon;
end;

procedure TfrmMain.btnSaveClick(Sender: TObject);
begin
  // Make sure the user specified a target
  if ecTarget.Text = '' then begin
    ShowMessage('Please specify a target file before saving.');
    exit;
  end;

  SaveShortcut(FLinkFile);
end;

procedure TfrmMain.btnOpenClick(Sender: TObject);
begin
  if OpenTarget.Execute then begin
    LoadShortcut(OpenTarget.FileName);
  end;
end;

procedure TfrmMain.ecTargetChange(Sender: TObject);
begin
  if not FLoading then begin
    FIconFile := ecTarget.Text;
    FIconIndex := 0;
```

```
    ShowIcon;
  end;
end;

end.
end.
```

---

**Listing 9.12**   *LinkDemo—NewLinkForm.pas*

```
unit NewLinkForm;

interface

uses
  Windows, Messages, SysUtils, Classes, Graphics, Controls, Forms,
  Dialogs, StdCtrls, ExtCtrls, ShlObj;

type
  TfrmNewShortcut = class(TForm)
    pnlBottom: TPanel;
    pnlClient: TPanel;
    btnOK: TButton;
    btnCancel: TButton;
    Label1: TLabel;
    cbLocation: TComboBox;
    Label2: TLabel;
    ecName: TEdit;
    procedure btnOKClick(Sender: TObject);
    procedure cbLocationClick(Sender: TObject);
    procedure FormCreate(Sender: TObject);
  private
    FFolder: Integer;
    { Private declarations }
  public
    { Public declarations }
    property Folder: Integer read FFolder;
  end;

implementation

type
  TFolderRec = record
    FolderName: string;
    FolderID: Integer;
  end;

const
{$IFDEF VER100}
  CSIDL_INTERNET = $0001;
  CSIDL_ALTSTARTUP = $001d;
  CSIDL_COMMON_ALTSTARTUP = $001e;
```

## Listing 9.12    *continued*

```
  CSIDL_COMMON_FAVORITES = $001f;
  CSIDL_INTERNET_CACHE = $0020;
  CSIDL_COOKIES = $0021;
  CSIDL_HISTORY = $0022;
{$ENDIF}

  MAX_FOLDERS = 30;

  Folders: Array[0 .. MAX_FOLDERS - 1] of TFolderRec = (
    (FolderName: 'Alt Startup'; FolderID: CSIDL_ALTSTARTUP),
    (FolderName: 'App Data'; FolderID: CSIDL_APPDATA),
    (FolderName: 'Bit Bucket'; FolderID: CSIDL_BITBUCKET),
    (FolderName: 'Common Alt Startup'; FolderID: CSIDL_COMMON_ALTSTARTUP),
    (FolderName: 'Common Desktop Directory'; FolderID: CSIDL_COMMON_DESKTOPDIRECTORY),
    (FolderName: 'Common Favorites'; FolderID: CSIDL_COMMON_FAVORITES),
    (FolderName: 'Common Programs'; FolderID: CSIDL_COMMON_PROGRAMS),
    (FolderName: 'Common Start Menu'; FolderID: CSIDL_COMMON_STARTMENU),
    (FolderName: 'Common Startup'; FolderID: CSIDL_COMMON_STARTUP),
    (FolderName: 'Controls'; FolderID: CSIDL_CONTROLS),
    (FolderName: 'Cookies'; FolderID: CSIDL_COOKIES),
    (FolderName: 'Desktop'; FolderID: CSIDL_DESKTOP),
    (FolderName: 'Desktop Directory'; FolderID: CSIDL_DESKTOPDIRECTORY),
    (FolderName: 'Drives'; FolderID: CSIDL_DRIVES),
    (FolderName: 'Favorites'; FolderID: CSIDL_FAVORITES),
    (FolderName: 'Fonts'; FolderID: CSIDL_FONTS),
    (FolderName: 'History'; FolderID: CSIDL_HISTORY),
    (FolderName: 'Internet'; FolderID: CSIDL_INTERNET),
    (FolderName: 'Internet Cache'; FolderID: CSIDL_INTERNET_CACHE),
    (FolderName: 'Network Neighborhood'; FolderID: CSIDL_NETHOOD),
    (FolderName: 'Network'; FolderID: CSIDL_NETWORK),
    (FolderName: 'Personal'; FolderID: CSIDL_PERSONAL),
    (FolderName: 'Printers'; FolderID: CSIDL_PRINTERS),
    (FolderName: 'Printer Neighborhood'; FolderID: CSIDL_PRINTHOOD),
    (FolderName: 'Programs'; FolderID: CSIDL_PROGRAMS),
    (FolderName: 'Recent Files'; FolderID: CSIDL_RECENT),
    (FolderName: 'Send To'; FolderID: CSIDL_SENDTO),
    (FolderName: 'Start Menu'; FolderID: CSIDL_STARTMENU),
    (FolderName: 'Startup'; FolderID: CSIDL_STARTUP),
    (FolderName: 'Templates'; FolderID: CSIDL_TEMPLATES)
  );

{$R *.DFM}

procedure TfrmNewShortcut.btnOKClick(Sender: TObject);
begin
  if ecName.Text = '' then begin
    ModalResult := mrNone;
    ShowMessage('Please enter a file name for the shortcut.');
  end;
end;
```

```
procedure TfrmNewShortcut.cbLocationClick(Sender: TObject);
begin
  FFolder := Folders[cbLocation.ItemIndex].FolderID;
end;

procedure TfrmNewShortcut.FormCreate(Sender: TObject);
var
  Index: Integer;
begin
  for Index := 0 to High(Folders) - 1 do
    cbLocation.Items.Add(Folders[Index].FolderName);
  cbLocation.ItemIndex := 0;
  FFolder := Folders[0].FolderID;
end;

end.
```

Figure 9.7 shows LinkDemo at runtime.

**Figure 9.7**    *LinkDemo with a newly created shortcut on the desktop.*

This section showed you how to take advantage of the Windows shell to create shortcuts on your desktop, in the Start menu, or in numerous other locations on your computer. In the next section, we'll take a look at tray icons.

## Tray Icons

Like the previous section, this section discusses a commonly used Windows shell phenomenon—tray icons. The tray sits, by default, at the lower right-hand side of the Windows desktop. Figure 9.8 shows the tray on my home machine.

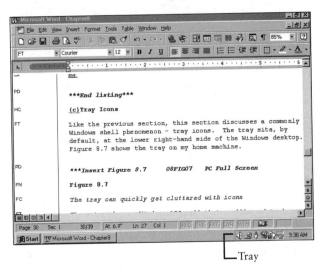

Tray

**Figure 9.8** *The tray can quickly get cluttered with icons.*

There is only one Windows API call that you'll need to learn to work with
tray icons. That function is Shell_NotifyIcon, and is defined in shellapi.pas
as follows:

```
function Shell_NotifyIcon(dwMessage: DWORD; lpData: PNotifyIconData): BOOL; stdcall;
```

Shell_NotifyIcon takes two parameters. The first, dwMessage, indicates the
operation you want to perform. Valid values for this parameter are listed in
Table 9.6.

*Table 9.6    Valid dwMessage Values for Shell_NotifyIcon*

| Value | Description |
| --- | --- |
| NIM_ADD | Adds an icon to the status area |
| NIM_DELETE | Deletes an icon from the status area |
| NIM_MODIFY | Modifies an icon in the status area |

The other parameter, lpData, contains supporting data for the operation. It
is a pointer to a TNotifyIconData structure, defined in shellapi.pas as

```
TNotifyIconData = record
  cbSize: DWORD;
  Wnd: HWND;
  uID: UINT;
  uFlags: UINT;
  uCallbackMessage: UINT;
  hIcon: HICON;
  szTip: array [0..63] of AnsiChar;
end;
```

As is the custom with many of Microsoft's newer APIs, cbSize contains the size in bytes of the TNotifyIconData structure. Wnd is the handle of a window that will receive notification messages on the tray icon's behalf (more on that in the section "Tray Icon Messages").

uID should contain a unique number that you can use to refer to the taskbar icon. uFlags contains a set of flags that indicates which of the other fields in the record contain valid data. Acceptable values for the uFlags field are listed in Table 9.7.

*Table 9.7    Valid uFlags Values for TnotifyIconData*

| Value | Description |
|---|---|
| NIF_ICON | The hIcon member is valid. |
| NIF_MESSAGE | The uCallback member is valid. |
| NIF_TIP | The szTip member is valid. |

uCallbackMessage is an application defined message identifier. Windows will specify this identifier when sending messages to the window specified in Wnd.

hIcon contains a handle to the icon to add, delete, or modify.

szTip contains a string to use as a tooltip for the tray icon.

## Tray Icon Messages

As I alluded to a moment ago, tray icons don't actually respond to any Windows messages. In order for your application to detect the user clicking the tray icon, for example, you must create a (hidden) window whose sole purpose is to respond to messages on the tray icon's behalf.

The act of creating this notification window is not particularly difficult, but it is cumbersome enough that you won't want to have to remember the details every time you use a tray icon in your application. For that reason, in this section we'll build a Delphi component that hides all the complexities from you.

## The TDCPTrayIcon Component

Listing 9.13 shows the entire source code for the TDCPTrayIcon component. I will not go through the code line by line, but there are a number of points that I will go over in a little detail.

First, the Create method uses AllocateHWnd to create a window handle responsible for responding to messages on the tray icon's behalf.

The Loaded method, called after the component has been created, takes care of assigning the application's icon to the component if the user hasn't explicitly assigned an icon.

NotificationWndProc is the window procedure for the window created by AllocateHWnd. It intercepts double-clicks and right-clicks the tray icon. Double-clicks are reported to the application through the OnDblClick event. Right-clicks are automatically used to display a popup menu, if the user assigned one to the component's FPopupMenu property.

SendTrayMessage is the method responsible for making calls to Shell_NotifyIcon. It automatically sets the flags necessary for the call, based on property settings of the component. Making all calls to Shell_NotifyIcon through a single access method reduces the chances of error. If there is only one place where parameters might be set incorrectly, there is only one place you need to look when something goes wrong.

ShowInTaskbar and RemoveFromTaskbar take care of showing and removing the application from the taskbar, respectively. When the application is minimized (and visible in the tray), you typically don't want the taskbar cluttered with an entry for the application. TDCPTrayIcon automatically makes calls to these methods to hide and show the application in the taskbar at the appropriate times.

ShowTrayIcon and RemoveTrayIcon show and remove the icon from the tray. These functions are called automatically when the component is created and destroyed, and also when the Active property of the component is toggled.

---

**Listing 9.13**  *TrayIcon.pas*

```
unit TrayIcon;

interface

uses
  Windows, Messages, SysUtils, Classes, Graphics, Controls, Forms,
  Dialogs, Menus, ShellAPI;

type
  TDCPTrayIcon = class(TComponent)
  private
    { Private declarations }
    FNotificationHandle: HWnd;
    FTrayIcon: TIcon;
    FShowHint: Boolean;
    FHint: string;
    FActive: Boolean;
    FCurrentlyActive: Boolean;
    FOnDblClick: TNotifyEvent;
    FPopupMenu: TPopupMenu;
    procedure NotificationWndProc(var Message : TMessage);
    procedure SetShowHint(const Value: Boolean);
    procedure SetHint(const Value: string);
```

```
    procedure SetTrayIcon(const Value: TIcon);
    procedure SetActive(const Value: Boolean);
    procedure SetPopupMenu(const Value: TPopupMenu);
  protected
    { Protected declarations }
    procedure DoDblClick;
    procedure Loaded; override;
    procedure OnAppMinimize(Sender: TObject);
    function SendTrayMessage(AMessage: DWORD): Boolean;
  public
    { Public declarations }
    constructor Create(AOwner: TComponent); override;
    destructor Destroy; override;
    procedure RemoveTrayIcon;
    procedure RestoreApp;
    procedure ShowTrayIcon;
    procedure RemoveFromTaskbar;
    procedure ShowInTaskbar;
  published
    { Published declarations }
    property Active: Boolean read FActive write SetActive;
    property Hint: string read FHint write SetHint;
    property OnDblClick: TNotifyEvent read FOnDblClick write FOnDblClick;
    property PopupMenu: TPopupMenu read FPopupMenu write SetPopupMenu;
    property ShowHint: Boolean read FShowHint write SetShowHint;
    property TrayIcon: TIcon read FTrayIcon write SetTrayIcon;
  end;

procedure Register;

implementation

const
  ID_TRAYICON = 1;
  UWM_TRAYICON = WM_USER + 1;

procedure Register;
begin
  RegisterComponents('DCP', [TDCPTrayIcon]);
end;

{ TDCPTrayIcon }

constructor TDCPTrayIcon.Create(AOwner: TComponent);
begin
  inherited Create(AOwner);

  FNotificationHandle := AllocateHWnd(NotificationWndProc);
  FTrayIcon := TIcon.Create;

  Application.OnMinimize := OnAppMinimize;
end;
```

*continues* ▶

**Listing 9.13**    *continued*

```
destructor TDCPTrayIcon.Destroy;
begin
  if FCurrentlyActive then
    RemoveTrayIcon;

  FTrayIcon.Free;

  if FNotificationHandle <> 0 then
    DeallocateHWnd(FNotificationHandle);

  inherited Destroy;
end;

procedure TDCPTrayIcon.DoDblClick;
begin
  if Assigned(OnDblClick) then
    OnDblClick(self);
end;

procedure TDCPTrayIcon.Loaded;
begin
  inherited Loaded;

  if not (csDesigning in ComponentState) then begin
    if FTrayIcon.Handle = 0 then
      FTrayIcon.Assign(Application.Icon);
  end;

  SetTrayIcon(FTrayIcon);

  if FActive then
    ShowTrayIcon;
end;

procedure TDCPTrayIcon.NotificationWndProc(var Message: TMessage);
var
  Pt: TPoint;
begin
  if Message.Msg = UWM_TRAYICON then begin
    case Message.lParam of
      WM_LBUTTONDBLCLK:
        DoDblClick;

      WM_RBUTTONDOWN:
        if Assigned(FPopupMenu) then begin
          SetForegroundWindow(FNotificationHandle);
          GetCursorPos(Pt);
          FPopupMenu.Popup(Pt.X, Pt.Y);
        end;
    end;
  end;
end;
```

```
procedure TDCPTrayIcon.OnAppMinimize(Sender: TObject);
begin
  if FCurrentlyActive then
    RemoveFromTaskbar;
end;

procedure TDCPTrayIcon.RemoveFromTaskbar;
begin
  if not (csDesigning in ComponentState) then begin
    ShowWindow(Application.Handle, SW_HIDE);
    ShowWindow(Application.MainForm.Handle, SW_HIDE);
  end;
end;

procedure TDCPTrayIcon.RemoveTrayIcon;
begin
  if FCurrentlyActive then
    if SendTrayMessage(NIM_DELETE) then begin
      FCurrentlyActive := False;

      ShowInTaskbar;
    end;
end;

procedure TDCPTrayIcon.RestoreApp;
begin
  ShowInTaskbar;
  SetForegroundWindow(Application.MainForm.Handle);
end;

function TDCPTrayIcon.SendTrayMessage(AMessage: DWORD): Boolean;
var
  Flags: Integer;
  NotifyIconData: TNotifyIconData;
begin
  Result := True;
  if csDesigning in ComponentState then
    exit;

  Flags := NIF_MESSAGE or NIF_ICON;
  if FShowHint then
    Flags := Flags or NIF_TIP;

  FillChar(NotifyIconData, SizeOf(NotifyIconData), 0);
  with NotifyIconData do begin
    cbSize := SizeOf(TNotifyIconData);
    Wnd := FNotificationHandle;
    uID := ID_TRAYICON;
    uFlags := Flags;
    uCallBackMessage := UWM_TRAYICON;
    hIcon := FTrayIcon.Handle;
    StrLCopy(szTip, PChar(FHint), SizeOf(szTip));
  end;
```

*continues* ▶

**Listing 9.13** *continued*

```
  Result := Shell_NotifyIcon(AMessage, @NotifyIconData);
end;

procedure TDCPTrayIcon.SetActive(const Value: Boolean);
begin
  FActive := Value;

  if FActive then
    ShowTrayIcon
  else
    RemoveTrayIcon;
end;

procedure TDCPTrayIcon.SetHint(const Value: string);
begin
  FHint := Value;

  SendTrayMessage(NIM_MODIFY);
end;

procedure TDCPTrayIcon.SetPopupMenu(const Value: TPopupMenu);
begin
  FPopupMenu := Value;
end;

procedure TDCPTrayIcon.SetShowHint(const Value: Boolean);
begin
  FShowHint := Value;

  SendTrayMessage(NIM_MODIFY);
end;

procedure TDCPTrayIcon.SetTrayIcon(const Value: TIcon);
begin
  FTrayIcon.Assign(Value);

  SendTrayMessage(NIM_MODIFY);
end;

procedure TDCPTrayIcon.ShowInTaskbar;
begin
  if not (csDesigning in ComponentState) then begin
    if Application.MainForm <> nil then
      ShowWindow(Application.MainForm.Handle, SW_SHOWNORMAL);
    ShowWindow(Application.Handle, SW_SHOWNORMAL);
  end;
end;

procedure TDCPTrayIcon.ShowTrayIcon;
```

```
begin
  if SendTrayMessage(NIM_ADD) then
    FCurrentlyActive := True;
end;

end.
```

This component certainly gets the job done, but it is not meant to be an industrial-strength component. There are third-party libraries available that provide much more functionality, such as animated tray icons. Again, the one that I am most familiar with is SysTools from TurboPower Software.

## A Sample Tray Application

Now that you've seen how to write a tray icon component, I'll show you a simple application that displays an icon in the tray. Listings 9.14 and 9.15 show the source code for a simple application that makes use of the TDCPTrayIcon component.

**Listing 9.14** *TrayDemo—TrayDemo.dpr*

```
program TrayDemo;

uses
  Forms,
  MainForm in 'MainForm.pas' {Form1};

{$R *.RES}

begin
  Application.Initialize;
  Application.CreateForm(TForm1, Form1);
  Application.Run;
end.
```

**Listing 9.15** *TrayDemo—MainForm.pas*

```
unit MainForm;

interface

uses
  Windows, Messages, SysUtils, Classes, Graphics, Controls, Forms, Dialogs,
  TrayIcon, Menus, StdCtrls;

type
  TForm1 = class(TForm)
    DCPTrayIcon1: TDCPTrayIcon;
    PopupMenu1: TPopupMenu;
    Restore1: TMenuItem;
```

```
    Close1: TMenuItem;
    Label1: TLabel;
    procedure DCPTrayIcon1DblClick(Sender: TObject);
    procedure Close1Click(Sender: TObject);
  private
    { Private declarations }
  public
    { Public declarations }
  end;

var
  Form1: TForm1;

implementation

{$R *.DFM}

procedure TForm1.DCPTrayIcon1DblClick(Sender: TObject);
begin
  DCPTrayIcon1.RestoreApp;
end;

procedure TForm1.Close1Click(Sender: TObject);
begin
  Close;
end;

end.
```

Figure 9.9 shows what the TrayDemo application looks like at runtime.

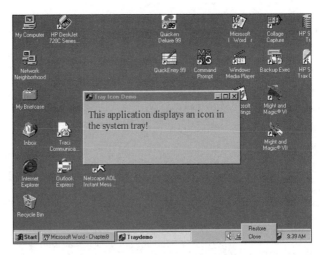

**Figure 9.9**   *TDCPTrayIcon can automatically inherit the application's icon.*

As you saw in this section, writing programs that make use of the Windows tray is not that complicated. With the creation of a Delphi component, the code required by the client application is only a handful of lines.

In the next section, we'll discuss a more complicated shell extension—property sheet handlers.

## Property Sheet Handlers

When you right-click a file in the Windows Explorer, you'll see a Properties... menu item. Selecting that menu item brings up properties for the selected file. For many files, all you see is a General tab, which shows the program name, location, and attributes. Figure 9.10 shows a properties dialog box for a bitmap file on my hard drive.

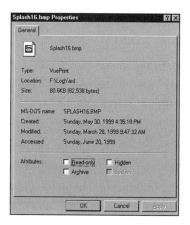

**Figure 9.10**    *Standard Windows Properties dialog box.*

For other files, such as application files and DLLs, you'll see an additional Version tab that shows version information stored in the file (see Figure 9.11).

Other file types may have additional property sheets displayed, showing other types of information. Wouldn't it be cool if you could define and display custom property sheets for file types used by your applications? Well, you can. The process isn't as clean as the previous shell features I've shown you, but if you follow the guidelines shown here carefully, it's not that difficult.

In Chapter 7, "Structured Storage," we created a CarDemo application that stores the vehicle name and model year in a separate stream within the structured storage file CARS.CAR. I'll show you how you can create a property sheet handler to display that information in a separate page of the Properties dialog box.

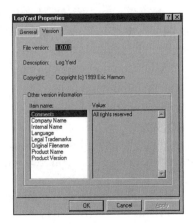

**Figure 9.11**    *Version Information displayed in the Properties dialog box.*

## Creating a Dialog Template

The first thing you need to do is create a dialog template for the new property sheet. If you're thinking 'Huh?,' then Delphi is probably your first programming language, and you have never seen a dialog template. If you've done other work with Visual C++ or Borland C++, you should know what a dialog template is.

At any rate, Delphi itself doesn't deal with dialog templates. This makes Delphi programming easier, but unfortunately, it makes this project slightly more difficult. You have three options for creating a property sheet template:

- You can use another programming tool, such as Visual C++, to create the dialog template. This is what I did to create this example.

- If you have Delphi 5 or later (or other Borland tools such as the Delphi 1 RAD pack or Borland C++), you can use the included Resource Workshop to create the dialog template.

- If all else fails, you can use any editor to manually create the .RC file containing the dialog template and then use Delphi's command line resource compiler, brcc, to compile the .RC file into a dialog template. I don't recommend this route unless you're *really* desperate, since it is extremely difficult to create a dialog box nonvisually. See Listing 9.16 for an example of a .RC file for a simple dialog box.

Regardless of which method you select, you'll wind up with an .RC file with a dialog template in it. Listing 9.16 shows PPage.RC, which contains the dialog template I created with Visual C++.

**Listing 9.16**    *PPage.rc: Dialog Template for Use with PropDemo.DLL*

```
#define IDD_CARPROPS              106
#define IDC_VEHICLENAME          1000
#define IDC_MODELYEAR            1001
#define IDC_STATIC                 -1

IDD_CARPROPS DIALOG DISCARDABLE  0, 0, 210, 154
STYLE WS_CHILD ¦ WS_VISIBLE ¦ WS_CAPTION
CAPTION "Car Information"
FONT 8, "MS Sans Serif"
BEGIN
    LTEXT           "Vehicle name:",IDC_STATIC,7,9,52,8
    LTEXT           "Model year:",IDC_STATIC,7,24,52,8
    EDITTEXT        IDC_VEHICLENAME,75,7,128,12,ES_AUTOHSCROLL ¦ WS_DISABLED
    EDITTEXT        IDC_MODELYEAR,75,22,40,12,ES_AUTOHSCROLL ¦ WS_DISABLED
END
```

Notice that the dialog box is defined with style WS_CHILD | WS_VISIBLE | WS_CAPTION. The symbol "|" is a bitwise, or operator, as those of you also familiar with C or C++ will recognize.

After you have an .RC file, you can create a .RES file from it by issuing the following command:

```
brcc32 PPage.rc
```

This will create the file PPage.res.

## Property Sheet Handler Interfaces

Property sheet handlers must implement the IShellExtInit and IShellPropSheetExt interfaces. As usual, you can use Delphi's COM Object Wizard to create the skeleton project (Delphi 3 users will enter the code shown in Listing 9.16 manually). From the main menu, select File, New. On the ActiveX page of the Object Repository, select ActiveX Library. Select File, New again, and on the ActiveX page of the Object Repository, select COM Object.

Fill out the COM Object wizard to look like Figure 9.12.

When you press OK, Delphi generates the code shown in Listing 9.17. Save the file as PropSheet.pas.

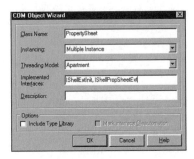

**Figure 9.12**    *COM Object Wizard for a Property Sheet Handler.*

**Listing 9.17**    *Skeleton File Generated by Delphi's COM Object Wizard*

```
unit PropSheet;

interface

uses
  Windows, ActiveX, ComObj;

type
  TPropertySheet = class(TComObject, IShellExtInit, IShellPropSheetExt)
  protected
    {Declare IShellExtInit methods here}
    {Declare IShellPropSheetExt methods here}
  end;

const
  Class_PropertySheet: TGUID = '{20F943E1-2751-11D3-B800-0040F67455FE}';

implementation

uses ComServ;

initialization
  TComObjectFactory.Create(ComServer, TPropertySheet, Class_PropertySheet,
    'PropertySheet', '', ciMultiInstance, tmApartment);
end.
```

By now, you're familiar with the IShellExtInit interface. IShellPropSheetExt is defined in shlobj.pas as follows:

```
  SID_IShellPropSheetExt = '{000214E9-0000-0000-C000-000000000046}';
  IShellPropSheetExt = interface(IUnknown)
    [SID_IShellPropSheetExt]
    function AddPages(lpfnAddPage: TFNAddPropSheetPage; lParam: LPARAM): HResult;
stdcall;
    function ReplacePage(uPageID: UINT; lpfnReplaceWith: TFNAddPropSheetPage;
      lParam: LPARAM): HResult; stdcall;
    end;
```

There are only two methods defined by this interface: AddPage and ReplacePage. AddPage is used to add a new page to the property sheet. ReplacePage is used to replace an existing page in the property sheet. We won't be using ReplacePage in this example (although we must provide an empty handler, because all methods of an interface must be provided by an implementation of that interface).

Listings 9.18 through 9.20 show the complete source code for the property sheet handler after the interfaces have been implemented. I won't discuss the implementation of the IShellExtInit interface, because I've already discussed it earlier in this chapter. Also, I've implemented a custom TObjectFactory descendent to handle registering and unregistering the COM server, just as in earlier projects.

At the top of the implementation section, you'll see the following constants:

```
const
  IDD_CARPROPS     = 106;
  IDC_VEHICLENAME  = 1000;
  IDC_MODELYEAR    = 1001;
```

These numbers mirror the constants defined at the top of PPage.rc, and are used to reference the dialog box and the edit controls placed on the dialog box.

Just below that, the line that reads

```
{$R PPAGE.RES}
```

ensures that the dialog template is linked into this project's DLL file.

Skipping down to the AddPages method, I've written some fairly generic code to add the new page to the property sheet. First, a TPropSheetPage record is filled out. The pszTemplate field specifies the resource that the new property page is created from. Notice that I've set this to IDD_ORDPROPS, the number assigned to the dialog box in the PPage.rc file. pfnDlgProc specifies a dialog procedure (much like a window procedure) to use when responding to dialog messages. pfnCallback specifies a callback procedure to use when certain events occur (such as, when the property page is destroyed). Also, note that I set psp.lParam to self. After control passes to the dialog procedure, I will have no other way to reference the TPropertySheetObject, so I store a "pointer" to it here.

After the property page is created by the CreatePropertySheetPage and lpfnAddPage calls, you'll see a call to _AddRef. In Chapter 1, I discussed the use of _AddRef and _Release, and told you that you'll seldom need to use these methods. I did so here because without it, the TPropertySheet class is destroyed before the COM server is destroyed (after the property page is created, the only procedures that need to run are the dialog procedure and the callback procedure, neither of which are methods of TPropertySheet). However, I've stored the name of the selected file in the private field FFileName of TPropertySheet. The call to _AddRef guarantees that TPropertySheet won't be destroyed at least until I call _Release.

**Listing 9.18**    *PropDemo—PropDemo.dpr*

```
library PropDemo;

uses
  Windows,
  ComServ,
  PropSheet in 'PropSheet.pas',
  PropDemo_TLB in 'PropDemo_TLB.pas';

exports
  DllGetClassObject,
  DllCanUnloadNow,
  DllRegisterServer,
  DllUnregisterServer;

{$R *.TLB}

{$R *.RES}

end.
```

**Listing 9.19**    *PropDemo—PropDemo_TLB.pas*

```
unit PropDemo_TLB;

// ********************************************************************* //
// WARNING                                                             //
// -------                                                             //
// The types declared in this file were generated from data read from a //
// Type Library. If this type library is explicitly or indirectly (via //
// another type library referring to this type library) re-imported, or the //
// 'Refresh' command of the Type Library Editor activated while editing the //
// Type Library, the contents of this file will be regenerated and all //
// manual modifications will be lost.                                  //
// ********************************************************************* //

// PASTLWTR : $Revision:   1.11.1.75  $
// File generated on 6/19/99 10:25:44 AM from Type Library described below.

// ********************************************************************* //
// Type Lib: J:\Book\samples\Chap9\PropDemo\PropDemo.tlb
// IID\LCID: {D01C8F62-264B-11D3-B7FE-0040F67455FE}\0
// Helpfile:
// HelpString: PropDemo Library
```

```
// Version:    1.0
// ********************************************************************** //

interface

uses Windows, ActiveX, Classes, Graphics, OleCtrls, StdVCL;

// **********************************************************************//
// GUIDS declared in the TypeLibrary. Following prefixes are used:    //
//    Type Libraries    : LIBID_xxxx                                  //
//    CoClasses         : CLASS_xxxx                                  //
//    DISPInterfaces    : DIID_xxxx                                   //
//    Non-DISP interfaces: IID_xxxx                                   //
// **********************************************************************//
const
  LIBID_PropDemo: TGUID = '{D01C8F62-264B-11D3-B7FE-0040F67455FE}';

implementation

uses ComObj;

end.
```

## Listing 9.20    *PropDemo—PropSheet.pas*

```
unit PropSheet;

interface

uses
  Windows, Messages, ActiveX, ComObj, CommCtrl, ShlObj;

type
  TPropertySheet = class(TComObject, IShellExtInit, IShellPropSheetExt)
  private
    FFileName: WideString;

    function IShellExtInit.Initialize = InitShellExtension;
  protected
    {Declare IShellExtInit methods here}
    function InitShellExtension(pidlFolder: PItemIDList;
      lpdobj: IDataObject; hKeyProgID: HKEY): HResult; stdcall;

    {Declare IShellPropSheetExt methods here}
    function AddPages(lpfnAddPage: TFNAddPropSheetPage; lParam: LPARAM): HResult; stdcall;
    function ReplacePage(uPageID: UINT; lpfnReplaceWith: TFNAddPropSheetPage;
      lParam: LPARAM): HResult; stdcall;
  end;
```

*continues* ▶

**Listing 9.20** *continued*

```
TPropertySheetFactory = class(TComObjectFactory)
public
  procedure UpdateRegistry(Register: Boolean); override;
end;

const
  Class_PropertySheet: TGUID = '{D01C8F61-264B-11D3-B7FE-0040F67455FE}';

implementation

uses Classes, SysUtils, ComServ, ShellAPI, AXCtrls;

const
  IDD_CARPROPS    = 106;
  IDC_VEHICLENAME = 1000;
  IDC_MODELYEAR   = 1001;

{$R PPAGE.RES}

function PropertySheetDlgProc(hDlg: HWND; uMessage: UINT;
  wParam: WPARAM; lParam: LPARAM): Boolean; stdcall;
var
  psp: PPropSheetPage;
  ps: TPropertySheet;
  stgRoot: IStorage;
  stmInfo: IStream;
  Res: HResult;
  OS: TOleStream;
  Reader: TReader;
  VehicleName: string;
  ModelYear: Integer;
begin
  Result := True;

  case uMessage of
    WM_INITDIALOG: begin
      psp := PPropSheetPage(lParam);
      ps := TPropertySheet(psp.lParam);

      Res := StgOpenStorage(PWideChar(ps.FFileName), nil, STGM_READ or
        STGM_SHARE_EXCLUSIVE, nil, 0, stgRoot);
      if SUCCEEDED(Res) then begin
        Res := stgRoot.OpenStream('Info', nil, STGM_READ or
          STGM_SHARE_EXCLUSIVE, 0, stmInfo);
        if SUCCEEDED(Res) then begin
          OS := TOleStream.Create(stmInfo);
          try
            Reader := TReader.Create(OS, 1024);
            try
              VehicleName := Reader.ReadString;
              ModelYear := Reader.ReadInteger;
```

```
            finally
              Reader.Free;
            end;
          finally
            OS.Free;
          end;

          SetDlgItemText(hDlg, IDC_VEHICLENAME, PChar(VehicleName));
          SetDlgItemText(hDlg, IDC_MODELYEAR, PChar(IntToStr(ModelYear)));
        end;
      end;
    end;

    WM_COMMAND: begin
      // If you have buttons on your dialog, you can handle
      // button presses here...
    end;

    WM_NOTIFY: begin
      case PNMHDR(lParam).code of
        PSN_APPLY: begin
          // The user clicked the OK or apply button.
        end;
      end;
    end;

    else
      Result := False;
  end;
end;

function PropertySheetCallback(hWnd: HWND; uMessage: UINT;
  var psp: TPropSheetPage): UINT; stdcall;
begin
  case uMessage of
    PSPCB_RELEASE:
      if psp.lParam <> 0 then
        TPropertySheet(psp.lParam)._Release;
  end;

  Result := 1;
end;

{ TPropertySheet }

function TPropertySheet.InitShellExtension(pidlFolder: PItemIDList; lpdobj: IDataObject;
     hKeyProgID: HKEY): HResult; stdcall;
var
  Medium: TStgMedium;
  Format: TFormatEtc;
  FileName: string;
```

*continues* ▶

**Listing 9.20** *continued*

```
begin
  // Fail if no data object was provided
  if lpdobj = nil then begin
    Result := E_FAIL;
    exit;
  end;

  // Set up the TFormatEtc structure...
  with Format do begin
    cfFormat := CF_HDROP;
    ptd := nil;
    dwAspect := DVASPECT_CONTENT;
    lIndex := -1;
    tymed := TYMED_HGLOBAL;
  end;

  // Fail if we can't get to the data
  Result := lpdobj.GetData(Format, Medium);
  if Failed(Result) then
    exit;

  try
    // Make sure the user only selected one file
    if DragQueryFile(Medium.hGlobal, $FFFFFFFF, nil, 0) = 1 then begin
      SetLength(FileName, MAX_PATH);
      DragQueryFile(Medium.hGlobal, 0, PChar(FileName), MAX_PATH);
      FFileName := FileName;
      Result := NOERROR;
    end else
      Result := E_FAIL;
  finally
    ReleaseStgMedium(Medium);
  end;
end;

function TPropertySheet.AddPages(lpfnAddPage: TFNAddPropSheetPage;
  lParam: LPARAM): HResult;
var
  psp: TPropSheetPage;
  hPage: HPropSheetPage;
begin
  FillChar(psp, sizeof(psp), 0);
  psp.dwSize := sizeof(psp);
  psp.dwFlags := PSP_USETITLE or PSP_USECALLBACK;
  psp.hInstance := hInstance;
  psp.pszTemplate := MAKEINTRESOURCE(IDD_CARPROPS);
  psp.pszTitle := 'Car Information';
  psp.pfnDlgProc := @PropertySheetDlgProc;
  psp.pfnCallback := @PropertySheetCallback;
  psp.lParam := Integer(self);
```

```
  hPage := CreatePropertySheetPage(psp);

  if hPage <> nil then begin
    if not lpfnAddPage(hPage, lParam) then
      DestroyPropertySheetPage(hPage);
  end;

  _AddRef;

  Result := NOERROR;
end;

function TPropertySheet.ReplacePage(uPageID: UINT;
  lpfnReplaceWith: TFNAddPropSheetPage; lParam: LPARAM): HResult;
begin
  Result := E_NOTIMPL;
end;

{ TPropertySheetFactory }

procedure TPropertySheetFactory.UpdateRegistry(Register: Boolean);
begin
  inherited UpdateRegistry(Register);

  if Register then begin
    CreateRegKey('.car', '', 'CarDemo');
    CreateRegKey('CarDemo\shellex\PropertySheetHandlers\' +
      ClassName, '', GUIDToString(ClassID));
  end else begin
    DeleteRegKey('CarDemo\shellex\PropertySheetHandlers\' +
      ClassName);
  end;
end;

initialization
{$IFDEF VER100}
  TPropertySheetFactory.Create(ComServer, TPropertySheet, Class_PropertySheet,
    'PropertySheet', '', ciMultiInstance);
{$ELSE}
  TPropertySheetFactory.Create(ComServer, TPropertySheet, Class_PropertySheet,
    'PropertySheet', '', ciMultiInstance, tmApartment);
{$ENDIF}
end.
```

# Implementing a Dialog Procedure

We're not working with a standard Delphi form—instead, we're working with a Windows dialog box—so we have to write some pretty low-level code to interface with the property page. After the property page is created, Windows sends a WM_INITDIALOG message to it. For this example, that's really the only message I need to respond to. However, I've included some boilerplate code to show you where you can respond to the WM_COMMAND message (sent when the user clicks a button on the property page, for example), and the WM_NOTIFY message (send when the user clicks the Apply or OK buttons on the property sheet).

As I indicated, the only message we need to concern ourselves with for this example is WM_INITDIALOG. The lParam parameter of PropertySheetDlgProc will contain a pointer to the TPropSheetPage structure that we set up in TPropertySheet.AddPages. You'll notice that I've retrieved the lParam field of that structure to obtain a reference back to the TPropertySheet class. After I have that class, I am able to retrieve the file name that the user clicked on in order to open it and retrieve the vehicle name and model year.

The code for reading the vehicle information from the file is the same as the code used in the CarDemo application, so I won't go over it again here. After the information is retrieved, I use the Windows API call SetDlgItemText to display that information in the edit controls of the property page.

SetDlgItemText performs the equivalent of what happens behind the scenes when you write the following code in Delphi:

```
Edit1.Text := 'Hello';
```

Obviously, it's much easier to just say Edit1.Text := "Hello"; but unfortunately, that's not possible here, so we grit our teeth and do things the hard way instead.

## Implementing the Callback Function

The only other point of interest in this example is the callback function PropertySheetCallback. It gets called when the property page is being destroyed. The psp parameter contains the TPropSheetPage record that we set up in TPropertySheet.AddPages, so again I convert the lParam field back to a TPropertySheet. I then call _Release to let Windows know that I'm finished using that interface, and it can destroy it whenever it sees fit.

**Note**

*When implementing the dialog procedure and callback function, you must be sure to mark them as stdcall. If you don't, all kinds of weird behavior will ensue, and your property sheet handler won't work correctly. ◆*

Well, the hard part is done. After you compile and register this COM server, you can right-click CARS.CAR from the Windows explorer. Select Properties from the popup menu, and you should see an additional tab named Car Information on the property sheet. Figure 9.13 shows what the Properties dialog box looks like on my home machine.

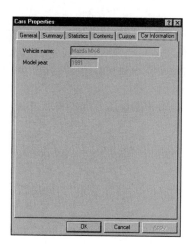

**Figure 9.13**   *Displaying information in a custom property page.*

# Where to Go from Here

In this chapter, we examined five of the most common Windows shell-related COM interfaces: namely, context-menu handlers, copy hook handlers, shell links, tray icons, and property sheet handlers.

In this book, I have provided you with the information you need to quickly and easily create COM clients and servers in Delphi. At times, I delved into the inner workings of Delphi and COM, but for the most part, I tried to give you the information you need to write COM applications without bogging you down with a lot of the inner details.

In order to drive home the points discussed in this book, I provided useful examples in each chapter, showing you that you can learn COM in small increments, while putting your newfound knowledge to work almost immediately.

There are plenty of additional references available that you can turn to for more information on Delphi programming in general, and COM programming specifically. The COM-specific books are not geared towards Delphi, but they will give you a deeper understanding of COM internals, should you be interested. Appendix A, "Suggested Readings and Resources," lists a number of references that I have personally found very useful in the past.

# Appendix **A**

## *Suggested Readings and Resources*

If, after completing this book, you want to delve further into the subjects of Delphi or COM/OLE programming, this appendix offers suggestions on where to turn.

## Delphi Programming

The books listed in this section apply to Delphi programming as a whole. Most discuss advanced programming issues (including COM development).

1. *Borland Delphi 4 Developer's Guide: The Authoritative Solution,* by **Xavier Pacheco and Steve Teixeira.** This is an excellent, advanced reference written by two ex-Borland employees. The book is packed with Delphi programming tips and techniques, and includes a CD containing a number of additional chapters that, due to space limitations, did not make it into the book itself.

2. *Delphi Component Design,* by **Danny Thorpe.** This book was written for earlier versions of Delphi, and is now out of print, but it is a must-have if you can get your hands on a copy. Thorpe's book goes beyond what the rest offer by giving you the inside story on the VCL.

3. *Delphi Developer's Handbook,* by **Marco Cantu, Tim Gooch, and John Lam.** Written for Delphi 3, this book also contains much useful information for Delphi 4 and Delphi 5 programmers. This book is not for beginners, but covers a number of topics that you will be hard-pressed to find elsewhere.

4. *Delphi 4 Unleashed,* by **Charlie Calvert.** This book covers a number of Delphi programming issues, ranging from Internet programming to MIDAS to ActiveX development. It is an advanced book for serious Delphi programmers.

5. *Mastering Delphi 4,* **by Marco Cantu.** This book is an indispensable addition to every Delphi programmer's library. It provides a detailed discussion of a wide array of Delphi features, from beginning topics to COM, CORBA, and ActiveX development.

# COM/OLE

This section lists two additional resources that you might find helpful for COM development. They are geared toward C/C++ developers, but if you want a deeper understanding of COM, you will find these references useful.

1. *Essential COM,* **by Don Box.** The code presented in this book is written in C++, but the book is still valuable for Delphi programmers who want to more fully understand the workings of COM. If you want to understand more about how COM works internally, this is an excellent book.

2. **Microsoft Developer's Network.** The Microsoft Developer's Network (MSDN) is available on CD on a subscription basis, or you can visit `http://msdn.microsoft.com` to access MSDN online. This is the definitive reference for new Microsoft technologies, including advances in COM, as well as new COM-based technologies, such as ADO, SAPI (Speech API), and more.

# *Index*

## Symbols

# C

# G

# New Riders Professional Library

Michael Masterson, Herman Knief, Scott Vinick, and Eric Roul:
*Windows NT DNS*
ISBN: 1-56205-943-2

Sandra Osborne:
*Windows NT Registry*
ISBN: 1-56205-941-6

Mark Edmead and Paul Hinsberg:
*Windows NT Performance: Monitoring, Benchmarking, and Tuning*
ISBN: 1-56205-942-4

Karanjit Siyan:
*Windows NT TCP/IP*
ISBN: 1-56205-887-8

Ted Harwood:
*Windows NT Terminal Server and Citrix MetaFrame*
ISBN: 1-56205-944-0

Anil Desai:
*Windows NT Network Management: Reducing Total Cost of Ownership*
ISBN: 1-56205-946-7

Eric K. Cone, Jon Boggs, and Sergio Perez:
*Planning for Windows 2000*
ISBN: 0-7357-0048-6

Doug Hauger, Marywynne Leon, and William C. Wade III:
*Implementing Exchange Server*
ISBN: 1-56205-931-9

Janice Rice Howd:
*Exchange System Administration*
ISBN: 0-7357-0081-8

Sean Baird and Chris Miller:
*SQL Server Systen Administration*
ISBN: 1-56205-955-6

Stu Sjouwerman and Ed Tittel:
*Windows NT Power Toolkit*
ISBN: 0-7357-0922-X

# The Circle Series from MTP

## April 1998

Richard Puckett:

*Windows NT Automated Deployment and Customization*
ISBN: 1-57870-045-0

Tim Hill:

*Windows NT Shell Scripting*
ISBN: 1-57870-047-7

## May 1998

Gene Henriksen:

*Windows NT and UNIX Integration*
ISBN: 1-57870-048-5

## November 1998

PeterViscarola/Anthony Mason:

*Windows NT Device Driver Development*
ISBN: 1-57870-058-2

Steve Thomas:

*Windows NT Heterogeneous Networking*
ISBN: 1-57870-064-7

Todd Mathers/Shawn Genoway:

*Windows NT Thin Client Solutions: Implementing Terminal Server and Citrix MetaFrame*
ISBN: 1-57870-065-5

## January 1999

David Roth:

*Win32 Perl Programming: The Standard Extensions*
ISBN: 1-57870-067-1

## February 1999

Gregg Branham:

*Windows NT Domain Architecture*
ISBN: 1-57870-112-0

## August 1999

Sean Deuby:

*Windows 2000 Server: Planning and Migration*
ISBN: 1-57870-023-X

## September 1999

David Iseminger:

*Windows 2000 Quality of Service*
ISBN: 1-57870-115-5

## October 1999

Tim Hill:

*Windows Script Host*
ISBN: 1-57870-139-2

Paul Hinsberg:

*Windows NT Applications: Measuring and Optimizing Performance*
ISBN: 1-57870-176-7

William Zack:

*Windows 2000 and Mainframe Integration*
ISBN: 1-57870-200-3

# Sample Applications

Each chapter in this book includes a number of sample programs to help you to get up to speed with Delphi COM programming as quickly and painlessly as possible.

## Chapter 1
- **GUIDDemo**—Shows how to generate Globally Unique IDentifiers (GUIDs) programmatically. *See page 14.*
- **IntfDemo**—Reinforces the concept of interface reference counting and lifetime management for COM objects. *See page 30.*
- **SortDemo**—Shows a concrete example of how to implement a generic algorithm (comparison/sorting routines) using interfaces. *See page 35.*
- **GrphDemo**—Implements a number of advanced interface features, such as multiple interfaces in a single class, method name resolution, and more. Shows how interfaces can be used to cleanly create a hierarchy of classes. *See page 53.*

## Chapter 2
- **Bin1Srv**—Demonstrates how to create a simple COM server that implements one-dimensional optimization (an NP-complete problem). *See page 80.*
- **Bin1Cli**—Shows a client that accesses the Bin1Srv server. *See page 87.*
- **Bin1Srv2**—Shows how to update an existing COM server without breaking existing client code. *See page 90.*
- **Bin1Cli2**—An updated version of Bin1Cli that takes advantage of the new features of Bin1Srv2. *See page 99.*

## Chapter 3
- **TIViewer**—Demonstrates how to read and interpret the contents of a type library. *See page 136.*

## Chapter 4
- **UnitSrv**—Demonstrates an in-process COM server that can convert between different units, such as feet, inches, meters, and so on. *See page 159.*
- **UnitCli**—A client application for UnitSrv. *See page 161.*
- **MemoDemo**—A simple application used as a base point for showing how to add automation to existing applications. *See page 166.*
- **MemoSrv**—The automated MemoDemo application. *See page 168.*
- **MemoCli**—A client application for MemoSrv. *See page 172.*
- **EventSrv**—A simple application used to demonstrate how to fire events from an automation server. *See page 180.*
- **EventCli**—A client application for EventSrv. *See page 189.*
- **EventMultSrv**—The EventSrv application enhanced to allow events to be sent to multiple clients at once. *See page 195.*
- **EventMultCli**—A client application for EventMultSrv. *See page 194.*
- **EventCli5**—A Delphi 5-specific client application for EventMultSrv. *See page 192.*
- **IntfSrv**—Shows how to implement callback interfaces in COM servers. *See page 200.*
- **IntfCli**—A client application for IntfSrv. *See page 209.*
- **ADO**—Demonstrates how to access Microsoft Active Data Objects (ADO) from Delphi. *See page 220.*